D1003876

Beginning iPhone Development with Swift 5

Exploring the iOS SDK

Fifth Edition

Wallace Wang

Apress®

Beginning iPhone Development with Swift 5: Exploring the iOS SDK

Wallace Wang
San Diego, CA, USA

ISBN-13 (pbk): 978-1-4842-4864-5   ISBN-13 (electronic): 978-1-4842-4865-2
https://doi.org/10.1007/978-1-4842-4865-2

Managing Director, Apress Media LLC: Welmoed Spahr
Acquisitions Editor: Aaron Black
Development Editor: James Markham
Coordinating Editor: Jessica Vakili

Cover image designed by Freepik (www.freepik.com)

Distributed to the book trade worldwide by Springer Science+Business Media New York, 233 Spring Street, 6th Floor, New York, NY 10013. Phone 1-800-SPRINGER, fax (201) 348-4505, e-mail orders-ny@springer-sbm.com, or visit www.springeronline.com. Apress Media, LLC is a California LLC and the sole member (owner) is Springer Science + Business Media Finance Inc (SSBM Finance Inc). SSBM Finance Inc is a **Delaware** corporation.

For information on translations, please e-mail rights@apress.com, or visit http://www.apress.com/rights-permissions.

Apress titles may be purchased in bulk for academic, corporate, or promotional use. eBook versions and licenses are also available for most titles. For more information, reference our Print and eBook Bulk Sales web page at http://www.apress.com/bulk-sales.

Any source code or other supplementary material referenced by the author in this book is available to readers on GitHub via the book's product page, located at www.apress.com/978-1-4842-4864-5. For more detailed information, please visit http://www.apress.com/source-code.

Printed on acid-free paper

This book is dedicated to everyone who has an idea for an app but didn't know what to do first or how to get started. First, believe in your idea. Second, trust that you have intelligence to achieve your dream even if you don't know how you'll get there. Third, keep learning and improving your skills all the time. Fourth, stay focused. Success will come one day as long as you persist and never give up on yourself.

Table of Contents

About the Author

Wallace Wang has written dozens of computer books over the years beginning with ancient MS-DOS programs like WordPerfect and Turbo Pascal, migrating to writing books on Windows programs like Visual Basic and Microsoft Office, and finally switching to Swift programming for Apple products like the Macintosh and the iPhone.

When he's not helping people discover the fascinating world of programming, he performs stand-up comedy and appears on two radio shows on KNSJ in San Diego (http://knsj.org) called *Notes from the Underground* (with Dane Henderson, Jody Taylor, and Kristen Yoder) and *Laugh In Your Face Radio* (with Chris Clobber, Sarah Burford, and Ikaika Patria).

He also writes a screenwriting blog called *The 15 Minute Movie Method* (http://15minutemoviemethod.com) and a blog about the latest cat news on the Internet called *Cat Daily News* (http://catdailynews.com).

About the Technical Reviewer

Wesley Matlock is a published author of books about iOS technologies. He has more than 20 years of development experience in several different platforms. He first started doing mobile development on the Compaq iPAQ in the early 2000s.

Today Wesley enjoys developing on the iOS platform and bringing new ideas to life for Major League Baseball in the Denver metro area.

CHAPTER 1

Understanding iOS Programming

All programming involves the same task of writing commands for a computer to follow. To learn iOS programming, you need to learn three different skills:

- How to write commands in the Swift programming language
- How to use Apple's software frameworks
- How to create user interfaces in Xcode

While it's possible to create an entire iOS app using nothing but Swift code, this is a tedious, time-consuming, and error-prone method. Trying to write an entire iOS app in Swift means you'll need to write code to create your user interface, write more code to work with the hardware of an iOS device such as an iPhone or iPad, and then write a third set of code to make your app actually work.

Rather than create your user interface entirely in code, you can design your user interface visually in Xcode. Not only does this make creating your user interface easier, faster, and more consistent with the user interfaces of other iOS apps, but it also frees your code from relying on any particular user interface design. By using Xcode, you can keep your user interface separate from the code that makes your app work. This gives you the flexibility to modify user interfaces without the need to modify your code at the same time.

Every iOS app needs to communicate with different hardware features of an iOS device such as its camera or touch screen. Rather than force you to write code to work with hardware, Apple provides several software libraries or frameworks that provide this code for you. Now instead of writing your own code to access the camera or touch screen, you can use Apple's proven frameworks to make your app work correctly right from the start.

1

© Wallace Wang 2019
W. Wang, *Beginning iPhone Development with Swift 5*, https://doi.org/10.1007/978-1-4842-4865-2_1

Essentially, every iOS app consists of three parts as shown in Figure 1-1:

- Your code to make an app do something useful

- A user interface that you can design visually in Xcode

- Access to hardware features of an iOS device through one or more of Apple's iOS frameworks

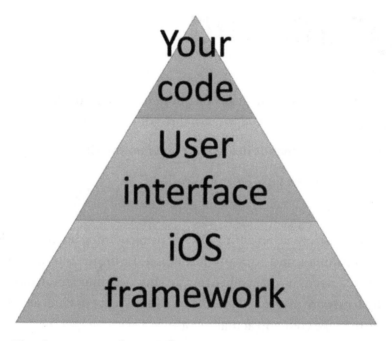

Figure 1-1. *The three parts of an iOS app*

Apple provides dozens of frameworks for iOS (and their other operating systems as well such as macOS, watchOS, and tvOS). By simply using Apple's frameworks, you can accomplish common tasks by writing little code of your own. Some of Apple's available frameworks include

- UIKit – iOS user interface and touch screen support

- ARKit – Augmented reality features

- Core Animation – Displays animation

- GameKit – Creates multiplayer interactive apps

- Contacts – Accesses the Contacts data on an iOS device

- SiriKit – Allows the use of voice commands through Siri

- AVKit – Allows playing of audio and video files

- MediaLibrary – Allows access to images, audio, and video stored on an iOS device

- CallKit – Provides voice calling features

Apple's frameworks essentially contain code that you can reuse. This makes apps more reliable and consistent while also saving developers' time by using proven code that works correctly. To see a complete list of Apple's available software frameworks, visit Apple's developer documentation site (`https://developer.apple.com/documentation`).

Apple's frameworks can give you a huge head start in creating an iOS app, but you still need to provide a user interface so users can interact with your app. While you could create a user interface from scratch, this would also be tedious, time-consuming, and error-prone. Even worse, if every app developer created a user interface from scratch, no two iOS apps would look or work exactly the same, confusing users.

That's why Apple's Xcode compiler helps you design user interfaces with standard features used in most apps such as views (windows on the screen), buttons, labels, text boxes, switches, and sliders. In Xcode, each window of a user interface is called a view. While simple iOS apps may consist of a single view (think of the Calculator app on an iPhone), more sophisticated iOS apps consist of multiple views.

To help you create and organize your user interface, Xcode stores an iOS app's user interface in a file called a storyboard, which gets its name from the movie industry. When making films, directors often use storyboards that visually show each scene the director wants to film. By viewing these storyboard images in a specific sequence, a director can see how to tell a story before actually filming the scene.

In iOS app development, storyboards contain views and segues. Views appear as rectangles that represent the screen size of different iOS devices such as an iPhone 8 or an iPad Pro, while segues appear as arrows that show the order that views appear to the user as shown in Figure 1-2.

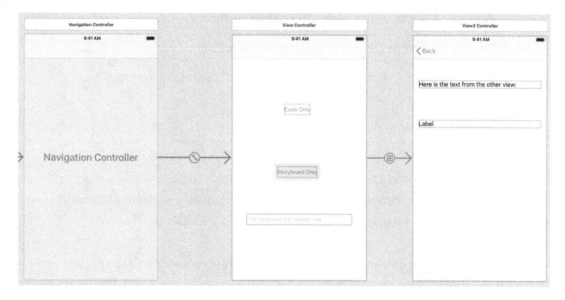

Figure 1-2. *Storyboards help you design the user interface of an iOS app*

Xcode keeps storyboards completely separate from your code. This way you can easily change your user interface without needing to retest your code again. Some developers create their user interface first to design the structure of their app before they write a single line of code. Other developers write their code first and then attach a user interface to the code later.

Most developers write code and create a user interface at the same time so they can test their app as they progress. Whatever method you choose, you'll be able to design your user interface visually for a variety of different iOS device screen sizes and orientation.

The heart of any iOS app is the unique code you write to make your app do something useful. When you write code, you could store it in a single file, but this would be like printing an entire novel on a long scroll of paper. It's possible, but it would be cumbersome to edit and modify later.

That's why most iOS apps consist of multiple files. Even a simple iOS app will consist of a handful of files, while a complicated app might contain hundreds or even thousands of separate files. By storing code in separate files, you can quickly identify the file that contains the code you want to edit and modify while safely ignoring code stored in other files.

When you create files to store Swift commands, your files will have a file extension of .swift to help you identify them from files that might contain code written in other programming languages such as Objective-C, which was Apple's original programming language.

To help you organize your files, you can store them in separate folders. These folders exist solely for your convenience in organizing your code. Figure 1-3 shows how Xcode can divide an app into folders and files.

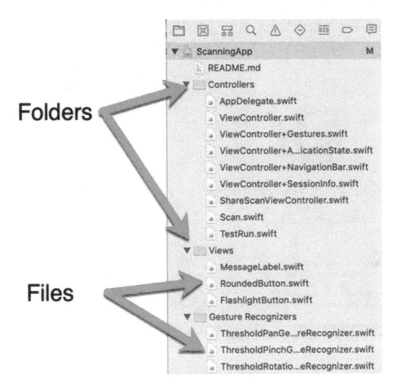

Figure 1-3. Xcode stores your code in files that you can organize in folders

Learning About Xcode

Learning iOS development is more than just learning how to write code in the Swift programming language. Besides knowing Swift, you must also know how to find and use Apple's different software frameworks, how to use Xcode to design your user interface using storyboards, and how to organize, create, and delete files that contain your Swift code. In addition, you must also learn how to write code using Xcode's editor.

To get acquainted with iOS app development, let's start with a simple project that will teach you

- How to understand the parts of a project
- How to view different files
- How the different parts of Xcode work

1. Start Xcode. A welcoming screen appears that lets you choose a recently used project or the option of creating a new project as shown in Figure 1-4. (You can always open this welcoming screen from within Xcode by choosing Windows ➤ Welcome to Xcode or by pressing Shift + Command + 1.)

Figure 1-4. *The Xcode welcoming screen*

2. Click the **Create a new Xcode project** option. Xcode displays templates for designing different types of apps as shown in Figure 1-5. Notice that the top of the template window displays different operating systems you can develop apps for, such as iOS, watchOS, tvOS, and macOS. By selecting different operating systems, you can create projects designed for the devices that run that particular operating system.

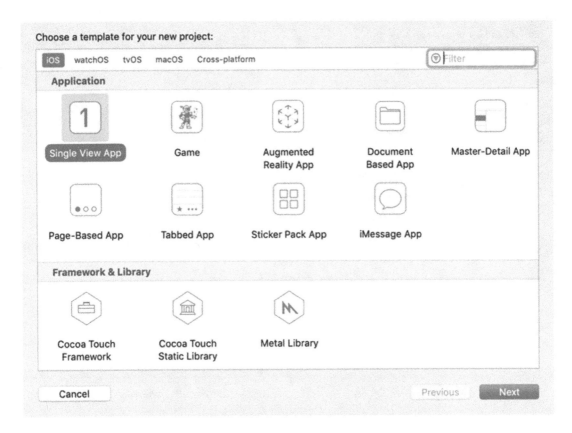

Figure 1-5. *Choosing a project template*

3. Click **iOS** and then click **Single View App**. The Single View App represents the simplest iOS project.

4. Click the **Next** button. Another window appears, asking for your project name along with an organization name and organization identifier as shown in Figure 1-6. You must fill out all three text fields, but the project name, organization name, and organization identifier can be any descriptive text that you want.

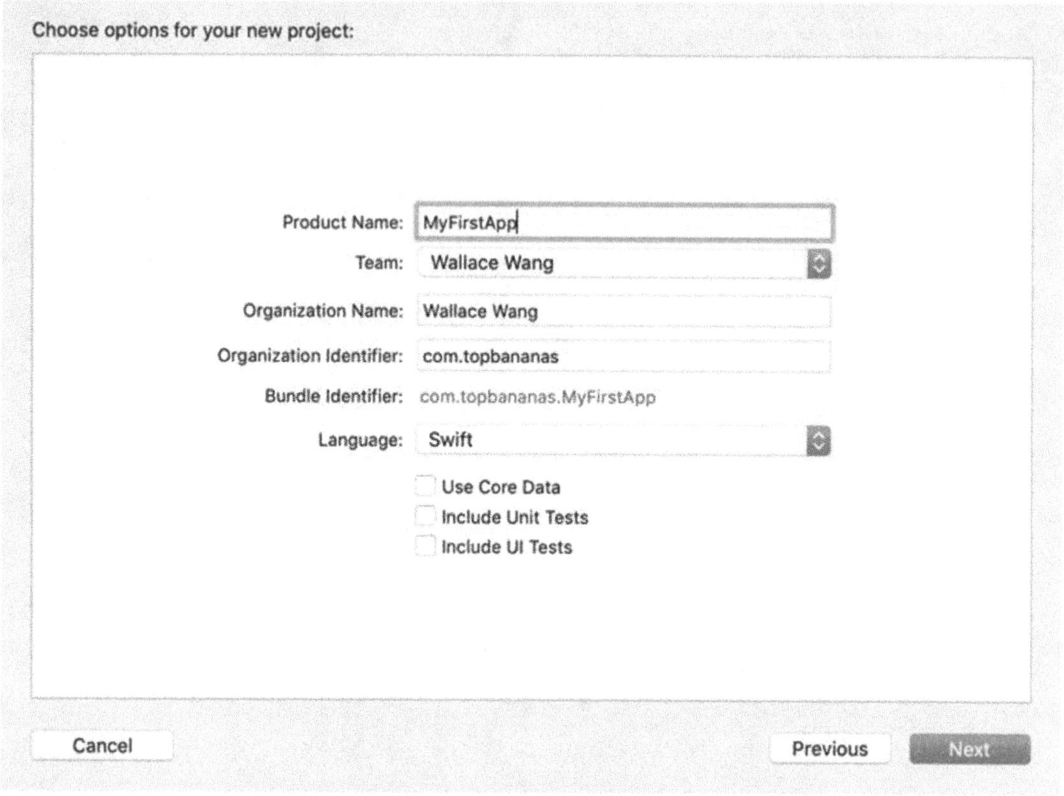

Choose options for your new project:

Product Name: MyFirstApp

Team: Wallace Wang

Organization Name: Wallace Wang

Organization Identifier: com.topbananas

Bundle Identifier: com.topbananas.MyFirstApp

Language: Swift

☐ Use Core Data
☐ Include Unit Tests
☐ Include UI Tests

Cancel   Previous   Next

Figure 1-6. *Defining a project name, organization name, and organization identifier*

5. Click in the Project Name text field and type a name for your project such as MyFirstApp.

6. Click in the Organization Name text field and type your name or company name.

7. Click in the Organization Identifier text field and type any identifying text you wish. Typically this identifier is your web site spelled backward such as com.microsoft.

8. Make sure the Language popup menu shows Swift and that all check boxes are clear. Then click the **Next** button. Xcode displays a dialog for you to choose which drive and folder to store your project in.

9. Choose a drive and folder and click the **Create** button. Xcode
    displays information about your newly created project as shown
    in Figure 1-7.

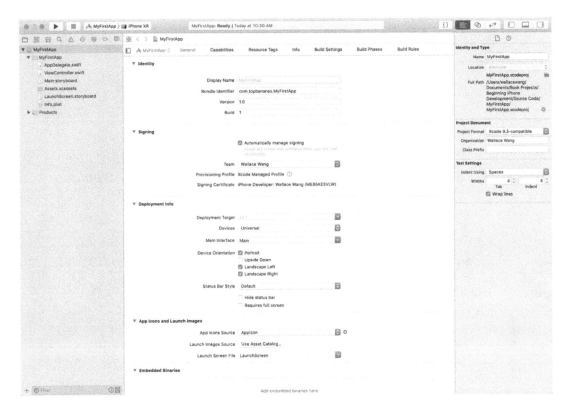

Figure 1-7. *Viewing details of a newly created iOS project*

Initially the Xcode window may look confusing because it displays so much
information on the screen at once, but Xcode organizes this information in several
panes.

The far left pane is called the Navigator pane. By clicking icons at the top of the
Navigator pane, you can view different parts of your project as shown in Figure 1-8.

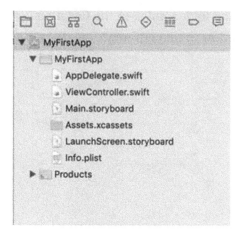

Figure 1-8. *The Navigator pane appears on the far left of the Xcode window*

The simplest iOS app consists of three files:

- AppDelegate.swift – Contains Swift code for monitoring the behavior of your app

- ViewController.swift – Contains Swift code for controlling the user interface of a single view

- Main.storyboard – Contains the storyboard that defines your app's user interface

In our simple app, we only have one view (window) so we only have one ViewController.swift file. In more complicated apps that consist of multiple views (windows), you'll need a separate ViewController.swift file (usually given a distinctive name) to work with each individual view.

The most common use of the Navigator pane is to display your project as folders and files. Folders exist solely to help you organize files. By clicking the gray disclosure triangles that appear to the left of a folder icon, you can expand or hide a folder's contents.

To see how the Navigator pane works, follow these steps:

1. Choose one of the following to make the Project Navigator appear in the Navigator pane:

    - Click the Project Navigator icon at the top, left of the Navigator pane.

- Choose View ➤ Navigators ➤ Show Navigator.

- Press Command + 1.

Just like on any computer, you can store folders within folders. Within each folder you can store one or more files. In our simple iOS app, the two types of files displayed in the Navigator pane end with the .swift and .storyboard extensions.

A .swift extension identifies a file that contains Swift code. A .storyboard extension identifies a file that contains the user interface.

2. Click the AppDelegate.swift file. Xcode displays the contents of that file in the middle pane as shown in Figure 1-9.

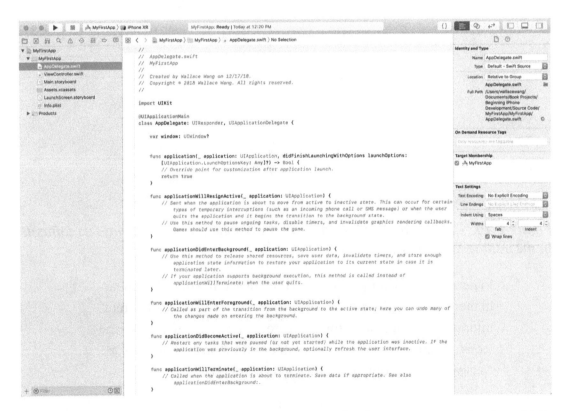

Figure 1-9. *Clicking a file in the Navigator pane displays its contents in the middle Xcode pane*

When you click a .swift file, the middle Xcode pane displays an editor where you can write and edit Swift code.

11

3. Click the Main.storyboard file. The middle Xcode pane displays
    the storyboard so you can see your user interface as shown in
    Figure 1-10.

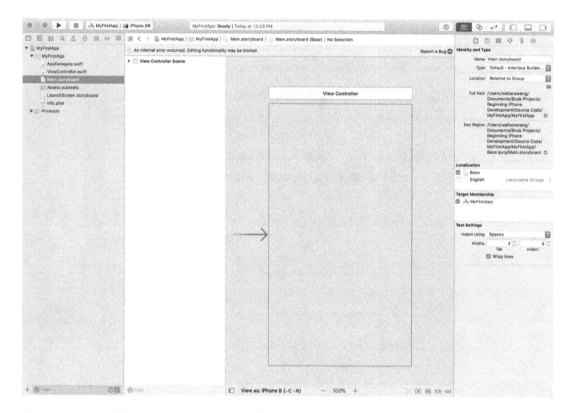

Figure 1-10. *Clicking a .storyboard file in the Navigator pane displays its contents
in the middle Xcode pane*

In general, whatever you select in the Navigator pane will appear
in more detail in the middle Xcode pane. You can select different
information to appear in the Navigator pane either by clicking the
icons at the top of the Navigator pane or by choosing the View ➤
Navigators menu option as shown in Figure 1-11.

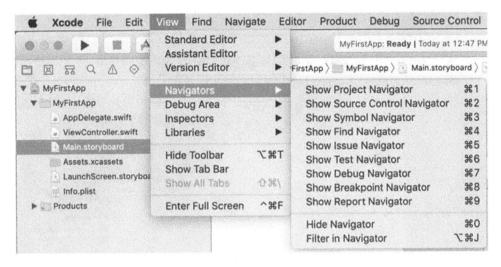

Figure 1-11. *The View ➤ Navigators menu lets you choose what to display in the Navigator pane*

4. Move the mouse pointer over the right border until the mouse pointer turns into a two-way pointing arrow. Then drag the mouse to widen or narrow the Navigator pane width. This lets you see more or less of the Navigator pane.

5. Choose View ➤ Navigators ➤ Hide/Show Navigator, or press Command + 0 (zero). This toggles between hiding the Navigator pane or showing it again. You may want to hide the Navigator pane to give you more space, but then you'll need to display the Navigator pane when you want to switch to a different file.

The far right Xcode pane is called the Inspector pane and is used to display information or allow you to customize items displayed in the middle pane. To see how the Inspector pane works, follow these steps:

1. Click the ViewController.swift file in the Navigator pane. The middle pane displays the contents of the ViewController.swift file.

2. Choose one of the following to display Quick Help in the Inspector pane:

    •   Click the Quick Help icon.

    •   Choose View ➤ Inspectors ➤ Show Quick Help Inspector.

    •   Press Option + Command + 2.

3. Move the cursor over the word "UIViewController". The Inspector pane displays information about the UIViewController as shown in Figure 1-12. By using Quick Help, you can get information about different commands stored in a .swift file.

Figure 1-12. *Quick Help displays additional information about code in the Inspector pane*

4. Click the Main.storyboard file in the Navigator pane. The middle Xcode pane now shows a Document Outline and a Storyboard as shown in Figure 1-13. The Document Outline lists all the items on the user interface in an outline, while the Storyboard displays the position of the user interface items as they appear to the user.

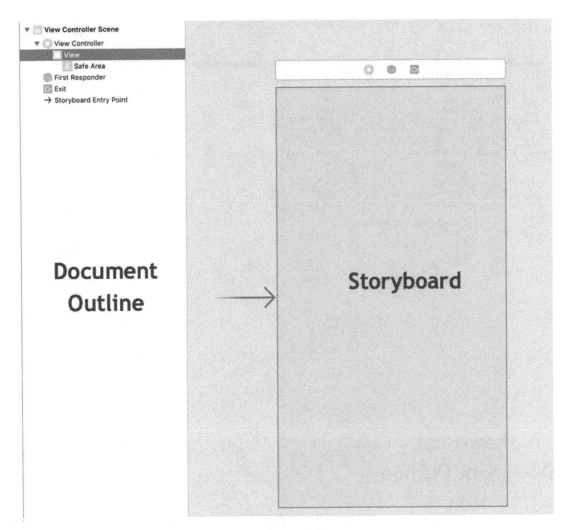

Figure 1-13. *The Document Outline and Storyboard display the user interface*

5. You can toggle between hiding and showing the Document Outline in two ways as shown in Figure 1-14:

    •   Choose Editor ➤ Show Document Outline.

    •   Click the Show/Hide Document Outline icon.

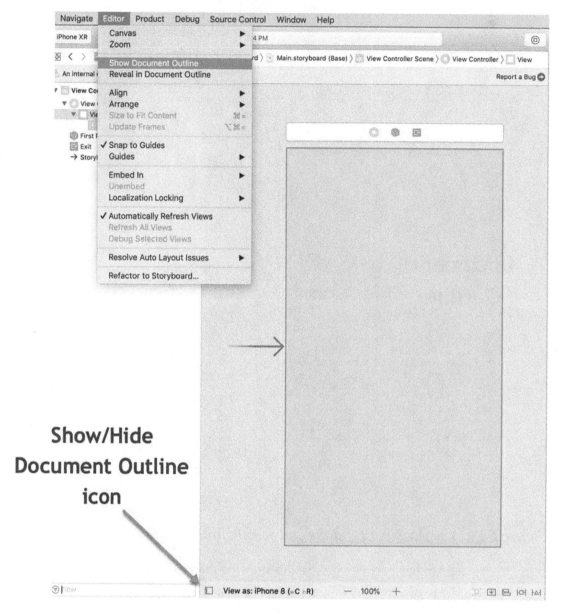

Figure 1-14. *How to display or hide the Document Outline*

6. Make sure the Document Outline is open and click the View icon that appears directly under the View Controller icon in the Document Outline.

7. Choose View ➤ Inspectors ➤ Show Quick Help Inspector. The Inspector pane displays help about the view, which displays a window, as shown in Figure 1-15.

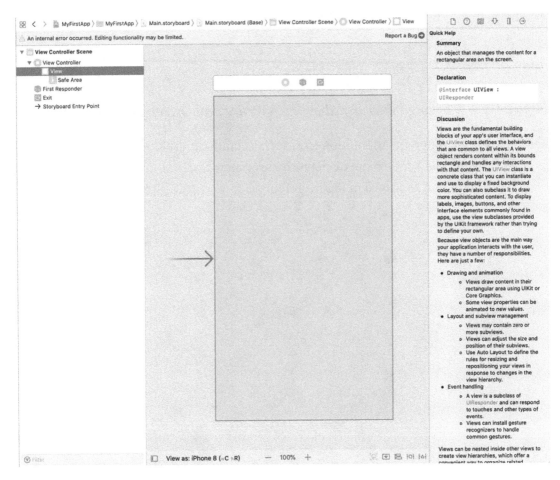

Figure 1-15. *Viewing Quick Help for a view on the user interface*

When you click a .storyboard file in the Navigator pane, the middle Xcode pane displays your app's user interface. Xcode can only display your user interface for a single iOS device at a time such as an iPhone 8. However, you can change the appearance of your app's user interface to see how it will look on a variety of different iOS devices such as an iPad Pro or an iPhone XR.

To change the type of iOS device to display, follow these steps:

1. Click a .storyboard file in the Navigator pane.

2. Click the "View as:" text at the bottom of the screen. In Figure 1-15, this text reads "View as: iPhone 8". A new bottom pane appears letting you choose a different device and orientation to use as shown in Figure 1-16.

Figure 1-16. *Clicking "View as:" displays a device and Orientation icon*

3. Click a different Orientation icon such as landscape. Notice how the middle Xcode pane displays the user interface in your new orientation as shown in Figure 1-17.

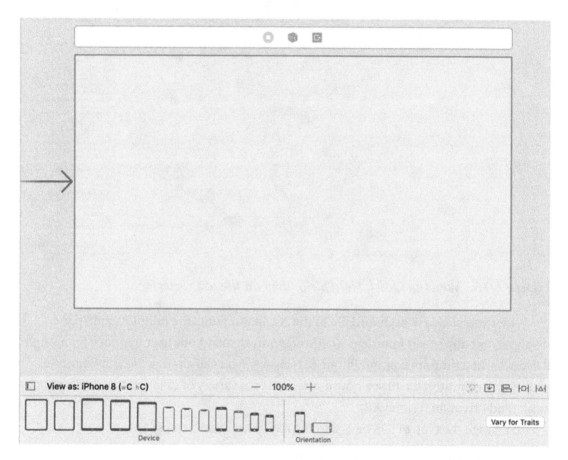

Figure 1-17. *Displaying a user interface as an iPhone in landscape orientation*

4. Click a different device icon such as an iPad. Notice that Xcode now displays your user interface in the larger iPad format. To help you view your user interface in a larger iPad screen, you can also change the magnification of the middle Xcode pane. Notice that the middle bottom bar displays the "View as:" text along with a minus sign, 100%, and a plus sign. The 100% tells you the current magnification and the minus and plus signs let you increase or decrease the magnification.

5. Click the minus sign to decrease the magnification (such as 50%) so you can view the iPad user interface easier as shown in Figure 1-18.

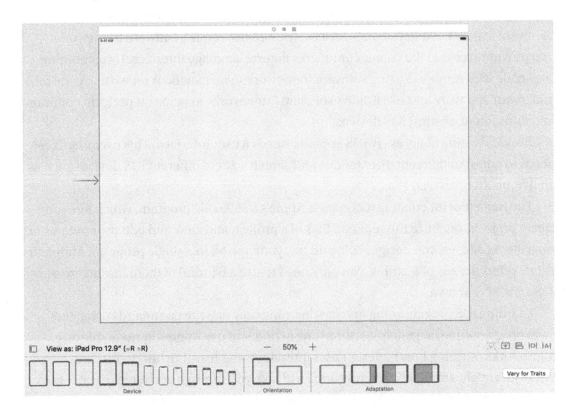

Figure 1-18. *Displaying an iPad Pro user interface at 50% magnification*

6. Click the "View as:" text to make the device and orientation pane disappear.

7. Choose File ➤ Save to save your project.

As you can see, the three Xcode panes work together to show you different information about your project. The Navigator pane (on the far left) lets you see an overview of your project. Clicking a specific item in the Navigator pane displays that item in the middle Xcode pane. The Inspector pane (on the far right) shows additional information about something displayed and selected in the middle pane.

If you explore Xcode, you'll see dozens of features, but it's not necessary to understand everything at once to start using Xcode. Just focus on using only those features you need and feel free to ignore the rest until you need them.

Summary

Creating iOS apps involves more than just writing code. To help your app access hardware features of different iOS devices, you can use Apple's software frameworks that provide access to the camera or to Siri's natural language interface. By combining your code with Apple's existing software frameworks, you can focus on writing code to make your app work and use Apple's software frameworks to help you perform common functions found on most iOS devices.

Besides writing code, every iOS app also needs a user interface. This user interface needs to adjust to different orientations and screen sizes of different iOS devices such as an iPhone XR or an iPad Pro.

The main tool for creating iOS apps is Apple's free Xcode program, which lets you create projects, organize the separate files of a project, and view and edit the contents of each file. Xcode lets you design, edit, and test your app all in a single program. Although Xcode offers dozens of features, you only need to use a handful of them to start creating iOS apps of your own.

Learning iOS programming involves learning how to write commands using the Swift programming language, learning how to find and use Apple's various software frameworks, learning how to design user interfaces, and learning how to use Xcode. While this might seem like a lot, this book will take you through each step of the way so you'll feel comfortable using Xcode and creating your own iOS apps in the near future.

CHAPTER 2

Designing User Interfaces

Every app needs a user interface. Unlike user interfaces for desktop operating systems like Windows or macOS that can display multiple windows on a screen at a time, iOS apps typically display a single window (called a view) that fills the entire screen at a time. Also unlike Windows or macOS user interfaces that users can manipulate using a keyboard or a mouse, users must be able to manipulate iOS apps solely through a touch screen although they can also be controlled through an optional keyboard as well. In iOS apps, Figure 2-1 shows how a user interface consists of

- Views
- Objects such as buttons, labels, text boxes, and switches
- Segues

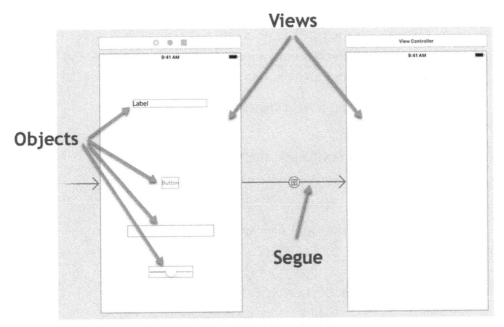

Figure 2-1. *The three parts of an iOS app user interface*

© Wallace Wang 2019
W. Wang, *Beginning iPhone Development with Swift 5*, https://doi.org/10.1007/978-1-4842-4865-2_2

The Single View App template that we used to create an app in Chapter 1 consists of a single view and no objects. Since there's also only one view, there are no segues because segues connect two views together to show the order that each view appears when the app runs.

By itself, a view with no objects on it is nothing more than a blank screen. To make a view useful, it needs one or more objects on it. With Xcode, there are often two ways to accomplish the exact same tasks:

- Programmatically

- Visually

Programmatically means writing code to do everything. In the case of creating objects that appear on a view, this means writing Swift code to define the object you want to display, its size, its position on the view, and any other custom settings such as its color.

Visually means using the mouse to drag and drop objects on a view. After placing an object on a view, you can then modify its size, position, or any other attribute without writing any code at all.

You can use one or both methods, but it's generally best to use one method for consistency. Also while you can create an entire user interface by writing code (programmatically), it's generally best not to do so because the less code you write, the easier it will be to modify and debug your program. The goal of programming is to write as little code as possible that does as much as possible.

First, let's see how to create objects programmatically so you can understand how the process works. Let's create a label and a button on a view.

1. Open your MyFirstApp project (or create a new Single View App iOS project).

2. Click the ViewController.swift file in the Navigator pane. The middle Xcode pane displays the contents of the ViewController. swift file.

3. Modify the code in the ViewController.swift file so it looks like this:

```swift
import UIKit

class ViewController: UIViewController {

    override func viewDidLoad() {
        super.viewDidLoad()
```

```swift
let label = UILabel()
label.frame = CGRect(x: 125, y: 125, width: 200,
height: 80)
label.text = "This is a label"
view.addSubview(label)

let button = UIButton()
button.frame = CGRect(x: 125, y: 300, width: 80,
height: 80)
button.setTitle("Button", for: .normal)
button.setTitleColor(UIColor.blue, for: .normal)
view.addSubview(button)
    }

}
```

4.   Choose Project ➤ Run or press Command + R. Xcode loads the
     Simulator program that lets you simulate an iOS device. When
     your app loads in the Simulator, it will display a label and a button
     as shown in Figure 2-2.

Figure 2-2. *The user interface displaying a label and a button, created programmatically*

5. Choose Simulator ➤ Quit Simulator or press Command + Q.
The Xcode window appears again.

Let's go over this code so you understand how it works. First, we must define the type of object we want to create such as a UILabel or UIButton:

```
let label = UILabel()
let button = UIButton()
```

Next, we need to define the object's position, width, and height. Keep in mind that the origin (0, 0) is defined as the upper left corner of the screen:

```
label.frame = CGRect(x: 125, y: 125, width: 200, height: 21)
button.frame = CGRect(x: 125, y: 300, width: 80, height: 30)
```
24

The first line of code defines the label to appear 125 points from the left side of the screen and down 125 points from the top of the screen. It also defines the width of the label to be 200 and the height to be 21.

The second line of code defines the button to appear 125 points from the left side of the screen and down 300 points from the top of the screen. It also defines the width of the button to be 80 and the height to be 30.

After defining the size and position of an object, the next step is to customize the object's appearance. The label contains the text "This is a label" based on this code:

```
label.text = "This is a label"
```

The button gets customized in two different ways. First, the button title gets set to "Button" and the color of the text gets set to blue:

```
button.setTitle("Button", for: .normal)
button.setTitleColor(UIColor.blue, for: .normal)
```

After defining the type of object to display, defining its size and position, and customizing it, the final step is to place it on the view:

```
view.addSubview(label)
view.addSubview(button)
```

If this looks like a lot of trouble just to create an object to appear on the user interface, you're right. That's why most developers design their user interface visually. Let's see how this works.

1. Click the ViewController.swift file in the Navigator pane. The middle Xcode pane displays the contents of the ViewController. swift file.

2. Modify the ViewController.swift file so it looks like this:

```
import UIKit

class ViewController: UIViewController {

    override func viewDidLoad() {
        super.viewDidLoad()

    }

}
```

3. Click the Main.storyboard file in the Navigator pane. Xcode displays the storyboard that contains the user interface, which consists of a single, blank view.

4. Click the Library icon. The Objects Library window appears, listing all the different objects you can add to your user interface as shown in Figure 2-3.

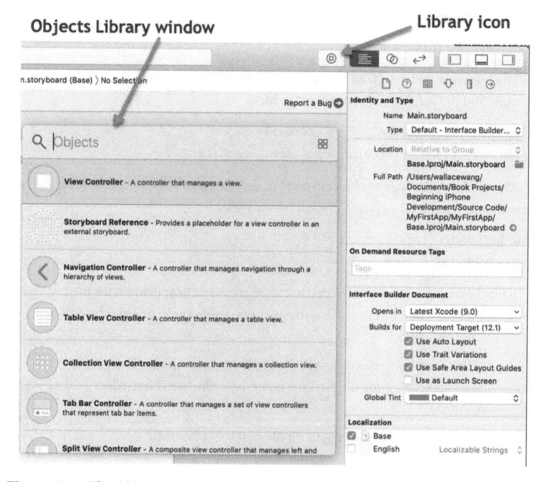

Figure 2-3. *The Objects Library lets you choose an object to place on a view*

5. Scroll through the Objects Library list until you find Label, or just click in the search field at the top of the Objects Library window, type **label**, and press ENTER. The Objects Library window displays the Label object as shown in Figure 2-4.

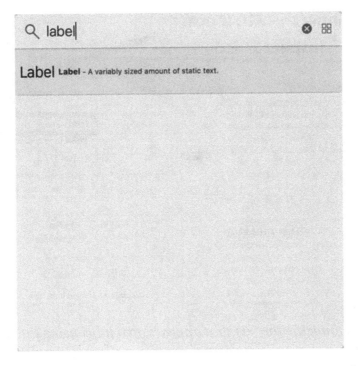

Figure 2-4. *Searching for a Label object in the Objects Library window*

6. Drag and drop the Label object from the Objects Library window to the view. As you drag the label, the Objects Library window disappears. When you release the left mouse button, the label appears on the view. We can resize and move the label to position it, but if you want to define precise values, you'll need to use the Inspector pane.

7. Click the label to select it. Handles appear around the label to show it's selected.

8. Choose View ➤ Inspectors ➤ Show Attributes Inspector (or click the Show the Attributes Inspector icon at the top of the Inspector pane).

9. Click in the text field that appears above the Color popup menu and type **This is a label** and press ENTER as shown in Figure 2-5. The Attributes Inspector pane lets us customize the text in a label. Now let's define the label's size and position.

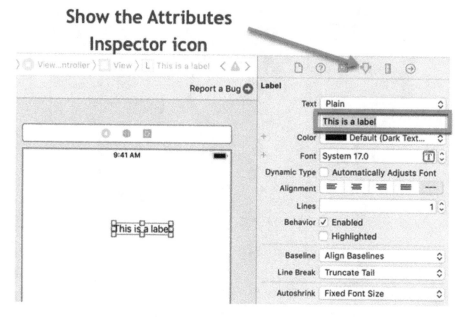

Figure 2-5. *Customizing the text that appears on a label using the Attributes Inspector pane*

10. Choose View ➤ Inspectors ➤ Show Size Inspector (or click the Show the Size Inspector icon). The Size Inspector pane appears.

11. Click in the X text field and type **125**. Then click in the Y text field and type **125**.

12. Click in the Width text field and type **200**. Then click the Height text field and type **21**. Press ENTER. This defines the size and position of the label as shown in Figure 2-6.

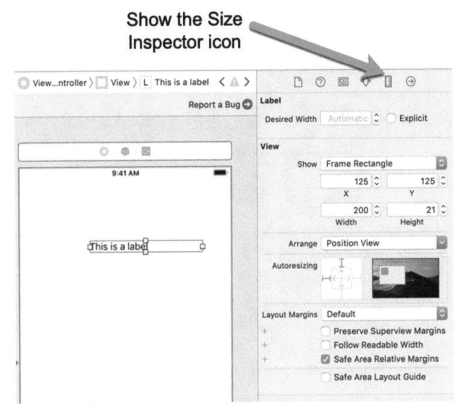

Figure 2-6. *Defining the size and position of a label using the Size Inspector pane*

13. Click the Library icon. The Objects Library window appears, listing all the different objects you can add to your user interface (see Figure 2-3).

14. Scroll through the Objects Library list until you find Label, or just click in the search field at the top of the Objects Library window, type **button**, and press ENTER. The Objects Library displays the Button object as shown in Figure 2-7.

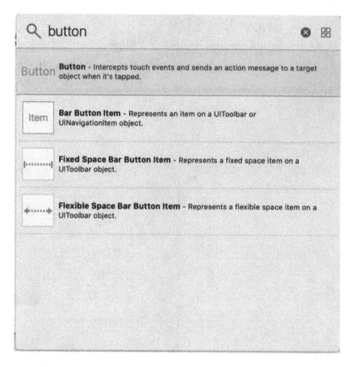

Figure 2-7. *Searching for a Button object in the Objects Library window*

15. Drag and drop the Button object from the Objects Library window to the view. As you drag the button, the Objects Library window disappears. When you release the left mouse button, the button appears on the view.

16. Click the button to select it. Handles appear around the button to show it's selected.

17. Choose View ➤ Inspectors ➤ Show Attributes Inspector (or click the Show the Attributes Inspector icon at the top of the Inspector pane). Notice that the Attributes Inspector pane already displays the word "Button" on the button and displays it in blue as shown in the Text Color popup menu in Figure 2-8.

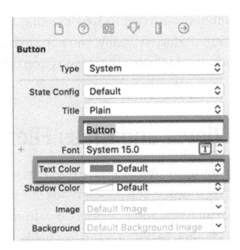

Figure 2-8. *Customizing the text and color that appears on a button using the Attributes Inspector pane*

18. Choose View ➤ Inspectors ➤ Show Size Inspector (or click the Show the Size Inspector icon). The Size Inspector pane appears.

19. Click in the X text field and type **125**. Then click in the Y text field and type **300**.

20. Click in the Width text field and type **80**. Then click the Height text field and type **30**. Press ENTER. This defines the size and position of the button.

21. Choose Project ➤ Run or press Command + R. Xcode loads the Simulator program that lets you simulate an iOS device. When your app loads in the Simulator, it will display a label and a button.

22. Choose Simulator ➤ Quit Simulator or press Command + Q. The Xcode window appears again.

23. Choose File ➤ Save to save your project.

Notice that when you create objects on the user interface programmatically, you had to write code to do everything from creating the object to defining its size and position, to placing it on the view. On the other hand, designing a user interface visually means dragging and dropping objects on a view and then resizing or moving them using the mouse. Then to define the appearance, exact size, and position of an object, you can open the Attributes Inspector and Size Inspector to choose specific values.

Many Xcode projects combine both methods for creating a user interface. While it's generally easier to create user interfaces visually, you need to be familiar with writing code to create user interfaces programmatically because you may see this in projects created by others.

Learning About Views and Class Files

The most important part of any app's user interface is a view, which displays information on an iOS device's screen. The simplest app contains just one view but most apps contain multiple views. You can easily add or delete views from a project. While a view contains user interface objects such as buttons and text fields, you may wonder how does a view store data that a user might type in from the user interface. The answer is that each view needs a class file that contains Swift code that can store data and handle interactions such as the user tapping a button.

Before we go on, be aware that Xcode uses confusing terms to describe parts of the user interface. A user interface is stored in a storyboard where each individual window displayed on the screen is called a scene. Most apps contain multiple scenes, so the Document Outline lets you selectively hide or display the details of each scene as shown in Figure 2-9. By clicking each scene in the Document Outline, you can quickly see the different scenes that make up your user interface.

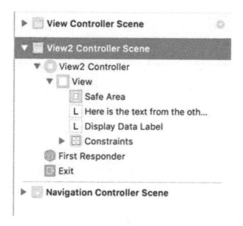

Figure 2-9. *The Document Outline makes it easy to find and view scenes*

Within each scene is a controller. A controller defines how that scene appears on the screen. You can select the controller by clicking the controller name in the Document Outline or by clicking the controller icon in the storyboard as shown in Figure 2-10.

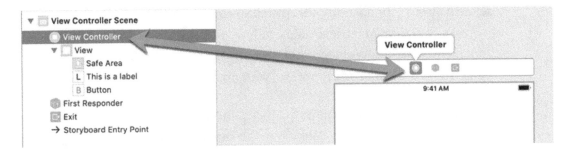

Figure 2-10. *You can select a controller in the Document Outline or in the storyboard*

Within each controller is typically a view, which defines what appears on the screen when the app runs. Objects such as buttons or labels appear on the view, so if you delete a view, you also delete any objects stored on that view.

Let's take a look at the two .swift files in the Single View App project we've created so far and see how the hierarchy of the Document Outline works:

1. Click the AppDelegate.swift file in the Navigator pane. Xcode's middle pane displays the contents of the AppDelegate.swift file. You'll notice several functions already created for you that contain no code. These functions let you handle different conditions when your app runs:

   - didFinishLaunchingWithOptions – Runs after your app starts

   - applicationWillResignActive – Runs before your app no longer remains the active app on the screen

   - applicationDidEnterBackground – Runs as soon as your app is pushed into the background so the user can use a different app

   - applicationWillEnterForeground – Runs right before your app becomes active again on the screen

   - applicationDidBecomeActive – Runs after the app becomes active on the screen

   - applicationWillTerminate – Runs right before your app closes

   In many cases, you won't need to write code for all of these functions. For example, you may want your app to save data before it closes (applicationWillTerminate) and then you may want your app to retrieve data again when it first starts (didFinishLaunchingWithOptions). The AppDelegate.swift file is where you write Swift code to control your app's behavior.

2. Click the Main.storyboard file in the Navigator pane. Xcode displays your user interface. Make sure the Document Outline appears. (You can toggle between showing and hiding the Document Outline by choosing Editor ➤ Show/Hide Document Outline or by clicking the Document Outline icon.)

3. Click the controller icon either in the Document Outline or in the storyboard (see Figure 2-10).

4. Choose View ➤ Inspectors ➤ Show the Identity Inspector, or click the Show the Identity Inspector icon at the top of the Inspector pane. Notice that the Class text field displays the text **ViewController** as shown in Figure 2-11. This name refers to the ViewController.swift file in the Navigator pane and links the controller to the file named ViewController.swift. You can always change the name of your files, but if you change a file name, you must also make sure any controllers use the correct file name.

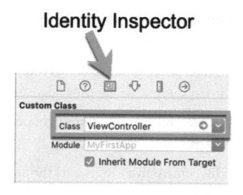

Figure 2-11. The Identity Inspector lets you link .swift files to a controller

5. Choose View ➤ Inspectors ➤ Show Attributes Inspector, or click the Show the Attributes Inspector icon as shown in Figure 2-12.

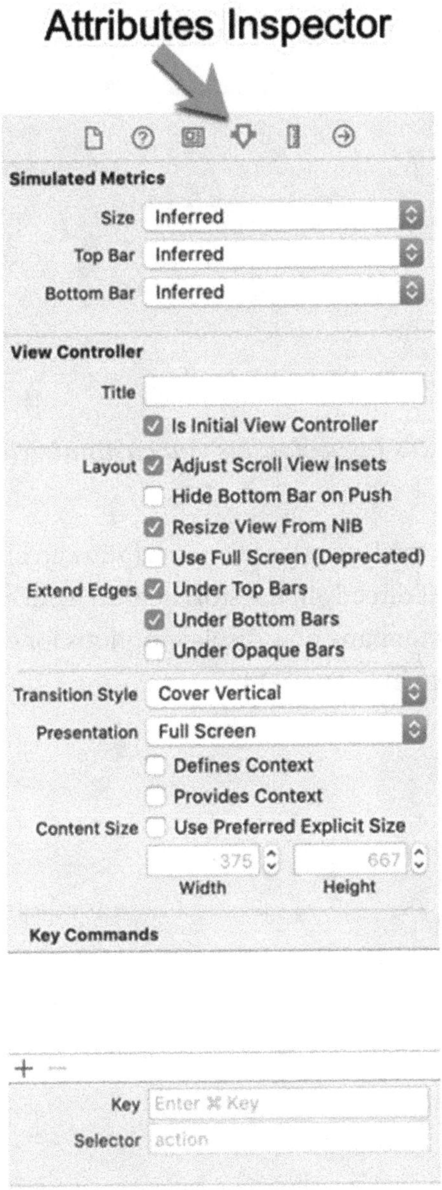

Figure 2-12. *The Attributes Inspector lets you customize how the scene appears*

6. Click **View** in the Document Outline. Notice how the Attributes Inspector pane now displays different options for customizing the view as shown in Figure 2-13.

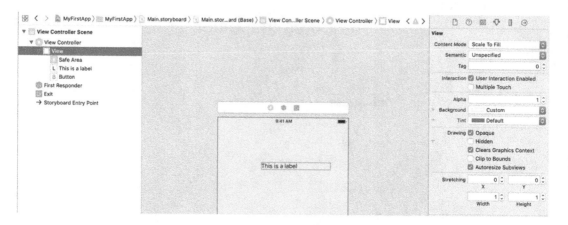

Figure 2-13. *The Attributes Inspector lets you customize how the view appears*

7. Click the label in the Document Outline. (You can also select the
    label by clicking it directly in the storyboard.) Notice how the
    Attributes Inspector pane now displays options for customizing
    the label as shown in Figure 2-14.

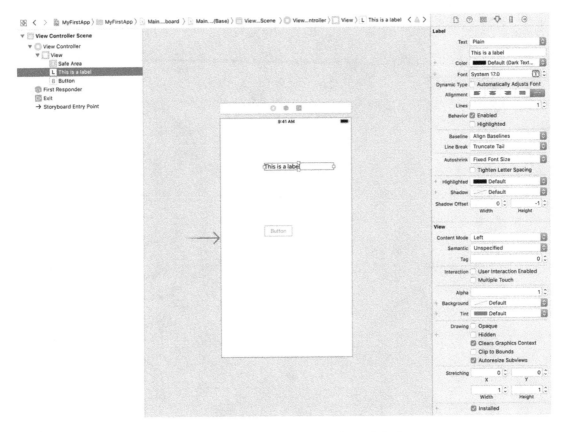

Figure 2-14. *Displaying the Attributes Inspector for a label*

8. Click the button in the Document Outline. (You can also select the button by clicking it directly in the storyboard.) Notice how the Attributes Inspector pane now displays options for customizing the button as shown in Figure 2-15.

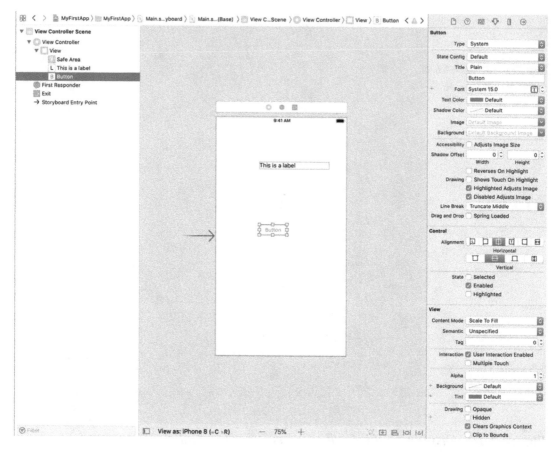

Figure 2-15. *Displaying the Attributes Inspector for a button*

At this point you've seen how to use the Document Outline and the different Inspector panes. The main point is that every storyboard scene has a controller, and every controller needs to be linked to a .swift file. In our Single View App, we just have a single scene.

The controller is given a generic name of View Controller and it's linked to a .swift file called ViewController.swift. When creating your own app, you'll likely want to give both your controller and its linked .swift file a more descriptive name.

To change the name of any controller displayed in the Document Outline, follow these steps:

1. Click the Main.storyboard file in the Navigator pane.

2. Make sure the Document Outline appears by choosing Editor ➤ Show Document Outline or click the Document Outline icon.

3. Click a controller displayed in the Document Outline and press
    ENTER. Xcode highlights the controller name as shown in
    Figure 2-16. Now you can edit the controller name by using the
    arrow keys or BACKSPACE and DELETE keys.

Figure 2-16. *You can edit a controller name in the Document Outline by pressing*
ENTER

Selecting items and pressing ENTER also lets you change the names of files displayed
in the Navigator pane or in the macOS Finder as well.

Working with Different Screen Sizes

When you design a user interface, you have to choose the iOS device screen and
orientation such as an iPhone 8 in portrait orientation or an iPad in landscape
orientation. Since your iOS app might be run on different iOS devices, you need to test
your app on all different screen sizes and orientations.

Xcode gives you three different ways to view your app's user interface in different iOS
device screen sizes and orientations:

*   Click the "View as:" text at the bottom of the Xcode window and
    choose a different iOS device screen size and orientation.

*   Choose a different iOS device and orientation for the Simulator to
    mimic.

*   Preview your views in Xcode.

The first option (clicking the "View as:" text) lets you quickly switch between different iOS screen sizes and orientations. The second option (using the Simulator) lets you test your app as if it were running in an actual iOS device.

You'll likely use the first option while designing your user interface and use the second option to verify everything works. Let's see how to test our Single View App project with different screen sizes and orientations:

1. Make sure you have loaded your MyFirstApp project in Xcode.

2. Click the Main.storyboard file in the Navigator pane. Xcode displays the storyboard of your project.

3. Click the "View as:" text at the bottom of the Xcode window to display the different iOS device and orientation options as shown in Figure 2-17.

Figure 2-17. *Choosing a different iOS device screen size and orientation*

4. Click an iPad Pro icon. Notice that Xcode changes the storyboard to match the size of an iPad Pro screen as shown in Figure 2-18. (You may need to click the minus sign icon to lower the magnification so you can see the entire iPad Pro screen.)

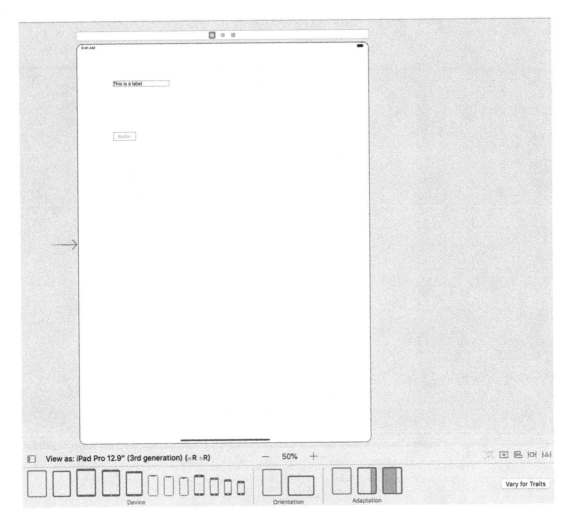

Figure 2-18. *Viewing the app user interface on an iPad Pro screen*

5. Click the smaller iPhone SE icon. Notice how Xcode now displays your user interface to show how it would appear on the smaller iPhone SE screen as shown in Figure 2-19.

41

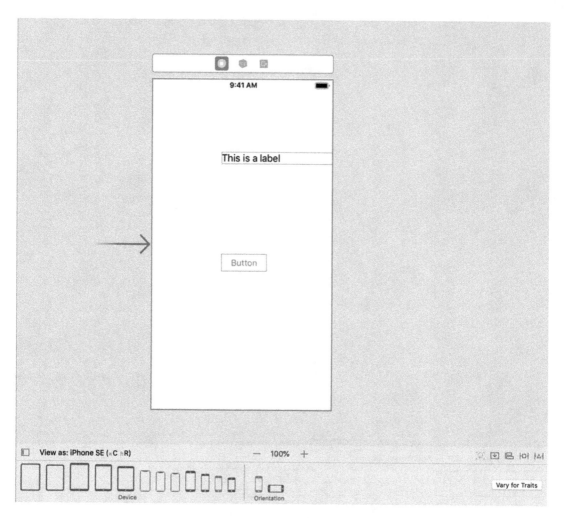

Figure 2-19. *Viewing the app user interface on a smaller iPhone SE screen*

6. Look in the upper left corner of the Xcode window for the name of
    your project (MyFirstApp) followed by the name of an iOS device
    such as iPhone XR as shown in Figure 2-20.

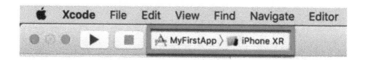

Figure 2-20. *Identifying the type of iOS device the Simulator will mimic*

7. Click the name of the currently displayed iOS device in the upper left corner of the Xcode window. A menu of different iOS devices appears as shown in Figure 2-21.

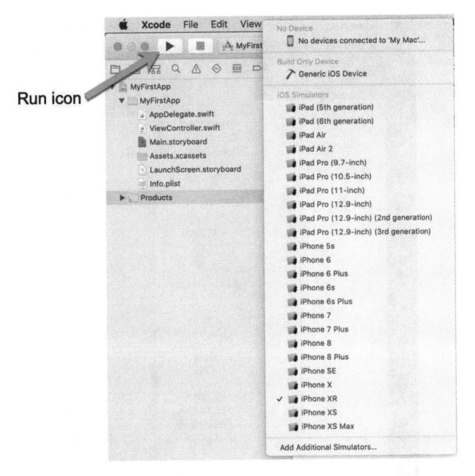

Figure 2-21. *Viewing different iOS devices for the Simulator to mimic*

8. Click a different iOS device than the one currently displayed in the upper left corner of the Xcode window such as iPad Air or iPhone 8 Plus. Once you choose an iOS device for the Simulator to mimic, you need to run the Simulator.

9. Choose Product ➤ Run, press Command + R, or click the Run icon. The Simulator window appears, mimicking your chosen iOS device.

10. Click the Hardware menu and you'll see options to change the orientation of the iOS device such as Rotate Left or Rotate Right as shown in Figure 2-22.

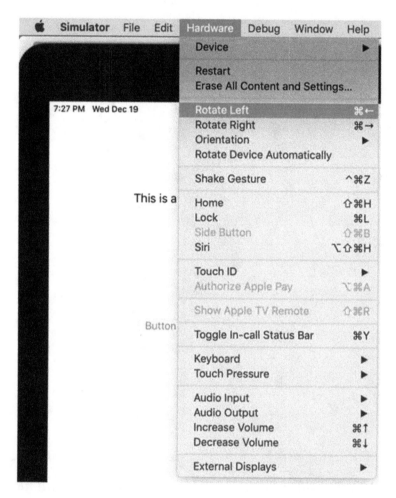

Figure 2-22. *The Hardware menu of the Simulator program*

11. Choose Simulator ➤ Quit Simulator. The Xcode window appears again.

By viewing your user interface in different iOS device screen sizes and orientations, you can make sure your app appears correctly. Since you likely won't have every possible iOS device available to test your app on, you'll have to rely on Xcode and the Simulator program to help you verify that your app looks the way it should no matter what screen size and orientation a user might have.

Previewing the User Interface

Another way to see how your app will look on different iOS device screen sizes is to use the Preview feature. This lets you select a controller in the storyboard and then see how that controller will look in different types of iOS devices.

To see how to preview a controller, follow these steps:

1. Make sure you have loaded your MyFirstApp project in Xcode.

2. Click the Main.storyboard file in the Navigator pane.

3. Choose View ➤ Assistant Editor ➤ Show Assistant Editor or click the Assistant Editor icon. Xcode displays the Main.storyboard file side by side with the ViewController.swift file as shown in Figure 2-23.

Figure 2-23. *Opening the Assistant Editor*

4. Click the double circles that appear at the top of the .swift file. A menu appears as shown in Figure 2-24.

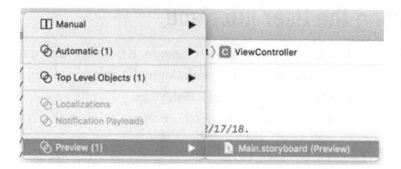

Figure 2-24. *Displaying the double circle menu*

5. Choose Preview ➤ Main.storyboard (Preview). Xcode displays
    your user interface in the current iOS device you've chosen as
    shown in Figure 2-25.

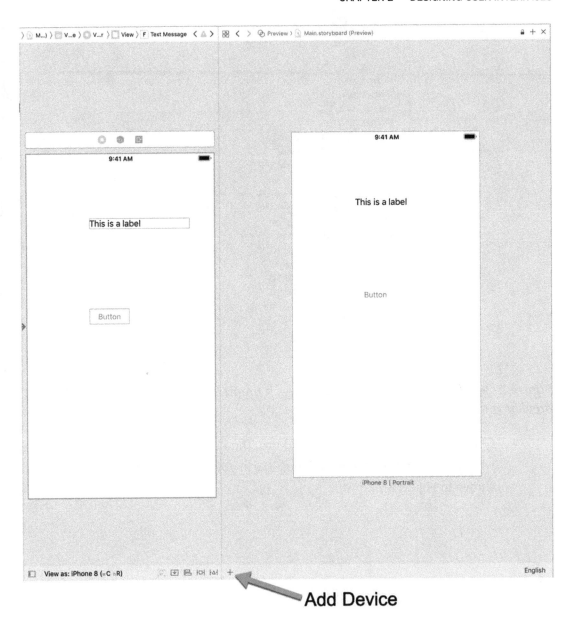

Figure 2-25. *Previewing a user interface*

6. Click the Add Device icon (+). A menu appears, listing all the different iOS devices you can choose as shown in Figure 2-26.

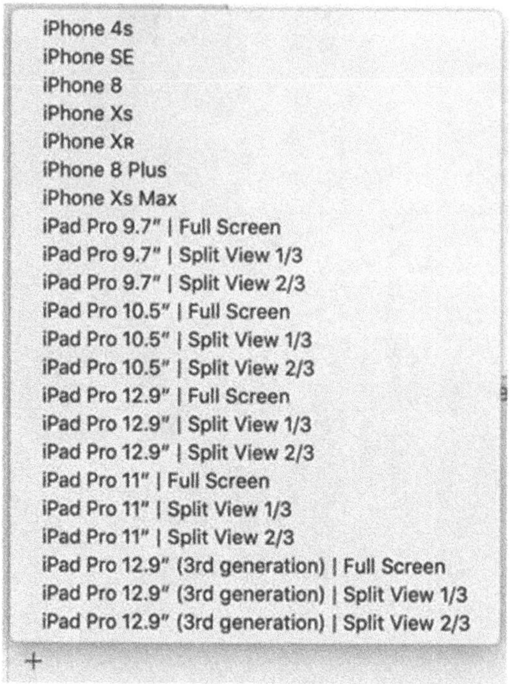

Figure 2-26. *The Add Device icon displays a menu listing different iOS devices to preview a user interface*

7. Click an iOS device such as an iPad Pro. The Preview pane shows what your user interface would look like in your chosen device as shown in Figure 2-27.

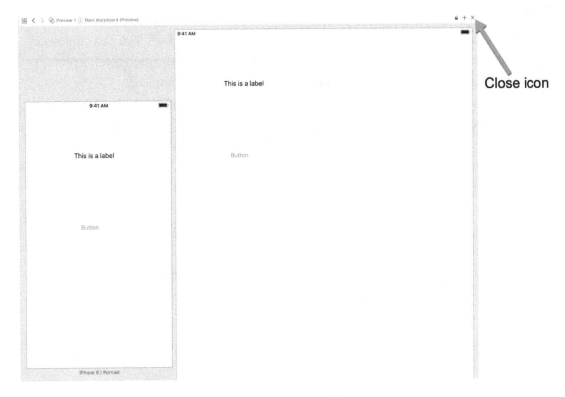

Figure 2-27. *Displaying previews on multiple iOS devices*

8.   Click a preview and press BACKSPACE or DELETE to remove it.

9.   Click the Close icon in the upper right corner of the Preview pane to make the Preview pane disappear.

By using the Preview pane, you can see how your user interface will look on different size iOS devices. Even better, you can compare different size screens side by side.

Summary

Every app needs a user interface. That user interface gets stored in a storyboard that consists of one or more views where a view represents information displayed on a single screen. You can add objects on a view such as buttons, text fields, labels, and sliders. If you have two or more views, you'll also need segues to connect views, showing the order that they appear to the user.

You can add objects to a view programmatically (by writing code) or visually. Programmers often use both methods to design their user interface. You can customize objects (buttons, labels, text fields, etc.) either through code or through the Inspector pane. Each view in your storyboard needs to be linked to a .swift file.

Since iOS apps can run on different types of devices, you need to make sure your app looks good no matter what the screen size or orientation might be. To help you view your app's user interface in different screen sizes and orientations, you can change the iOS device screen size that Xcode uses to display your storyboard.

Another way to test your app's user interface in different screen sizes is to run the Simulator program and define it to mimic different iOS devices such as an iPad Pro or an iPhone 8. If you want to compare how your app will look on different iOS device screens, you can use the Preview feature.

User interfaces represent what users see, so it's important that your user interface always looks good no matter what type of iOS device the user runs it on.

CHAPTER 3

Writing Swift Code

Every iOS app needs a user interface, but that user interface won't do anything until you write Swift code to make it work. While you could write all your code in a single file, it's better to divide your code into files where each file contains related code. A simple app might only contain a handful of files, but a more complicated app could contain dozens or even hundreds of separate files that contain related Swift code. Within each file, you can further organize your Swift code into separate functions.

Swift code is necessary to

- Retrieve data from the user interface

- Calculate some result from retrieved data

- Display that result back on the user interface again

To retrieve data from the user interface, you need to define special variables known as IBOutlets. An IBOutlet is a variable that represents an object displayed on the user interface. Through an IBOutlet, the rest of your Swift code can access and manipulate that data somehow.

To calculate a result from retrieved data, you can write Swift code to manipulate data, but it's far more common to also use Apple's frameworks as well. Apple's frameworks contain dozens of functions that you can use to perform common tasks. That way you can use tested code and spend more time writing code that makes your app do something useful and unique.

To make your app do something, you can create special functions known as IBActions. An IBAction makes a user interface object interactive such as responding if the user taps a button, types text in a text field, or manipulates a slider.

Once your app finishes calculating some result, the final step is to display that result back on the user interface again. To do that, you store the data back in an IBOutlet variable so that the data can appear in the user interface.

© Wallace Wang 2019
W. Wang, *Beginning iPhone Development with Swift 5*, https://doi.org/10.1007/978-1-4842-4865-2_3

IBOutlet variables and IBAction functions are stored in the .swift file linked to the View Controller displaying the user interface objects connected to an IBOutlet variable or an IBAction function. Remember, each View Controller is linked to a .swift file.

To see how IBOutlets and IBAction functions work, follow these steps:

1. Open your MyFirstApp project (or create a new Single View App iOS project).

2. Click the Main.storyboard file in the Navigator pane. The middle Xcode pane displays the contents of your app's user interface. It should display a button and a label.

3. Click the Library icon to open the Object Library window. Then type **text field**.

4. Drag the text field from the Object Library window to the user interface as shown in Figure 3-1.

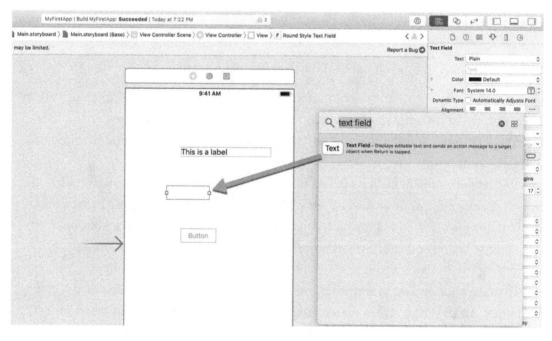

Figure 3-1. *Adding a text field to the view*

5. Resize the width of the text field to make it wider. The exact width isn't important. At this point, your user interface should consist of a label, a text field, and a button. If we ran this app, the user could tap on the button or type in the text field, but nothing would happen. That's because we haven't written any Swift code to make anything work yet.

Creating IBOutlet Variables

An IBOutlet is nothing more than a variable that connects your Swift code to a user interface object such as a text field or a label. By using an IBOutlet, you can retrieve data from a user interface object or put information to appear inside that user interface object.

When creating a variable in Swift, you normally need to declare a variable name and the type of data it can hold such as:

```
var age : Int
```

The preceding code declares a variable called "age" that can hold an integer (Int) value. When you create IBOutlets, you must also declare a variable name. The two differences are that you must also identify the variable as an IBOutlet and you must declare its type as a user interface object such as:

```
@IBOutlet var age: UITextField!
```

To identify an IBOutlet, you must use @IBOutlet in front of "var". Next, you must define the type of user interface object the IBOutlet connects to. In the preceding example, the "age" IBOutlet connects to a text field (UITextField). Some other common types of user interface objects an IBOutlet can connect to include UILabel, UIButton, or UISlider.

Note   Any user interface object that needs to retrieve or display data must be connected to a single IBOutlet variable. However, not all user interface objects need to be connected to an IBOutlet if they won't be used to retrieve or display data.

One way to create an IBOutlet is to type the code yourself. Then you have to link the IBOutlet from your code to the user interface object on the storyboard. A second option is to first create a link from a user interface object to your .swift file and then type just the IBOutlet variable name while Xcode types the rest of the code.

To link code to a storyboard, we have to divide the middle Xcode pane in half using a feature called the Assistant Editor. This will display the storyboard side by side next to a .swift file. Let's see how this works.

1. Open the MyFirstApp project that displays a label, button, and text field on a view (see Figure 3-1). First, we're going to look at the user interface of the app.

2. Click the Main.storyboard file in the Navigator pane. The middle Xcode pane displays the app's storyboard that contains the user interface.

3. Click the controller icon (a yellow circle with a white square inside) either in the Document Outline or at the top of the view as shown in Figure 3-2. This selects the controller that contains the user interface objects to link. In our simple app, there's only one controller, but in a more complicated app, there will be multiple controllers so you need to tell Xcode which one you want to use.

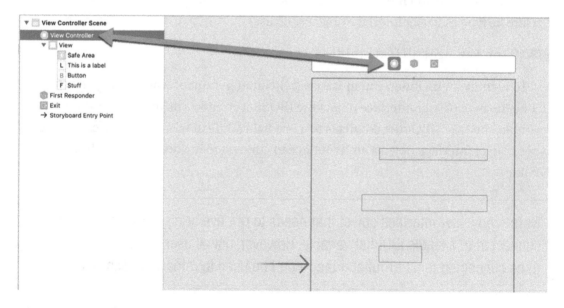

Figure 3-2. *Selecting a controller*

4. Choose View ➤ Assistant Editor ➤ Show Assistant Editor or click
    the Assistant Editor icon. Xcode displays the controller and the
    .swift file that it's linked to as shown in Figure 3-3.

Figure 3-3. *Opening the Assistant Editor*

5. Click in the ViewController.swift file and type @IBOutlet var
    labelResult: UILabel! So the entire code in the ViewController.
    swift file should look like this:

```
import UIKit

class ViewController: UIViewController {

    @IBOutlet var labelResult: UILabel!

    override func viewDidLoad() {
        super.viewDidLoad()

    }

}
```

Notice that an empty circle appears to the left of your newly
created IBOutlet as shown in Figure 3-4. This empty circle
represents the link to your user interface object. Because it's
empty, that means this IBOutlet hasn't been linked to any user
interface object yet.

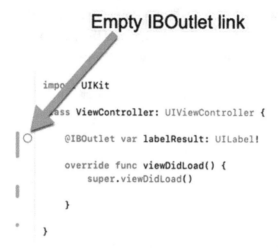

Figure 3-4. *An IBOutlet that hasn't been linked to a user interface object*

6. Move the mouse pointer over this empty circle, hold down the left
    mouse button, and drag the mouse until it appears over the label
    either on the storyboard or in the Document Outline as shown in
    Figure 3-5.

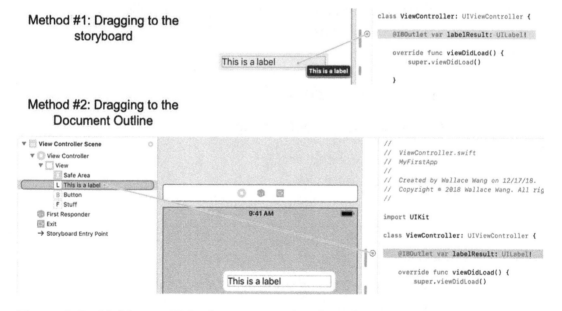

Figure 3-5. *Linking an IBOutlet to a user interface object*

7. Release the left mouse button. Move the mouse pointer over the circle (which should no longer appear empty) that appears to the left of the IBOutlet. Xcode highlights the user interface object linked to that IBOutlet and displays the name of that IBOutlet underneath as shown in Figure 3-6.

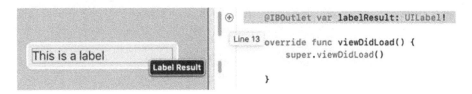

Figure 3-6. *Verifying a connection between an IBOutlet and a user interface object*

8. Click the label on the storyboard or in the Document Outline to select it. Then choose View ➤ Inspectors ➤ Show Connections Inspector, or click the Show the Connections Inspector icon. Xcode shows that the labelResult IBOutlet is connected to the ViewController.swift file as shown in Figure 3-7.

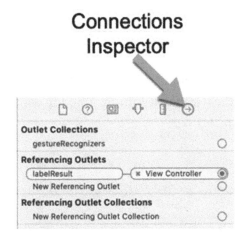

Figure 3-7. *Verifying that an IBOutlet is connected to a user interface object in the Connections Inspector*

Writing code is one way to create an IBOutlet, but you need to know what type of user interface object you're connecting to such as a UITextField or a UILabel. A faster and simpler way to create an IBOutlet is to Ctrl-drag from the user interface object (such as a text field or label) into the .swift file. We'll use this method for the text field.

9. Move the mouse over the text field on the storyboard or in the Document Outline, hold down the Control key, and Ctrl-drag the mouse from the text field to the area in the ViewController.swift file underneath the existing IBOutlet as shown in Figure 3-8.

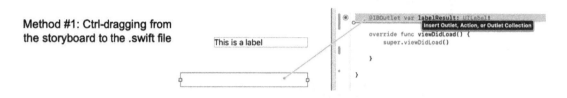

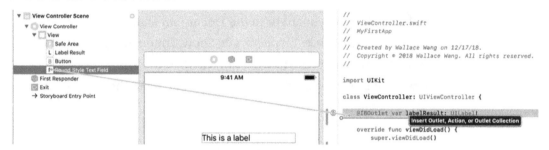

Figure 3-8. *Ctrl-dragging from a user interface object to a .swift file*

10. When a horizontal line appears inside the .swift file, release the Control key and the left mouse button. A popup window appears as shown in Figure 3-9.

Figure 3-9. *Customizing the text that appears on a label using the Attributes Inspector pane*

11. Click in the Name text field and type **textMessage**. This name for your IBOutlet can be anything you want.

12. Click the Connect button. Xcode creates an IBOutlet in your .swift file:

@IBOutlet var textMessage: UITextField!

Notice that when you Ctrl-drag from a user interface object in the storyboard or Document Outline, Xcode automatically types most of the necessary code. All you need to do is type a descriptive name for your IBOutlet. Because this method involves less typing (which decreases your chances of making a mistake), it's often easier and more reliable to use this Ctrl-drag method instead to create IBOutlets.

13. Right-click the text field. Xcode displays a popup menu showing you the Connections Inspector as shown in Figure 3-10. Right-clicking an object can be faster than opening the Connections Inspector pane.

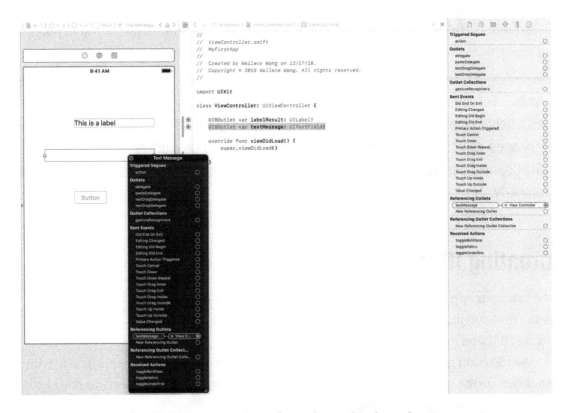

Figure 3-10. *Right-clicking a user interface object displays the Connections Inspector*

14.   Click the Close (X) icon in the upper left corner of the popup menu to make it go away.

15.   Choose View ➤ Standard Editor ➤ Show Standard Editor, or click the Standard Editor icon as shown in Figure 3-11. The Standard Editor appears, displaying the contents of only one file in the middle Xcode pane.

Figure 3-11. *Returning to the Standard Editor*

At this point, we've connected our label and text field to two different IBOutlets. This allows us to retrieve data from the user interface and display new information on the user interface. Of course, IBOutlets simply represent user interface objects, but to make an app truly interactive, we need to create something called IBAction methods.

Note   Forgetting to connect IBOutlets to user interface objects (or connecting IBOutlets to the wrong object) is a common source of errors when developing iOS apps. Any time your user interface doesn't seem to be working right, open the Connections Inspector pane and check to see if your IBOutlets are connected properly.

Creating IBAction Methods

If we run our app right now, the user will see a button on the screen, but the button won't do anything. To make any part of the user interface actually work, we need to create IBAction methods.

An IBAction method contains Swift code that runs every time the user interacts with an object on the user interface such as a button, slider, or switch. IBAction methods let users make an app do something useful.

To create an IBAction method, you need to use the Assistant Editor to display the storyboard side by side with the .swift file linked to a particular controller. Let's see how this works.

1. Click the Main.storyboard file in the Navigator pane. Xcode's middle pane displays the storyboard that contains your app's user interface.

2. Click the controller icon (a yellow circle with a white square inside) either in the Document Outline or at the top of the view (see Figure 3-2). This selects the controller that contains the user interface objects to link.

3. Choose View ➤ Assistant Editor ➤ Show Assistant Editor or click the Assistant Editor icon. Xcode displays the controller and the .swift file that it's linked to (see Figure 3-3).

4. Click the button to select it.

5. Hold down the Control key and Ctrl-drag the mouse from the button to the area above the last curly bracket in the ViewController.swift file as shown in Figure 3-12.

Figure 3-12. *Ctrl-dragging from a button to the .swift file*

6. Release the Control key and the left mouse button. A popup window appears. Make sure the Connection popup menu displays Action.

Note   One common mistake is to create an IBOutlet variable (when the Connection popup menu displays Outlet) instead of an IBAction method (when the Connection popup menu displays Action). Always check the Connection popup menu to make sure it displays Outlet or Action, depending on what you want to create.

---

7. Click in the Name text field and type **changeButton**.

8. Click in the Type popup menu and choose UIButton as shown in
    Figure 3-13.

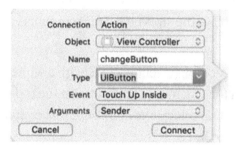

Figure 3-13. *The Attributes Inspector lets you customize how the scene appears*

9. Click the Connect button. Xcode creates an IBAction method:

    ```
    @IBAction func changeButton(_ sender: UIButton) {
    }
    ```

    This IBAction method runs every time the user taps on the button.
    Now we need to write Swift code inside this IBAction method to
    make it actually do something.

10. Modify this IBAction method as follows:

    ```
    @IBAction func changeButton(_ sender: UIButton) {
        labelResult.text = textMessage.text
    }
    ```

    Notice that as you type, Xcode displays a list of commands it
    thinks you want to type as shown in Figure 3-14. Rather than type
    a complete command, you can simply select the command you
    want and press ENTER to make Xcode type this command for you
    automatically.

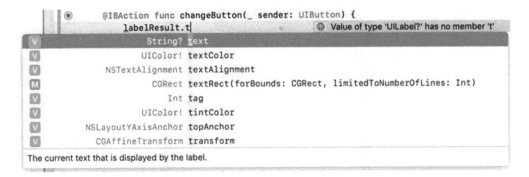

Figure 3-14. *Xcode's auto-complete feature tries to guess the command you want to type*

The preceding code for the IBAction method simply takes the text stored in the textMessage IBOutlet (which is connected to the text field) and displays it in the labelResult IBOutlet (which is connected to the label). Let's see it actually work.

11.   Choose Product ➤ Run, or click the Run button. The Simulator appears.

12.   Click in the text field and type **Hello there!**

13.   Click the button. Notice that the label now displays *Hello there!* as shown in Figure 3-15.

Figure 3-15. *Running the app in the Simulator*

14. Choose Simulator ➤ Quit Simulator. The Xcode window appears again.

15. Choose View ➤ Standard Editor ➤ Show Standard Editor, or click the Standard Editor icon (see Figure 3-11). The Standard Editor appears, displaying the contents of only one file in the middle Xcode pane.

This example demonstrates several key principles of writing Swift code:

- Every user interface object that needs to retrieve or display data must be connected to an IBOutlet variable.

- Every user interface object that the user interacts with must be connected to an IBAction method.

- The Assistant Editor helps you create IBOutlet variables and IBAction methods.

- As you type Swift code, Xcode displays lists of commands it thinks you want to type.

Using Apple's Frameworks

While it's possible to write Swift code to perform various tasks, it's often easier to use Apple's frameworks instead. Apple provides several commonly needed functions so you don't have to re-invent the wheel and rewrite code that Apple has already written for you. This lets you use Apple's proven and tested code so your app will be more reliable as a result.

In our example, our app simply takes any text typed into the text field and displays it in the label. Let's make this fancier and have the label take any text typed into the text field and display that same text in uppercase.

To do this, we could write Swift code to substitute each letter and replace it with its uppercase equivalent, but this would take time to write and even more time to test. As a simpler alternative, we can just use a special function that Apple's framework provides for us called uppercased().

This uppercased() function already works and doesn't require us to write our own code to replace lowercase letters with uppercase letters so it will save us time and increase the reliability of our app. As a general rule, rely on Apple's frameworks as much as possible and only write code when Apple's frameworks can't help you.

To use one of Apple's frameworks, you have to import it into your .swift file. If you look in either the AppDelegate.swift or ViewController.swift file, you'll see the following line:

```
import UIKit
```

The preceding line allows that particular file to use any code stored in the UIKit framework. More complicated apps typically use more than one framework such as:

```
import UIKit
import SceneKit
import ARKit
```

The preceding code allows access to code stored in the UIKit, SceneKit, and ARKit frameworks. Whenever you need to use code stored in a different framework, you can simply add it to your .swift file by adding an import line at the top of your .swift file.

Let's see how to use the uppercased() function in our code:

1. Open the MyFirstApp project in Xcode.

2. Click the ViewController.swift file in the Navigator pane.

3. Modify the IBAction method as follows:

```
@IBAction func changeButton(_ sender: UIButton) {
    labelResult.text = textMessage.text?.uppercased()
}
```

   By simply using the uppercased() function, we can change lowercase letters into uppercase without wasting time writing our own code to do this.

4. Choose Product ➤ Run, or click the Run button. The Simulator appears.

5. Click in the text field and type **Hello there!**

6. Click the button. Notice that the label now displays *HELLO THERE!* as shown in Figure 3-16.

Figure 3-16. *Running the app in the Simulator using the uppercased() function*

7.   Choose Simulator ➤ Quit Simulator. The Xcode window appears again.

Using the Xcode Editor

When you type and edit Swift code, Xcode displays certain text in different colors to help you understand the different parts of your commands. These different colors highlight the following:

- Black – Arbitrary commands that the user typed

- Magenta – Swift keywords such as func (function) or @IBOutlet

- Purple – Classes, properties, or methods such as UIButton, text, or uppercased

- Green – Variable names

- Red – Strings

Users can always customize how Xcode uses different colors to identify the parts of Swift code. To see what colors may be assigned to display different Swift code, follow these steps:

1. Choose Xcode ➤ Preferences. A Preferences window appears.

2. Click the Fonts & Colors icon. A list of different themes appears in the left pane.

3. Click the theme currently being used by Xcode to view which colors are being used to identify different Swift commands as shown in Figure 3-17. (You can identify the theme currently being used by Xcode if you choose Editor ➤ Theme.)

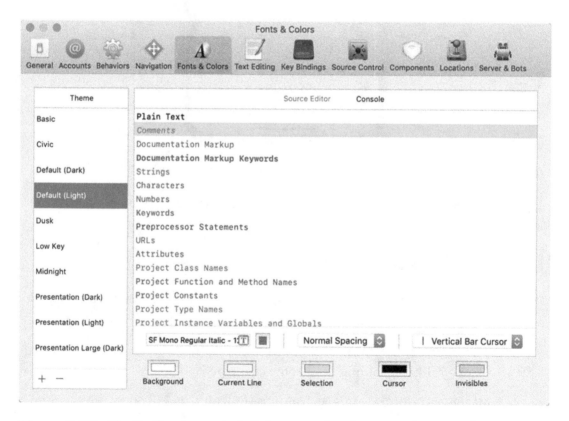

Figure 3-17. *The Preferences window lets you view how Xcode uses different colors to identify Swift code*

4. Click the red Close button in the upper left corner of the Preferences window to make it go away.

Getting Help with Swift Commands

The code in a typical app will contain a mixture of your own code along with methods and properties. To help you understand what various code might mean, you can get help on specific commands by holding down the Option key and clicking a particular command. To see how this works, follow these steps:

1. Load the MyFirstApp project in Xcode.

2. Click the ViewController.swift file in the Navigator pane.

3. Hold down the Option key and move the mouse pointer over the uppercased() function near the bottom of the ViewController.swift file. The mouse pointer turns into a question mark.

4. Click the uppercased() function while holding down the Option key. Xcode displays a window that explains how the uppercased() function works as shown in Figure 3-18.

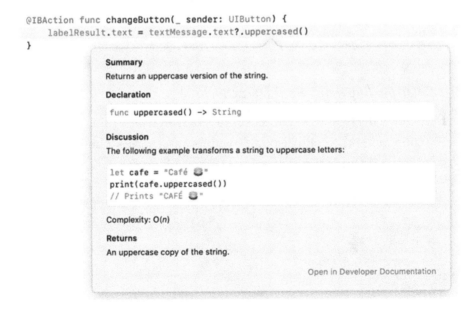

Figure 3-18. Getting help by holding down the Option key and clicking a command

5.   Hold down the Option key and click UITextField! Xcode displays
     another window that explains more about the UITextField!
     Command as shown in Figure 3-19.

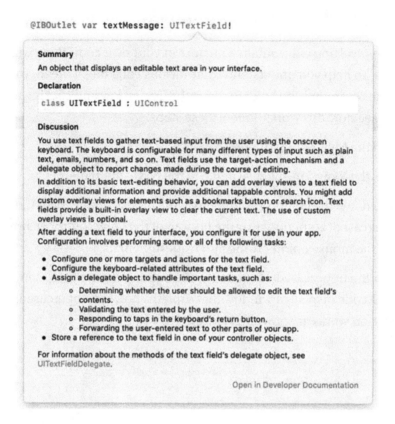

Figure 3-19. *Displaying help about UITextField*

6.   Hold down the Option key and click labelResult inside the
     IBAction method. Xcode displays a window that shows where the
     labelResult IBOutlet was declared as shown in Figure 3-20.

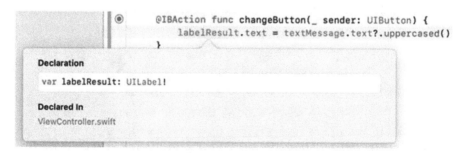

Figure 3-20. *Displaying additional information about the labelResult IBOutlet*

By holding down the Option key and clicking different Swift commands, you can get quick help on that command right within the Xcode editor.

Folding and Unfolding Functions

In complicated apps, a single .swift file will likely contain multiple functions. This can make finding a specific line of code difficult. To temporarily hide code stored in functions, Xcode can fold and unfold functions. Folding collapses a function so you can see its name but not any code stored inside. Unfolding expands a function so you can see all of its code.

To see how to fold and unfold functions in a .swift file, follow these steps:

1. Load the MyFirstApp project in Xcode.

2. Click the ViewController.swift file in the Navigator pane.

3. Choose Editor ➤ Code Folding ➤ Fold Methods and Functions. Xcode now only displays all function names but not any of the code inside each function as shown in Figure 3-21. Notice that each folded function displays an ellipsis (…) to show that it's hiding its code from sight.

```
override func viewDidLoad() { ••• }

@IBAction func changeButton(_ sender: UIButton) { ••• }
```

Figure 3-21. *Folded functions*

4. Double-click the ellipsis at the end of the viewDidLoad folded function. Xcode now displays that function's code.

By folding functions, you can hide code that you don't want to see and focus just on the code you do want to see. Code folding is one more simple way Xcode makes viewing and editing code a little bit easier.

Summary

Swift code tells your app what to do. To retrieve or display data on the user interface, you need to create IBOutlet variables and link them to different user interface objects such as text fields and labels. If a user interface object won't retrieve or display data, then you won't need to create an IBOutlet variable for that object.

To make certain user interface objects interactive such as buttons, you need to write IBAction methods. When you create an IBAction method, you also need to write Swift code that does something useful. Both IBOutlet variables and IBAction methods get stored in the .swift file connected to a particular controller.

To keep you from rewriting commonly used code, Apple offers frameworks that contain functions that you can use. These framework functions have been tested so you can use them and write apps faster by focusing solely on the unique code that makes your app work. Apple provides dozens of different frameworks that your app can use although it's unlikely you'll ever use or need all of them in a single app.

To help you write and understand Swift code, Xcode lets you hold down the Option key and click different commands. This displays a window that offers further explanations for how a particular command works. Since many .swift files contain lots of code, Xcode lets you temporarily hide code in functions so you can focus on only the code you want to see.

Swift code makes your app do something useful, so you'll spend lots of time writing, rewriting, and studying code. Knowing how to use Swift is just the first step to creating iOS apps. You also need to know how to use Xcode as well.

CHAPTER 4

Using Xcode

Before you start writing Swift code and designing user interfaces, take a moment to get acquainted with Xcode, Apple's free tool for creating apps. Xcode offers so many features because it's designed to handle all your needs in creating an app from start to finish. Fortunately, you won't have to learn every single feature of Xcode to start creating apps. Instead, you can just focus on learning only the features you need and gradually learn any additional features of Xcode later. Xcode provides the following features to help you create apps for all of Apple's products:

- Writing and editing Swift code

- Designing a user interface

- Debugging your app to find and fix problems

- Running and testing your app

Xcode is both an editor and a compiler. The editor lets you write and modify Swift code along with designing and customizing user interfaces. Once you're done creating your user interface and Swift code, you can use Xcode to compile and run your app to make sure it works.

Changing Xcode's Appearance

Whether you're working on a small laptop screen or a much larger desktop monitor, chances are good you won't always have enough room to see everything in Xcode. That's why Xcode offers several ways to hide or display information. That way you can focus on what you want to see and avoid the clutter of additional information that might get in your way.

© Wallace Wang 2019
W. Wang, *Beginning iPhone Development with Swift 5*, https://doi.org/10.1007/978-1-4842-4865-2_4

Some of the different parts that Xcode can hide or display include the following:

- Navigator pane

- Toolbar

- Tab bar

- Debug Area

- Inspector pane

- Document Outline

- Object Library

The Navigator Pane

The Navigator pane appears on the left side of the Xcode window. You can toggle between hiding and displaying the Navigator pane by choosing any of the following commands:

- Choose View ➤ Navigators ➤ Show/Hide Navigator.

- Press Command + 0 (zero).

You can also resize the width of the Navigator pane by moving the mouse pointer over the border of the Navigator pane and dragging the mouse left or right. By making the Navigator pane too narrow, you can hide it completely.

Note   Dragging the mouse to the left can hide the Navigator pane, but then you'll need to choose View ➤ Navigators ➤ Show Navigator or press Command + 0 (zero) to make the Navigator pane appear again.

Although the Navigator pane can display different information, the three most common types of information to use include the following:

- Project Navigator (Command + 1) – Displays all the folders and files that make up your project including your .swift files and .storyboard user interface.

- Symbol Navigator (Command + 3) – Lists all the functions stored in each .swift file.

- Issue Navigator (Command + 5) – Displays possible problems with your project.

To see how these three different types of navigators work, follow these steps:

1. Open the MyFirstApp project that displays a label, button, and text field on a view.

2. Choose View ➤ Navigators ➤ Show Project Navigator, press Command + 1, or click the Project Navigator icon. Xcode shows a list of folders and files that make up your project as shown in Figure 4-1. The Project Navigator is used when you want to view a different file in the middle Xcode pane.

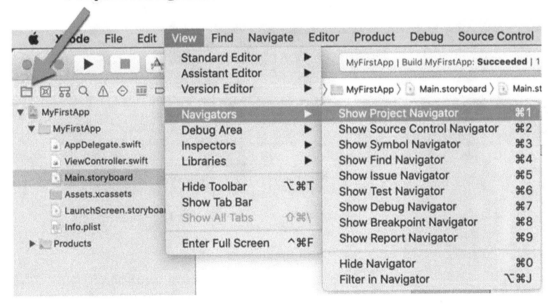

Figure 4-1. *Choosing the Project Navigator*

3. Click the ViewController.swift file in the Navigator pane. Xcode's middle pane displays the contents of the ViewController.swift file so you can write and edit Swift code in that file.

4. Click the Main.storyboard file in the Navigator pane. Xcode's
    middle pane displays the user interface of your app so you can
    design and edit the user interface such as adding buttons or
    labels.

5. Choose View ➤ Navigators ➤ Show Symbol Navigator, press
    Command + 3, or click the Symbol Navigator icon. Xcode shows
    a list of .swift files that make up your project. By clicking the gray
    disclosure triangle to the left of each .swift file name, you can
    expand or collapse the list of functions and variables used in each
    .swift file as shown in Figure 4-2.

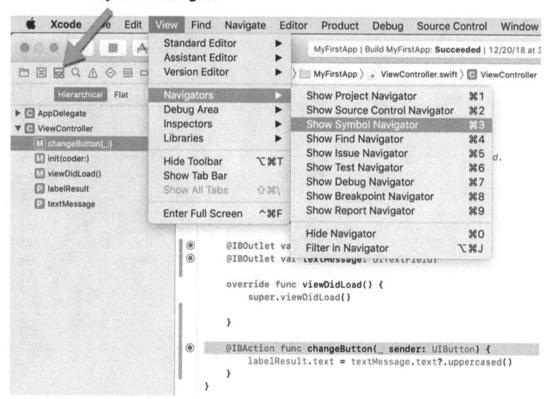

Figure 4-2. *The Symbol Navigator lets you quickly find a function or variable
stored in a .swift file*

6. Click the gray disclosure triangle to the left of the ViewController file to display the list of functions (also known as methods, identified by a capital M icon) and variables (also known as properties, identified by a capital P icon) in that file.

7. Click the changeButton method. Xcode highlights the changeButton method in the ViewController.swift file (see Figure 4-2).

8. Click the labelResult property. Xcode highlights the labelResult property in the ViewController.swift file. The Symbol Navigator helps you quickly jump to a specific property or method in your project.

9. Choose View ➤ Navigators ➤ Show Project Navigator, press Command + 1, or click the Project Navigator icon. Then click the Main.storyboard file to view your app's user interface.

10. Choose View ➤ Navigators ➤ Show Issue Navigator, press Command + 5, or click the Issue Navigator icon. The Issue Navigator displays warnings about your project as shown in Figure 4-3. Yellow icons represent problems that let your app still work but could cause problems with the user interface's appearance or code not being completely safe to run. Red icons represent problems that keep your app from working at all.

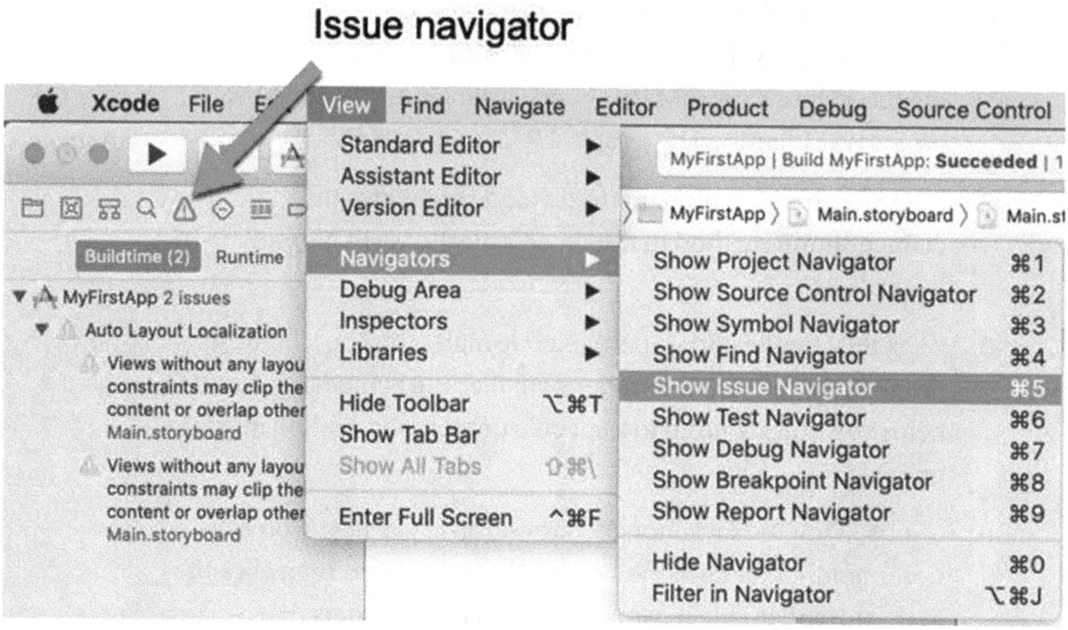

Issue navigator

Figure 4-3. *The Issue Navigator lets you view possible problems with your project*

The Toolbar

The Toolbar appears at the top of the Xcode window and displays icons that give you one-click access to common commands as shown in Figure 4-4 such as

- Run – Runs your iOS project so you can test it in the Simulator (which mimics an iOS device) or an actual iOS device connected to your Macintosh

- Stop – Stops running your iOS project

- Scheme – Lets you choose which iOS device to mimic in the Simulator or which iOS device to use if connected to your Macintosh

- Library – Opens the Object Library for designing a user interface (when viewing a .storyboard file in Xcode's middle pane) or the Code library (when viewing a .swift file in Xcode's middle pane)

- Standard Editor – Displays the Standard Editor in Xcode's middle pane

- Assistant Editor – Displays two editors side by side in Xcode's middle pane

- Show/Hide Navigator pane – Toggles between hiding and showing the Navigator pane on the left side of the Xcode window

- Show/Hide Debug Area – Toggles between hiding and showing the Debug Area at the bottom of the Xcode window

- Show/Hide Inspector pane – Toggles between hiding and showing the Inspector pane on the right side of the Xcode window

Figure 4-4. *The Toolbar at the top of the Xcode window*

You can toggle between hiding and showing the Toolbar by choosing one of the following:

- Choose View ➤ Show/Hide Toolbar.

- Press Option + Command + T.

When you want to test your app, you can click the Scheme popup menu to choose an iOS device. Then click the Run and Stop icons on the Toolbar to start or stop your app from running on your chosen iOS device.

When you want to edit a .swift or .storyboard file, you can click the Standard Editor icon on the Toolbar. When you need to view two files side by side, such as a .swift and a .storyboard file, you can click the Assistant Editor icon. When editing a .storyboard file, you can click the Library icon to access different objects to place on your user interface.

Finally, you can selectively hide or show the Navigator pane, Debug Area, or Inspector pane. Hiding any of these areas gives the middle pane more room to appear in Xcode.

To see how these common icons work in Xcode, follow these steps:

1. Make sure your MyFirstApp project is loaded in Xcode.

2. Choose View ➤ Hide Toolbar. The Toolbar disappears from the top of the Xcode window.

3. Choose View ➤ Show Toolbar. The Toolbar appears again at the top of the Xcode window.

4. Click the Show/Hide Navigator pane icon on the far right of the Toolbar. Notice that the Navigator pane disappears.

5. Click the Show/Hide Navigator pane icon again to make the Navigator pane appear.

6. Click the Show/Hide Inspector icon. Notice that the Inspector pane disappears.

7. Click the Show/Hide Inspector pane icon again to make the Inspector pane appear again.

8. Click the Scheme popup menu on the far left of the Toolbar. A menu appears listing different iOS devices you can select for the Simulator to mimic as shown in Figure 4-5.

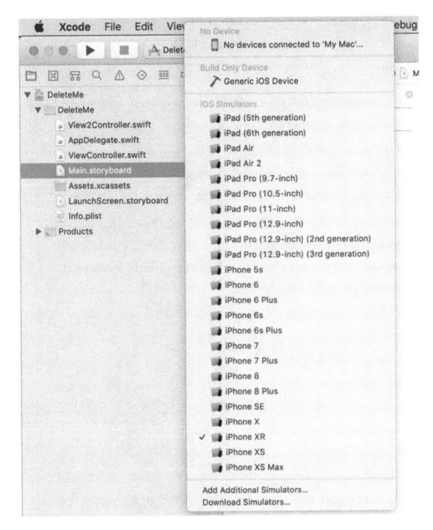

Figure 4-5. *The Scheme popup menu displays different iOS devices you can test your app on*

9. Select an iOS device such as iPhone 8 or iPhone XR.

10. Click the ViewController.swift file in the Navigator pane.

11. Edit the ViewController.swift file so the changeButton method looks like this:

```
@IBAction func changeButton(_ sender: UIButton) {
    labelResult.text = textMessage.text?.uppercased()
    print (labelResult.text!)
}
```

12. Click the Run icon on the Toolbar. The Simulator appears, displaying the MyFirstApp's user interface.

13. Click in the text field on the user interface and type **Hello, world!**

14. Click the button on the user interface. The label displays HELLO, WORLD!

15. Click the Stop icon on the Toolbar in the Xcode window. Notice that this stops your app from running on the Simulator, but the Simulator window still remains on the screen.

16. Choose Simulator ➤ Quit Simulator to make the Simulator window go away. Notice that the bottom of the Xcode window displays the Debug Area because the print (labelResult.text!) command prints HELLO, WORLD! in the Debug Area as shown in Figure 4-6.

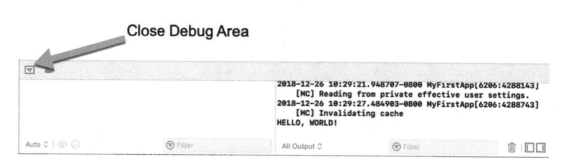

Figure 4-6. The Debug Area appears at the bottom of the Xcode pane

17. Click the Show/Hide Debug Area icon on the far right of the Toolbar, or click the Close Debug Area in the upper left corner of the Debug Area pane. Notice that the Debug Area disappears.

The Tab Bar

One problem with Xcode is that you can normally view one file at a time by clicking that file in the Navigator pane. The Assistant Editor lets you see two files side by side, but each file appears narrow. To help you switch back and forth between files quickly, you can use the Tab bar.

By default, the Tab bar remains hidden. To toggle between showing and hiding the Tab bar, choose View ➤ Show/Hide Tab Bar.

The main purpose of the Tab bar is to display tabs representing different .swift or .storyboard files. By clicking a tab, you can quickly switch between files within clicking the file name in the Navigator pane first.

To see how to use the Tab bar, follow these steps:

1. Make sure the MyFirstApp project is loaded in Xcode.

2. Click the Main.storyboard file in the Navigator pane. Xcode displays the .storyboard file in the middle pane.

3. Choose View ➤ Show Tab Bar. The Tab bar appears at the Xcode window. Initially there's only one tab that displays the name of the Main.storyboard file as shown in Figure 4-7.

Tab   Create new tab

Figure 4-7. *Each tab displays the name of the file displayed by that tab*

4. Click the New tab icon (+) on the far right of the Tab bar. Xcode displays a second tab.

5. Click the ViewController.swift file in the Navigator pane. Notice that the Tab bar now displays two tabs: one representing the Main. storyboard file and the other representing the ViewController.swift file.

6. Click the Main.storyboard tab. Xcode displays the .storyboard file.

7. Click the ViewController.swift tab. Xcode displays the .swift file. By using tabs, you can load the files you need to edit most often and switch back and forth between them.

8. Choose View ➤ Show All Tabs, or press Shift + Command + \. Xcode displays thumbnail images of all your open tabs. This lets you quickly view all your currently open files as shown in Figure 4-8. (You can create a new tab by clicking the + thumbnail.)

Figure 4-8. *Tabs displayed as thumbnail images*

9. Choose View ➤ Show All Tabs or press Shift + Command + \ to hide thumbnail images of your tabs.

10. Move the mouse pointer to the left of the ViewController.swift tab. A Close icon (X) appears as shown in Figure 4-9.

Figure 4-9. *The Close icon appears on the far left of each tab*

11. Click the Close icon on the ViewController.swift tab. The tab disappears. Notice that you must always have at least one tab in the Tab bar.

12. Chose View ➤ Hide Tab Bar. Xcode now hides the Tab bar.

Note   You can only hide the Tab bar when you only have exactly one tab open. If you have multiple tabs open, the Hide Tab Bar command appears grayed out.

Marking Swift Code

By using the Symbol Navigator, you can view all the .swift files in your project and jump to the properties and methods stored in each file. However, if you want to divide a .swift file into arbitrary sections, you can create a special MARK comment that lets you define a group of related code. The MARK command looks like this:

```
// MARK: <description>
```

The two // symbols define this line as a comment.

The MARK: command defines this command as a markup section.

The <description> text represents any arbitrary text you want to define the name of your section. If you wanted to name your section All Properties, then the markup line would look like this:

```
// MARK: All Properties
```

By dividing your Swift code with the MARK comment, you can quickly jump to different parts of any .swift file. To see how this works, follow these steps:

1. Open the MyFirstApp project in Xcode.

2. Click the ViewController.swift file in the Navigator pane.

3. Modify the ViewController.swift file with two // MARK: comments above the IBOutlet properties and IBAction method so it looks like this:

```
import UIKit

class ViewController: UIViewController {

    // MARK: Properties
    @IBOutlet var labelResult: UILabel!
    @IBOutlet var textMessage: UITextField!

    override func viewDidLoad() {
        super.viewDidLoad()

    }

    // MARK: Methods
    @IBAction func changeButton(_ sender: UIButton) {
        labelResult.text = textMessage.text?.uppercased()
        print (labelResult.text!)
    }
}
```

Notice that the top of the middle pane in Xcode displays a hierarchy such as MyFirstApp ➤ MyFirstApp ➤ ViewController. swift as shown in Figure 4-10.

Figure 4-10. *The hierarchy list of project, folder, and file*

4. Click the last item that appears after ViewController.swift > (in Figure 4-10, that item is viewDidLoad()). A menu appears as shown in Figure 4-11.

Figure 4-11. *A popup menu for jumping to a different part of the currently open .swift file*

5. Click Properties. Xcode highlights the // MARK: Properties line.

6. Click the last item that appears after ViewController.swift > to display the popup menu again.

7. Click Methods. Xcode highlights the // MARK: Methods line.

In a short file like our current ViewController.swift file, using the // MARK: comments may not be necessary, but in a large file with lots of Swift code, you can see that dividing a large file into named sections will make finding and jumping to a specific part of a .swift file much faster and easier.

Even if you don't add // MARK: comments to any of your .swift files, you can still click the hierarchy list of items to jump to different parts of your .swift file. Instead of clicking Properties or Methods (defined by // MARK: comments) in Figure 4-11, you could easily click the different properties (labelResult or textMessage) or the different methods (viewDidLoad or changeButton) to jump to that particular spot in the .swift file.

Renaming and Deleting IBOutlet Variables

When you need to link Swift code to a user interface object, you need to create an IBOutlet variable that represents that user interface object such as

@IBOutlet var petLabel: UILabel!

If you want to rename an IBOutlet, you might think you can just edit the IBOutlet variable name, but if you do this, you'll also get an error when running your project. The problem is that if you rename an IBOutlet in a .swift file, the Connections Inspector is still looking for a connection to the previous IBOutlet name.

To rename an IBOutlet variable, you must let Xcode change the IBOutlet name in both the .swift file and in the Connections Inspector pane by using the Refactor command.

To see how the Refactor command works to rename an IBOutlet, follow these steps:

1. Open the MyFirstApp project in Xcode.

2. Click the ViewController.swift file in the Navigator pane.

3. Select the textMessage IBOutlet. You can manually select the entire "textMessage" name or simply double-click it to select it. Make sure the entire "textMessage" appears selected.

4. Choose Editor ➤ Refactor ➤ Rename as shown in Figure 4-12. Xcode highlights all areas in your project where it found your selected text (such as "textMessage") as shown in Figure 4-13.

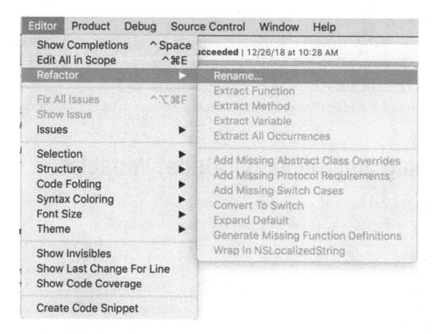

Figure 4-12. *The Refactor command appeared on the Editor menu*

Figure 4-13. *The Refactor command lets Xcode rename text throughout your project*

5. Edit the textMessage IBOutlet by changing its name to **textDisplay**.

6. Click the Rename button in the upper right corner of the middle Xcode pane. Xcode automatically renames your IBOutlet and changes "textMessage" to "textDisplay" everywhere in your project.

7. Click Main.storyboard in the Navigator pane and click the text field (which is linked to the IBOutlet variable now named "textDisplay").

8. Choose View ➤ Inspectors ➤ Show Connections Inspector, or click the Connections Inspector icon in the upper right corner of the Xcode window. Notice that the Connections Inspector now displays the connection to an IBOutlet named "textDisplay" as shown in Figure 4-14.

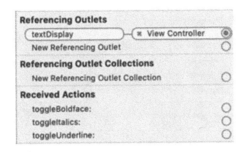

Figure 4-14. *The Connections Inspector displays the updated IBOutlet textDisplay*

What happens if you want to delete an IBOutlet that you may have misspelled or simply don't need anymore? You might think that you can simply delete the IBOutlet from your .swift file, but if you do this and try running your project, you'll get an error.

To delete an IBOutlet variable, you must follow two steps:

•   First, you must delete the IBOutlet variable in your .swift file.

•   Second, you must break the connection of that IBOutlet in the Connections Inspector pane.

To break the connection between a user interface object and its IBOutlet variable, follow these steps:

1. Click the .swift file that contains the IBOutlet you want to delete.

2. Select the IBOutlet and press BACKSPACE or DELETE. This deletes the IBOutlet from the .swift file, but we still need to break its connection to the user interface object.

3. Click Main.storyboard in the Navigator pane.

4. Click the user interface object that was linked to the IBOutlet.

5. Choose View ➤ Inspectors ➤ Show Connections Inspector, or click the Connections Inspector icon in the upper right corner of the Xcode window. The Connections Inspector pane displays the IBOutlet name and the .swift file that it's connected to as shown in Figure 4-15.

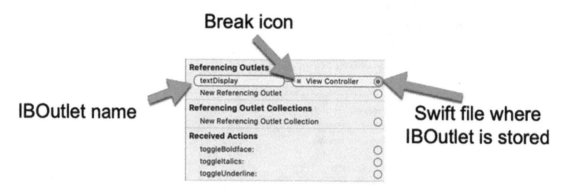

Figure 4-15. *The Connections Inspector displays the IBOutlet name and the .swift file it's connected to*

6. Click the X icon to break the connection.

Summary

Xcode is the only tool you need to edit your Swift code, design your user interface, and test your app to see if it works. By getting familiar with Xcode, you can learn how to take advantage of its different features to make viewing your files and editing Swift code easier and more convenient.

The simplest way to adjust the appearance of Xcode is to temporarily hide the Navigator pane, the Inspector pane, or the Debug Area. Xcode gives you multiple ways to hide and display these different areas so you can choose the method you like best.

Rather than rely on Xcode's pull-down menus all the time, you might find it easier to use the icons on the Toolbar to give you one-click access to common commands such as Run (to run your app), Stop (to exit out of your app), Assistant Editor (to open the Assistant Editor), or Show/Hide the Navigator pane/Debug Area/Inspector pane.

If you find yourself switching back and forth between files, you may want to display the Tab bar. Now you'll be able to open two or more tabs to represent different files so you can click and open each file without going through the Navigator pane over and over again.

If your project won't run because of error messages and your Swift code looks fine, check the connections between all your user interface objects. If you have too many (or not enough) connections, you may need to break some existing connections and relink or rename your IBOutlets so the names in the .swift files exactly match the names displayed in the Connections Inspector pane.

Xcode is a powerful, professional programming tool, so take some time to get familiar with the more common features of Xcode and feel free to ignore any features you don't understand or need. As you get more familiar with Xcode, you'll gradually learn and need some of its more advanced features. Just remember that few people ever need to use every possible feature in Xcode. The more you use Xcode, the more comfortable you'll feel using it over time.

CHAPTER 5

Working with Controllers

There's a saying that you don't get a second chance to make a first impression. In the world of app development, that first impression always comes through your app's user interface. It doesn't matter how useful, fun, and creative your app might be if the user interface is sloppy, poorly designed, or confusing. If users don't like your app's user interface, nothing else will really matter.

Designing a user interface is both an art and a science. As a general rule, the best user interface is one that appears to be invisible. Always remember that there will be multiple ways to accomplish the same task, so create and test out radically different user interface designs to see which one might be best suited for your particular app.

For example, consider the task of enlarging a picture. In a traditional user interface from desktop computers, a user interface could display a list of menus for the user to choose. Then after choosing the right menu, the user could choose a command to enlarge a picture. Then a dialog box could appear to give the user options for how much to enlarge that picture.

While this type of user interface might work, it's obviously clumsier and less intuitive than simply pinching on the screen and moving your fingertips apart to enlarge a picture. The best user interface is usually one that requires the fewest steps to achieve a desired task.

Understanding Controllers

The visual part of any app is its user interface, which is created by using one or more controllers. Every controller consists of two parts:

- The actual view displayed as part of the user interface

- The .swift file that contains Swift code for retrieving and displaying data to the user interface (IBOutlets) or methods for running Swift code to respond to the user (IBAction functions)

93

© Wallace Wang 2019
W. Wang, *Beginning iPhone Development with Swift 5*, https://doi.org/10.1007/978-1-4842-4865-2_5

A view fills the entire screen of an iOS device. To create a user interface, you need to add objects to the view such as buttons, text fields, and labels. To control those user interface objects, you need to use Swift code stored in a .swift file that's linked to the view.

Xcode provides several different types of controllers you can use to create your app's user interface as shown in Figure 5-1:

- View Controller – Displays a blank screen

- Navigation Controller – Displays other views on the screen with back buttons automatically displayed in the upper left corner

- Table View Controller – Displays a table view on the screen

- Collection View Controller – Displays a Collection View on the screen

- Tab bar controller – Displays other views on the screen, accessible through tabs at the bottom of the screen

- Split View Controller – Displays two views on the screen at the same time

- Page View Controller – Displays other views like pages in a book

- GLKit View Controller – Displays a view for showing graphics based on the OpenGL cross-platform graphics library (Apple has mostly switched to its own Metal graphics library, so OpenGL is largely obsolete and is provided for backward compatibility with older apps that still use OpenGL.)

- AVKit player View Controller – Displays a view for displaying video on the screen

Figure 5-1. *The different types of controllers available for creating a user interface*

The Object Library displays all available controllers you can add to create a user interface although you likely won't need all these different controllers. You can always modify any controller to display Tab bars, tables, or other items at any time, so it's possible to design the exact same user interface by using a basic View Controller and modifying it, or by using a specialized controller such as the Split View or Table View Controller. Starting with a specialized controller simply gives you unique features right away.

To see how to add (and delete) controllers to create a user interface, follow these steps:

1. Create a new iOS project using the Single View App template (see Chapter 1) and name this new project MySecondApp. This creates a single view for the user interface.

2. Click the Main.storyboard file in the Navigator pane. Xcode displays the single view.

3. Choose Editor ➤ Show Document Outline or click the Document Outline icon if the Document Outline is not visible.

4. Click View Controller in the Document Outline as shown in Figure 5-2.

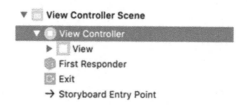

Figure 5-2. *Selecting a View Controller*

5. Press the BACKSPACE or DELETE key. Xcode deletes the entire View Controller from your storyboard. At this point, your app has no user interface.

6. Click the Library icon to open the Object Library window (see Figure 5-1).

7. Drag and drop a View Controller from the Library window to Xcode as shown in Figure 5-3. Xcode displays the new View Controller in the storyboard. If you run the app now, this view won't appear on the screen because we need to make this view the first view to display, otherwise known as the Initial View Controller.

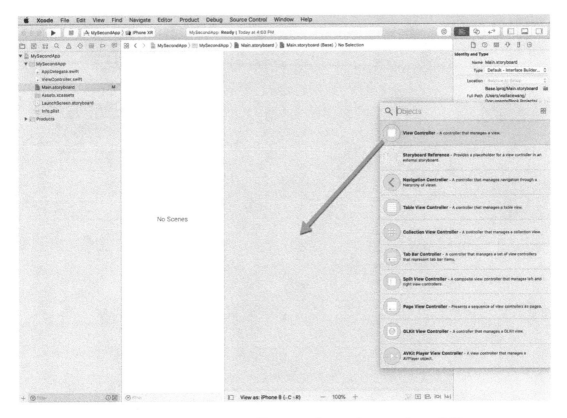

Figure 5-3. *Dragging a View Controller into the Main.storyboard file*

8. Click View Controller in the Document Outline to select it and choose View ➤ Inspectors ➤ Show Attributes Inspector, or click the Show the Attributes Inspector icon at the top of the Inspector pane.

9. Select the Is Initial View Controller check box as shown in Figure 5-4. When the Is Initial View Controller check box is selected, an arrow appears pointing to the left side of the View Controller to show you which view is the initial View Controller, which is the first view that appears when your app runs. The next step is to connect this View Controller to the existing ViewController.swift file.

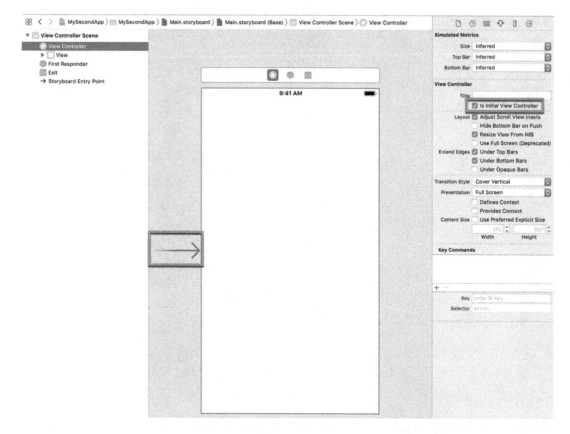

Figure 5-4. *The Is Initial View Controller check box*

Note   Only one View Controller can ever be the initial View Controller at a time.

---

10.   Click View Controller in the Document Outline to select it.

11.   Choose View ➤ Inspectors ➤ Show Identity Inspector, or click the Show the Identity Inspector icon at the top of the Inspector pane.

12.   Click the downward-pointing arrow that appears to the right of the Class text field. A menu appears. Scroll down this menu until you find ViewController as shown in Figure 5-5.

Figure 5-5. *Choosing a .swift class file to connect to a View Controller*

At this point, you've deleted a View Controller, added a new controller, made it the initial view, and connected it to the ViewController.swift file.

Working with Multiple Controllers

A simple iOS app might consist of a single view such as the Calculator app. However, most apps will consist of two or more controllers that display different views to appear on the screen. That means you need to know how to work with multiple controllers in a storyboard that make up an iOS app's user interface.

When a storyboard contains two or more controllers, you need to define one to be the initial View Controller, which is the first screen to appear when your app runs. To see how this works, follow these steps:

1. Make sure your MySecondApp project is loaded in Xcode.

2. Click the Main.storyboard file in the Navigator pane.

3. Click the Library icon to display the Object Library.

4. Drag and drop a second View Controller onto the storyboard as shown in Figure 5-6.

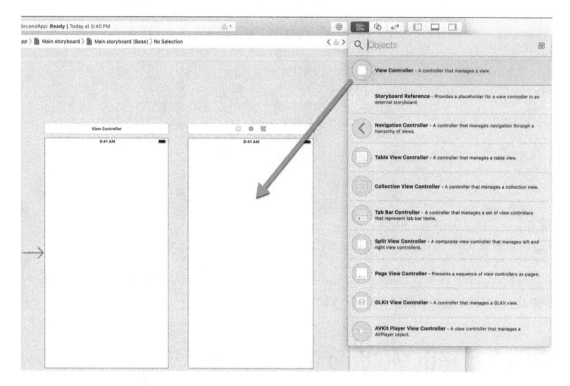

Figure 5-6. *Adding a second View Controller to a storyboard*

5.   Click the View that appears underneath the second View Controller you just added in the Document Outline.

6.   Choose View ➤ Inspectors ➤ Show Attributes Inspector, or click the Attributes Inspector icon that appears at the top of the Inspector pane.

7.   Click the Background popup menu to display a color palette as shown in Figure 5-7.

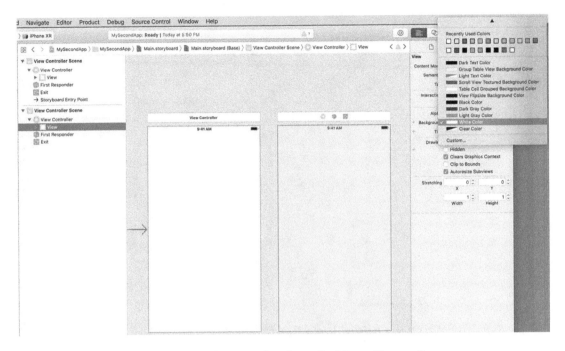

Figure 5-7. *Changing the background color of a View Controller*

8. Click a color such as blue or yellow. The goal is to choose a different background color other than white to make it easy to see which controller appears when you run the app. Xcode displays your chosen color in the view. Now let's make this colored view appear as the initial View Controller so it appears when the app first runs.

9. Click the second View Controller that contains the view with the colored background that you chose in step 8.

10. Drag the arrow from the first controller to the second. (You can also choose View ➤ Inspectors ➤ Show Attributes Inspector and then select the Is Initial View Controller check box.) The initial View Controller arrow should now be pointing at the View Controller with the non-white background as shown in Figure 5-8.

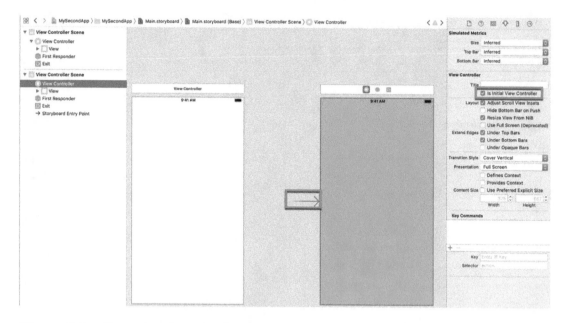

Figure 5-8. *Changing the initial View Controller*

11. Click the Run button or choose Product ➤ Run. The Simulator runs your app. Notice that the colored view appears.

12. Choose Simulator ➤ Quit Simulator to return to Xcode.

13. Drag the arrow from the second (colored) controller to the first (with the white background).

14. Click the Run button or choose Product ➤ Run. The Simulator appears. Notice that the white background appears.

15. Choose Simulator ➤ Quit Simulator to return to Xcode.

Transitioning Between Controllers

Right now our app has two controllers, but only one can appear at any given time (the one defined as the initial View Controller). To allow an app to display more than one view while running, you have several options. First, you can manually create links between two controllers. Second, you can place two or more controllers inside a Navigation or Tab Bar Controller.

To see how to manually link controllers together, follow these steps:

1. Make sure the MySecondApp project is loaded in Xcode.

2. Click the Main.storyboard file in the Navigator pane. Xcode displays the two existing views where one has a white background and the other has a colored background. An arrow should be pointing at the white view to show that this is the initial View Controller that appears when the app runs.

3. Click the Library icon to display the Object Library window. Then drag and drop a button onto the view of the first (white background) controller. (The exact location of the button doesn't matter.)

4. Move the mouse pointer over this button, hold down the Control key, and Ctrl-drag the mouse to point over the second view, which Xcode highlights as shown in Figure 5-9. (As an alternative, you can also Ctrl-drag from the button to the second View Controller in the Document Outline as shown in Figure 5-10.)

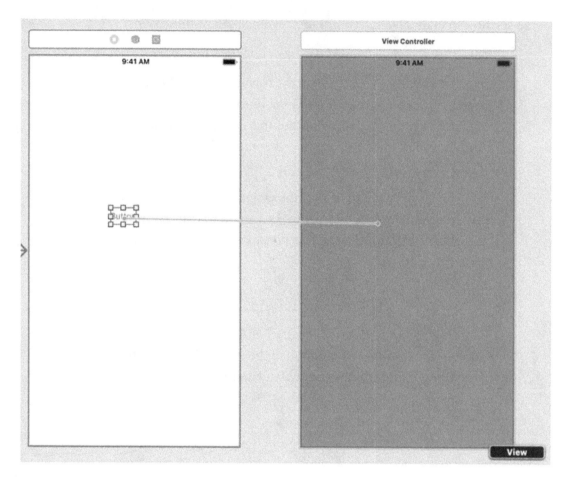

Figure 5-9. *Ctrl-dragging from a button to another view creates a segue link*

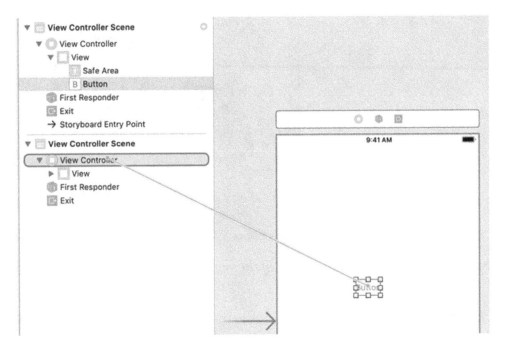

Figure 5-10. *Ctrl-dragging from a button to another View Controller in the Document Outline also creates a segue link*

5. Release the left mouse button and Control key. A popup menu appears as shown in Figure 5-11.

Figure 5-11. *After Ctrl-dragging, a menu appears to define how to display the next controller*

6. Choose Show. Xcode creates a segue between the two controllers.

7. Click the segue to select it. Then choose View ➤ Inspectors ➤ Show Attributes Inspector, or click the Attributes Inspector icon at the top of the Inspector pane. Notice that the Kind popup menu lets you define the segue as well as shown in Figure 5-12.

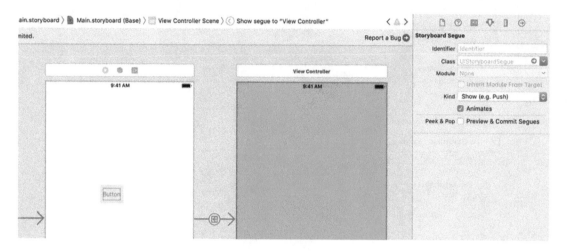

Figure 5-12. *The Attributes Inspector of the segue lets you change the type of segue*

8.   Click the Library icon again to display the Object Library window. Then drag and drop a button anywhere on the second (colored) view.

9.   Ctrl-drag from this button on the colored view to the first (white) controller. Release the Control key and left mouse button to display a popup menu (see Figure 5-11).

10.   Choose Show. Xcode creates a second segue linking the two controllers together as shown in Figure 5-13. Before we run this app, we need to make sure the storyboard choice of an iOS device matches with the Simulator's choice of an iOS device.

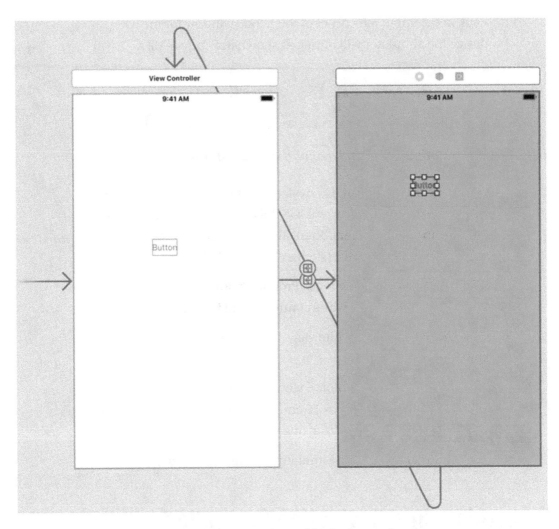

Figure 5-13. *Two controllers in a storyboard linked together by two segues*

11. Look at the bottom of the middle Xcode pane to see which type of
     iOS device your storyboard currently mimics. In Figure 5-14, the
     storyboard mimics an iPhone 8. You can click this "View as:" text
     to display different iOS devices to mimic.

Figure 5-14. *Identifying the iOS device the storyboard mimics*

107

12. Look in the upper left corner of the Xcode window for the iOS device the Simulator will mimic as shown in Figure 5-15.

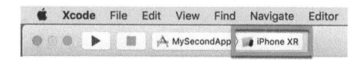

Figure 5-15. *Identifying the iOS device the Simulator mimics*

13. Make sure the Simulator iOS device matches the storyboard iOS device. If not, click the current iOS device the Simulator mimics so a popup menu appears. Then click the iOS device that matches the storyboard iOS device (such as iPhone 8 in Figure 5-14).

14. Click the Run button or choose Product ➤ Run. The Simulator appears, displaying the white controller and its button.

15. Click the button in the white view. The colored controller view appears.

16. Click the button in the colored view. The white controller view appears again. Repeat steps 15 and 16 to see how the buttons and the segues let you switch from one view to the other.

17. Choose Simulator ➤ Quit Simulator to return to Xcode.

Embedding in a Navigation Controller

Manually linking two controllers together can work, but it can be clumsy to create. As an alternative, you can use a Navigation Controller. A Navigation Controller encloses other controllers and takes care of letting the user navigate back and forth between the two controllers. That way you don't need to add buttons on both controllers to let users switch back and forth between the two.

If you already have two or more controllers in a storyboard, you can embed them inside a Navigation Controller. To see how to embed existing controllers inside a Navigation Controller, follow these steps:

1. Make sure the MySecondApp project is loaded in Xcode.

2. Click the Main.storyboard file in the Navigator pane.

3. Click the first View Controller Scene (the one with the white background) in the Document Outline to select it as shown in Figure 5-16.

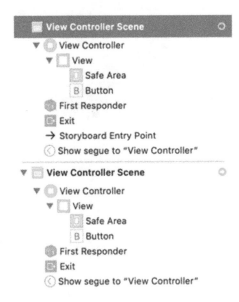

Figure 5-16. *Selecting the first View Controller in the Document Outline*

4. Choose Editor ➤ Embed In ➤ Navigation Controller. Xcode displays a Navigation Controller in the storyboard as shown in Figure 5-17.

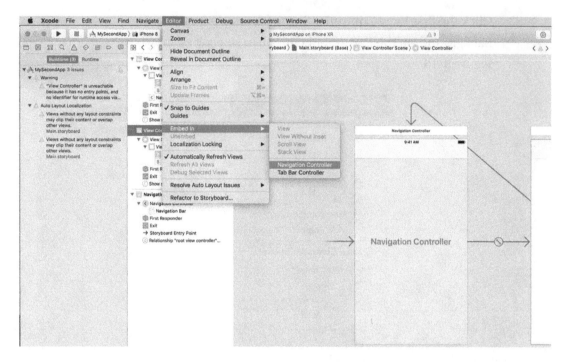

Figure 5-17. *Embedding existing controllers inside a Navigation Controller*

5. Click the Run button or choose Product ➤ Run. The Simulator
    appears, displaying the first (white) controller with a button on it.

6. Click the button. Notice that the second (colored) controller slides
    into view and displays a < Back button in the upper left corner as
    shown in Figure 5-18.

Figure 5-18. *The Navigation Controller displays a < Back button to return to the previous view*

7. Click the < Back button in the upper left corner. Notice that the first (white) controller appears again. Repeat steps 6 and 7 to see how the Navigation Controller lets you move forward to the colored controller and then back to the white controller.

8. Choose Simulator ➤ Quit Simulator to return to Xcode.

Using a Navigation Controller

Choosing the Embed In command from the Editor menu is one way to add a Navigation Controller to a storyboard. A second way is to add a Navigation Controller from the Object Library window. When you add a Navigation Controller from the Object Library, you'll also add a Table View Controller that you'll need to delete. Then you'll need to connect the Navigation Controller to your existing controller and make sure the Navigation Controller is the initial View Controller.

To see how to add a Navigation Controller from the Object Library, follow these steps:

1. Make sure the MySecondApp project is loaded in Xcode.

2. Click the Main.storyboard file in the Navigator pane.

3. Click the Navigation Controller Scene in the Document Outline and press the BACKSPACE or DELETE key to delete the existing Navigation Controller from your storyboard.

4. Click the Library icon to open the Object Library window.

5. Drag and drop a Navigation Controller onto the storyboard. This will include a Navigation Controller and a Table View Controller as shown in Figure 5-19.

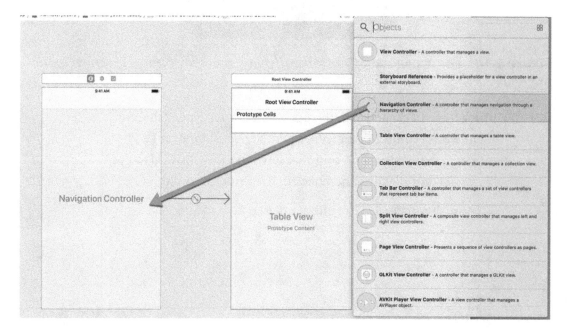

Figure 5-19. *Adding a Navigation Controller from the Object Library window*

6. Click the Root View Controller Scene in the Document Outline
    and press BACKSPACE or DELETE to delete the controller
    currently linked to the Navigation Controller.

7. Click the Navigation Controller Scene in the Document Outline to
    select it.

8. Choose View ➤ Inspectors ➤ Show Attributes Inspector, or click
    the Attributes Inspector icon at the top of the Inspector pane.

9. Select the Is Initial View Controller check box. This makes the
    Navigation Controller the first controller that appears when the app
    runs.

10. Move the mouse pointer over the middle of the Navigation
     Controller, hold down the Control key, and Ctrl-drag to the middle
     of the controller with the white background as shown in Figure 5-20.

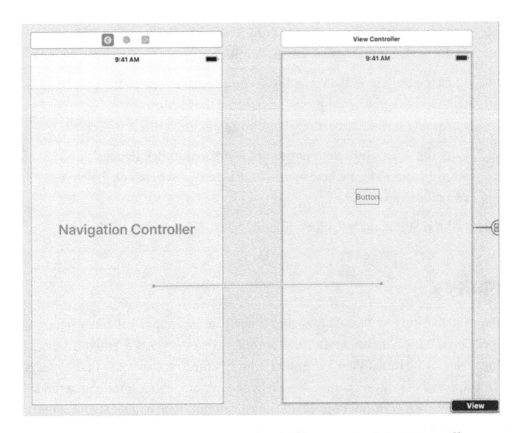

Figure 5-20. *Connecting a Navigation Controller to an existing controller*

11.   Release the Control key and the left mouse button. A popup menu appears as shown in Figure 5-21.

Figure 5-21. *A popup menu appears to define the segue between the Navigation Controller and the other controller*

12.   Choose root View Controller under the Relationship Segue category.

13.   Click the Run button or choose Product ➤ Run. The first view (the white background) appears in the Simulator.

14.   Click the button on the view. The second controller (with the colored background) appears. Notice that the Navigation Controller now displays the < Back button in the upper left corner.

15.   Click the < Back button to return to the first controller. Repeat steps 14 and 15 to see how to move back and forth between the two different views.

16.   Choose Simulator ➤ Quit Simulator.

Summary

The simplest iOS apps consist of just a single view, but most apps will likely need multiple views. When you have multiple controllers in a storyboard, you must designate one controller as the initial View Controller, which is the first controller that appears when the app runs. Only one controller can be the initial View Controller at a time.

To change which controller appears at any given time, you can create links between controllers called segues. To create a segue, you can Ctrl-drag the mouse from an object such as a button to another controller. However, creating segues manually can be tedious, so another alternative is to use a Navigation Controller.

A Navigation Controller encloses or embeds other controllers. That way the other controllers can focus on displaying information while the Navigation Controller focuses on providing a way for users to go back to the previous controller.

CHAPTER 6

Adding User Interface Objects

Controllers contain the user interface that appears on an iOS screen. At the simplest level, a controller can contain a view, which represents an iOS screen. By default, this view is blank, so to make it display information or provide interaction to the user, you can add a variety of user interface objects such as buttons, text fields, labels, or sliders.

User interface objects typically perform two different tasks. One, they either display information or allow the user to type or input information. Common types of user interface objects that display or allow input include text fields and labels.

Two, they provide a way for the user to interact with the user interface to give commands. Examples of interactive user interface objects include buttons, sliders, and switches.

To place an object on the user interface, you must open the Object Library window and drag and drop an object. Then you'll need to connect most objects to a .swift file through IBOutlet properties or IBAction methods. No matter what type of object you add to a user interface, you'll need to adjust the following:

- Size

- Position

- Other attributes such as color, text displayed, etc.

Every user interface object offers multiple properties you can modify, but you'll likely not need to modify all of them. You can modify an object's properties either through the Inspector pane or through Swift code.

© Wallace Wang 2019
W. Wang, *Beginning iPhone Development with Swift 5*, https://doi.org/10.1007/978-1-4842-4865-2_6

Changing the Size and Position of Objects

After placing an object on the user interface, you can change its size or position using the mouse or by defining specific values for its height and width or its X and Y values measured from the upper left corner of the view as shown in Figure 6-1.

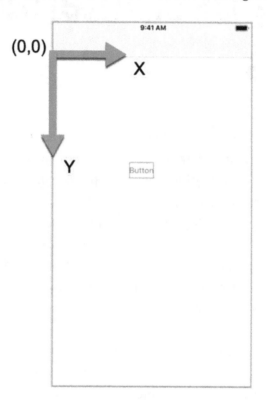

Figure 6-1. *Measuring the X and Y position of an object from the upper left corner*

By using the mouse, you can change an object's size or position easily, but defining specific values for an object's height, width, X, and Y values gives you precise control over that object's size and position.

To see how to change the size and position of an object on a user interface, follow these steps:

1. Create a new iOS project using the Single View App template (see Chapter 1) and name this new project ObjectApp. This creates a single view for the user interface.

2. Click the Main.storyboard file in the Navigator pane. Xcode displays the single view.

3. Make sure the "View as:" text at the bottom of the Xcode middle pane displays an iPhone 8 as shown in Figure 6-2.

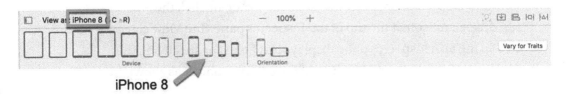

Figure 6-2. *Defining your storyboard user interface to mimic the iPhone 8 screen*

4. Click the Library icon to open the Object Library window.

5. Drag and drop a button anywhere on the view. Handles appear around the button as shown in Figure 6-3. Any time you select an object, handles appear around to show which objects you've selected it.

Figure 6-3. *Handles appear around a selected object*

6. Move the mouse pointer over the handles around the button until the mouse pointer turns into a two-way pointing arrow.

7. Drag the mouse to resize the button by making it wider or narrower, taller or shorter. As you change the size of an object, Xcode displays its current width and height in the upper left corner of that object as shown in Figure 6-4.

Figure 6-4. *Viewing the height and width of an object while dragging the mouse*

119

8. Make sure handles still appear around your button. (If not, click the button to select it.)

9. Choose View ➤ Inspectors ➤ Size Inspector, or click the Size Inspector icon at the top of the Inspector pane. The View category in the Size Inspector pane displays text fields for specifying the height, width, X, and Y values of the selected object as shown in Figure 6-5.

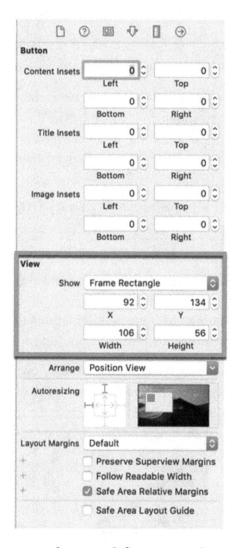

Figure 6-5. *The View category lets you define size and position values in the Size Inspector pane*

10. Click in the Width text field, type 80, and press ENTER.

11. Click in the Height text field, type 30, and press ENTER.

12. Move the mouse pointer over the button. As soon as the mouse pointer turns into a hand icon, drag the button to the upper left corner of the view until you see two blue guidelines appear as shown in Figure 6-6.

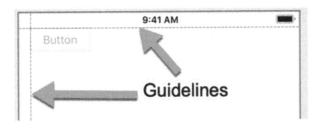

Figure 6-6. *Guidelines appear to help you align objects using the mouse*

13. Release the mouse button. Notice that the blue guidelines disappear after you stop moving the mouse.

14. Click the up/down arrows in the X text field to change the value displayed within. Notice that as you increase the X value, the button moves further to the right, and when you decrease the X value, the button moves further to the left.

15. Make sure a value of 16 appears in the X text field and then click in the Y text field.

16. Click the up/down arrows in the Y text field. Notice that as you increase the Y value, the button moves further down, and when you decrease the Y value, the button moves further up.

17. Make sure a value of 20 appears in the Y text field. Notice that when you define specific X or Y values to define the button's position on the view, no blue guidelines appear because they only appear when you're moving an object using the mouse.

Changing an Object's Attributes

Every object lets you define its size and position, but you can also modify other attributes as well, depending on the object. For example, a button lets you change a Title attribute that defines the text that appears on a button, while a text field has a Text attribute that defines the text that appears inside the text field.

To see how different objects offer different types of attributes, follow these steps:

1. Make sure your ObjectApp project is loaded in Xcode.

2. Click the Main.storyboard file in the Navigator pane.

3. Click the Library icon to display the Object Library.

4. Drag and drop a text field anywhere onto the storyboard.

5. Move the mouse pointer over the text field. When the mouse pointer turns into a hand icon, drag the mouse underneath the button at the upper left corner of the view. Notice that when you bring two objects near each other, guidelines appear to help you align one object next to a second one as shown in Figure 6-7.

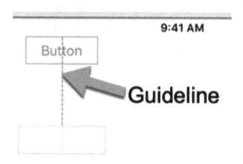

Figure 6-7. *Guidelines appear when dragging an object near another object*

6. Click the text field to select it so handles appear around it.

7. Choose View ➤ Inspectors ➤ Show Attributes Inspector, or click the Attributes Inspector icon that appears at the top of the Inspector pane.

8. Click in the Text text field and type **Hello** and press ENTER. Notice that the text appears in the Text text field and on the text field on the user interface as shown in Figure 6-8.

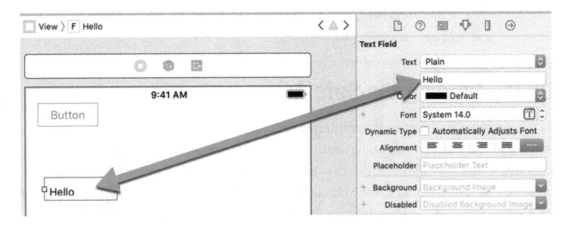

Figure 6-8. *Changing the Text attribute of a text field*

9. Click the button so handles appear around it. Notice that the Attributes Inspector pane changes to display attributes for the selected button.

10. Click in the Title text field and type **OK** and press ENTER. Notice that OK now appears on the button as well as shown in Figure 6-9.

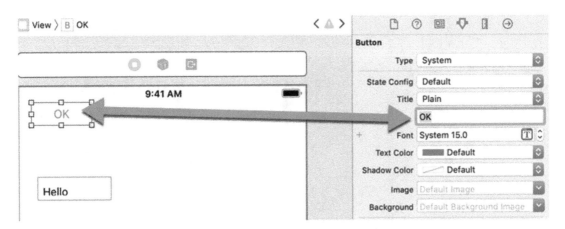

Figure 6-9. *Changing the Title attribute of a button*

11. Click the text field to select it.

12. Choose View ➤ Inspectors ➤ Show Size Inspector, or click the Size Inspector icon at the top of the Inspector pane.

13. Click in the X text field, type 16, and press ENTER. Notice that the text field moves close to the left border of the view.

14. Click in the Y text field, type 115, and press ENTER. Notice that the text field appears under the button.

Understanding the Safe Area

At this point, your ObjectApp user interface contains a button in the upper left corner and a text field that appears underneath the button. Since we started the storyboard currently mimics an iPhone 8, our user interface will look perfect as long as it's running on an iPhone 8 or running in the Simulator when it's mimicking an iPhone 8. However, if we switch our storyboard to mimic an iPhone XR, suddenly the placement of the button no longer looks right as shown in Figure 6-10.

Figure 6-10. *Viewing the ObjectApp user interface on an iPhone XR screen*

The problem is that we placed the button based on the size of the iPhone 8 screen, but the iPhone XR screen has slightly different dimensions. When you're designing an iOS app, you never know which iOS device someone might run your app on such as a smaller screen iPhone SE or a larger screen iPad Pro. Apple keeps introducing different size iPhones and iPads every year, so you can never predict how screen sizes may change in the future.

To help you design iOS apps that will look good on any iOS device, now and in the future, Xcode offers two features:

- Safe Area

- Auto Layout

The Safe Area defines the area where you should place your user interface objects, so they will always appear properly on any iOS device's screen. To view the Safe Area of any iOS device, follow these steps:

1. Make sure the ObjectApp project is loaded in Xcode.

2. Click the Main.storyboard file in the Navigator pane to view the app's user interface.

3. Click Safe Area in the Document Outline. (If the Document Outline is not visible, choose Editor ➤ Show Document Outline, or click the Document Outline icon near the bottom of the Xcode window.) Xcode shades the Safe Area so you can see where you need to place user interface objects as shown in Figure 6-11. Notice that the button in Figure 6-11 appears outside the Safe Area, which explains why it doesn't look right.

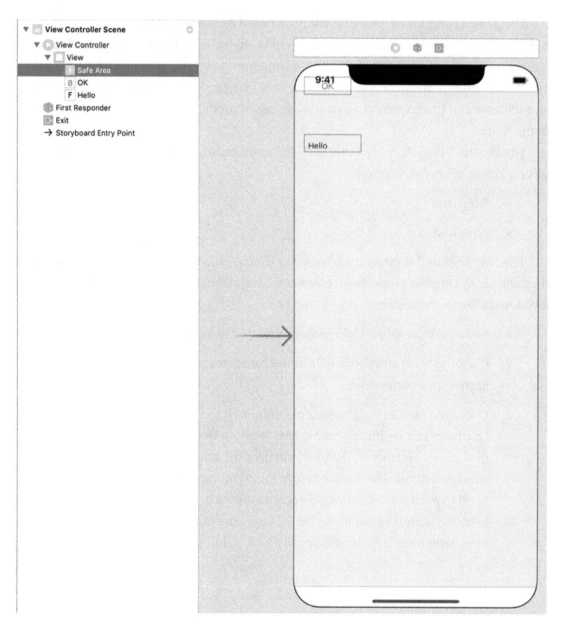

Figure 6-11. *Viewing the Safe Area of an iOS device*

4.   Click the "View as:" button at the bottom of the Xcode window
      and choose a different iOS device for the storyboard to mimic,
      such as an iPhone 8 Plus. Notice that the button didn't appear
      correctly on one iOS device but now appears correctly on a
      different iOS device as shown in Figure 6-12.

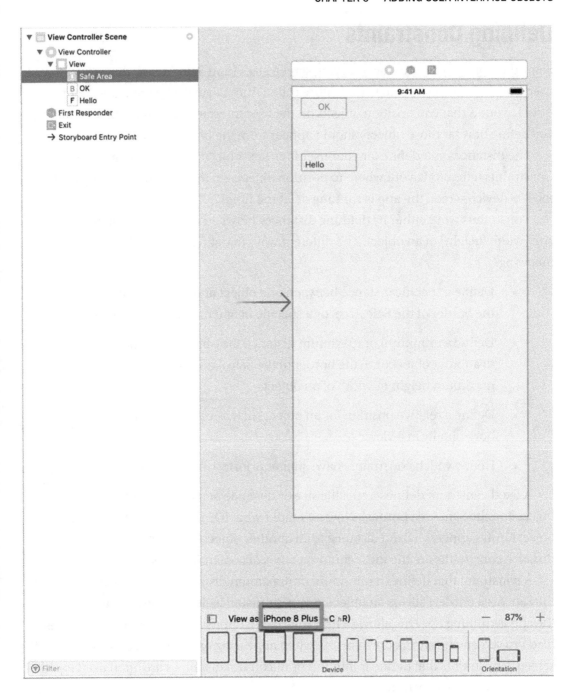

Figure 6-12. *Viewing the storyboard as an iPhone 8 Plus*

Defining Constraints

Since different iOS devices have varying screen sizes (and Safe Areas), the way to design user interfaces correctly is to use a feature called Auto Layout. The main idea behind Auto Layout is that you position objects on the user interface, within the Safe Area, then you define how far those objects should appear from the borders of the Safe Area.

The distances you define for your user interface objects are called constraints. Constraints tell Auto Layout where to position objects on the user interface regardless of the iOS device screen the app is running on at the time.

Constraints work either by defining distances between objects or by defining the size (width/height) of an object. The different ways to define a constraint include the following:

- Define a specific distance between one object and another object or the border of the Safe Area, or a specific height or width of an object.

- Define a minimum or maximum distance the object can appear to another object or to the border of the Safe Area, or a minimum/maximum height or width of an object.

- Define a relative position for an object such as centered vertically or horizontally in a view.

- Define which constraints have greater priority over other constraints.

A fixed constraint defines a specific size or distance between two objects (or one object and the Safe Area border). Now no matter what iOS device the app runs on, that object always appears a fixed distance from another object or Safe Area border. Fixed distance constraints are the most common types of constraints used.

A constraint that defines a minimum or maximum distance between two objects (or the Safe Area border) allows an object to vary its distance depending on the iOS device the app is running on. This allows a user interface to adjust its appearance for a larger iPad Pro screen and shrink down in size when appearing on the much smaller iPhone SE screen. Constraints that define minimum or maximum distances are often used together with fixed distance constraints.

When designing simple user interfaces, you may only need to design fixed distance constraints. When designing more complicated user interfaces, you may also need constraints that can vary distances between objects. However, the more constraints you place on different user interface objects, the more likely you risk creating contradictory constraints.

Contradictory constraints commonly occur when you use two or more fixed distance constraints. For example, you might want a button to appear a fixed width and a fixed distance from the left and right side of the screen. However, it's impossible to keep an object a fixed width and a fixed distance from both the left and right sides of the screen on both large and small iOS device screens.

The solution is to assign priorities to different constraints where one constraint is more important than another. Now if your app runs on different iOS device screens, the constraints with the highest priority define the user interface first and then the constraints with lower priorities define the user interface next.

Defining Constraints Automatically

The simplest way to define constraints is to let Xcode do it for you automatically. The drawback with this method is that Xcode may not always create the constraints you might want for your user interface, but you can always delete or modify its constraints later if necessary.

To see how to define constraints automatically, follow these steps:

1. Make sure the ObjectApp project is loaded in Xcode.

2. Click the Main.storyboard file in the Navigator pane.

3. Choose Editor ➤ Resolve Auto Layout Issues. A menu appears as shown in Figure 6-13. The top half of this submenu applies to any selected objects. The bottom half of this submenu applies to all objects whether you selected them or not.

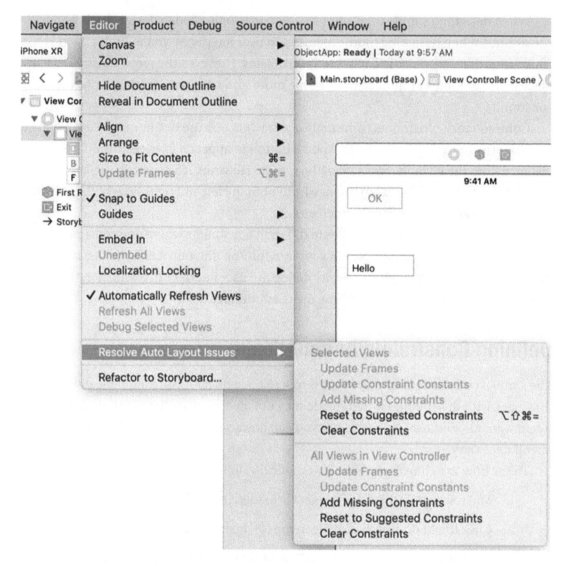

Figure 6-13. *The Resolve Auto Layout Issues submenu*

4. Choose Add Missing Constraints in the bottom half of the submenu.

5. Hold down the SHIFT key and click the button and the text field so handles appear around both objects. Notice that Xcode displays constraints as lines defining distances between objects or the Safe Area boundaries as shown in Figure 6-14.

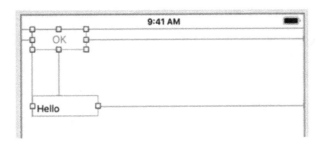

Figure 6-14. *Viewing constraints for selected objects*

6. Click the "View as:" button at the bottom of the Xcode window and choose iPhone XR to make the storyboard mimic the iPhone XR screen. Notice that after we defined constraints, Xcode correctly displays the button in the upper left corner of the iPhone XR screen as shown in Figure 6-15.

Figure 6-15. *Constraints correctly define objects in any size iOS screen*

Xcode displays constraints in different colors to help you identify possible problems. The different color constraints Xcode can display include

- Blue – Your constraints are sufficient to define the position of your user interface object on different size iOS screens.

- Orange – You do not have enough constraints to properly define the position of your user interface object on different size iOS screens.

- Red – Your constraints are contradictory or insufficient and will not display the position of your user interface object correctly.

Viewing and Deleting Constraints

Once you've defined constraints, you can always view or delete them later. Viewing constraints gives you a chance to modify how they behave. Deleting constraints lets you remove any constraints you don't need.

To see how to view and delete constraints, follow these steps:

1. Make sure the ObjectApp project is loaded in Xcode.

2. Click the Main.storyboard file in the Navigator pane.

3. If the Document Outline isn't visible, choose Editor ➤ Show Document Outline or click the Document Outline icon at the bottom of the Xcode window.

4. Click the hierarchy of gray disclosure triangles (View Controller Scene ➤ View Controller ➤ View ➤ Constraints) to see a list of all constraints currently defined as shown in Figure 6-16.

Figure 6-16. *Viewing constraints in the Document Outline*

5. Click any constraint to select it. Notice that details of that
    constraint appear in the Inspector pane as shown in Figure 6-17.

Figure 6-17. *The Inspector pane lets you modify different parts of a constraint*

6. Click the constraint you want to delete and press the BACKSPACE or DELETE key. Repeat this step until you have deleted all the constraints. Notice that as you delete constraints, Xcode may change the colors of any remaining constraints to show you do not have enough constraints to properly define an object's position on the user interface. (You can also remove constraints by choosing Editor ➤ Resolve Auto Layout Issues ➤ Clear Constraints. If you choose the top half of the submenu, you'll only clear constraints from the selected objects. If you choose the bottom half of the submenu, you'll clear constraints from all objects whether you've selected them or not.)

Adding Constraints Manually

You can let Xcode define constraints automatically, but you might want to add constraints manually. To add constraints manually, you need to follow a two-step process. First, select one or more objects. Second, click one of the icons at the bottom of the Xcode window to choose the type of constraints you want as shown in Figure 6-18:

- Align

- Add new constraints

- Resolve Auto Layout Issues (equivalent to choosing Editor ➤ Resolve Auto Layout Issues)

Figure 6-18. *Icons for manually adding constraints*

The Align icon lets you position an object in relation to another one such as aligning two objects by their bottoms or left sides. In addition, the Align icon also lets you position an object to appear horizontally or vertically within a view as shown in Figure 6-19.

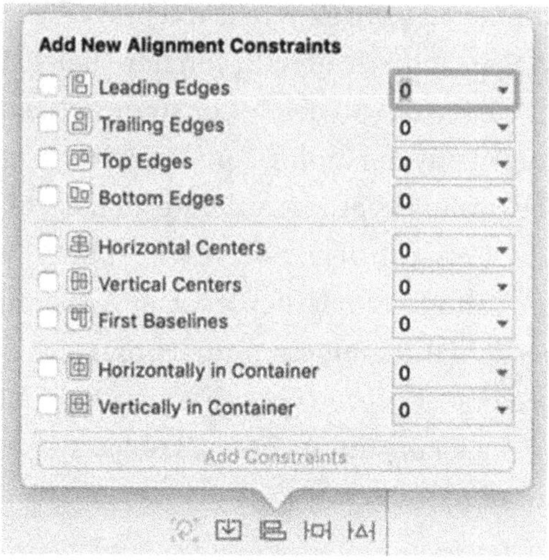

Figure 6-19. *The Align popup menu options*

The Add new constraints icon lets you define size constraints or distance constraints to nearby objects or Safe Area borders as shown in Figure 6-20. Grayed-out options become visible only when you select two or more objects so you can define all selected objects with the same width or height.

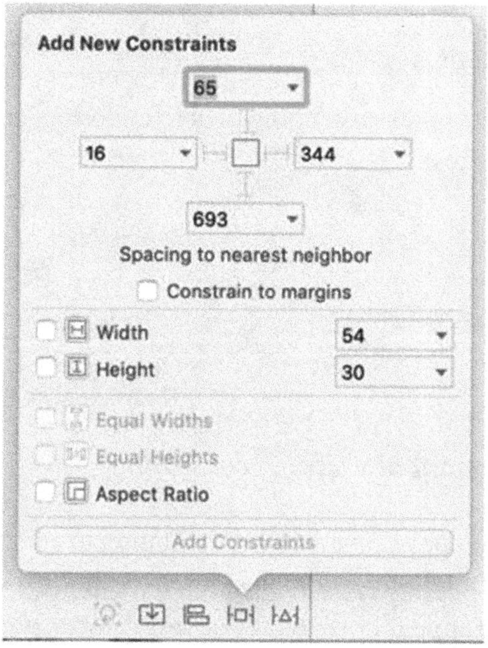

Figure 6-20. *The Add new constraints popup menu options*

The Resolve Auto Layout Issues icon displays the same submenu as choosing Editor
➤ Resolve Auto Layout Issues as shown in Figure 6-21. Reset to Suggested Constraints
removes any current constraints on the selected object and adds new constraints that
Xcode thinks your objects need. If you have already added constraints to an object, then
Add Missing Constraints simply adds the constraints Xcode thinks your object needs.

Figure 6-21. *The Resolve Auto Layout icon menu*

To see how to define constraints manually, follow these steps:

1. Make sure the ObjectApp project is loaded in Xcode.

2. Click the Main.storyboard file in the Navigator pane.

3. Click the button to select it so handles appear.

4. Click the Align icon. A popup menu appears (see Figure 6-19).

5. Select the Horizontally in Container check box and click the Add
    1 Constraint button as shown in Figure 6-22. Xcode moves the
    button to the top middle of the screen.

Figure 6-22. *Adding a constraint to place an object horizontally in a view*

6. Hold down the SHIFT key and click the text field. Handles should now appear around both the button and the text field to show that both objects are selected.

7. Click the Align icon, and when a popup menu appears, select the Horizontal Centers check box, then click the Add 1 Constraint button as shown in Figure 6-23. Xcode moves the text field centered under the button.

Figure 6-23. *Aligning two objects vertically by the center*

8. Click the text field to select it (handles appear around it) and unselect the button. Then click the Add new constraints icon at the bottom of the Xcode window. A popup menu appears.

9. Click the top line that defines how far the text field must appear from the nearest object or border. This defines a fixed distance constraint as shown in Figure 6-24.

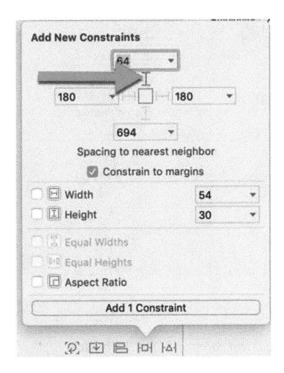

Figure 6-24. *Defining a fixed distance from the top of an object to its nearest neighbor*

10. Click the Add 1 Constraint button. Xcode displays a constraint between the top of the text field and the bottom of the button. However, this constraint appears in orange, which tells us that there aren't enough constraints to make the text field appear properly in different size iOS screens.

11. Click the text field again to select it, and then click the Add new constraints icon at the bottom of the Xcode window. A popup menu appears again.

12. Click the button near the top to select it.

13. Click the Add new constraints icon at the bottom of the Xcode window. A popup menu appears.

14. Click the top line to define how far the button appears from the top of the screen as shown in Figure 6-25.

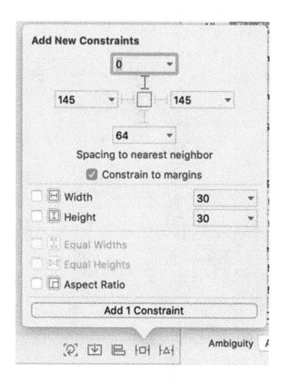

Figure 6-25. *Defining a top constraint for the button*

15. Click the Add 1 Constraint button. Xcode adds a top constraint to the button. Notice that Xcode no longer displays any orange constraints because you have defined enough constraints to define the appearance of all user interface objects.

16. Click the "View as:" button at the bottom of the Xcode window and choose a different iOS device to mimic such as an iPhone SE or iPhone 8 Plus. Notice that no matter which iOS device you choose, the button and text field appear correctly centered and spaced on the screen.

As you can see, Auto Layout and constraints let you define where objects should appear on the user interface. In this example, we defined a fixed distance constraint (between the top of the text field and the bottom of the button) along with a relative constraint that defined the button and text field to be centered horizontally.

The fixed distance constraint defines that exact distance no matter what the screen size, but the relative constraint automatically centers the button and text field horizontally based on the size of the iOS device screen. Here are some general rules for using constraints:

- Use the fewest constraints possible. The more constraints you add, the more likely constraints will contradict each other on different size iOS device screens.

- Avoid fixed distance constraints. On extremely large or small iOS device screens, fixed distance constraints increase the chance of skewering the appearance of the user interface.

To avoid using fixed values, Xcode offers two options. First, when you define a constant value for a constraint, you'll have a choice between typing a number and choosing between a Standard Value and a Canvas Value as shown in Figure 6-26.

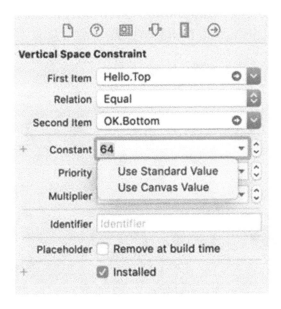

Figure 6-26. *You can choose to use a Standard or Canvas Value for a constraint*

Rather than use a specific value, you can choose to define a constraint using a Canvas Value, which uses the distance of the current storyboard size, or a Standard Value, which lets Xcode decide the best value to use for different iOS screen sizes. In most cases, try a Standard Value first, and if that doesn't work, then try Canvas Value.

A specific value defines a fixed distance, but you can use that fixed value to define a minimum or maximum distance. This allows the distance between two objects (or an object and the edge of the screen) to vary within a minimum or maximum value depending on the iOS screen size.

To see how to change a fixed value for a constraint to a Standard or Canvas Value, or define a minimum or maximum distance, follow these steps:

1. Make sure the ObjectApp project is loaded in Xcode.

2. Click the Main.storyboard file in the Navigator pane.

3. If the Document Outline isn't visible, choose Editor ➤ Show Document Outline or click the Document Outline icon at the bottom of the Xcode window.

4. Click the hierarchy of gray disclosure triangles (View Controller Scene ➤ View Controller ➤ View ➤ Constraints) to see a list of all constraints currently defined.

5. Click the **Hello.top = OK.bottom + 64** constraint. The Inspector pane shows the constraint's values in Figure 6-27.

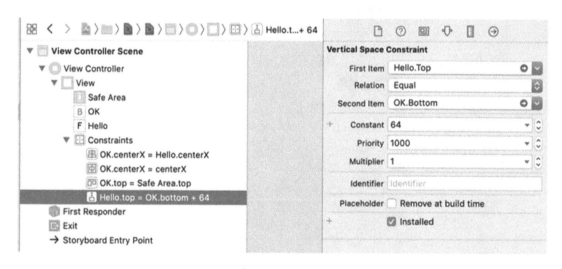

Figure 6-27. *Viewing attributes for a constraint*

6. Click in the Constant popup menu. A menu appears, letting you choose Standard Value or Canvas Value (see Figure 6-26).

7. Click the Relationship popup menu to display different options such as Less Than or Equal, Equal, or Greater Than or Equal as

shown in Figure 6-28. Less Than or Equal means the distance can shrink down to a minimum value defined by the Constant value. Equal means the distance must always be exactly equal to the Constant value. Greater Than or Equal means the distance can equal the Constant value or increase to a greater value.

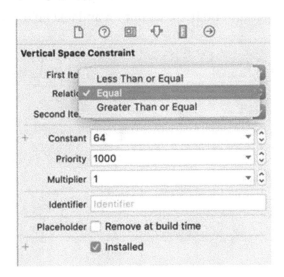

Figure 6-28. *Changing the relationship of a constraint*

Using Stack Views

Many app user interfaces use multiple objects. The problem comes from defining constraints for all those numerous objects. Move one object to a new position or resize it and you'll need to modify all constraints of nearby objects as well. Since this can be cumbersome and tedious, Xcode offers a solution called stack views.

The idea behind stack views is to group multiple objects together and treat them as a single object. The stack view defines the position of objects between themselves, and constraints define how the stack appears in relation to the screen edges. Stack views let you move multiple objects without worrying about modifying the individual constraints between them.

To see how stack views work, follow these steps:

1. Make sure the ObjectApp project is loaded in Xcode.

2. Click the Main.storyboard file in the Navigator pane.

3. Hold down the SHIFT key and click the button and text field to select them both.

4. Choose Editor ➤ Embed In ➤ Stack View, or click the Stack View icon at the bottom of the Xcode window, and when a menu appears, choose Stack View as shown in Figure 6-29. Xcode displays handles around both the button and text field.

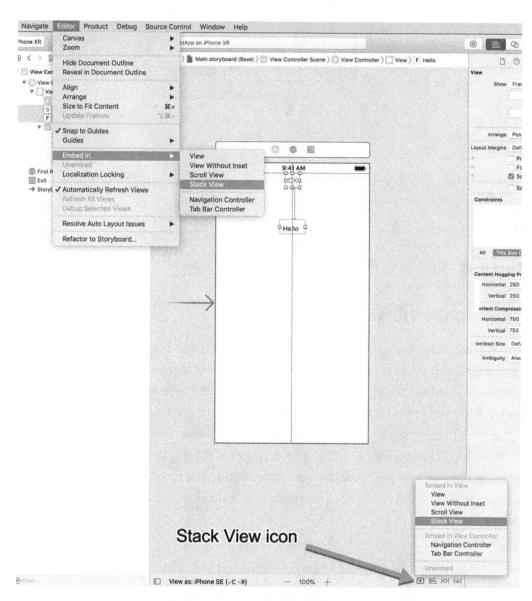

Figure 6-29. *Two ways to choose the Stack View command*

5. Click the Align icon at the bottom of the Xcode window and select the Horizontally in Container check box. Then click the Add 1 Constraint button as shown in Figure 6-30.

Figure 6-30. *Placing a constraint to center the stack horizontally*

6. Click the Add new constraints icon at the bottom of the Xcode window. When a popup menu appears, click the line defining the distance from the top of the stack to the top of the screen as shown in Figure 6-31.

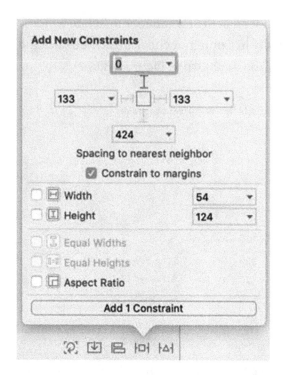

Figure 6-31. *Defining a constraint from the top of the stack to the top of the screen*

7. Click the Add 1 Constraint button. Xcode adds a constraint. Your user interface should now have just two constraints, one defining the distance of the stack to the top of the screen and one centering the stack horizontally in the screen as shown in Figure 6-32.

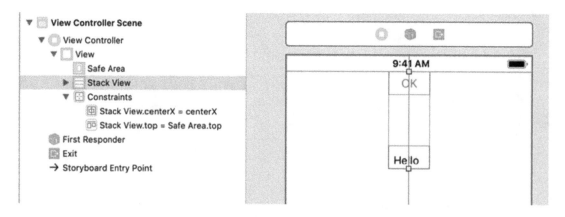

Figure 6-32. *Two constraints define the position of the stack, which consists of a button and a text field*

8. Click the "View as:" button at the bottom of the Xcode window and choose a different iOS device for the storyboard to mimic such as an iPhone XR or an iPhone SE. No matter which iOS device you choose, the stack and constraints keep the button and text field displayed on every screen correctly.

9. Make sure the stack (button and text field) is selected. Then choose Editor ➤ Unembed or click the Stack View icon at the bottom of the Xcode window, and when a menu appears, choose Unembed as shown in Figure 6-33. Xcode now separates the button and text field so you can manipulate and select them individually once more.

Figure 6-33. *The Unembed command separates objects in a stack view*

Summary

When you place objects on a user interface, you need to define each object's size (width and height) and position (X and Y values measured from the upper left corner of the screen). Every user interface object needs to define its size and position. Each user interface object may offer additional attributes to customize such as text to appear or a background color. By changing different attributes of an object, you can customize its appearance on the user interface.

Because apps may run on iOS devices that have different screen sizes, you must use constraints to define distances between objects and each other or the screen borders.

Every iOS device offers a Safe Area to place objects. As long as objects appear in this Safe Area, they will never risk getting cut off on different iOS screens. You'll need to use constraints to define the distance you want to place objects near the borders of this Safe Area or between neighboring objects.

Constraints can define the distance between objects or the size (width and height) of an object. Constraints can use fixed values, but it's usually better to place objects near each other and then use a Standard or Canvas Value instead, which helps adjust the position of user interface objects better on different size iOS screens.

When using fixed values, you can define a distance that's exactly equal to the fixed value. For more flexibility, you might want to choose to use the fixed value to define a minimum or maximum value instead. This allows the distance between objects or screen borders to vary, bound only by a minimum or maximum value.

If you have multiple objects, you can group them in a stack view. A stack view locks objects in their current relative position and lets you move and add constraints to the entire stack view rather than to each object individually.

CHAPTER 7

Using Common User Interface Objects

A user interface must display information to the user. In addition, a user interface must also allow the user to input data such as text or numbers. Finally, a user interface must allow the user to control the app. Displaying data, accepting data, and accepting commands form the heart of any user interface.

The three most common types of user interface objects are

- Labels

- Text fields

- Buttons

Labels simply display text. Text fields can display text but are most often used to allow the user to type in text. Buttons can also display text (usually the name of the command that the button represents) but are most often used to let the user control the app.

Although Xcode offers dozens of different user interface objects, their purpose is either to display information, allow the user to input data, or offer a way for the user to give a command to the app. These other user interface objects exist to provide different ways to display information, allow input, or offer a way to choose a command.

For example, labels can display data as text, but a Progress View object displays data visually in the form of a bar that changes over time to show how much a task has been completed. A label could display this exact same information as a number, but a Progress View makes it easier to see at a glance while also visually showing how much further a task has to go before it's done as shown in Figure 7-1.

© Wallace Wang 2019
W. Wang, *Beginning iPhone Development with Swift 5*, https://doi.org/10.1007/978-1-4842-4865-2_7

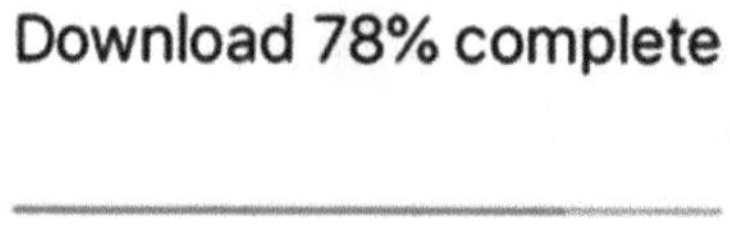

Download 78% complete

Figure 7-1. *Displaying information as text and a visual progress bar*

A text field allows users to input text as data, but when inputting numbers as data, typing a number can be clumsy. As an alternative to using a text field to input numbers, you could use a slider instead. By dragging a slider, the user can quickly choose a numeric value without the hassle of typing a number instead or typing a letter instead of a number as shown in Figure 7-2.

74

Figure 7-2. *A slider lets the user choose a numeric value without any typing*

A button represents a single command, but if you need to display multiple commands, displaying multiple buttons can clutter the screen. As an alternative to cluttering a screen with buttons to choose different commands, an app can offer gesture recognizers instead where each gesture performs a different command such as shrinking or moving an item. Gestures eliminate the need to display commands on the screen and allow users to manipulate objects directly using their fingers in different ways as shown in Figure 7-3.

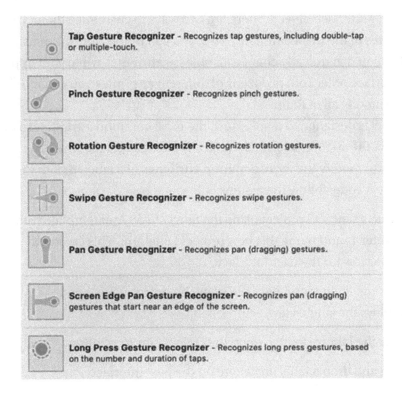

Figure 7-3. *A slider lets the user choose a numeric value without any typing*

By using common user interface objects, you can quickly design an app then add Swift code to make it actually work. Just remember to try different user interface designs until you find the one that works best for your app.

Using Labels

The main purpose of a label is to display text on the screen. Sometimes that text helps describe the purpose of a neighboring object (such as a switch) and sometimes that text is meant to provide more detailed information to the user as shown in Figure 7-4.

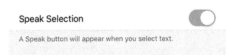

Figure 7-4. *Labels display text to provide information to the user*

With all user interface objects, there are two ways to customize them. One, you can modify attributes in the Inspector pane. Two, you can modify attributes using Swift code. Swift code lets you dynamically change an object's attributes while your app is running. Every user interface object offers dozens of different attributes you can modify, but you'll rarely need to modify all of them.

Since a label is designed to display text, the most common attributes to modify are those that affect the appearance of text such as color, font, or alignment.

To see how to modify the more common attributes of a label in both the Inspector pane and in Swift code, follow these steps:

1. Create a new iOS project using the Single View App template (see Chapter 1) and name this new project LabelApp. This creates a single view for the user interface.

2. Click the Main.storyboard file in the Navigator pane. Xcode displays the single view.

3. Click the Library icon to open the Object Library window.

4. Drag and drop a label anywhere on the user interface.

5. Choose View ➤ Inspectors ➤ Show Attributes Inspector, or click the Attributes Inspector icon at the top of the Inspector pane. The Inspector pane shows all attributes available for a label.

6. Click in the text field underneath the Text popup menu. By default, every label displays "Label" as shown in Figure 7-5.

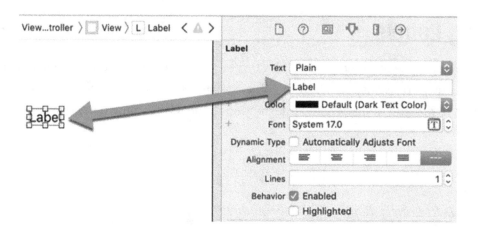

Figure 7-5. *The attribute for modifying the text that appears in a label*

7. Use the BACKSPACE or DELETE key to delete the text, type **This is a label**, and press ENTER. Xcode displays "This is a label" on the label on your user interface. (You can also double-click a label to edit the text directly on that label.)

8. Click the square icon that displays a T inside at the far right of the Font text field. A popup menu appears allowing you to choose a different font and font size as shown in Figure 7-6.

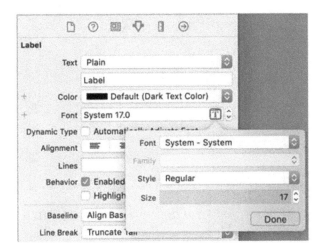

Figure 7-6. *Defining a font and font size for text displayed in a label*

9. Click in the Font popup menu. When another menu appears, choose Custom as shown in Figure 7-7.

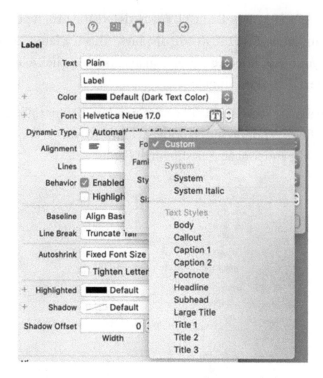

Figure 7-7. *Choosing Custom lets you define a font for text in a label*

10. Click the Family popup menu. A list of all available fonts appears.

11. Click a font you want to use such as Helvetica.

12. Click in the Size text field and type a new value (such as 24) or click the up/down arrows at the far right of the text field to increase/decrease the displayed value.

13. Click the Done button. Xcode displays the label text in your chosen font and font size.

Changing the text, font, and font size is the most common way to modify a label. Some other ways to customize a label include changing its background, how many lines of text the label can display, and whether text appears enabled (dark) or not (gray). To see how to change these attributes of a label, follow these steps:

1. Select (or clear) the Enabled check box. If the Enabled check box is selected, then text appears normally, but if the Enabled check box is clear, then text appears grayed out as shown in Figure 7-8.

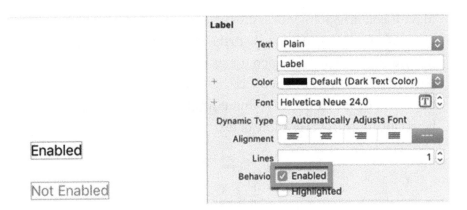

Enabled

Not Enabled

Figure 7-8. *The Enabled check box defines the appearance of text*

2. Click the Background popup menu. A menu of different colors appears as shown in Figure 7-9.

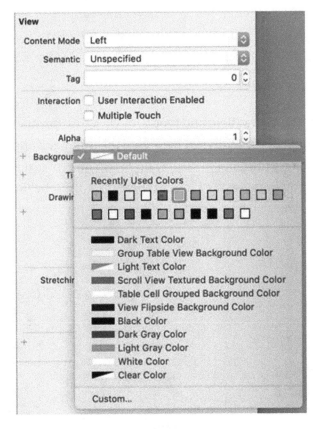

Figure 7-9. *Choosing a background color for a label*

3. Move the mouse pointer over the handle on the far right edge of the label and drag the mouse to the left and down to shrink the width of the label and increase its height. Notice that the text inside the label appears cut off as shown in Figure 7-10. That's because the Lines text field contains a value of 1, which means the label can only display one line of text.

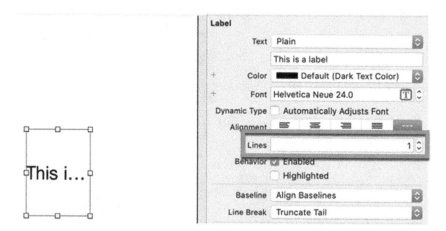

Figure 7-10. *Resizing a label*

4. Click in the Lines text field and type 2, or click the up/down arrow at the far right of the Lines text field until the number 2 appears. This now allows the label to display up to two lines of text. Notice that when you increase the Lines property to 2, the label now displays text on two lines as shown in Figure 7-11.

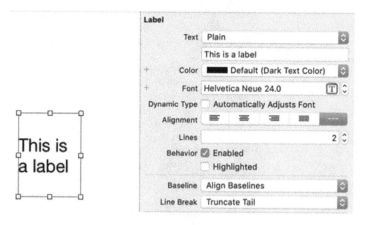

Figure 7-11. *Displaying text on two lines in a label*

Note If you need a label to display multiple lines of text, increase the value in the Lines text field. If you specify a value of 0 (zero) in the Lines text field, then the label will be able to hold an unlimited number of lines of text.

Modifying a label's attributes in the Inspector pane is fine when you know how you want the text to appear in a label before your app runs. However in certain cases, you may need to change a label's properties while your app is running. The most common property to change is the Text property, which defines the text that appears inside of a label, but any property displayed in the Inspector pane can be modified using Swift code as well. To modify any user interface object, you must first define an IBOutlet variable for each user interface object you want to modify with Swift code.

To see how to change a label's properties using Swift code, follow these steps:

1. With the Main.storyboard of your LabelApp visible in Xcode, click the Library icon to open the Object Library window.

2. Drag and drop a button anywhere on the view.

3. Choose Editor ➤ Resolve Auto Layout Issues ➤ Reset to Suggested Constraints (at the bottom half of the menu). Xcode adds constraints to the button and label.

4. Choose View ➤ Assistant Editor ➤ Show Assistant Editor, or click the Assistant Editor icon in the upper right corner of the Xcode window. Xcode displays the Main.storyboard file side by side with the ViewController.swift file.

5. Move the mouse pointer over the label, hold down the Control key, and Ctrl-drag from the label to the space underneath the "class ViewController" line in the ViewController.swift file as shown in Figure 7-12.

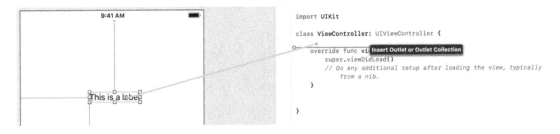

Figure 7-12. *Ctrl-dragging from the label to the ViewController.swift file*

6. Release the Control key and the left mouse button. A window appears as shown in Figure 7-13.

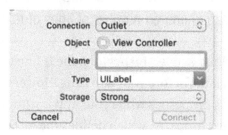

Figure 7-13. *A window appears to let you define an IBOutlet variable for the label*

7. Click in the Name text field and type a descriptive name such as **myLabel**.

8. Click the Connect button. Xcode creates an IBOutlet variable like this:

@IBOutlet var myLabel: UILabel!

9. Move the mouse pointer over the button, hold down the Control key, and Ctrl-drag from the button to the space above the last curly bracket in the ViewController.swift file as shown in Figure 7-14.

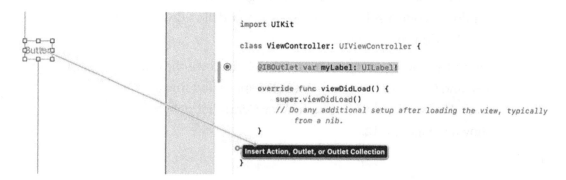

Figure 7-14. *Ctrl-dragging from the button to the ViewController.swift file*

10. Release the Control key and the left mouse button. A window appears as shown in Figure 7-15.

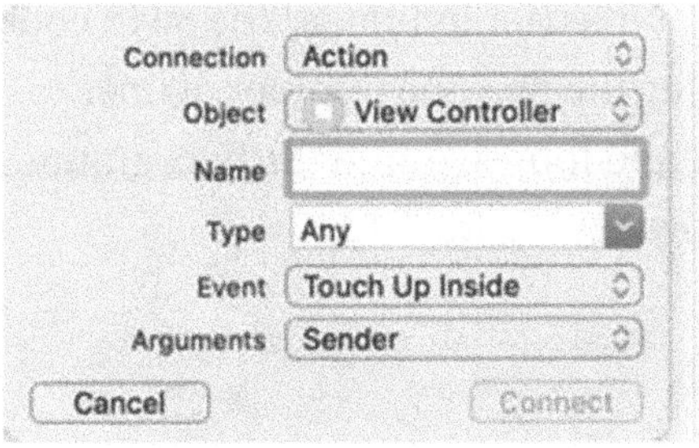

Figure 7-15. *Ctrl-dragging from a button to the ViewController.swift file*

11. Make sure the Connection popup menu displays Action and then click in the Name text field and type **changeLabel**.

12. Click in the Type popup menu and choose UIButton.

13. Click the Connect button. Xcode displays an IBAction method as follows:

```
@IBAction func changeLabel(_ sender: UIButton) {
}
```

14. Edit this changeLabel method as follows:

```
@IBAction func changeLabel(_ sender: UIButton) {
    myLabel.text = "Text created by Swift \ncode using Xcode"
    myLabel.numberOfLines = 2
    myLabel.font = UIFont(name: "Courier", size: 14)
    myLabel.backgroundColor = UIColor.yellow
    myLabel.isEnabled = false
}
```

Note   In the preceding Swift code, the \n symbol stands for new line. This forces the text to appear on the next line below.

15. Click the Run button or choose Product ➤ Run. The Simulator displays your app in a simulated iOS device.

16. Click the button on the user interface. The Swift code modifies the text by changing the text, the number of lines to display in the label, the font and font size, and the background color and disabling it as shown in Figure 7-16.

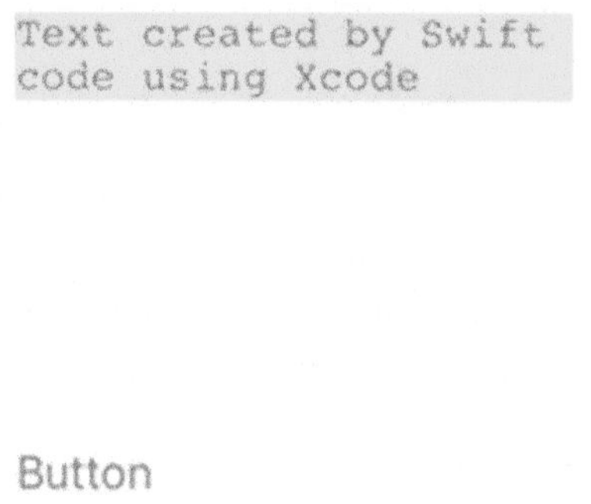

Text created by Swift
code using Xcode

Button

Figure 7-16. *Displaying modified text in a label using Swift code*

17. Choose Simulator ➤ Quit Simulator to return to Xcode.

Notice that Swift code can modify every property of the label. To learn the exact Swift command to use, you'll need to look in Apple's documentation. Since we need to access properties of a label, we need to look up what properties are available to a label. In iOS, Label objects are called UILabel.

To view Apple's documentation within Xcode, choose Help ➤ Developer Documentation to open the documentation window. Then type the word or phrase that you want to find. In this case, we want information about labels, so we'd type UILabel into the documentation window. This will display information about all the properties you can access and modify in a label as shown in Figure 7-17.

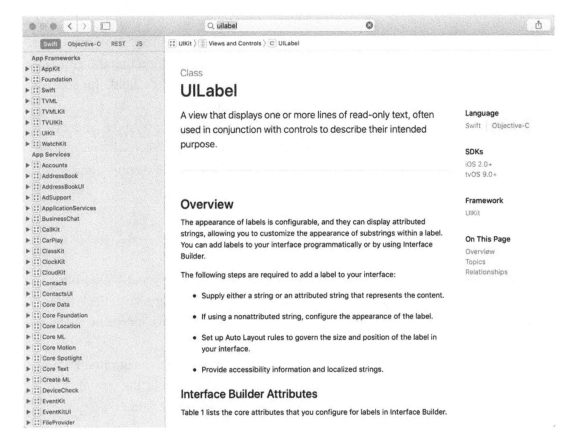

Figure 7-17. Viewing available properties in the documentation window

Using Text Fields

When you just want to display text, use a label. When you need the user to input text, then you need to use a text field. The key to using a text field is that your app must display a virtual keyboard on the screen. When using the virtual keyboard, you need to be aware of its position on the screen and the text fields.

If text fields appear near the top of the screen, then the virtual keyboard can slide up without risk of covering up the text fields. However, if the text fields appear too close to the bottom of the screen, the virtual keyboard will slide up and cover the text fields that the user wants to type in.

If this occurs, your app needs to slide its view up to keep the text field visible while allowing the virtual keyboard to fill the bottom of the screen. After the user gets done typing text in a text field, then the virtual keyboard needs to disappear and the text field needs to slide back down again.

161

To make the screen slide up and down to accommodate the appearance of the virtual keyboard, every app needs to use the iOS notification center, which detects when events will occur. When the user clicks in a text field, this sends a notification that the virtual keyboard needs to appear. When the user is done editing text in a text field, this sends another notification that the virtual keyboard needs to go away.

To receive notifications, an app needs to use the addObserver method that defines an object (the view) to receive notifications along with a method to run when it receives that specific notification. To detect when the virtual keyboard should appear and disappear, we'll need to detect two notifications:

- keyboardWillShowNotification

- keyboardWillHideNotification

Next, we'll need to write two functions to display the virtual keyboard and hide it. To show the virtual keyboard, we need to slide the view up by the size of the virtual keyboard's height, which varies depending on the type of iOS device it runs on such as a small screen like an iPhone SE or a larger screen like an iPad Pro.

To hide the virtual keyboard, we need to return the view back to its original Y position that determines its vertical position on the screen. However, the virtual keyboard will never go away as long as the cursor appears in a text field.

To tell our app to make the virtual keyboard go away, we also need to detect if the user taps anywhere outside of a text field. Tapping on the view tells the app to end editing in the text field, which sends a notification to remove the virtual keyboard. When the view receives notification that the virtual keyboard needs to go away (when the user taps outside the text field), we need a function to move the view back to its original position.

All of this requires writing code to receive the two notifications (keyboardWillShowNotification and keyboardWillHideNotification). Then we also need to detect the tap gesture outside of the text field.

Finally, we need to write three functions. One function displays the virtual keyboard by calculating the screen height and width, then sliding the view up by the height of the virtual keyboard. A second function ends editing in a text field, triggering the keyboardWillHideNotification. The third function moves the view back to its original position after the virtual keyboard disappears.

To see how to make the virtual keyboard appear and disappear with text fields, follow these steps:

1. Create a new iOS project using the Single View App template (see Chapter 1) and name this new project TextFieldApp. This creates a single view for the user interface.

2. Click the Main.storyboard file in the Navigator pane. Xcode displays the single view.

3. Click the Library icon to display the Object Library.

4. Drag and drop two text fields in the bottom one-third of the view, so when the virtual keyboard slides up from the bottom, it will cover the text fields as shown in Figure 7-18.

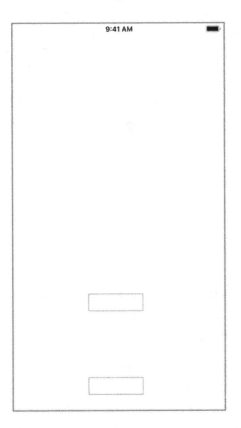

Figure 7-18. Placing two text fields in the bottom one-third of the view

5. Choose Editor ➤ Resolve Auto Layout Issues ➤ Reset to Suggested Constraints in the bottom half of the submenu. This applies constraints to both text fields.

6. Click the ViewController.swift file in the Navigator pane.

7. Add the following inside the viewDidLoad method:

```
NotificationCenter.default.addObserver(self, selector:
#selector(keyboardWillShow), name: UIResponder.
keyboardWillShowNotification, object: nil)
NotificationCenter.default.addObserver(self, selector:
#selector(keyboardWillHide), name: UIResponder.
keyboardWillHideNotification, object: nil)
```

The first line defines the view as an observer to receive the keyboardWillShowNotification. When this notification appears, then the app needs to run a function called keyboardWillShow. The second line defines the view as an observer to receive the keyboardWillHideNotification. When this notification appears, then the app needs to run a function called keyboardWillHide.

8. Add the following inside the viewDidLoad method:

```
let tap: UITapGestureRecognizer =
UITapGestureRecognizer(target: self, action:
#selector(self.dismissKeyboard))
view.addGestureRecognizer(tap)
```

This code allows the view to detect tap gestures (when the user taps outside of a text field). When this occurs, this line runs a function called dismissKeyboard. The entire viewDidLoad function should look like this:

```
override func viewDidLoad() {
    super.viewDidLoad()
    NotificationCenter.default.addObserver(self, selector:
    #selector(keyboardWillShow), name: UIResponder.
    keyboardWillShowNotification, object: nil)
```

```
NotificationCenter.default.addObserver(self, selector:
#selector(keyboardWillHide), name: UIResponder.
keyboardWillHideNotification, object: nil)

    let tap: UITapGestureRecognizer =
    UITapGestureRecognizer(target: self, action:
    #selector(self.dismissKeyboard))
    view.addGestureRecognizer(tap)
}
```

9. Type the following underneath the viewDidLoad function:

```
@objc func dismissKeyboard() {
    view.endEditing(true)
}
```

This function runs when the user taps outside of a text field, which
ends editing and sends the notification that the virtual keyboard
needs to go away (keyboardWillHideNotification).

10. Type the following underneath the dismissKeyboard function:

```
@objc func keyboardWillShow(notification: NSNotification) {
    if let keyboardSize = (notification.userInfo?[UIResponder.
    keyboardFrameEndUserInfoKey] as? NSValue)?.cgRectValue {
        if self.view.frame.origin.y == 0 {
            self.view.frame.origin.y -= keyboardSize.height
        }
    }
}
```

This function defines the keyboard size based on the size of the
iOS screen. (Remember, iPhone screens are narrower than iPad
screens.) Then this function uses the height of the virtual keyboard
to determine how far to slide the view (along with all its user
interface objects) up to make room for the virtual keyboard.

11. Type the following underneath the keyboardWillShow function:

```
@objc func keyboardWillHide(notification: NSNotification) {
    if ((notification.userInfo?[UIResponder.
    keyboardFrameEndUserInfoKey] as? NSValue)?.cgRectValue)
    != nil {
        if self.view.frame.origin.y != 0 {
            self.view.frame.origin.y = 0
        }
    }
}
```

This function checks if the virtual keyboard is visible. If not, then do nothing. If the virtual keyboard is visible, then move the view back down to cover and hide the virtual keyboard. The entire ViewController.swift file should look like this:

```
import UIKit

class ViewController: UIViewController {

    override func viewDidLoad() {
        super.viewDidLoad()
        NotificationCenter.default.addObserver(self, selector:
        #selector(keyboardWillShow), name: UIResponder.
        keyboardWillShowNotification, object: nil)
        NotificationCenter.default.addObserver(self, selector:
        #selector(keyboardWillHide), name: UIResponder.
        keyboardWillHideNotification, object: nil)

        let tap: UITapGestureRecognizer =
        UITapGestureRecognizer(target: self, action:
        #selector(self.dismissKeyboard))
        view.addGestureRecognizer(tap)
    }

    @objc func dismissKeyboard() {
        view.endEditing(true)
    }
```

```swift
@objc func keyboardWillShow(notification: NSNotification) {
    if let keyboardSize = (notification.userInfo?[UIResponder.
    keyboardFrameEndUserInfoKey] as? NSValue)?.cgRectValue {
        if self.view.frame.origin.y == 0 {
            self.view.frame.origin.y -= keyboardSize.height
        }
    }
}

@objc func keyboardWillHide(notification: NSNotification) {
    if ((notification.userInfo?[UIResponder.
    keyboardFrameEndUserInfoKey] as? NSValue)?.cgRectValue)
    != nil {
        if self.view.frame.origin.y != 0 {
            self.view.frame.origin.y = 0
        }
    }
}
}
```

12. Click the Run button or choose Product ➤ Run. The Simulator
    appears, displaying your two text fields near the bottom of the
    screen.

13. Click in any text field. Notice that the virtual keyboard slides
    up and moves the view (and the two text fields) up as shown
    in Figure 7-19. (If the virtual keyboard does not appear for
    any reason, you can make it appear or disappear by choosing
    Hardware ➤ Keyboard ➤ Toggle Software Keyboard, or pressing
    Command + K.)

Figure 7-19. *The virtual keyboard appears when the user clicks in a text field*

14. Click the keys on the virtual keyboard to type a word in the text field.

15. Click in the second text field and type another word using the virtual keyboard.

16. Click anywhere outside of the text field. Notice that the virtual keyboard disappears.

17. Choose Simulator ➤ Quit Simulator to return to Xcode.

Defining Different Keyboards

Once you know how to make a virtual keyboard appear and disappear without covering up text fields, the next step is to learn how to customize the type of keyboard that appears when the user clicks in a text field. The default virtual keyboard simply displays letters (see Figure 7-19). However, what if a text field needs to store numbers instead? Then you could display a numeric virtual keyboard as shown in Figure 7-20.

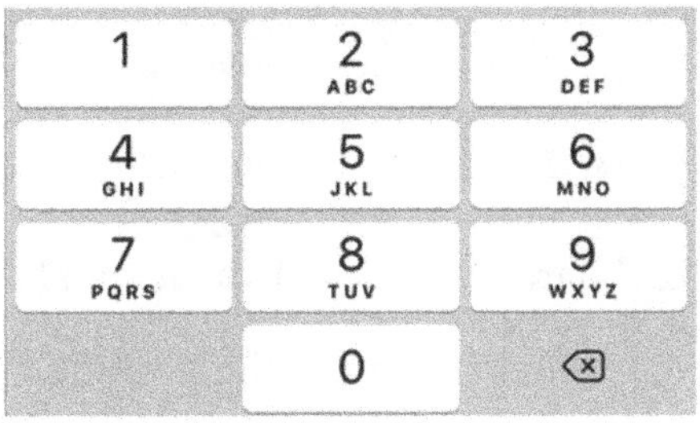

Figure 7-20. *A numeric virtual keyboard*

By giving you different options for a keyboard, Xcode lets you choose the best keyboard for a particular text field. For example, if you expect the user to type in a URL (web site) address, you can choose a virtual keyboard that displays a .com key to make it easy for users to type common web site addresses. If a text field expects a telephone number, then the virtual keyboard can display a typical phone number keypad (see Figure 7-20). By choosing different virtual keyboards, you can make it easy for users to type certain data into a text field.

In our TextFieldApp project, we have two text fields. To see how to choose and display different virtual keyboards for each text field, follow these steps:

1. Make sure the TextFieldApp project is loaded in Xcode.

2. Click the Main.storyboard file in the Navigator pane to view the app's user interface.

3. Click in a text field and choose View ➤ Inspectors ➤ Show Attributes Inspector, or click the Attributes Inspector icon at the top of the Inspector pane.

4. Click in the Keyboard Type popup menu to display a popup menu as shown in Figure 7-21.

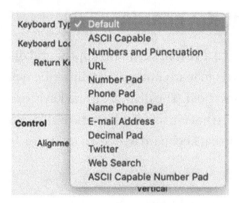

Figure 7-21. *Choosing different virtual keyboards to appear*

5. Choose a virtual keyboard such as URL or Decimal Pad.

6. Click in the second text field and click the Keyboard Type popup menu to choose a different virtual keyboard such as E-mail Address or Web Search.

7. Click the Run button or choose Product ➤ Run. The Simulator window appears.

8. Click in a text field. Notice the appearance of the virtual keyboard you defined for that text field.

9. Click in the second text field. Notice that the virtual keyboard is different for that text field such as shown in Figure 7-22.

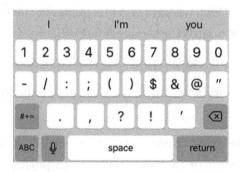

Figure 7-22. *The Numbers and Punctuation virtual keyboard*

10. Choose Simulator ➤ Quit Simulator to return to Xcode.

Defining the Content of a Text Field

Text fields capture text input from the user, but every text field has a different purpose. One text field might capture names, while a second text field might capture numeric data such as telephone numbers. Yet another text field might need to capture a password.

To define different ways a text field can accept data, the Attributes Inspector pane displays a Text Input Traits category with different options you can choose as shown in Figure 7-23.

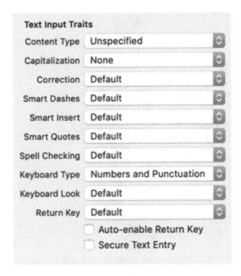

Figure 7-23. *The Text Input Traits category on the Attributes Inspector pane*

Some of the different options you can customize include

- Content Type – Defines the type of data the text field should expect such as a telephone number or name

- Capitalization – Defines whether to capitalize every word, only the beginning of sentences, or every character

- Correction – Defines whether Auto-correct is turned on or off

- Keyboard Look – Defines a dark or light appearance

- Return Key – Defines the title that appears on the Return Key such as Return, Join, Next, Search, or Done

The Secure Text Entry check box lets you configure a text field to hide the actual characters typed by a user, which can be useful to mask a password.

To see how these different text field options can work, follow these steps:

1. Make sure the TextFieldApp project is loaded in Xcode.

2. Click the Main.storyboard file in the Navigator pane.

3. Click in a text field and choose View ➤ Inspectors ➤ Show Attributes Inspector, or click the Attributes Inspector icon at the top of the Inspector pane.

4. Click the Content Type popup menu and choose Password as shown in Figure 7-24.

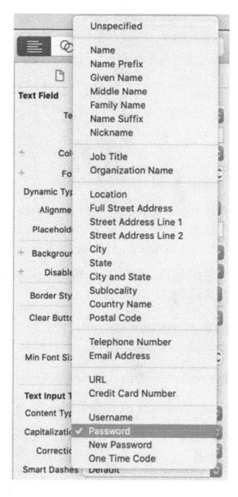

Figure 7-24. *Changing the content type of a text field to Password*

5.   Click the Keyboard Type popup menu and choose Default.

6.   Click the Return Key popup menu and choose Done.

7.   Select the Secure Text Entry check box.

8.   Click in the other text field.

9.   Click the Content Type popup menu and choose E-mail Address.

10.   Click the Keyboard Type popup menu and choose E-Mail Address.

11.   Click the Return Key popup menu and choose Send.

12.   Click the Run button or choose Product ➤ Run. The Simulator window appears.

13.   Click in the text field defined as Password content type. The virtual keyboard appears and displays Done in the bottom right corner.

14.   Click the virtual keyboard keys. Notice that as you type, the text field masks the actual characters as shown in Figure 7-25.

Figure 7-25. *Masking typed characters in a text field*

15.   Click in the other text field. Notice that the Web Search virtual keyboard appears that displays a @ key and a Send button in the bottom right corner as shown in Figure 7-26.

Figure 7-26. *Displaying a virtual keyboard with a Send return key*

16.   Choose Simulator ➤ Quit Simulator to return to Xcode.

By configuring the text field and the virtual keyboard that appears, you can customize a text field for allowing the user to enter specific types of information using a virtual keyboard optimized for that task.

Modifying the Appearance of a Text Field

Once you know the type of data a text field will hold and the best virtual keyboard to appear for that particular text field, the final step involves modifying the text field's appearance. Several ways you can modify a text field's appearance include

- Text – Stores the text that appears in a text field

- Placeholder – Defines text that appears in light gray to explain to the user the type of text the text field expects such as a password or name

- Color – Defines the color of text in a text field

- Font – Defines the font and font size of text in a text field

- Clear button – Defines whether a clear button appears in a text field, which allows the user to delete everything in a text field

While you can modify these properties in the Inspector pane, you can also define them using Swift code. First, we'll need to create an IBOutlet for the text field we want to modify using Swift code. Then we'll need to write Swift code to modify each property of the text field. To see all properties you can modify in a text field, choose Help ➤ Developer Documentation and search for UITextField.

To see how to customize the appearance of a text field using Swift code, follow these steps:

1. Make sure the TextFieldApp project is loaded in Xcode.

2. Click the Main.storyboard file in the Navigator pane.

3. Choose View ➤ Assistant Editor ➤ Show Assistant Editor or click the Assistant Editor icon in the upper right corner of the Xcode window. Xcode displays the ViewController.swift file next to the Main.storyboard file.

4. Move the mouse pointer over the text field that does not have the Secure Text Entry check box selected, hold down the Control key, and Ctrl-drag from the text field to the ViewController.swift file underneath the "class ViewController" line.

5. Release the Control key and the left mouse button. A popup menu appears.

6. Click in the Name text field and type **myTextField**.

7. Click the Connect button. Xcode creates an IBOutlet as shown here:

    @IBOutlet var myTextField: UITextField!

8. Click the ViewController.swift file in the Navigator pane.

9. Choose View ➤ Standard Editor ➤ Show Standard Editor, or click the Standard Editor icon in the upper right corner of the Xcode window. Xcode displays the ViewController.swift file.

10. Add the following code to the viewDidLoad function:

```
myTextField.placeholder = "Email address here"
myTextField.textColor = UIColor.red
myTextField.font = UIFont(name: "Courier", size: 16)
myTextField.clearButtonMode = .whileEditing
```

The entire ViewController.swift file should look like this:

```swift
import UIKit

class ViewController: UIViewController {

    @IBOutlet var myTextField: UITextField!

    override func viewDidLoad() {
        super.viewDidLoad()
        NotificationCenter.default.addObserver(self, selector:
        #selector(keyboardWillShow), name: UIResponder.
        keyboardWillShowNotification, object: nil)
        NotificationCenter.default.addObserver(self, selector:
        #selector(keyboardWillHide), name: UIResponder.
        keyboardWillHideNotification, object: nil)

        let tap: UITapGestureRecognizer =
        UITapGestureRecognizer(target: self, action:
        #selector(self.dismissKeyboard))
        view.addGestureRecognizer(tap)

        myTextField.placeholder = "Email address here"
        myTextField.textColor = UIColor.red
        myTextField.font = UIFont(name: "Courier", size: 16)
        myTextField.clearButtonMode = .whileEditing
    }

    @objc func dismissKeyboard() {
        view.endEditing(true)
    }

    @objc func keyboardWillShow(notification: NSNotification) {
        if let keyboardSize = (notification.userInfo?[UIResponder.
        keyboardFrameEndUserInfoKey] as? NSValue)?.cgRectValue {
            if self.view.frame.origin.y == 0 {
                self.view.frame.origin.y -= keyboardSize.height
            }
        }
    }
```

```
@objc func keyboardWillHide(notification: NSNotification) {
    if ((notification.userInfo?[UIResponder.
    keyboardFrameEndUserInfoKey] as? NSValue)?.cgRectValue)
    != nil {
        if self.view.frame.origin.y != 0 {
            self.view.frame.origin.y = 0
        }
    }
}
```

}

11. Click the Run button or choose Product ➤ Run. The Simulator appears.

12. Click in the text field that you connected to the myTextField IBOutlet. (This text field should display "Email address" in light gray, which is defined by the placeholder property.)

13. Click the virtual keyboard. Notice that as you type, the letters appear in red and in Courier font. Notice that as soon as you type one character, the clear button appears on the far right.

14. Choose Simulator ➤ Quit Simulator to return to Xcode.

When defining the clear button in a text field, your four choices are

- .never – The clear button never appears in the text field.

- .whileEditing – The clear button only appears when the user starts editing text in the text field.

- .unlessEditing – The clear button only appears when the user is not editing text in the text field.

- .always – The clear button always appears in the text field.

By modifying properties in the Inspector pane or using Swift code, you can customize the appearance and behavior of a text field.

Using Buttons

Buttons represent a single command that the user can tap. A button can display text (by changing the Title property) or a graphic image (by changing the Image property). The main purpose of a button is to allow the user to choose a command that makes the app do something.

Unlike objects like labels that do not always need to link to a .swift file, you always need to link a button to an IBAction method in a .swift file. The IBAction method contains Swift code to make the button perform a specific task.

To see how to create an IBAction method to a button, follow these steps:

1. Make sure the TextFieldApp project is loaded in Xcode.

2. Click the Main.storyboard file in the Navigator pane.

3. Click the Library icon to open the Object Library window.

4. Drag and drop a button on the view.

5. Choose Editor ➤ Resolve Auto Layout Issues ➤ Add Missing Constraints from the top half of the submenu. Xcode adds constraints to the button.

6. Choose View ➤ Assistant Editor ➤ Show Assistant Editor or click the Assistant Editor icon in the upper right corner of the Xcode window. Xcode displays the ViewController.swift file next to the Main.storyboard file.

7. Move the mouse pointer over the text field that has the Secure Text Entry check box selected.

8. Hold down the Control key and Ctrl-drag from the text field underneath the existing IBOutlet variable in the ViewController. swift file.

9. Release the Control key and the left mouse button. A popup menu appears.

10. Click in the Name text field and type **passwordTextField**, then click the Connect button. Xcode creates an IBOutlet variable like this:

    ```
    @IBOutlet var passwordTextField: UITextField!
    ```

11.   Move the mouse pointer over the button, hold down the Control key, and Ctrl-drag from the button to the ViewController.swift file just above the last curly bracket near the bottom of the file as shown in Figure 7-27.

```
@objc func keyboardWillHide(notification: NSNotification) {
    if ((notification.userInfo?[UIResponder.keyboardFrameEndUserInfoKey] as?
    NSValue)?.cgRectValue) != nil {
        if self.view.frame.origin.y != 0 {
            self.view.frame.origin.y = 0
        }
    }
}
```

Insert Action, Outlet, or Outlet Collection

Figure 7-27. *Ctrl-dragging to create an IBAction method for the button*

12.   Release the Control key and the left mouse button. A popup menu appears.

13.   Click in the Name text field and type **displayPassword**.

14.   Click the Type popup menu and choose UIButton.

15.   Click the Connect button. Xcode creates an IBAction method like this:

```
@IBAction func displayPassword(_ sender: UIButton) {
}
```

16.   Edit the displayPassword IBAction method as follows:

```
@IBAction func displayPassword(_ sender: UIButton) {
    myTextField.text = passwordTextField.text?.uppercased()
}
```

This IBAction method runs every time the user taps on the button. It takes whatever text appears in the passwordTextField, changes the text to uppercase, and then displays that text in the myTextField.

17.   Click the Run button or choose Product ➤ Run. The Simulator window appears.

18. Click in the Password text field and type a word using the virtual keyboard.

19. Click the button. Notice that the text you typed in the Password text field now appears all uppercase in the other text field.

20. Choose Simulator ➤ Quit Simulator to return to Xcode.

By this point, you should start feeling more comfortable understanding how user interfaces work. To access data stored or displayed in an object, you need to create IBOutlet variables. To perform some type of action, you need to create an IBAction method.

Summary

The three most common functions of any user interface involve displaying data, allowing the user to input data, and allowing the user to give commands. The most common object to display data is the label. The most common object to allow input is the text field. The most common object to accept commands is the button.

With any object, you can modify it through the Inspector pane or through Swift code. Use the Inspector pane when you need to define the initial appearance of an object. In many cases, those initial settings will be all you'll need.

However, sometimes you may need to change an object's property while the app runs. To do this, you need to write Swift code that modifies an object's property. To find the property name to use when writing Swift code, you need to read Apple's documentation for different objects such as UIButton or UITextField. You can access Apple's documentation by choosing Help ➤ Developer Documentation.

When using text fields, you may need to move them out of the way when the virtual keyboard appears. To do this, you need to use Swift code to detect when the virtual keyboard will appear so your Swift code can slide the view up. When the virtual keyboard is no longer needed anymore, then your Swift code must make it slide back down and move the view back in its original position as well.

Since text fields can be used to store different types of data, you can customize common types of data for the text field to hold such as names, telephone numbers, or e-mail addresses. Besides defining what type of data a text field can hold, you can also define what type of virtual keyboard appears when the user wants to type in a particular text field. Different virtual keyboards specialize in helping the user enter different types of data such as text, numbers, or e-mail addresses.

The basic purpose of any user interface object is to display information, accept input, and allow the user to choose commands. Labels, text fields, and buttons represent the most common types of objects you'll need for any user interface. All other types of user interface objects perform one or more of these functions but just in different ways.

When designing your own user interface, experiment with the best way to display data, accept input from the user, and offer commands for the user to choose. Once you understand the basics of labels, text fields, and buttons, you'll have little trouble using other user interface objects.

CHAPTER 8

Steppers, Sliders, Progress Views, and Activity Indicator Views

Labels, text fields, and buttons are the three most common types of user interface objects, but they aren't the only ones used to display information, allow input, and allow interaction from the user. Four other user interface objects that can display information, allow input, and allow interaction in different ways include

- Steppers

- Sliders

- Progress Views

- Activity Indicator Views

Steppers display a minus/plus icon that users can click to increment a value by a fixed amount, up or down. By using a stepper, users can define a value without typing a specific number.

Sliders give users another way to input a specific value without any typing whatsoever. Both steppers and sliders can define minimum and maximum values to restrict users into choosing only valid numeric values. For many people, it's easier to click to choose a value than to type that number itself.

Progress Views visually show how far a task needs to go before completion. A Progress View displays a bar and highlights part of that bar until the entire bar appears highlighted. By visually displaying the completion of a task, a Progress View makes it easy to see how much further a task needs to go before it's done.

© Wallace Wang 2019
W. Wang, *Beginning iPhone Development with Swift 5*, https://doi.org/10.1007/978-1-4842-4865-2_8

Activity Indicator Views provide an animated display to let users know that a task is being worked on. Although an Activity Indicator View does not display how much further a task needs to go before it's done, it does provide animation to make it obvious that a task is currently being worked on.

Steppers and sliders make it easy to input numeric data quickly and accurately. Progress Views make it easy to see how much further a task needs to go before it's done, while Activity Indicator Views simply let users know that something is happening.

Using Steppers

Steppers store a value that users can increment by a fixed increment such as 1 or 2.5. You can define a minimum and maximum value that the stepper can represent such as a range between 1 and 10. Furthermore, you can define whether the stepper wraps or not. Wrapping means if you keep incrementing the stepper beyond its maximum value, it goes back to its minimum value. Likewise if you keep decrementing the stepper below its minimum value, it jumps to its maximum value. This can make it easy for users to choose different values without having to exhaustively step from one extreme value to the other.

To see how a stepper works, follow these steps:

1. Create a new iOS project using the Single View App template (see Chapter 1) and name this new project StepperApp. This creates a single view for the user interface.

2. Click the Main.storyboard file in the Navigator pane. Xcode displays the single view.

3. Click the Library icon to open the Object Library window.

4. Drag and drop a stepper anywhere on the view.

5. Choose View ➤ Inspectors ➤ Show Attributes Inspector, or click the Attributes Inspector icon at the top of the Inspector pane. The Inspector pane shows all attributes available for a stepper as shown in Figure 8-1.

Figure 8-1. *Modifying attributes for a stepper in the Inspector pane*

The default settings for a stepper define its current value as 0, its minimum value as 0, its maximum value as 100, and its increment value as 1.

In addition, its Autorepeat option is selected, which means the user doesn't need to click the stepper each time to increment or decrement its value. Instead, the user can simply hold down left mouse down over the stepper.

The Continuous check box is also selected, which means the value of the stepper constantly changes to reflect the latest value. If this Continuous check box is clear, then the value of the stepper only changes once the user stops clicking it.

The Wrap check box is clear, which means once the stepper reaches its minimum or maximum value, it won't decrement or increment anymore. If the Wrap check box is selected, then the user can move past the maximum value defined (100) and return to 0 again, or move below the minimum value defined (0) and return to 100 again.

6. Click the Library icon to open the Object Library window.

7. Drag and drop a label near the stepper.

8. Click the Library icon to open the Object Library window and drag and drop a button near the stepper and label. At this point, your user interface should contain a stepper, a label, and a button as shown in Figure 8-2.

185

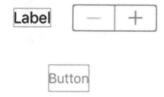

Figure 8-2. *A stepper, label, and button on the user interface*

9. Choose Editor ➤ Resolve Auto Layout Issues ➤ Reset to Suggested Constraints at the bottom half of the submenu. This adds constraints to all your objects.

10. Choose View ➤ Assistant Editor ➤ Show Assistant Editor, or click the Assistant Editor icon. Xcode displays the Main.storyboard and ViewController.swift file side by side.

11. Move the mouse pointer over the label, hold down the Control key, and Ctrl-drag from the label to the ViewController.swift file underneath the "class ViewController" line.

12. Release the Control key and the left mouse button. A popup window appears.

13. Click in the Name text field, type **labelValue**, and click the Connect button. Xcode creates an IBOutlet variable as follows:

    @IBOutlet var labelValue: UILabel!

14. Move the mouse pointer over the stepper, hold down the Control key, and Ctrl-drag from the stepper to the ViewController.swift file underneath the IBOutlet line.

15. Release the Control key and the left mouse button. A popup window appears.

16. Click in the Name text field, type **stepperValue**, and click the Connect button. Xcode creates an IBOutlet variable as follows:

    @IBOutlet var stepperValue: UIStepper!

17. Move the mouse pointer over the stepper, hold down the Control key, and Ctrl-drag from the stepper to the ViewController.swift file above the last curly bracket at the bottom.

18. Release the Control key and the left mouse button. A popup window appears.

19. Click in the Name text field, type **stepperChanged**, click in the Type popup menu and choose UIStepper, and click the Connect button. Xcode creates an IBAction method as follows:

```
@IBAction func stepperChanged(_ sender: UIStepper) {

}
```

20. Move the mouse pointer over the button, hold down the Control key, and Ctrl-drag from the button to the ViewController.swift file above the last curly bracket at the bottom.

21. Release the Control key and the left mouse button. A popup window appears.

22. Click in the Name text field, type **changeStepper**, click in the Type popup menu and choose UIButton, and click the Connect button. Xcode creates an IBAction method as follows:

```
@IBAction func changeStepper(_ sender: UIButton) {
}
```

23. Edit the stepperChanged IBAction method as follows:

```
@IBAction func stepperChanged(_ sender: UIStepper) {
    labelValue.text = "\(stepperValue.value)"
}
```

This IBAction method retrieves the current value of the stepper, which is a number, and displays it as text. Then it puts this text into the label.

Note   The "\()" symbol is called string interpolation. You can place any value inside the parentheses to convert that value into a string.

---

24. Choose View ➤ Standard Editor ➤ Show Standard Editor, or click the Standard Editor icon.

25. Click the Run button or choose Product ➤ Run.

26. Click the + icon on the stepper multiple times. Notice that each time you click the + icon of the stepper, its numeric value increases by 1 in the label.

27. Click the – icon on the stepper multiple times. Notice that each time you click the – icon of the stepper, its numeric value decreases by 1 in the label.

28. Choose Simulator ➤ Quit Simulator to return to Xcode.

The stepper increments by 1 and has a minimum value of 0 and a maximum value of 100 because of its default settings as displayed in the Attributes Inspector pane. We could change those settings in the Inspector pane but let's change them using Swift code instead.

To see how to change a stepper's properties using Swift code, follow these steps:

1. Click the ViewController.swift file in the Navigator pane.

2. Edit the changeStepper IBAction method as follows:

```
@IBAction func changeStepper(_ sender: UIButton) {
    stepperValue.minimumValue = -10
    stepperValue.maximumValue = -5
    stepperValue.stepValue = 0.5
    stepperValue.isContinuous = true
    stepperValue.autorepeat = true
    stepperValue.wraps = true
}
```

Setting the stepper's isContinuous, autorepeat, and wraps properties to true is equivalent to selecting the Continuous, Autorepeat, and Wraps check boxes in the Inspector pane.

3. Click the Run button or choose Product ➤ Run. The Simulator window appears.

4. Click the + icon on the stepper. Notice that the value in the label increases by 1 each time you click the + icon.

5. Click the button. This runs the Swift code in the changeStepper IBAction method.

6. Click the – and + icons in the stepper. Notice that it now increments or decrements by 0.5 because the Swift code defined its stepValue property to 0.5.

7. Chose Simulator ➤ Quit Simulator to return to Xcode.

The entire ViewController.swift file should look like this:

```swift
import UIKit

class ViewController: UIViewController {

    @IBOutlet var labelValue: UILabel!
    @IBOutlet var stepperValue: UIStepper!

    override func viewDidLoad() {
        super.viewDidLoad()
        // Do any additional setup after loading the view, typically from a nib.
    }

    @IBAction func stepperChanged(_ sender: UIStepper) {
        labelValue.text = "\(stepperValue.value)"
    }

    @IBAction func changeStepper(_ sender: UIButton) {
        stepperValue.minimumValue = -10
        stepperValue.maximumValue = -5
        stepperValue.stepValue = 0.5
        stepperValue.isContinuous = true
        stepperValue.autorepeat = true
        stepperValue.wraps = true
    }

}
```

Using Sliders

Like a stepper, a slider lets the user choose a numeric value without typing a specific number. While a stepper forces users to increment/decrement values by a fixed amount, sliders make it easy for users to choose between a range of values quickly by simply changing the slider's position.

One drawback of sliders is that they take up more space than steppers. Another drawback is that steppers let you define a fixed increment/decrement value, while a slider does not.

A slider consists of three parts as shown in Figure 8-3:

- A thumb

- A minimum track

- A maximum track

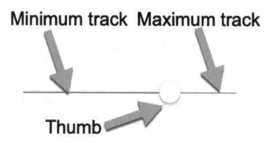

Figure 8-3. *The three parts of a slider*

The minimum track and maximum track typically appear in different colors to make it easy to see the position of the thumb. However, you can define colors for the thumb, minimum, and maximum track to make them more visible.

To see how to use a slider, follow these steps:

1. Create a new iOS project using the Single View App template (see Chapter 1) and name this new project SliderApp. This creates a single view for the user interface.

2. Click the Main.storyboard file in the Navigator pane. Xcode displays the single view.

3. Click the Library icon to display the Object Library.

4. Drag and drop a label, a button, and a slider onto the view.

5.   Expand the width of the slider to make it longer.

6.   Choose Editor ➤ Resolve Auto Layout Issues ➤ Reset to Suggested
     Constraints in the bottom half of the submenu. This applies
     constraints to the label, button, and slider.

7.   Choose View ➤ Assistant Editor ➤ Show Assistant Editor, or click
     the Assistant Editor icon. Xcode displays the Main.storyboard and
     ViewController.swift file side by side.

8.   Move the mouse pointer over the label, hold down the Control
     key, and Ctrl-drag from the label to the ViewController.swift file
     underneath the "class ViewController" line.

9.   Release the Control key and the left mouse button. A popup
     window appears.

10. Click in the Name text field, type **labelValue**, and click the
     Connect button. Xcode creates an IBOutlet variable as follows:

     @IBOutlet var labelValue: UILabel!

11. Move the mouse pointer over the slider, hold down the Control
     key, and Ctrl-drag from the slider to the ViewController.swift file
     underneath the IBOutlet line.

12. Release the Control key and the left mouse button. A popup
     window appears.

13. Click in the Name text field, type **sliderValue**, and click the
     Connect button. Xcode creates an IBOutlet variable as follows:

     @IBOutlet var sliderValue: UISlider!

14. Move the mouse pointer over the button, hold down the Control
     key, and Ctrl-drag from the button to the ViewController.swift file
     above the last curly bracket at the bottom of the file.

15. Release the Control key and the left mouse button. A popup
     window appears.

16. Click in the Name text field, type **changeSlider**, click the Type popup menu and choose UIButton, and click the Connect button. Xcode creates an IBAction method as follows:

```
@IBAction func changeSlider(_ sender: UIButton) {
}
```

17. Move the mouse pointer over the slider, hold down the Control key, and Ctrl-drag from the slider to the ViewController.swift file above the last curly bracket at the bottom of the file.

18. Release the Control key and the left mouse button. A popup window appears.

19. Click in the Name text field, type **sliderValueChanged**, click the Type popup menu and choose UISlider, and click the Connect button. Xcode creates an IBAction method as follows:

```
@IBAction func sliderValueChanged(_ sender: UISlider) {
}
```

20. Choose View ➤ Standard Editor ➤ Show Standard Editor, or click the Standard Editor icon in the upper right corner of the Xcode window.

21. Click the ViewController.swift file in the Navigator pane to edit it.

22. Modify the sliderValueChanged method as follows:

```
@IBAction func sliderValueChanged(_ sender: UISlider) {
    labelValue.text = "\(sliderValue.value)"
}
```

The entire ViewController.swift file should look like this:

```
import UIKit

class ViewController: UIViewController {

    @IBOutlet var labelValue: UILabel!
    @IBOutlet var sliderValue: UISlider!

    override func viewDidLoad() {
```

```swift
        super.viewDidLoad()
        // Do any additional setup after loading the view,
        typically from a nib.
    }

    @IBAction func changeSlider(_ sender: UIButton) {
    }

    @IBAction func sliderValueChanged(_ sender: UISlider) {
        labelValue.text = "\(sliderValue.value)"
    }
}
```

23. Click the Run button or choose Product ➤ Run. The Simulator window appears.

24. Drag the slider left and right. Notice that if you drag the slider thumb to the far left, the value 0 (zero) appears in the label, but if you drag the thumb to the far right, the value of 1.0 appears. That's because the default minimum and maximum values of the slider are 0 and 1, respectively.

25. Choose Simulator ➤ Quit Simulator to return to Xcode.

Modifying a Slider with Swift Code

Just as you can customize a slider through the Attributes Inspector pane, so can you modify a slider using Swift code. Some of the common properties to modify on a slider include

- .value – Defines the initial value displayed by the slider

- .minimumValue – Defines the minimum value the slider can represent

- .maximumValue – Defines the maximum value the slider can represent

- .thumbTintColor – Defines the color of the thumb on the slider

- .minimumTrackTintColor – Defines the color of the minimum track

- .maximumTrackTintColor – Defines the color of the maximum track

To see how to use Swift code to modify a slider, follow these steps:

1. Make sure the SliderApp project is loaded in Xcode.

2. Click the ViewController.swift file in the Navigator pane to edit the ViewController.swift file.

3. Modify the changeSlider IBAction method as follows:

```
@IBAction func changeSlider(_ sender: UIButton) {
    sliderValue.minimumValue = 1
    sliderValue.maximumValue = 25
    sliderValue.value = 7
    sliderValue.minimumTrackTintColor = UIColor.red
    sliderValue.maximumTrackTintColor = UIColor.green
    sliderValue.thumbTintColor = UIColor.black
}
```

The entire ViewController.swift file should look like this:

```
import UIKit

class ViewController: UIViewController {

    @IBOutlet var labelValue: UILabel!
    @IBOutlet var sliderValue: UISlider!

    override func viewDidLoad() {
        super.viewDidLoad()
        // Do any additional setup after loading the view,
        typically from a nib.
    }

    @IBAction func changeSlider(_ sender: UIButton) {
        sliderValue.minimumValue = 1
        sliderValue.maximumValue = 25
        sliderValue.value = 7
        sliderValue.minimumTrackTintColor = UIColor.red
        sliderValue.maximumTrackTintColor = UIColor.green
        sliderValue.thumbTintColor = UIColor.black
    }
```

```
@IBAction func sliderValueChanged(_ sender: UISlider) {
    labelValue.text = "\(sliderValue.value)"
    }
}
```

4. Click the Run button or chose Product ➤ Run. The Simulator
    window appears.

5. Drag the slider left and right. Notice that the label displays a value
    between 0 and 1, which are the minimum and maximum values
    defined by the Attributes Inspector pane.

6. Click the button. This runs the Swift code to modify the slider.

7. Drag the slider left and right. Notice that the label now displays
    a value between 1 and 25. In addition, the slider appears with
    the thumb, minimum track, and maximum track displayed in
    different colors.

8. Choose Simulator ➤ Quit Simulator to return to Xcode.

Using the Progress and Activity Indicator Views

The Progress View displays a horizontal bar that fills with color to visually show the
progress of a task. When the Progress View is empty, that means the task hasn't started yet.
When the Progress View is completely filled with color, that means the task is completed.
When the Progress View is partially filled, that indicates the task is partially completed.

However, it's not always possible to know exactly when a task might be completed.
In that case, the Progress View would appear stagnant, giving the illusion that nothing
is happening or that the app may have crashed. When the completion of a task can't be
determined, it's better to use the Activity Indicator View, which displays an animated
spinner that shows something's happening.

The main differences between the Progress View and the Activity Indicator View are

- The Progress View shows how far a task has been completed, while
  an Activity Indicator View does not.

- The Activity Indicator View constantly shows that something is
  happening, while a Progress View may not.

To see how to use the Progress and Activity Indicator Views, follow these steps:

1. Create a new iOS project using the Single View App template (see Chapter 1) and name this new project ProgressApp. This creates a single view for the user interface.

2. Click the Main.storyboard file in the Navigator pane. Xcode displays the single view.

3. Click the Library icon to display the Object Library.

4. Drag and drop a button and Activity Indicator View onto the user interface as shown in Figure 8-4.

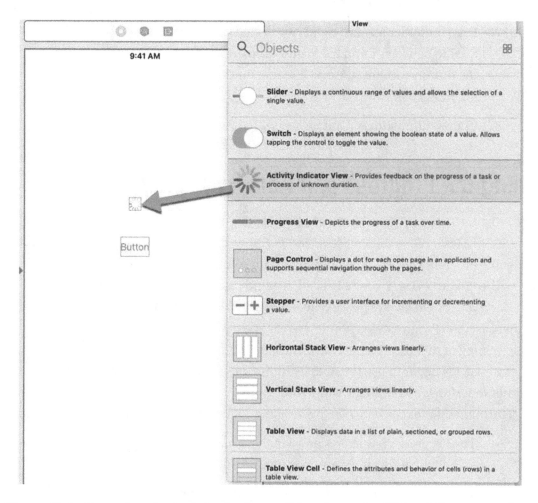

Figure 8-4. *Dragging the Activity Indicator View from the Object Library window to the user interface*

5. Choose Editor ➤ Resolve Auto Layout Issues ➤ Reset to Suggested Constraints on the bottom half of the submenu. This will add constraints to all objects on the user interface.

6. Click the Main.storyboard file in the Navigator pane.

7. Choose View ➤ Assistant Editor ➤ Show Assistant Editor, or click the Assistant Editor icon in the upper right corner of the Xcode window. Xcode displays the Main.storyboard file side by side with the ViewController.swift file.

8. Move the mouse over the Activity Indicator View, hold down the Control key, and Ctrl-drag to the ViewController.swift file underneath the IBOutlet line.

9. Release the Control key and the left mouse button. A popup window appears.

10. Click in the Name text field and type **activityView**, and click the Connect button. Xcode creates an IBOutlet as follows:

@IBOutlet var activityView: UIActivityIndicatorView!

11. Move the mouse over the button, hold down the Control key, and Ctrl-drag to the ViewController.swift file above the last curly bracket at the bottom of the file.

12. Release the Control key and the left mouse button. A popup window appears.

13. Click in the Name text field and type **runButton**, click in the Type popup menu and choose UIButton, and click the Connect button. Xcode creates an IBAction method as follows:

```
@IBAction func runButton(_ sender: UIButton) {
}
```

14. Choose View ➤ Standard Editor ➤ Show Standard Editor, or click the Standard Editor icon in the upper right corner of the Xcode window.

15. Click the ViewController.swift file in the Navigator pane.

16. Add this line above the IBOutlet variables:

var counter = 0

17. Add this line inside the viewDidLoad function:

```
activityView.hidesWhenStopped = true
```

18. Edit this runButton IBAction method as follows:

```
@IBAction func runButton(_ sender: UIButton) {
    Timer.scheduledTimer(withTimeInterval: 1.0, repeats: true)
    { timer in
        self.activityView.startAnimating()
        self.counter += 1

        if self.counter >= 5 {
            self.activityView.stopAnimating()
            timer.invalidate()
        }
    }
}
```

This code runs a timer that counts in 1-second increments. While the timer runs, it runs the startAnimating method to make the Activity Indicator View appear to spin around. As soon as the Activity Indicator View starts spinning, it appears on the screen.

After 5 seconds, the timer stops running and runs the stopAnimating method to make the Activity Indicator View stop spinning. As soon as it stops spinning, it disappears from the screen. The entire ViewController.swift file should look like this:

```
import UIKit

class ViewController: UIViewController {

    var counter = 0

    @IBOutlet var activityView: UIActivityIndicatorView!

    override func viewDidLoad() {
        super.viewDidLoad()
        activityView.hidesWhenStopped = true
```

```
        // Do any additional setup after loading the view,
        typically from a nib.
    }

    @IBAction func runButton(_ sender: UIButton) {

        Timer.scheduledTimer(withTimeInterval: 1.0, repeats: true)
{ timer in
            self.activityView.startAnimating()
            self.counter += 1

            if self.counter >= 5 {
                self.activityView.stopAnimating()
                timer.invalidate()
                self.counter = 0
            }
        }
    }
}
```

19. Click the Run button or choose Product ➤ Run. The Simulator screen appears.

20. Click the button. The Activity Indicator View appears spinning around, then after 5 seconds, it disappears.

21. Chose Simulator ➤ Quit Simulator to return to Xcode.

Using a Progress View

A Progress View gradually fills up to show the completion of a task. That means your app needs to know when a task will be completed. Since a Progress View visually displays progress, it's best to make sure that the Progress View appears to fill up fairly quickly to give users feedback that the app is working and to show that the task is nearly completion. If the Progress View fills up too slowly, the app may appear frozen.

To see how a Progress View can work, follow these steps:

1. Make sure the ProgressApp is loaded in Xcode.

2. Click the Main.storyboard file in the Navigator pane. Xcode displays the single view.

3. Click the Library icon to display the Object Library.

4. Drag and drop a label, a stepper, and a Progress View onto the user interface where the label appears above the Progress View and the stepper appears below the Progress View as shown in Figure 8-5.

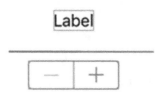

Figure 8-5. *Organizing the Progress View in between the label and stepper*

5. Click the label and expand the width of the label until it stretches past both ends of the Progress View.

6. Hold down the SHIFT key and click the label, Progress View, and stepper so handles appear around all three objects.

7. Choose Editor ➤ Resolve Auto Layout Issues ➤ Reset to Suggested Constraints in the bottom half of the submenu. This sets constraints on the label, Progress View, and stepper.

8. Move the mouse over the label, hold down the Control key, and Ctrl-drag to the ViewController.swift file underneath the IBOutlet line.

9. Release the Control key and the left mouse button. A popup window appears.

10. Click in the Name text field and type **labelProgress**, and click the Connect button. Xcode creates an IBOutlet as follows:

    @IBOutlet var labelProgress: UILabel!

11. Move the mouse over the Progress View, hold down the Control key, and Ctrl-drag to the ViewController.swift file underneath the "class ViewController" line.

12. Release the Control key and the left mouse button. A popup window appears.

13. Click in the Name text field and type **progressView**, and click the Connect button. Xcode creates an IBOutlet as follows:

     @IBOutlet var progressView: UIProgressView!

14. Move the mouse over the stepper, hold down the Control key, and Ctrl-drag to the ViewController.swift file underneath the IBOutlet line.

15. Release the Control key and the left mouse button. A popup window appears.

16. Click in the Name text field and type **stepperObject**, and click the Connect button. Xcode creates an IBOutlet as follows:

     @IBOutlet var stepperObject: UIStepper!

17. Move the mouse over the stepper, hold down the Control key, and Ctrl-drag to the ViewController.swift file above the last curly bracket at the bottom of the file.

18. Release the Control key and the left mouse button. A popup window appears.

19. Click in the Name text field, type **stepperChanged**, click in the Type popup menu and choose UIStepper, and click the Connect button. Xcode creates an IBAction method as follows:

     ```
     @IBAction func stepperChanged(_ sender: UIStepper) {
     }
     ```

20. Choose View ➤ Standard Editor ➤ Show Standard Editor, or click the Standard Editor icon in the upper right corner of the Xcode window.

21. Click the ViewController.swift file in the Navigator pane.

22. Edit the stepperChanged IBAction method as follows:

```
@IBAction func stepperChanged(_ sender: UIStepper) {
    labelProgress.text = "Completed \(Int(stepperObject.value
    * 10)) of 10 tasks"
    progressView.progress = Float(stepperObject.value)
}
```

The first line retrieves the value from the stepper, multiplies it by 10, and converts the value to an integer. The second line takes the value of the stepper, converts it to a Float value, and stores this value in the Progress View, which displays the value by filling the Progress View.

23. Edit the viewDidLoad method to add the following three lines:

```
progressView.progress = 0
stepperObject.stepValue = 0.1
stepperObject.maximumValue = 1.0
```

The first line sets the Progress View value to 0 so it appears on the user interface completely empty. The second line defines the stepper to increment values by 0.1. The third line defines the maximum stepper value as 1.0. The entire ViewController.swift file should look like this:

```
import UIKit

class ViewController: UIViewController {

    var counter = 0

    @IBOutlet var labelProgress: UILabel!
    @IBOutlet var progressView: UIProgressView!
    @IBOutlet var stepperObject: UIStepper!
    @IBOutlet var activityView: UIActivityIndicatorView!

    override func viewDidLoad() {
        super.viewDidLoad()
        activityView.hidesWhenStopped = true
        progressView.progress = 0
```

```swift
    stepperObject.stepValue = 0.1
    stepperObject.maximumValue = 1.0
    // Do any additional setup after loading the view,
    typically from a nib.
}

@IBAction func runButton(_ sender: UIButton) {

    Timer.scheduledTimer(withTimeInterval: 1.0, repeats: true)
    { timer in
        self.activityView.startAnimating()
        self.counter += 1

        if self.counter >= 5 {
            self.activityView.stopAnimating()
            timer.invalidate()
            self.counter = 0
        }
    }
}

@IBAction func stepperChanged(_ sender: UIStepper) {
    labelProgress.text = "Completed \(Int(stepperObject.value
    * 10)) of 10 tasks"
    progressView.progress = Float(stepperObject.value)
}
}
```

24. Click the Run button or choose Product ➤ Run. The Simulator window appears.

25. Click the + icon on the stepper multiple times. Notice that each time you click the + icon on the stepper, the Progress View appears more filled and the label displays the progress as shown in Figure 8-6.

Completed 3 of 10 tasks

Figure 8-6. *Using the stepper to increase/decrease values in the label and the Progress View*

26.   Choose Simulator ➤ Quit Simulator to return to Xcode.

Summary

When your app needs the user to input numeric data, a text field can work, but it might be clumsy, especially if you only want to accept a limited range of numeric values. To make it easy to input numeric data, use a stepper or a slider.

Both a stepper and slider can define a minimum and maximum value so that way the user can't input numeric data below a minimum value or above a maximum value. A stepper has the added advantage of letting the user increment/decrement values by a fixed value.

A stepper takes up less space, but a slider makes it easier to change values from one extreme to another by simply dragging the thumb (circle) on the slider. Steppers force users to increment/decrement values so steppers can be much slower to define values if the range of acceptable values is large.

To display progress of a task, your app could display a message using a label, but it's often easier to use a Progress View or Activity Indicator View instead. A Progress View can let users know how close a task is to completion, while an Activity Indicator View lets the user know that something is happening.

You can use Progress Views or Activity Indicator Views separately or together. An Activity Indicator View typically appears to display animation and then disappears when the task is done.

By using steppers and sliders, you can make it easy for users to input numeric data. By using Progress Views and Activity Indicator Views, you can make it easy for your app to let the user know when a task is working.

CHAPTER 9

Image Views and Text Views

Text fields can display text and let users edit or input new text. However if you need to display large amounts of text, a text field can be too limiting. To overcome the limited size of a text field, you can use a text view instead. A text view is essentially a larger version of a text field that can display large amounts of text or allow users to edit and input large amounts of text.

Since not all data is text, you can use an image view to display graphic images. Image views can display graphics for purely decorative purposes or to provide additional information to the user, such as changing images based on what the user is doing. Both text views and image views let you display information of any size on an iOS user interface.

Using Image Views

At the simplest level, an image view can display a graphic image such as a .jpg or .png image. However, an image view can also allow interaction so it can respond to touch or gestures from the user. This lets an image view double as both a way to display graphic images and a way to recognize touch input from the user.

To see how an image view works, follow these steps:

1. Create a new iOS project using the Single View App template (see Chapter 1) and name this new project ImageViewApp. This creates a single view for the user interface.

2. Click the Main.storyboard file in the Navigator pane. Xcode displays the single view.

205

© Wallace Wang 2019
W. Wang, *Beginning iPhone Development with Swift 5*, https://doi.org/10.1007/978-1-4842-4865-2_9

3. Click the Library icon to open the Object Library window.

4. Drag and drop an image view anywhere on the view. At this point, the image view is empty so we need to put something in to display it. Find a .jpg or .png image stored on your Macintosh. You can also find and download plenty of free images from `www.pexels. com`, `free-images.com`, or `www.nasa.gov`.

5. Drag and drop a .jpg or .png image from the Finder window to the Navigator pane as shown in Figure 9-1.

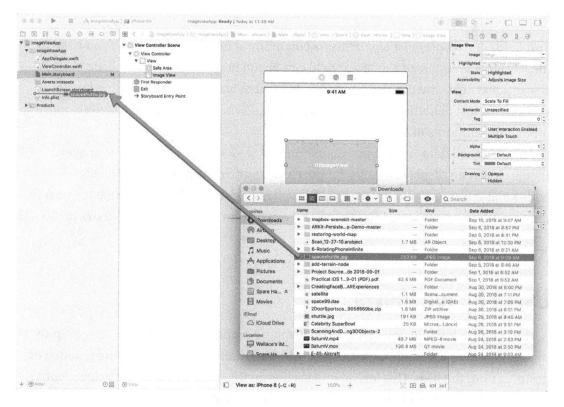

Figure 9-1. *Dragging and dropping an image to an Xcode project*

6. Release the left mouse button when a horizontal line appears in the Navigator pane. Xcode displays a dialog to complete the process of copying a graphic image into your Xcode project.

7. Select the "Copy items if needed" check box as shown in Figure 9-2.

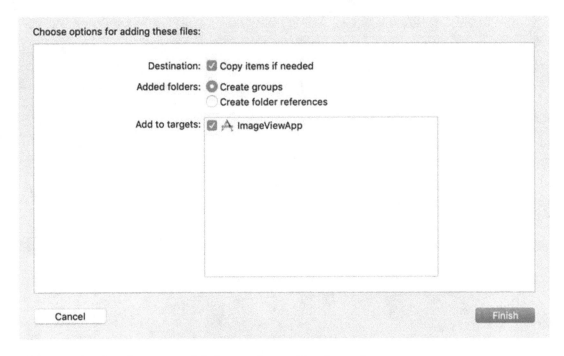

Figure 9-2. *Storing a graphic image in an Xcode project*

8.   Click the Finish button. Xcode displays the name of your graphic file in the Navigator pane.

9.   Click the graphic image name in the Navigator pane. The middle Xcode pane displays the contents of your graphic image.

10.   Click the image view object to select it.

11.   Choose View ➤ Inspectors ➤ Show Attributes Inspector, or click the Attributes Inspector icon in the upper right corner of the Xcode window.

12.   Click in the Image popup menu and choose the name of your graphic image such as spaceshuttle.jpg as shown in Figure 9-3. Xcode displays your graphic image inside the image view.

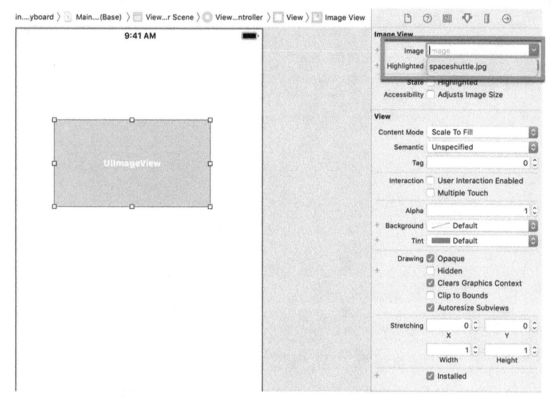

Figure 9-3. *Selecting a graphic image to display in an image view*

The Content Mode popup menu offers several options for how to display an image in an image view:

- Scale to Fill – Alters the size of an image to fill the image view no matter what the height or width of the image view may be. This could create skewered images if an image view is too high or wide.

- Aspect Fit – Fits an image within the width and height of the image view while retaining the aspect ratio of the original image's height and width. This means the image may not completely fill the height or width of the image view as shown in Figure 9-4.

 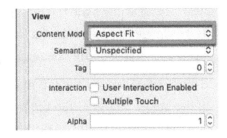

Figure 9-4. *Aspect Fit may leave empty space inside the image view*

- Aspect Fill – Expands an image to fill the width or height of an image view. This means the image may extend over the width or height of the image view.

- Redraw – Stretches the image to fill the width and height of the image view.

- Center – Displays the image center within the image view. If the image is larger than the image view, then the rest of the image appears outside of the image view.

- Top – Displays the image top within the image view. If the image is larger than the image view, then the rest of the image appears outside of the image view.

- Bottom – Displays the image bottom within the image view. If the image is larger than the image view, then the rest of the image appears outside of the image view.

- Left – Displays the image left center within the image view. If the image is larger than the image view, then the rest of the image appears outside of the image view.

- Right – Displays the image right center within the image view. If the image is larger than the image view, then the rest of the image appears outside of the image view.

- Top Left – Displays the top left of the image within the image view. If the image is larger than the image view, then the rest of the image appears outside of the image view.

- Top Right – Displays the top right of the image within the image view. If the image is larger than the image view, then the rest of the image appears outside of the image view.

- Bottom Left – Displays the bottom left of the image within the image view. If the image is larger than the image view, then the rest of the image appears outside of the image view.

- Bottom Right – Displays the bottom right of the image within the image view. If the image is larger than the image view, then the rest of the image appears outside of the image view.

Making the Image View Interactive

By default, an image view ignores all touch interaction. To make an image view respond to touches, you can turn on user interaction in one of two ways as shown in Figure 9-5:

- Select the User Interaction Enabled check box.

- Set the .isUserInteractionEnabled property to true using Swift code.

Figure 9-5. *Allowing an image view to respond to touch gestures*

To see how to make an image view respond to touch gestures, follow these steps:

1. Click the Main.storyboard file in the Navigator pane of the ImageViewApp project.

2. Choose View ➤ Assistant Editor ➤ Show Assistant Editor, or click the Assistant Editor icon. Xcode displays the Main.storyboard and ViewController.swift file side by side.

3. Move the mouse pointer over the image view, hold down the Control key, and Ctrl-drag from the image view to the ViewController.swift file underneath the "class ViewController" line.

4. Release the Control key and the left mouse button. A popup window appears.

5. Click in the Name text field, type **imageView**, and click the Connect button. Xcode creates an IBOutlet variable as follows:

```
@IBOutlet var imageView: UIImageView!
```

6. Choose View ➤ Standard Editor ➤ Show Standard Editor, or click the Standard Editor icon.

7. Click the ViewController.swift file in the Navigator pane.

8. Add the following line to the viewDidLoad method:

```
imageView.isUserInteractionEnabled = true
```

9. Type the following underneath the viewDidLoad method:

```
override func touchesBegan(_ touches: Set<UITouch>, with
event: UIEvent?) {
    let touch = touches.first

    if touch?.view == imageView {
        print ("Touched")
    } else {
        print ("Nothing ")
    }
}
```

The preceding touchesBegan method runs any time the user taps the screen. (In the Simulator, clicking the mouse mimics a finger tap.) The if-else statement checks to see if the user tapped the image view. If so, then it prints "Touched". If the user tapped away from the image view, then it prints "Nothing".

The entire ViewController.swift file should look like this:

```
import UIKit
```

```
class ViewController: UIViewController {
```

```
    @IBOutlet var imageView: UIImageView!
```

```swift
override func viewDidLoad() {
    super.viewDidLoad()
    imageView.isUserInteractionEnabled = true
    // Do any additional setup after loading the view,
    typically from a nib.
}

override func touchesBegan(_ touches: Set<UITouch>, with
event: UIEvent?) {
    let touch = touches.first

    if touch?.view == imageView {
        print ("Touched")
    } else {
        print ("Nothing ")
    }
}

}
```

10. Click the Run button or choose Product ➤ Run. The Simulator screen appears.

11. Click the graphic image you stored in the image view. Notice that the Debug Area at the bottom of the Xcode window displays "Touched" each time you click the image view.

12. Click anywhere else on the Simulator screen away from the image view. Notice that the Debug Area at the bottom of the Xcode window displays "Nothing" each time you click away from the image view.

13. Choose Simulator ➤ Quit Simulator to return to Xcode.

Using a Text View

A text view acts just like a text field. The big difference is that a text view can be much larger and acts more like a miniature word processor that allows the user to move the cursor around and view or edit large amounts of text. Since a text view can both display text and allow the user to input text, the first property to modify is whether you want a text view to be editable or not.

An editable text view means the user can modify the text displayed inside. A non-editable text view means the user cannot modify the text so the text view acts like a large label. There are two ways to modify a text view's editable property:

- Select the Editable check box in the Attributes Inspector (selected by default) as shown in Figure 9-6.

- Set the text view's .editable property to true using Swift code.

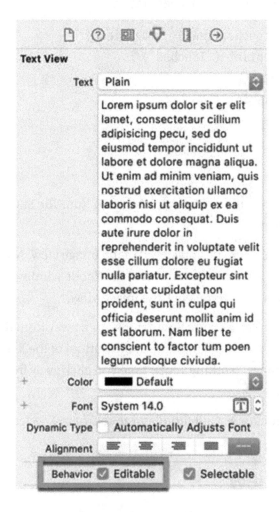

Figure 9-6. *Making a text view editable*

To see how to use a text view, follow these steps:

1. Create a new iOS project using the Single View App template (see Chapter 1) and name this new project TextViewApp. This creates a single view for the user interface.

2. Click the Main.storyboard file in the Navigator pane. Xcode displays the single view.

3. Click the Library icon to open the Object Library window.

4. Drag and drop a text view and a button near the top of the view.

5. Choose Editor ➤ Resolve Auto Layout Issues ➤ Reset to Suggested Constraints at the bottom half of the submenu. This adds constraints to both the text view and the button.

6. Choose View ➤ Assistant Editor ➤ Show Assistant Editor, or click the Assistant Editor icon. Xcode displays the Main.storyboard and ViewController.swift file side by side.

7. Move the mouse pointer over the text view, hold down the Control key, and Ctrl-drag from the text view to the ViewController.swift file underneath the "class ViewController" line.

8. Release the Control key and the left mouse button. A popup window appears.

9. Click in the Name text field, type **textView**, and click the Connect button. Xcode creates an IBOutlet variable as follows:

   @IBOutlet var textView: UITextView!

10. Move the mouse pointer over the button, hold down the Control key, and Ctrl-drag from the button to the ViewController.swift file underneath the IBOutlet line.

11. Release the Control key and the left mouse button. A popup window appears.

12. Click in the Name text field, type **buttonObject**, and click the Connect button. Xcode creates an IBOutlet variable as follows:

   @IBOutlet var buttonObject: UIButton!

13. Move the mouse pointer over the button, hold down the Control key, and Ctrl-drag just above the last curly bracket at the bottom of the ViewController.swift file.

14. Release the Control key and the left mouse button. A popup window appears.

15. Click in the Name text field, type **buttonTapped**, click in the Type popup menu and choose UIButton, and click the Connect button. Xcode creates an IBAction method as follows:

```
@IBAction func buttonTapped(_ sender: UIButton) {
}
```

16. Edit the buttonTapped IBAction method as follows:

```
@IBAction func buttonTapped(_ sender: UIButton) {

    if textView.isEditable == true {

        textView.isEditable = false

    } else {

        textView.isEditable = true

    }

}
```

Note   When assigning a value to a variable, you use a single (=) equal sign, but when comparing two values, you use a double equal sign (==).

This IBAction method toggles the text view between making it editable or not. When a text view is editable, you can modify the text. When a text view is not editable, you cannot edit the text. The entire ViewController.swift file should look like this:

```
import UIKit

class ViewController: UIViewController {

    @IBOutlet var textView: UITextView!
    @IBOutlet var buttonObject: UIButton!
```

```swift
override func viewDidLoad() {
    super.viewDidLoad()
    // Do any additional setup after loading the view,
    typically from a nib.
}

@IBAction func buttonTapped(_ sender: UIButton) {
    if textView.isEditable == true {
        textView.isEditable = false
    } else {
        textView.isEditable = true
    }
}
```

17. Click the Run button or choose Product ➤ Run. The Simulator window appears.

18. Click in the text view. Press the BACKSPACE and DELETE keys to delete text.

19. Click the button. This runs the Swift code in the buttonTapped IBAction method, which makes the text view non-editable.

20. Click in the text view. Notice that you cannot edit the text in the text view anymore.

21. Repeat steps 18–20 to see how you can switch the text view from being editable to not being editable.

22. Chose Simulator ➤ Quit Simulator to return to Xcode.

Changing Text Appearance in a Text View

Unlike a word processor that lets you selectively change the appearance of different text, all text inside a text view always appears in the same text color, background color, font, and font size. The properties to modify text color, background color, font, and font size in Swift are as follows:

- .text – Defines the actual text that appears in the text view

- .backgroundColor – Defines the background of the text view

- .textColor – Defines the color of the text

- .font – Defines the font and font size of text

To see how to modify the appearance of text using Swift code, follow these steps:

1. Choose View ➤ Standard Editor ➤ Show Standard Editor, or click the Standard Editor icon in the upper right corner of the Xcode window.

2. Click the ViewController.swift file in the Navigator pane. Xcode displays the ViewController.swift file.

3. Modify the buttonTapped IBAction method as follows:

```
@IBAction func buttonTapped(_ sender: UIButton) {
    if textView.isEditable == true {
        textView.isEditable = false
        textView.backgroundColor = UIColor.yellow
        textView.textColor = UIColor.blue
        textView.font = UIFont(name: "Courier", size: 24)
    } else {
        textView.isEditable = true
        textView.backgroundColor = UIColor.blue
        textView.textColor = UIColor.white
        textView.font = UIFont(name: "Ariel", size: 10)

    }
}
```

4. Click the Run button or choose Product ➤ Run. The Simulator window appears.

5. Click the button. Notice how the text changes appearance in the text view with a yellow background and blue text color.

6. Click the button again. Notice that now the text appears with a blue background and a white text color along with a smaller font size.

7. Choose Simulator ➤ Quit Simulator to return to Xcode.

Creating Clickable Text in a Text View

If you type in an iOS app like Notes or Messages, you may notice that if you type a phone number, web site URL, or date, that text gets highlighted so you can tap on it to take action. For example, if you type a phone number in the Notes app, that phone number text appears highlighted. If you tap this highlighted text, then an iPhone can call this phone number.

To make clickable text appear in a text view, the text view must not be editable. Some of the different types of clickable text a text view can highlight include

- .address – Detects street addresses

- .calendarEvent – Detects times and dates

- .flightNumber – Detects airline flight numbers

- .link – Detects URLs

- .lookupSuggestion – Detects words or phrases such as restaurant names, movie titles, celebrity names, etc.

- .phoneNumber – Detects phone numbers

You can define clickable text using Swift code or by selecting a check box in the Data Detectors category in the Attributes Inspector pane as shown in Figure 9-7.

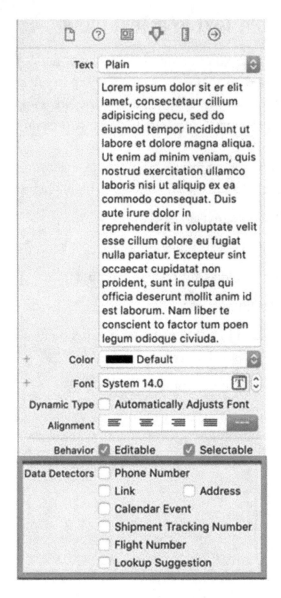

Figure 9-7. *Defining clickable text in the Data Detectors category of the Attributes Inspector pane*

To see how to make text clickable in a text view, follow these steps:

1. Make sure the TextViewApp project is loaded in Xcode.

2. Click the ViewController.swift file in the Navigator pane to edit the ViewController.swift file.

3. Edit the viewDidLoad method as follows:

```
override func viewDidLoad() {
    super.viewDidLoad()
    textView.dataDetectorTypes = UIDataDetectorTypes.link
    textView.isEditable = false
    textView.isSelectable = true
    textView.text = "This is an example of clickable text www.
    yahoo.com"
    // Do any additional setup after loading the view,
    typically from a nib.
}
```

The entire ViewController.swift file should look like this:

```
import UIKit

class ViewController: UIViewController {

    @IBOutlet var textView: UITextView!
    @IBOutlet var buttonObject: UIButton!

    override func viewDidLoad() {
        super.viewDidLoad()
        textView.dataDetectorTypes = UIDataDetectorTypes.link
        textView.isEditable = false
        textView.isSelectable = true
        textView.text = "This is an example of clickable text www.
        yahoo.com"
        // Do any additional setup after loading the view,
        typically from a nib.
    }

    @IBAction func buttonTapped(_ sender: UIButton) {
        if textView.isEditable == true {
            textView.isEditable = false
            textView.backgroundColor = UIColor.yellow
            textView.textColor = UIColor.blue
            textView.font = UIFont(name: "Courier", size: 24)
```

```
        } else {
            textView.isEditable = true
            textView.backgroundColor = UIColor.blue
            textView.textColor = UIColor.white
            textView.font = UIFont(name: "Ariel", size: 10)

        }
    }
}
```

4. Click the Run button or chose Product ➤ Run. The Simulator window appears. Notice that the URL www.yahoo.com appears highlighted as a blue hyperlink.

5. Click the www.yahoo.com hyperlink. The Simulator displays the Safari browser and the www.yahoo.com web site, which is exactly what would happen if this app were running on a real iPhone or iPad.

6. Choose Simulator ➤ Quit Simulator to return to Xcode.

Displaying the Virtual Keyboard with a Text View

For users to type in the text view, you need to display (and hide) the virtual keyboard. When the user taps in the text view to edit its contents, the virtual keyboard should appear, moving the text view up if necessary. When the user is done editing text in a text view, then the virtual keyboard needs to go away.

First, you need to define the View Controller to be notified of two events: keyboardWillShowNotification and keyboardWillHideNotification. Second, you need to create a keyboardWillShow and keyboardWillHide function to show the virtual keyboard (and move the view up) and hide the virtual keyboard when it's no longer needed. Finally, you need to dismiss the virtual keyboard if the user taps away from the text view.

To add code to show and hide the virtual keyboard, follow these steps:

1. Click the Main.storyboard file in the Navigator pane of the TextViewApp project.

2. Click the Library icon to display the Object Library.

3. Drag and drop a text view near the bottom of the user interface.

4. Choose Editor ➤ Resolve Auto Layout Issues ➤ Reset to Suggested Constraints on the top half of the submenu. This will add constraints to the new text view on the user interface.

5. Add the following to the viewDidLoad method:

```
NotificationCenter.default.addObserver(self, selector:
#selector(keyboardWillShow), name: UIResponder.
keyboardWillShowNotification, object: nil)
NotificationCenter.default.addObserver(self, selector:
#selector(keyboardWillHide), name: UIResponder.
keyboardWillHideNotification, object: nil)

let tap: UITapGestureRecognizer =
UITapGestureRecognizer(target: self, action:
#selector(self.dismissKeyboard))
view.addGestureRecognizer(tap)
```

6. Add the following code above the buttonTapped IBAction method as follows:

```
@objc func dismissKeyboard() {
        view.endEditing(true)
    }

    @objc func keyboardWillShow(notification: NSNotification) {
        if let keyboardSize = (notification.userInfo?[UIResponder.
        keyboardFrameEndUserInfoKey] as? NSValue)?.cgRectValue {
            if self.view.frame.origin.y == 0 {
                self.view.frame.origin.y -= keyboardSize.height
            }
        }
    }

    @objc func keyboardWillHide(notification: NSNotification) {
        if ((notification.userInfo?[UIResponder.
        keyboardFrameEndUserInfoKey] as? NSValue)?.cgRectValue)
        != nil {
            if self.view.frame.origin.y != 0 {
```

```
                    self.view.frame.origin.y = 0
            }
        }
    }
```

The entire ViewController.swift file should look like this:

```swift
import UIKit

class ViewController: UIViewController {

    @IBOutlet var textView: UITextView!
    @IBOutlet var buttonObject: UIButton!

    override func viewDidLoad() {
        super.viewDidLoad()
        textView.dataDetectorTypes = UIDataDetectorTypes.link
        textView.isEditable = false
        textView.isSelectable = true
        textView.text = "This is an example of clickable text www.
        yahoo.com"

        NotificationCenter.default.addObserver(self, selector:
        #selector(keyboardWillShow), name: UIResponder.
        keyboardWillShowNotification, object: nil)
        NotificationCenter.default.addObserver(self, selector:
        #selector(keyboardWillHide), name: UIResponder.
        keyboardWillHideNotification, object: nil)

        let tap: UITapGestureRecognizer =
        UITapGestureRecognizer(target: self, action:
        #selector(self.dismissKeyboard))
        view.addGestureRecognizer(tap)

        // Do any additional setup after loading the view,
        typically from a nib.
    }

    @objc func dismissKeyboard() {
        view.endEditing(true)
    }
```

```
@objc func keyboardWillShow(notification: NSNotification) {
    if let keyboardSize = (notification.userInfo?[UIResponder.
    keyboardFrameEndUserInfoKey] as? NSValue)?.cgRectValue {
        if self.view.frame.origin.y == 0 {
            self.view.frame.origin.y -= keyboardSize.height
        }
    }
}

@objc func keyboardWillHide(notification: NSNotification) {
    if ((notification.userInfo?[UIResponder.
    keyboardFrameEndUserInfoKey] as? NSValue)?.cgRectValue)
    != nil {
        if self.view.frame.origin.y != 0 {
            self.view.frame.origin.y = 0
        }
    }
}

@IBAction func buttonTapped(_ sender: UIButton) {
    if textView.isEditable == true {
        textView.isEditable = false
        textView.backgroundColor = UIColor.yellow
        textView.textColor = UIColor.blue
        textView.font = UIFont(name: "Courier", size: 24)
    } else {
        textView.isEditable = true
        textView.backgroundColor = UIColor.blue
        textView.textColor = UIColor.white
        textView.font = UIFont(name: "Ariel", size: 10)
    }
}
```

7. Click the Run button or choose Product ➤ Run. The Simulator screen appears.

8. Click in the bottom text view. (If the virtual keyboard does not appear, press Command + K or choose Hardware ➤ Keyboard ➤ Toggle Virtual Keyboard.)

9. Add and delete text inside the text view using the virtual keyboard.

10. Click anywhere but inside a text view. The virtual keyboard disappears.

11. Chose Simulator ➤ Quit Simulator to return to Xcode.

Summary

Image views and text views let your app display data on the user interface. An image view displays information visually as images. These images can be static and serve purely decorative purposes or display useful information such as a chart. Image views can also be interactive that can respond to taps.

Text views can both display text and allow the user to edit and input text. A text view behaves much like a text field except it can display large amounts of text at once, much like a miniature word processor. You can modify the appearance of text but any changes affect all text in a text view.

If you make a text view non-editable, then you can also create clickable text where the text view can recognize common types of words and phrases such as telephone numbers, street addresses, URLs, and calendar events such as dates and times.

Text views can simply display information to the user or they can allow input. Image views can display visual data or allow interaction so your app can respond if the user taps on the image view. By using both text views and image views, you have another way to display data, allow input, and accept interaction from the user.

CHAPTER 10

Buttons, Switches, and Segmented Controls

Besides displaying data or letting users input data, the second most important purpose of a user interface is to allow users to control an app. At the simplest level, users can use buttons where each button represents a single command. Of course if you want to display multiple options, displaying multiple buttons on the screen can get crowded.

For two alternatives for giving commands, Xcode offers switches and segmented controls. A switch lets users choose to turn a setting on or off. A segmented control acts like multiple buttons, in a condensed area, that the user can tap to select different options. Figure 10-1 shows the visual appearance of a button, switch, and segmented control.

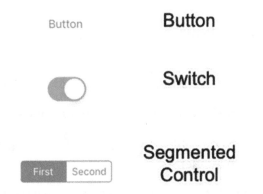

Figure 10-1. *Comparing the visual appearance of a button, switch, and segmented control*

© Wallace Wang 2019
W. Wang, *Beginning iPhone Development with Swift 5*, https://doi.org/10.1007/978-1-4842-4865-2_10

Understanding Events

User interface objects that represent commands, such as buttons, switches, and segmented controls, respond to events. The simplest event occurs when the user taps or touches inside an object. A more complicated event might occur when the user drags or slides a finger inside an object.

All types of user interface objects can respond to events such as when the user taps on an object such as a button. The combination of an object plus an event defines an IBAction method. If you want an object to respond to two different events, you'll need to create two different IBAction methods for that particular object.

The different available types of events an object can respond to include

- Touch Up Inside – A tap inside the bounds of an object with the finger lifting up

- Touch Up Outside – A tap outside the bounds of an object

- Touch Down – A tap inside the bounds of an object

- Touch Down Repeat – Two or more taps inside the bounds of an object

- Touch Drag Enter – Where a finger touches outside the object and slides over the object

- Touch Drag Exit – Where a finger touches inside an object and slides away from it

- Touch Drag Inside – Where a finger slides inside an object

- Touch Drag Outside – Where a finger slides just outside an object

- Value Changed – Where manipulating an object changes its stored value such as with a slider

- Editing Changed – When text changes inside a text field

- Editing Did Begin – When a finger taps inside a text field

- Editing Did End – When a finger taps outside a text field

By choosing which events a particular object can respond to, you can allow the user to interact with user interface objects in different and unique ways. In most cases, user interface objects only need to respond to the most likely event such as Touch Up Inside, which detects when the user taps an object.

Using Buttons

A button typically responds to the Touch Up Inside event and displays the command that it represents such as OK, Cancel, or Done. The text that appears on a button can be modified in three ways:

- In the Attributes Inspector pane
- By double-clicking the button
- Through Swift code

To see how we define the title on a button, follow these steps:

1. Create a new iOS project using the Single View App template (see Chapter 1) and name this new project ControlApp. This creates a single view for the user interface.

2. Click the Main.storyboard file in the Navigator pane. Xcode displays the single view.

3. Click the Library icon to open the Object Library window.

4. Drag and drop a button anywhere on the view. By default, the title on a button displays "Title".

5. Choose View ➤ Inspectors ➤ Show Attributes Inspector.

6. Click in the Title text field as shown in Figure 10-2, delete the existing text ("Title"), and type **Cancel**. Then press ENTER. Notice that Xcode now displays the word "Cancel" on the button.

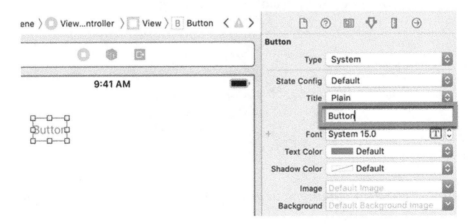

Figure 10-2. *Changing the title of a button in the Attributes Inspector*

7. Double-click the button to select the title.

8. Type **Done** and press ENTER. Notice that now the button displays Done.

9. Choose Editor ➤ Resolve Auto Layout Issues ➤ Set to Suggested Constraints. Xcode adds constraints to your button.

10. Choose View ➤ Assistant Editor ➤ Show Assistant Editor. Xcode displays the Main.storyboard and ViewController.swift file side by side.

11. Move the mouse pointer over the button, hold down the Control key, and Ctrl-drag from the image view to the ViewController.swift file underneath the "class ViewController" line.

12. Release the Control key and the left mouse button. A popup window appears.

13. Click in the Name text field, type **buttonObject**, and click the Connect button. Xcode creates an IBOutlet variable as follows:

    @IBOutlet var buttonObject: UIButton!

14. Move the mouse pointer over the button, hold down the Control key, and Ctrl-drag from the image view to the ViewController.swift file above the last curly bracket at the bottom of the file.

15. Release the Control key and the left mouse button. A popup window appears. Notice that the Event popup menu already chooses the Touch Up Inside event by default as shown in Figure 10-3.

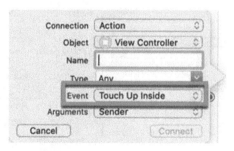

Figure 10-3. *The Event popup menu displays Touch Up Inside by default for buttons*

16. Click in the Name text field, type **touchInside**, click in the Type popup menu and choose UIButton, and click the Connect button. Xcode creates an IBAction method.

17. Edit this touchInside IBAction method as follows:

```
@IBAction func touchInside(_ sender: UIButton) {
    buttonObject.setTitle("New", for: UIControl.State.normal)
}
```

This IBAction runs every time the user taps on the button, and the Swift code changes the button title to "New". By using setTitle, your Swift code can change a button's title while your app runs.

The entire ViewController.swift file should look like this:

```
import UIKit

class ViewController: UIViewController {

    @IBOutlet var buttonObject: UIButton!

    override func viewDidLoad() {
        super.viewDidLoad()
        // Do any additional setup after loading the view,
        typically from a nib.
    }

    @IBAction func touchInside(_ sender: UIButton) {
        buttonObject.setTitle("New", for: UIControl.State.normal)
    }

}
```

18. Click the Run button or choose Product ➤ Run. The Simulator screen appears. Notice that the button title currently displays Done.

19. Click the button. Notice that the button title now changes to "New".

20. Choose Simulator ➤ Quit Simulator to return to Xcode.

Using a Switch

In many apps, users can turn features on or off. Whenever users have a choice between exactly two options, that's a perfect time to use a switch. As its name implies, a switch can slide right or left to represent an on or off value. When a switch is turned on, a color appears and the switch appears on the right. When a switch is turned off, the switch displays a different color and the switch appears on the left as shown in Figure 10-4.

Figure 10-4. *Switches are often used to turn settings on or off*

The three common properties of a switch to modify include

- isOn – Determines if a switch has a value of true (on) or false (off)

- onTintColor – Determines the color to display when a switch's isOn property is true (on)

- tintColor – Determines the color to display when a switch's isOn property is false (off)

To see how to use a switch, follow these steps:

1. Make sure your ControlApp project is loaded in Xcode.

2. Click the Main.storyboard file in the Navigator pane. Xcode displays the single view.

3. Click the Library icon to open the Object Library window.

4. Drag and drop a label and a switch on the view.

5. Hold down the SHIFT key and click the switch and label to select both of them.

6. Choose Editor ➤ Resolve Auto Layout Issues ➤ Reset to Suggested Constraints at the top half of the submenu. This adds constraints to switch and label.

7. Choose View ➤ Assistant Editor ➤ Show Assistant Editor, or click the Assistant Editor icon. Xcode displays the Main.storyboard and ViewController.swift file side by side.

8. Move the mouse pointer over the label, hold down the Control key, and Ctrl-drag from the label to the ViewController.swift file underneath the IBOutlet line.

9. Release the Control key and the left mouse button. A popup window appears.

10. Click in the Name text field, type **labelSwitch**, and click the Connect button. Xcode creates an IBOutlet variable as follows:

    @IBOutlet var labelSwitch: UILabel!

11. Move the mouse pointer over the switch, hold down the Control key, and Ctrl-drag from the button to the ViewController.swift file underneath the IBOutlet line.

12. Release the Control key and the left mouse button. A popup window appears.

13. Click in the Name text field, type **switchObject**, and click the Connect button. Xcode creates an IBOutlet variable as follows:

    @IBOutlet var switchObject: UISwitch!

14. Move the mouse pointer over the switch, hold down the Control key, and Ctrl-drag just above the last curly bracket at the bottom of the ViewController.swift file.

15. Release the Control key and the left mouse button. A popup window appears.

16. Click in the Name text field, type **switchChanged**, click in the Type popup menu and choose UISwitch, and click the Connect button. Xcode creates an IBAction method as follows:

    ```
    @IBAction func switchChanged(_ sender: UISwitch) {
    }
    ```

17. Edit the switchChanged IBAction method as follows:

```
@IBAction func switchChanged(_ sender: UISwitch) {
    if switchObject.isOn {
        labelSwitch.text = "On"
    } else {
        labelSwitch.text = "Off"
    }
}
```

18. Edit the touchInside IBAction method as follows:

```
@IBAction func touchInside(_ sender: UIButton) {
    buttonObject.setTitle("New", for: UIControl.State.normal)
    switchObject.onTintColor = UIColor.red
    switchObject.tintColor = UIColor.blue
}
```

The touchInside IBAction changes the color of the switch. Each time you tap on the switch, it changes from on to off (or vice versa), displays the text "On" or "Off" in the labelSwitch object, and displays different on and off colors. The entire ViewController.swift file should look like this:

```
import UIKit

class ViewController: UIViewController {

    @IBOutlet var buttonObject: UIButton!
    @IBOutlet var labelSwitch: UILabel!
    @IBOutlet var switchObject: UISwitch!

    override func viewDidLoad() {
        super.viewDidLoad()
        // Do any additional setup after loading the view,
        typically from a nib.
    }

    @IBAction func touchInside(_ sender: UIButton) {
        buttonObject.setTitle("New", for: UIControl.State.normal)
        switchObject.onTintColor = UIColor.red
```

```
        switchObject.tintColor = UIColor.blue
    }

    @IBAction func switchChanged(_ sender: UISwitch) {
        if switchObject.isOn {
            labelSwitch.text = "On"
        } else {
            labelSwitch.text = "Off"
        }
    }
}
```

19. Choose View ➤ Standard Editor ➤ Show Standard Editor, or click the Standard Editor icon in the upper right corner of the Xcode window.

20. Click the Run button or choose Product ➤ Run. The Simulator window appears.

21. Click the switch. Notice that each time you click the switch, it changes its appearance from on and off and displays "On" or "Off" in the label nearby as shown in Figure 10-5.

Figure 10-5. *The label displays whether a switch is on or off*

22. Click the button. This runs the Swift code in the touchInside IBAction method, which changes the colors of the switch.

23. Click the switch. Notice that each time you click the switch, you can see the colors red and blue appear instead of the default colors.

24. Chose Simulator ➤ Quit Simulator to return to Xcode.

Using a Segmented Control

A button is fine for displaying a single command, but when you need to display multiple commands, then multiple buttons can make a user interface appear cluttered. When you need to display multiple buttons in a limited amount of space, you can use a segmented control.

A segmented control can contain two or more segments where each segment acts like an individual button. You can define the number of segments through the Attributes Inspector pane, but you can also later add more segments using Swift code.

In the Attributes Inspector, you can customize a segmented control in the following ways as shown in Figure 10-6:

- Segments – Defines the number of segments (buttons) in a segmented control

- Segment – A popup menu that lets you choose which segment to modify

- Title – Defines the text that appears on the segment defined by the Segment popup menu

- Image – Defines an image to appear on the segment defined by the Segment popup menu

- Selected – A check box that defines which segment appears selected (highlighted) where only one segment in an entire segmented control can be selected

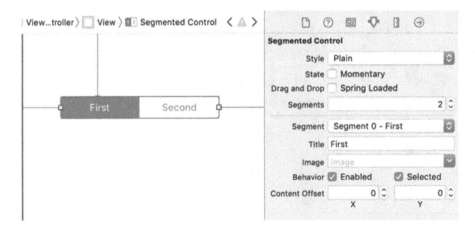

Figure 10-6. *Modifying a segmented control in the Attributes Inspector*

236

Every segmented control identifies its different segments by an index number where the segment on the far left is at index 0, the next segment to the right is at index 1, and so on. Xcode automatically assigns an index number to each segment based on the position of that segment. You can use the segment index number to identify which segment the user taps.

Once you've added a segmented control to a view, you can add or remove segments using Swift code. To see how to modify a segmented control, follow these steps:

1.   Click the Main.storyboard file in the Navigator pane. Xcode displays the storyboard user interface.

2.   Click the Library icon to display the Object Library window.

3.   Drag and drop a segmented control anywhere onto the view.

4.   Choose Editor ➤ Resolve Auto Layout Issues ➤ Reset to Suggested Constraints on the top half of the submenu. Xcode adds constraints to the segmented control.

5.   Double-click the segment labeled "First" on the left of the segmented control. Xcode highlights the title on the segment as shown in Figure 10-7.

Figure 10-7. *Double-clicking directly a segmented control title lets you edit that title*

6.   Type **One** and press ENTER to replace the First label. Double-clicking directly an object that displays text is one way to modify the text. A second way is to use the Attributes Inspector pane.

7.   Choose View ➤ Inspectors ➤ Show Attributes Inspector, or click the Attributes Inspector icon in the upper right corner of the Xcode window.

8.   Click in the Segment popup menu and choose Segment 1 – Second. The Title text field displays the current title for the chosen segment as shown in Figure 10-8.

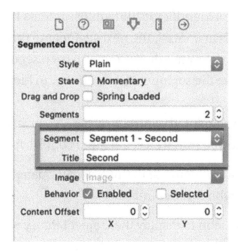

Figure 10-8. *Changing a segment title in the Attributes Inspector pane*

9. Click in the Title text field and change the text to **Two**. Then press ENTER. Notice that you can change the title on each segment either by double-clicking directly the title or by changing the Title text field of the segment.

10. Choose View ➤ Assistant Editor ➤ Show Assistant Editor, or click the Assistant Editor icon. Xcode displays the Main.storyboard and ViewController.swift file side by side.

11. Move the mouse pointer over the segmented control, hold down the Control key, and Ctrl-drag from the segmented control to the ViewController.swift file underneath the IBOutlet line.

12. Release the Control key and the left mouse button. A popup window appears.

13. Click in the Name text field, type **segmentedControl**, and click the Connect button. Xcode creates an IBOutlet variable as follows:

    @IBOutlet var segmentedControl: UISegmentedControl!

14. Move the mouse pointer over the segmented control, hold down the Control key, and Ctrl-drag from the segmented control to the ViewController.swift file above the last curly bracket at the bottom of the file.

15. Release the Control key and the left mouse button. A popup window appears.

16. Click in the Name text field, type **segmentedControlTapped**, and click the Connect button. Xcode creates an IBAction method.

17. Modify this segmentedControlTapped IBAction method as follows:

```
@IBAction func segmentedControlTapped(_ sender:
UISegmentedControl) {
switch segmentedControl.selectedSegmentIndex {
case 0:
    labelSwitch.text = "One"
case 1:
    labelSwitch.text = "Two"
default:
    labelSwitch.text = "Three"
}
}
```

This segmentedControlTapped IBAction method uses the .selectedSegmentIndex property to identify which segment the user tapped. Then a switch statement determines which segment the user tapped (based on its index number) and displays One, Two, or Three in the label to identify which segment the user tapped.

18. Edit the viewDidLoad method as follows:

```
override func viewDidLoad() {
    super.viewDidLoad()
    segmentedControl.insertSegment(withTitle: "Three", at: 2,
    animated: true)
    segmentedControl.setWidth(50, forSegmentAt: 0)
    segmentedControl.setWidth(50, forSegmentAt: 1)
    segmentedControl.setWidth(50, forSegmentAt: 2)
    // Do any additional setup after loading the view,
    typically from a nib.
}
```

This Swift code adds a third segment to the existing segmented control and it sets the width of each segment in the segmented control. The entire ViewController.swift file should look like this:

```swift
import UIKit

class ViewController: UIViewController {

    @IBOutlet var buttonObject: UIButton!
    @IBOutlet var labelSwitch: UILabel!
    @IBOutlet var switchObject: UISwitch!
    @IBOutlet var segmentedControl: UISegmentedControl!

    override func viewDidLoad() {
        super.viewDidLoad()
        segmentedControl.insertSegment(withTitle: "Three", at: 2,
        animated: true)
        segmentedControl.setWidth(50, forSegmentAt: 0)
        segmentedControl.setWidth(50, forSegmentAt: 1)
        segmentedControl.setWidth(50, forSegmentAt: 2)
        // Do any additional setup after loading the view,
        typically from a nib.
    }

    @IBAction func touchInside(_ sender: UIButton) {
        buttonObject.setTitle("New", for: UIControl.State.normal)
        switchObject.onTintColor = UIColor.red
        switchObject.tintColor = UIColor.blue
    }

    @IBAction func switchChanged(_ sender: UISwitch) {
        if switchObject.isOn {
            labelSwitch.text = "On"
        } else {
            labelSwitch.text = "Off"
        }
    }
}
```

```swift
@IBAction func segmentedControlTapped(_ sender:
UISegmentedControl) {
    switch segmentedControl.selectedSegmentIndex {
    case 0:
        labelSwitch.text = "One"
    case 1:
        labelSwitch.text = "Two"
    default:
        labelSwitch.text = "Three"
    }
}
}
```

19. Click the Run button or choose Product ➤ Run. The Simulator window appears.

20. Click the second or third segment in the segmented control. Notice that the segment you clicked now appears highlighted and the label displays the name of the segment you clicked such as "Two" or "Three".

21. Click any segment. Notice that each time you click a different segment, that segment appears highlighted and the label displays different text.

22. Choose Simulator ➤ Quit Simulator to return to Xcode.

Connecting Multiple Objects to the Same IBAction Method

Most of the time when you use objects to interact with the user such as buttons, switches, or segmented controls, you create a separate IBAction method for each object. However, it's possible to connect two or more objects to the same IBAction method.

First, you need to create an IBAction method with one object such as a button. Then you can connect another object to that existing IBAction method. That way both objects can respond to the same IBAction method. This can be useful because instead of writing two or more separate IBAction methods that do mostly the same thing, you can write a single IBAction method that responds slightly differently based on which object the user tapped.

When connecting two or more objects to the same IBAction method, you need to decide if you only want identical objects (such as buttons) to connect to the same IBAction method or whether you want to allow different objects (such as a button and an image view) to connect to the same IBAction method.

Whenever you create an IBAction method, you can define the type of object the IBAction method will respond to. By default, the type is set to Any, which means different objects can connect to the same IBAction method, but you can choose to allow only the same type of object to connect to the IBAction method such as UIButtons as shown in Figure 10-9.

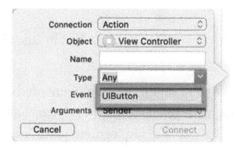

Figure 10-9. *Choosing the type of object an IBAction method can respond to*

If you define the Type to a specific object such as UIButton, your IBAction method will define the sender (the object that called the IBAction method) as that specific object such as:

```
@IBAction func buttonTapped(_ sender: UIButton) {
}
```

The preceding IBAction method can only be called from UIButton objects. If you accept the Type default of Any when creating an IBAction method, then your IBAction method will define the sender as Any such as:

```
@IBAction func buttonTapped(_ sender: Any) {
}
```

Any type of object can connect to an IBAction method where the sender is defined as Any.

When two or more objects connect to the same IBAction method, you need a way to identify which object called that IBAction method. One way to identify different user interface objects is to give each one a unique Tag number in the Attributes Inspector pane as shown in Figure 10-10.

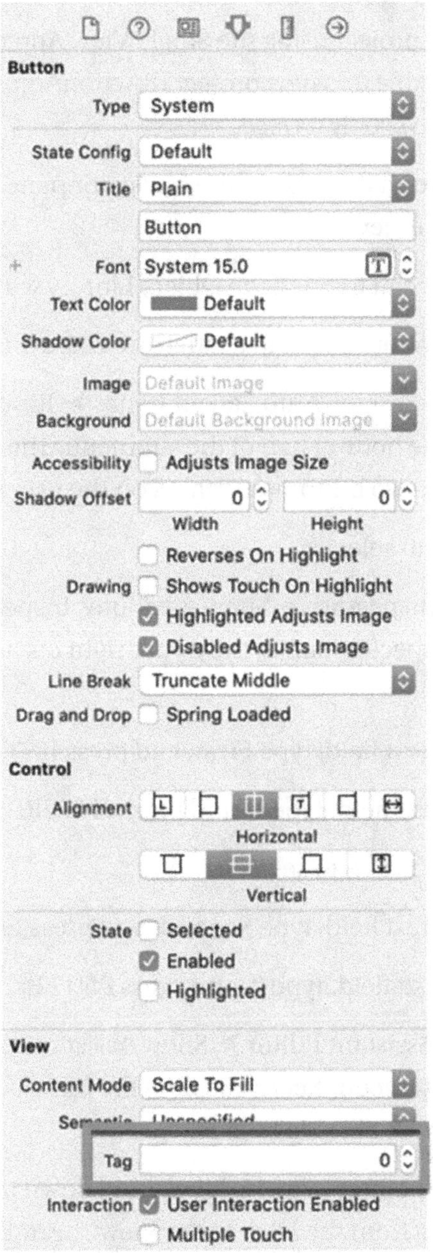

Figure 10-10. *The Tag property can be modified in the Attributes Inspector pane*

By default, every object has a Tag value of 0, but you can change this so each object has a distinct value such as 1, 24, or 894. By identifying the Tag value, an IBAction method can determine which object to respond to.

To show how to link multiple objects to an IBAction method and detect which object to respond to, follow these steps:

1. Create a new iOS project using the Single View App template (see Chapter 1) and name this new project IBActionApp. This creates a single view for the user interface.

2. Click the Main.storyboard file in the Navigator pane. Xcode displays the single view.

3. Click the Library icon to open the Object Library window.

4. Drag and drop two buttons and a label anywhere on the view.

5. Choose Editor ➤ Resolve Auto Layout Issues ➤ Reset to Suggested Constraints on the bottom half of the submenu. This will add constraints to the two buttons and label on the user interface.

6. Click one button to select it.

7. Choose View ➤ Inspectors ➤ Show Attributes Inspector, or click the Attributes Inspector icon in the upper right corner of the Xcode window.

8. Click in the Title text field, type **First**, and press ENTER.

9. Click in the Tag text field, type **1**, and press ENTER.

10. Click the second button to select it.

11. Click in the Title text field, type **Second**, and press ENTER.

12. Click in the Tag text field, type **2**, and press ENTER.

13. Choose View ➤ Assistant Editor ➤ Show Assistant Editor, or click the Assistant Editor icon. Xcode displays the Main.storyboard and ViewController.swift file side by side.

14. Move the mouse pointer over the label, hold down the Control key, and Ctrl-drag from the label to the ViewController.swift file underneath the IBOutlet line.

15. Release the Control key and the left mouse button. A popup window appears.

16. Click in the Name text field, type **labelResult**, and click the Connect button. Xcode creates an IBOutlet variable as follows:

    @IBOutlet var labelResult: UILabel!

17. Move the mouse pointer over the button titled "First", hold down the Control key, and Ctrl-drag from the button to the ViewController.swift file above the last curly bracket in the ViewController.swift file.

18. Release the Control key and the left mouse button. A popup window appears.

19. Click in the Name text field, type **buttonTapped**, make sure the Type popup menu displays Any, and click the Connect button. Xcode creates an IBAction method as follows:

    @IBAction func buttonTapped(**_** sender: **Any**) {
    }

20. Move the mouse pointer over the button titled "Second", hold down the Control key, and Ctrl-drag from the button to the buttonTapped IBAction method until the entire IBAction method appears highlighted as shown in Figure 10-11.

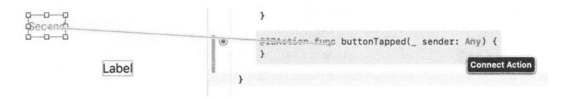

Figure 10-11. *Connecting a second object to an existing IBAction method*

21. Release the Control key and left mouse button.

22. Move the mouse pointer over the circle in the left margin of the buttonTapped IBAction method. Xcode highlights the two buttons to verify that both buttons are connected to the buttonTapped IBAction method as shown in Figure 10-12.

Figure 10-12. *Verifying all objects connected to a single IBAction method*

23.   Modify the buttonTapped IBAction method as follows:

```
@IBAction func buttonTapped(_ sender: Any) {
    switch (sender as AnyObject).tag {
    case 1:
        labelResult.text = "Button 1"
    case 2:
        labelResult.text = "Button 2"
    default:
        labelResult.text = "Default"
    }
}
```

24.   Modify the viewDidLoad method as follows:

```
override func viewDidLoad() {
    super.viewDidLoad()
    labelResult.frame.size.width = 120
    // Do any additional setup after loading the view,
    typically from a nib.
}
```

The entire ViewController.swift file should look like this:

```
import UIKit

class ViewController: UIViewController {

    @IBOutlet var labelResult: UILabel!
```

```swift
override func viewDidLoad() {
    super.viewDidLoad()
    labelResult.frame.size.width = 120
    // Do any additional setup after loading the view,
    typically from a nib.
}

@IBAction func buttonTapped(_ sender: Any) {
    switch (sender as AnyObject).tag {
    case 1:
        labelResult.text = "Button 1"
    case 2:
        labelResult.text = "Button 2"
    default:
        labelResult.text = "Default"
    }
}
}
```

25. Click the Run button or choose Product ➤ Run. The Simulator screen appears.

26. Click the button titled "First". Notice that the label displays "Button 1".

27. Click the button titled "Second". Notice that the label displays "Button 2".

28. Chose Simulator ➤ Quit Simulator to return to Xcode.

In the preceding example, two buttons connect to the same IBAction method, but because the IBAction type is Any, you could connect any objects to this IBAction method. In most cases, it's better to restrict an IBAction method to specific types of objects such as UIButton.

Besides reducing the risk that an unintended object could connect to an IBAction method, restricting an IBAction method to a specific object type also lets you access that specific object's properties. For example, an IBAction method linked only to UIButtons will then be able to access all the properties that a UIButton object contains such as titleLabel.text.

Before we link the two existing buttons to a new IBAction method, we need to break the connection between the current IBAction method in the Connections Inspector pane. After we break the connection between an IBOutlet and an IBAction method, we can delete the actual IBOutlet or IBAction method in the .swift file.

Note   Just deleting an IBOutlet variable or IBAction method will not break its link to an object on the user interface. You must break the actual link in the Connections Inspector pane. If you fail to break the link in the Connections Inspector pane, running your app will not work and Xcode will display an error message.

To see how to break a connection between an existing IBAction method and a user interface object and create an IBAction method for specific types of objects only, follow these steps:

1. Make sure the IBActionApp project is loaded in Xcode.

2. Click the Main.storyboard file in the Navigator pane.

3. Click the button titled "First" to select it.

4. Choose View ➤ Inspectors ➤ Show Connections Inspector, or click the Connections Inspector icon in the upper right corner of the Xcode window. The Connections Inspector pane appears, showing all IBOutlets and IBAction methods linked to the selected object. In Figure 10-13, the selected button is linked to an IBAction method called buttonTapped, which responds to the Touch Up Inside event.

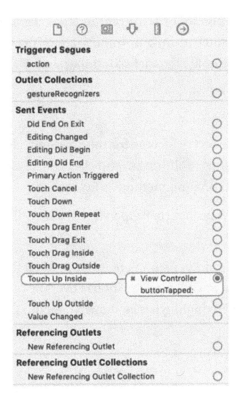

Figure 10-13. *The Connections Inspector pane displays all links to IBOutlets and IBAction methods*

5.   Click the Close icon (X) that appears to the left of View Controller buttonTapped. This breaks the link between the selected button and the buttonTapped IBAction method stored in the ViewController.swift file.

6.   Click the button titled "Second" to select it.

7.   Click the Close icon (X) that appears to the left of View Controller buttonTapped. This breaks the link between the second button and the buttonTapped IBAction method stored in the ViewController.swift file.

8.   Choose View ➤ Assistant Editor ➤ Show Assistant Editor, or click the Assistant Editor icon. Xcode displays the Main.storyboard and ViewController.swift file side by side.

9.   Move the mouse pointer over the button titled "First", hold down the Control key, and Ctrl-drag the mouse above the last curly bracket at the bottom of the ViewController.swift file.

10.   Release the Control key and the left mouse button. A popup window appears.

11.   Click in the Name text field, type **buttonRespond**, click the Type popup menu to choose UIButton, and click the Connect button. Xcode creates an IBAction method as follows:

```
@IBAction func buttonRespond(_ sender: UIButton) {
}
```

12.   Move the mouse pointer over the button titled "First", hold down the Control key, and Ctrl-drag the mouse over the buttonRespond IBAction method to highlight it as shown in Figure 10-14.

Figure 10-14.   *Connecting a button to an existing IBAction method*

13.   Release the Control key and the left mouse button.

14.   Edit the buttonRespond IBAction method as follows:

```
@IBAction func buttonRespond(_ sender: UIButton) {
    switch sender.tag {
    case 1:
        labelResult.text = sender.titleLabel?.text
    case 2:
        labelResult.text = sender.titleLabel?.text
    default:
        labelResult.text = "Default"
    }
}
```

The entire ViewController.swift file should look like this:

```swift
import UIKit

class ViewController: UIViewController {

    @IBOutlet var labelResult: UILabel!

    override func viewDidLoad() {
        super.viewDidLoad()
        labelResult.frame.size.width = 120
        // Do any additional setup after loading the view,
        typically from a nib.
    }

    @IBAction func buttonTapped(_ sender: Any) {
        switch (sender as AnyObject).tag {
        case 1:
            labelResult.text = "Button 1"
        case 2:
            labelResult.text = "Button 2"
        default:
            labelResult.text = "Default"
        }
    }

    @IBAction func buttonRespond(_ sender: UIButton) {
        switch sender.tag {
        case 1:
            labelResult.text = sender.titleLabel?.text
        case 2:
            labelResult.text = sender.titleLabel?.text
        default:
            labelResult.text = "Default"
        }
    }
}
```

15.   Click the Run button or choose Product ➤ Run. The Simulator screen appears.

16.   Click the button titled "First". Notice that the label displays "First".

17.   Click the button titled "Second". Notice that the label displays "Second".

18.   Chose Simulator ➤ Quit Simulator to return to Xcode.

Summary

Buttons, switches, and segmented controls offer ways for users to control an app. By using the Inspector pane or Swift code, you can modify buttons, switches, and segmented controls to customize them for your particular app.

Buttons represent a single command. Switches let users choose exactly two settings, on (true) and off (false). Segmented controls act like multiple buttons but take up less space than multiple buttons.

Typically you link a button, switch, or segmented control to a single IBAction method. However, you can connect two or more objects to a single IBAction method. When creating an IBAction method, you can allow any type of object to connect to it or you can define that only a specific type of object (such as a UIButton) can connect to the IBAction method. If you define that only a specific type of object can connect to an IBAction method, then you'll be able to access properties of that object.

Once you connect an object to an IBOutlet or IBAction method, you can always break that connection later. You must break that connection in the Connections Inspector pane. If you fail to break a connection and later delete an IBOutlet or IBAction method, then Xcode will give an error message if you try to run the app.

CHAPTER 11

Touch Gestures

Allowing the user to control an app through buttons, switches, or segmented controls is handy, but all of these controls take up space on the screen. To eliminate the need for extra objects on the user interface, your app can also detect and respond to touch gestures that allow direct manipulation of items displayed on the screen.

The different types of touch gestures that an iOS app can detect and respond to include

- Tap – A fingertip touches the screen and lifts up.

- Pinch – Two fingertips come together or move apart.

- Rotation – Two fingertips rotate left or right in a circular motion.

- Pan – A fingertip slides in a dragging motion across the screen.

- Swipe – A fingertip slides up, down, left, or right across the screen and lifts up.

- Screen edge pan – A fingertip slides in a dragging motion that starts near the edge of the screen.

- Long press – A fingertip touches and presses down on the screen.

You can create touch gestures on an app's user interface solely through Swift code or by placing gesture recognizer objects on a view from the Object Library as shown in Figure 11-1.

© Wallace Wang 2019
W. Wang, *Beginning iPhone Development with Swift 5*, https://doi.org/10.1007/978-1-4842-4865-2_11

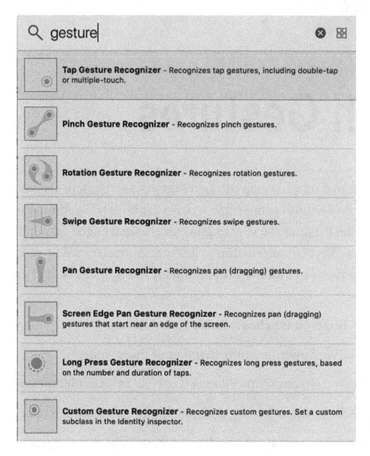

Figure 11-1. *The list of gestures available in the Object Library window*

To detect gestures in an app, you need to do the following:

- Add a gesture recognizer to a view.

- Create an IBAction method to respond to the gesture.

- Define which object needs to respond to the gesture.

Detecting Tap Gestures

Tap gestures simply detect when a user taps on the screen. By default, a tap gesture recognizes a single tap by one fingertip, but you can define multiple taps by two or more fingertips.

To see how to detect tap gestures, follow these steps:

1. Create a new iOS project using the Single View App template (see Chapter 1) and name this new project TapApp. This creates a single view for the user interface.

2. Click the Main.storyboard file in the Navigator pane. Xcode displays the single view.

3. Click the Library icon to open the Object Library window and look for the Tap Gesture Recognizer as shown in Figure 11-2.

Tap Gesture Recognizer - Recognizes tap gestures, including double-tap or multiple-touch.

Figure 11-2. The Tap Gesture Recognizer in the Object Library

4. Drag and drop a Tap Gesture Recognizer anywhere on the view. Notice that a gesture recognizer doesn't appear directly on the view but appears at the top of the view and in the Document Outline as shown in Figure 11-3.

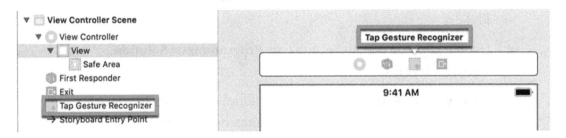

Figure 11-3. A Tap Gesture Recognizer appears in the Document Outline and at the top of the View Controller

5. Click the Tap Gesture Recognizer in the Document Outline or at the top of the View Controller.

6. Choose View ➤ Inspectors ➤ Show Attributes Inspector, or click
    the Attributes Inspector icon in the upper right corner of the
    Xcode window. Notice that the Attributes Inspector lets you define
    how many taps and touches (fingertips) needed to recognize a tap
    gesture. By default, a tap gesture only requires 1 tap with 1 touch
    (fingertip) as shown in Figure 11-4.

Figure 11-4. *A Tap Gesture Recognizer appears in the Document Outline and at the top of the View Controller*

7. Click the Library icon to open the Object Library window and drag
    and drop two labels anywhere on the view.

8. Double-click one label and type **Visual Solution** and press
    ENTER.

9. Double-click the other label and type **Programmatic Solution**
    and press ENTER.

10. Choose Editor ➤ Resolve Auto Layout Issues ➤ Reset to Suggested
    Constraints at the bottom half of the submenu. Xcode adds
    constraints to both labels.

11. Click the Visual Solution label and choose View ➤ Inspectors ➤
    Show Attributes Inspector, or click the Attributes Inspector icon in
    the upper right corner of the Xcode window.

12. Select the User Interaction Enabled check box as shown in Figure 11-5. With User Interaction Enabled selected, the label can respond to the user touching it.

Figure 11-5. *Selecting the User Interaction Enabled check box*

13. Move the mouse pointer over the Visual Solution label, hold down the Control key, and Ctrl-drag from the label to the Tap Gesture Recognizer in the Document Outline or above the View Controller as shown in Figure 11-6.

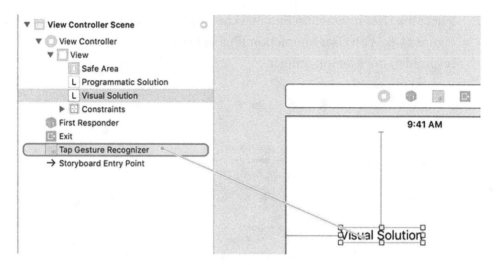

Figure 11-6. *Ctrl-dragging from the label to the Tap Gesture Recognizer links the label to the tap gesture*

14. Release the Control key and the left mouse button. A popup menu appears as shown in Figure 11-7.

Figure 11-7. *A popup menu lets you choose what to connect to the label*

15. Click gestureRecognizers.

16. Choose View ➤ Inspectors ➤ Show Connections Inspector, or click the Collections Inspector icon in the upper right corner of the Xcode window. The Connections Inspector pane shows that the label is linked to the Tap Gesture Recognizer, as shown in Figure 11-8, which means only the label can respond to tap gestures.

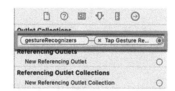

Figure 11-8. *The Connections Inspector verifies that the label is linked to the Tap Gesture Recognizer*

17. Choose View ➤ Assistant Editor ➤ Show Assistant Editor, or click the Assistant Editor icon in the upper right corner of the Xcode window.

18. Move the mouse pointer over the Tap Gesture Recognizer icon in the Document Outline or at the top of the View Controller, hold down the Control key, and Ctrl-drag above the last curly bracket at the bottom of the ViewController.swift file.

19. Release the Control key and the left mouse button. A popup window appears.

20. Click in the Name text field and type **tapDetected**, click the Type popup menu and choose UITapGestureRecognizer, and click the Connect button. Xcode creates an IBAction method.

21. Modify this tapDetected IBAction method as follows:

```
@IBAction func tapDetected(_ sender: UITapGestureRecognizer) {
    print ("Tap detected")
}
```

The entire ViewController.swift file should look like this:

```
import UIKit

class ViewController: UIViewController {

    override func viewDidLoad() {
        super.viewDidLoad()
        // Do any additional setup after loading the view,
        typically from a nib.
    }

    @IBAction func tapDetected(_ sender: UITapGestureRecognizer) {
        print ("Tap detected")
    }
}
```

22. Click the Run button or choose Product ➤ Run. The Simulator screen appears.

23. Click the Visual Solution label. Notice that the message "Tap detected" appears in the Xcode Debug Area at the bottom of the Xcode window.

24. Click anywhere but on the Visual Solution label. Notice that each time you click away from the Visual Solution label or on the Programmatic Solution label, nothing else appears in the Debug Area of the Xcode window.

25. Choose Simulator ➤ Quit Simulator to return to Xcode.

The preceding steps allowed a label to detect a tap gesture, but the only code we needed to create was the tapDetected IBAction method. We can also define gesture recognizers solely through Swift code, which we'll do with the Programmatic Solution label.

1. Make sure the TapApp project is loaded in Xcode.

2. Click the Main.storyboard file in the Navigator pane. Xcode displays the single view.

3. Choose View ➤ Assistant Editor ➤ Show Assistant Editor, or click the Assistant Editor icon in the upper right corner of the Xcode window. Xcode displays the Main.storyboard and ViewController. swift files side by side.

4. Move the mouse pointer over the Programmatic Solution label, hold down the Control key, and Ctrl-drag from the label underneath the "class ViewController" line in the ViewController. swift file.

5. Release the Control key and the left mouse button. A popup window appears.

6. Click in the Name text field, type **labelCode**, and click the Connect button. Xcode creates an IBOutlet as follows:

```
@IBOutlet var labelCode: UILabel!
```

7. Edit the viewDidLoad method as follows:

```
override func viewDidLoad() {
    super.viewDidLoad()
    labelCode.isUserInteractionEnabled = true
    let tapGesture = UITapGestureRecognizer(target: self,
                    action: #selector(handleTap))
    labelCode.addGestureRecognizer(tapGesture)
    // Do any additional setup after loading the view,
    typically from a nib.
}
```

Instead of selecting the User Interaction Enabled check box in the Attributes Inspector pane, we can simply set the .isUserInteractionEnabled property to true for the second label that displays "Programmatic Solution".

Rather than drag and drop a Tap Gesture Recognizer from the Object Library onto the view, we can create a UITapGestureRecognizer using Swift code. This means we also need to define a function to respond to the tap gesture, which is defined by #selector(handleTap). Finally, we need to add this tap gesture to the label instead of linking it through the Connections Inspector pane.

8. Add the following underneath the viewDidLoad method:

```
@objc func handleTap() {
    print ("Tap on second label detected")
}
```

The entire ViewController.swift file should look like this:

```
import UIKit

class ViewController: UIViewController {

    @IBOutlet var labelCode: UILabel!

    override func viewDidLoad() {
        super.viewDidLoad()
        labelCode.isUserInteractionEnabled = true
```

```
        let tapGesture = UITapGestureRecognizer(target: self,
        action: #selector(handleTap))
        labelCode.addGestureRecognizer(tapGesture)
        // Do any additional setup after loading the view,
        typically from a nib.
    }

    @objc func handleTap() {
        print ("Tap on second label detected")
    }

    @IBAction func tapDetected(_ sender: UITapGestureRecognizer) {
        print ("Tap detected")
    }
}
```

9. Click the Run button or choose Product ➤ Run. The Simulator screen appears.

10. Click the Programmatic Solution label. Notice that the message "Tap on second label detected" appears in the Xcode Debug Area at the bottom of the Xcode window.

11. Click the Visual Solution label. Notice that the message "Tap detected" appears in the Xcode Debug Area at the bottom of the Xcode window.

12. Click anywhere but on either of the two labels. Notice that even though you're tapping on the screen, the tap gesture isn't being recognized because both tap gestures are linked to the labels.

13. Choose Simulator ➤ Quit Simulator to return to Xcode.

When using gesture recognizers, you can define them visually through the Object Library and the Inspector pane, or you can create gesture recognizers through Swift code. Both methods are identical so it depends on whether you prefer writing Swift code or using the Object Library.

When customizing a tap gesture using Swift code, you can define the following two properties:

- .numberOfTapsRequired – Defines how many taps needed to recognize a tap gesture such as one tap (default)

- .numberOfTouchesRequired – Defines how many fingertips (touches) are needed to recognize a tap gesture

Detecting Pinch Gestures

A pinch gesture occurs when two fingertips either move toward each other or move away from each other. During a pinch gesture, an app can recognize scale and velocity. The scale defines the relative position of the two fingertips, while velocity detects the speed of the pinching motion.

To see how to detect a pinch gesture, follow these steps:

1. Create a new iOS project using the Single View App template (see Chapter 1) and name this new project PinchApp. This creates a single view for the user interface.

2. Click the Main.storyboard file in the Navigator pane. Xcode displays the single view.

3. Click the Library icon to open the Object Library window and look for the Pinch Gesture Recognizer as shown in Figure 11-9.

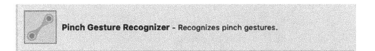

Figure 11-9. *The Pinch Gesture Recognizer in the Object Library window*

4. Drag and drop the Pinch Gesture Recognizer onto the view. Xcode displays the Pinch Gesture Recognizer in the Document Outline and above the View Controller.

5. Click the Library icon to open the Object Library window and drag and drop an image view in the center of the user interface.

6. Choose View ➤ Inspectors ➤ Show Attributes Inspector or click the Attributes Inspector icon in the upper right corner of the Xcode window.

7. Click in the Background popup menu and choose a color such as green or blue. This will make the image view easy to find when you run the app in the Simulator. Without a background color, the default white background of the image view will blend in with the white background of the view.

8. Select the User Interaction Enabled check box. This allows the image view to respond to the user.

9. Click the Align icon in the bottom of the middle Xcode pane. A window appears.

10. Select the Horizontally in Container and Vertically in Container check boxes and then click the Add 2 Constraints button as shown in Figure 11-10. The image view needs to be in the center to make it easy to mimic pinching gestures in the Simulator.

Figure 11-10. *Centering an image view*

11. Choose Editor ➤ Resolve Auto Layout Issues ➤ Add Missing Constraints in the top half of the submenu. Xcode adds additional constraints to the image view.

12. Move the mouse pointer over the image view, hold down the Control key, and Ctrl-drag from the image view to the Pinch Gesture Recognizer icon in the Document Outline or at the top of the View Controller.

13. Release the Control key and the left mouse button. A window appears.

14. Choose gestureRecognizers. This link lets the image view detect pinch gestures.

15. Choose View ➤ Assistant Editor ➤ Show Assistant Editor, or click the Assistant Editor icon. Xcode displays the Main.storyboard and ViewController.swift file side by side.

16. Move the mouse pointer over the image view, hold down the Control key, and Ctrl-drag from the image view to the ViewController.swift file underneath the IBOutlet line.

17. Release the Control key and the left mouse button. A popup window appears.

18. Click in the Name text field, type **topImageView**, and click the Connect button. Xcode creates an IBOutlet variable as follows:

```
@IBOutlet var topImageView: UIImageView!
```

19. Move the mouse pointer over the Pinch Gesture Recognizer icon in the Document Outline or at the top of the View Controller, hold down the Control key, and Ctrl-drag from the Pinch Gesture Recognizer above the last curly bracket in the ViewController.swift file.

20. Release the Control key and the left mouse button. A popup window appears.

21. Click in the Name text field, type **pinchDetected**, click in the Type popup menu and choose UIPinchGestureRecognizer, and click the Connect button. Xcode creates an IBAction method.

22. Edit the pinchDetected IBAction method as follows:

```swift
@IBAction func pinchDetected(_ sender: UIPinchGestureRecognizer) {
    topImageView.transform = CGAffineTransform(scaleX: sender.
    scale, y: sender.scale)
}
```

The pinchDetected IBAction method changes the size of the image view based on the scale property of the pinch gesture where the scale property defines the distance of the pinch gesture. The entire ViewController.swift file should look like this:

```swift
import UIKit

class ViewController: UIViewController {

    @IBOutlet var topImageView: UIImageView!

    override func viewDidLoad() {
        super.viewDidLoad()
        // Do any additional setup after loading the view,
        typically from a nib.
    }

    @IBAction func pinchDetected(_ sender: UIPinchGestureRecognizer) {
        topImageView.transform = CGAffineTransform(scaleX: sender.
        scale, y: sender.scale)
    }

}
```

23. Choose View ➤ Standard Editor ➤ Show Standard Editor, or click the Standard Editor icon in the upper right corner of the Xcode window.

24. Click the Run button or choose Product ➤ Run. The Simulator window appears. To mimic a pinch gesture, you need to use the mouse and hold down the Option key.

25. Move the mouse pointer over the image view, then hold down the Option key. Two gray dots appear to simulate two fingertips on the screen as shown in Figure 11-11.

Figure 11-11. *Holding down the Option key while dragging the mouse simulates a two-finger pinch gesture in the Simulator*

26. Hold down the left mouse button and the Option key, then drag the mouse to simulate a pinch gesture. Notice that as the pinch gesture changes, the image view also changes in size.

27. Chose Simulator ➤ Quit Simulator to return to Xcode.

This example defined the pinch gesture visually by dragging the Pinch Gesture Recognizer from the Object Library. Now let's see how to duplicate this process through Swift code alone.

1. Create a new iOS project using the Single View App template (see Chapter 1) and name this new project PinchCodeApp. This creates a single view for the user interface.

2. Click the Main.storyboard file in the Navigator pane. Xcode displays the single view.

3. Click the Library icon to open the Object Library window and drag and drop an image view in the center of the user interface.

4. Click the Align icon in the bottom of the middle Xcode pane. A window appears.

5. Select the Horizontally in Container and Vertically in Container check boxes and then click the Add 2 Constraints button (see Figure 11-10). The image view needs to be in the center to make it easy to mimic pinching gestures in the Simulator.

6. Choose Editor ➤ Resolve Auto Layout Issues ➤ Add Missing Constraints in the top half of the submenu. Xcode adds additional constraints to the image view.

7. Choose View ➤ Assistant Editor ➤ Show Assistant Editor, or click the Assistant Editor icon. Xcode displays the Main.storyboard and ViewController.swift file side by side.

8. Move the mouse pointer over the image view, hold down the Control key, and Ctrl-drag from the image view to the ViewController.swift file underneath the IBOutlet line.

9. Release the Control key and the left mouse button. A popup window appears.

10. Click in the Name text field, type **topImageView**, and click the Connect button. Xcode creates an IBOutlet variable as follows:

    @IBOutlet var topImageView: UIImageView!

11. Choose View ➤ Standard Editor ➤ Show Standard Editor, or click the Standard Editor icon in the upper right corner of the Xcode window.

12. Click the ViewController.swift file in the Navigator pane.

13. Add the following line underneath the IBOutlet:

    var pinchMe: UIPinchGestureRecognizer?

    This defines a global variable that represents the pinch gesture.

14. Edit the viewDidLoad method as follows:

    ```
    override func viewDidLoad() {
        super.viewDidLoad()
        topImageView.isUserInteractionEnabled = true
        topImageView.backgroundColor = UIColor.green
        let pinchGesture = UIPinchGestureRecognizer(target: self,
        action: #selector(handlePinch))
        topImageView.addGestureRecognizer(pinchGesture)
        pinchMe = pinchGesture
        // Do any additional setup after loading the view,
        typically from a nib.
    }
    ```

This code turns on the User Interaction Enabled setting for the image view and defines its background color as green to make it visible. Next, it defines a pinch gesture recognizer (instead of dragging and dropping a Pinch Gesture Recognizer from the Object Library window), defines a function called handlePinch to respond to the pinch gesture, and links the pinch gesture to the image view so pinches only affect the image view. Finally, it assigns the pinch gesture recognizer to the pinchMe variable.

15. Add the following function underneath the viewDidLoad method:

```
@objc func handlePinch() {
    topImageView.transform = CGAffineTransform(scaleX:
    pinchMe!.scale, y: pinchMe!.scale)
}
```

The entire ViewController.swift file should look like this:

```
import UIKit

class ViewController: UIViewController {

    @IBOutlet var topImageView: UIImageView!
    var pinchMe: UIPinchGestureRecognizer?

    override func viewDidLoad() {
        super.viewDidLoad()
        topImageView.isUserInteractionEnabled = true
        topImageView.backgroundColor = UIColor.green
        let pinchGesture = UIPinchGestureRecognizer(target: self,
        action: #selector(handlePinch))
        topImageView.addGestureRecognizer(pinchGesture)
        pinchMe = pinchGesture
        // Do any additional setup after loading the view,
        typically from a nib.
    }
```

```
@objc func handlePinch() {
    topImageView.transform = CGAffineTransform(scaleX:
    pinchMe!.scale, y: pinchMe!.scale)
}

}
```

16. Click the Run button or choose Product ➤ Run. The Simulator window appears. To mimic a pinch gesture, you need to use the mouse and hold down the Option key.

17. Move the mouse pointer over the image view, then hold down the Option key. Two gray dots appear to simulate two fingertips on the screen (see Figure 11-11).

18. Hold down the left mouse button and the Option key, then drag the mouse to simulate a pinch gesture. Notice that as the pinch gesture changes, the image view also changes in size.

19. Choose Simulator ➤ Quit Simulator to return to Xcode.

Detecting Rotation Gestures

A rotation gesture is similar to a pinch gesture because they both use two fingertips. The main difference is that rotation gesture detects when the two fingertips move in a circular motion clockwise or counterclockwise. During a rotation gesture, an app can recognize rotation (measured in radians) and velocity (measured in radians per second).

To see how to use a rotation gesture, follow these steps:

1. Create a new iOS project using the Single View App template (see Chapter 1) and name this new project RotateApp. This creates a single view for the user interface.

2. Click the Main.storyboard file in the Navigator pane. Xcode displays the single view.

3. Click the Library icon to open the Object Library window and look for the Rotate Gesture Recognizer as shown in Figure 11-12.

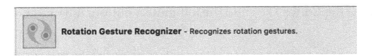

Figure 11-12. *The Rotate Gesture Recognizer in the Object Library window*

4. Drag and drop the Rotate Gesture Recognizer onto the view. Xcode displays the Rotate Gesture Recognizer in the Document Outline and above the View Controller.

5. Click the Library icon to open the Object Library window and drag and drop an image view on the user interface.

6. Choose View ➤ Inspectors ➤ Show Attributes Inspector or click the Attributes Inspector icon in the upper right corner of the Xcode window.

7. Click in the Background popup menu and choose a color such as green or blue. This will make the image view easy to find when you run the app in the Simulator. Without a background color, the default white background of the image view will blend in with the white background of the view.

8. Select the User Interaction Enabled check box. This allows the image view to respond to the user.

9. Click the Align icon in the bottom of the middle Xcode pane. A window appears.

10. Select the Horizontally in Container and Vertically in Container check boxes and then click the Add 2 Constraints button (see Figure 11-10). The image view needs to be in the center to make it easy to mimic pinching gestures in the Simulator.

11. Choose Editor ➤ Resolve Auto Layout Issues ➤ Add Missing Constraints in the top half of the submenu. Xcode adds additional constraints to the image view.

12. Move the mouse pointer over the image view, hold down the Control key, and Ctrl-drag from the image view to the Rotation Gesture Recognizer icon in the Document Outline or at the top of the View Controller.

13. Release the Control key and the left mouse button. A window appears.

14. Choose gestureRecognizers. This link lets the image view detect rotation gestures.

15. Choose View ➤ Assistant Editor ➤ Show Assistant Editor, or click the Assistant Editor icon. Xcode displays the Main.storyboard and ViewController.swift file side by side.

16. Move the mouse pointer over the image view, hold down the Control key, and Ctrl-drag from the image view to the ViewController.swift file underneath the "class ViewController" line.

17. Release the Control key and the left mouse button. A popup window appears.

18. Click in the Name text field, type **topImageView**, and click the Connect button. Xcode creates an IBOutlet variable as follows:

    @IBOutlet var topImageView: UIImageView!

19. Move the mouse pointer over the Rotation Gesture Recognizer icon in the Document Outline or at the top of the View Controller, hold down the Control key, and Ctrl-drag from the Rotation Gesture Recognizer above the last curly bracket in the ViewController.swift file.

20. Release the Control key and the left mouse button. A popup window appears.

21. Click in the Name text field, type **rotationDetected**, click in the Type popup menu and choose UIRotationGestureRecognizer, and click the Connect button. Xcode creates an IBAction method.

22. Edit the rotationDetected IBAction method as follows:

    ```
    @IBAction func rotationDetected(_ sender:
    UIRotationGestureRecognizer) {
        topImageView.transform = CGAffineTransform(rotationAngle:
        sender.rotation)
    }
    ```

The rotationDetected IBAction method rotates the image view based on the rotation property of the rotation gesture where the scale property defines the distance of the pinch gesture. The entire ViewController.swift file should look like this:

```swift
import UIKit

class ViewController: UIViewController {

    @IBOutlet var topImageView: UIImageView!

    override func viewDidLoad() {
        super.viewDidLoad()
        // Do any additional setup after loading the view,
        typically from a nib.
    }

    @IBAction func rotationDetected(_ sender:
    UIRotationGestureRecognizer) {
        topImageView.transform = CGAffineTransform(rotationAngle:
        sender.rotation)
    }

}
```

23. Choose View ➤ Standard Editor ➤ Show Standard Editor, or click the Standard Editor icon in the upper right corner of the Xcode window.

24. Click the Run button or choose Product ➤ Run. The Simulator window appears. To mimic a rotation gesture, you need to use the mouse and hold down the Option key.

25. Move the mouse pointer over the image view and then hold down the Option key. Two gray dots appear to simulate two fingertips on the screen (see Figure 11-11).

26. Hold down the left mouse button and the Option key, then drag the mouse in a circular motion to simulate a rotation gesture. Notice that as the rotation gesture changes, the image view also changes as it rotates.

27. Choose Simulator ➤ Quit Simulator to return to Xcode.

This example defined the rotation gesture visually by dragging the Rotation Gesture Recognizer from the Object Library. Now let's see how to duplicate this process through Swift code alone.

1. Create a new iOS project using the Single View App template (see Chapter 1) and name this new project RotateCodeApp. This creates a single view for the user interface.

2. Click the Main.storyboard file in the Navigator pane. Xcode displays the single view.

3. Click the Library icon to open the Object Library window and drag and drop an image view in the center of the user interface.

4. Click the Align icon in the bottom of the middle Xcode pane. A window appears.

5. Select the Horizontally in Container and Vertically in Container check boxes and then click the Add 2 Constraints button (see Figure 11-10). The image view needs to be in the center to make it easy to mimic pinching gestures in the Simulator.

6. Choose Editor ➤ Resolve Auto Layout Issues ➤ Add Missing Constraints in the top half of the submenu. Xcode adds additional constraints to the image view.

7. Choose View ➤ Assistant Editor ➤ Show Assistant Editor, or click the Assistant Editor icon. Xcode displays the Main.storyboard and ViewController.swift file side by side.

8. Move the mouse pointer over the image view, hold down the Control key, and Ctrl-drag from the image view to the ViewController.swift file underneath the "class ViewController" line.

9. Release the Control key and the left mouse button. A popup window appears.

10. Click in the Name text field, type **topImageView**, and click the Connect button. Xcode creates an IBOutlet variable as follows:

```
@IBOutlet var topImageView: UIImageView!
```

11. Choose View ➤ Standard Editor ➤ Show Standard Editor, or click the Standard Editor icon in the upper right corner of the Xcode window.

12. Click the ViewController.swift file in the Navigator pane.

13. Add the following line underneath the IBOutlet:

```
var rotateMe: UIRotationGestureRecognizer?
```

This defines a global variable that represents the rotation gesture.

14. Edit the viewDidLoad method as follows:

```
override func viewDidLoad() {
    super.viewDidLoad()
    topImageView.isUserInteractionEnabled = true
    topImageView.backgroundColor = UIColor.green
    let rotationGesture = UIRotationGestureRecognizer(target:
    self, action: #selector(handleRotation))
    topImageView.addGestureRecognizer(rotationGesture)
    rotateMe = rotationGesture
    // Do any additional setup after loading the view,
    typically from a nib.
}
```

This code turns on the User Interaction Enabled setting for the image view and defines its background color as green to make it visible. Next, it defines a rotation gesture recognizer (instead of dragging and dropping a Rotation Gesture Recognizer from the Object Library window), defines a function called handleRotation to respond to the rotation gesture, and links the rotation gesture to the image view so rotations only affect the image view. Finally, it assigns the rotation gesture recognizer to the rotateMe variable.

15. Add the following function underneath the viewDidLoad method:

```
@objc func handleRotation() {
    topImageView.transform = CGAffineTransform(rotationAngle:
    rotateMe!.rotation)
}
```

The entire ViewController.swift file should look like this:

```
import UIKit

class ViewController: UIViewController {

    @IBOutlet var topImageView: UIImageView!
    var rotateMe: UIRotationGestureRecognizer?

    override func viewDidLoad() {
        super.viewDidLoad()
        topImageView.isUserInteractionEnabled = true
        topImageView.backgroundColor = UIColor.green
        let rotationGesture = UIRotationGestureRecognizer(target:
        self, action: #selector(handleRotation))
        topImageView.addGestureRecognizer(rotationGesture)
        rotateMe = rotationGesture
        // Do any additional setup after loading the view,
        typically from a nib.
    }

    @objc func handleRotation() {
        topImageView.transform = CGAffineTransform(rotationAngle:
        rotateMe!.rotation)
    }
}
```

16. Click the Run button or choose Product ➤ Run. The Simulator window appears. To mimic a pinch gesture, you need to use the mouse and hold down the Option key.

17. Move the mouse pointer over the image view and then hold down the Option key. Two gray dots appear to simulate two fingertips on the screen (see Figure 11-11).

18. Hold down the left mouse button and the Option key and then drag the mouse in a circular motion to simulate a rotation gesture. Notice that as the rotation gesture rotates, the image view also rotates.

19. Choose Simulator ➤ Quit Simulator to return to Xcode.

Detecting Pan Gestures

A pan gesture occurs when the user holds a fingertip on the screen and moves the fingertip, keeping it pressed on the screen. A pan is similar to a dragging motion on a Macintosh and lets you define the minimum and maximum number of fingertips needed to define the pan gesture such as at least two fingers but no more than four fingertips.

A pan gesture tracks the velocity and translation where the velocity measures the speed of the pan gesture while the translation measures the movement of the pan gesture.

To see how to use a pan gesture, follow these steps:

1. Create a new iOS project using the Single View App template (see Chapter 1) and name this new project PanApp. This creates a single view for the user interface.

2. Click the Main.storyboard file in the Navigator pane. Xcode displays the single view.

3. Click the Library icon to open the Object Library window and look for the Pan Gesture Recognizer as shown in Figure 11-13.

Pan Gesture Recognizer - Recognizes pan (dragging) gestures.

Figure 11-13. *The Pan Gesture Recognizer in the Object Library window*

4. Drag and drop the Pan Gesture Recognizer onto the view. Xcode displays the Pan Gesture Recognizer in the Document Outline and above the View Controller.

5. Click the Library icon to open the Object Library window and drag and drop an image view in the center of the user interface.

6. Choose View ➤ Inspectors ➤ Show Attributes Inspector or click the Attributes Inspector icon in the upper right corner of the Xcode window.

7. Click in the Background popup menu and choose a color such as green or blue. This will make the image view easy to find when you run the app in the Simulator. Without a background color, the default white background of the image view will blend in with the white background of the view.

8. Select the User Interaction Enabled check box. This allows the image view to respond to the user.

9. Click the Align icon in the bottom of the middle Xcode pane. A window appears.

10. Select the Horizontally in Container and Vertically in Container check boxes and then click the Add 2 Constraints button (see Figure 11-10). The image view needs to be in the center to make it easy to mimic pinching gestures in the Simulator.

11. Choose Editor ➤ Resolve Auto Layout Issues ➤ Add Missing Constraints in the top half of the submenu. Xcode adds additional constraints to the image view.

12. Move the mouse pointer over the image view, hold down the Control key, and Ctrl-drag from the image view to the Pan Gesture Recognizer icon in the Document Outline or at the top of the View Controller.

13. Release the Control key and the left mouse button. A window appears.

14. Choose gestureRecognizers. This link lets the image view detect pan gestures.

15. Choose View ➤ Assistant Editor ➤ Show Assistant Editor, or click the Assistant Editor icon. Xcode displays the Main.storyboard and ViewController.swift file side by side.

16. Move the mouse pointer over the image view, hold down the Control key, and Ctrl-drag from the image view to the ViewController.swift file underneath the "class ViewController" line.

17. Release the Control key and the left mouse button. A popup window appears.

18. Click in the Name text field, type **topImageView**, and click the Connect button. Xcode creates an IBOutlet variable as follows:

```
@IBOutlet var topImageView: UIImageView!
```

19. Add the following two lines underneath the IBOutlet:

```
var xOrigin:CGFloat = 0
    var yOrigin:CGFloat = 0
```

Note that both variables are defined to hold CGFloat data types, which are used for measuring distances. Without explicitly defining both variables as CGFloat, Xcode would assume both variables would just hold integers.

20. Edit the viewDidLoad method as follows:

```
override func viewDidLoad() {
    super.viewDidLoad()
    xOrigin = topImageView.center.x
    yOrigin = topImageView.center.y
    // Do any additional setup after loading the view,
    typically from a nib.
}
```

21. Move the mouse pointer over the Pan Gesture Recognizer icon in the Document Outline or at the top of the View Controller, hold down the Control key, and Ctrl-drag from the Pan Gesture Recognizer above the last curly bracket in the ViewController. swift file.

22. Release the Control key and the left mouse button. A popup window appears.

23. Click in the Name text field, type **panDetected**, click in the Type popup menu and choose UIPanGestureRecognizer, and click the Connect button. Xcode creates an IBAction method.

24. Edit the panDetected IBAction method as follows:

```
@IBAction func panDetected(_ sender: UIPanGestureRecognizer) {
    let translation = sender.translation(in: view)
    topImageView.center = CGPoint(x: xOrigin + translation.x,
    y: yOrigin + translation.y)
}
```

The panDetected IBAction method captures the translation distance that the user's fingertip moved. Then it adds these distances to the image view's center. The entire ViewController. swift file should look like this:

```
import UIKit

class ViewController: UIViewController {

    @IBOutlet var topImageView: UIImageView!
    var xOrigin:CGFloat = 0
    var yOrigin:CGFloat = 0

    override func viewDidLoad() {
        super.viewDidLoad()
        xOrigin = topImageView.center.x
        yOrigin = topImageView.center.y
        // Do any additional setup after loading the view,
        typically from a nib.
    }
```

```
@IBAction func panDetected(_ sender: UIPanGestureRecognizer) {
    let translation = sender.translation(in: view)
    topImageView.center = CGPoint(x: xOrigin + translation.x,
    y: yOrigin + translation.y)
    }
}
```

25. Choose View ➤ Standard Editor ➤ Show Standard Editor, or click the Standard Editor icon in the upper right corner of the Xcode window.

26. Click the Run button or choose Product ➤ Run. The Simulator window appears.

27. Hold down the left mouse button and move the mouse to simulate a pan gesture. Notice that as the pan gesture changes, the image view also moves.

28. Choose Simulator ➤ Quit Simulator to return to Xcode.

This example defined the pan gesture visually by dragging the Pan Gesture Recognizer from the Object Library. Now let's see how to duplicate this process through Swift code alone.

1. Create a new iOS project using the Single View App template (see Chapter 1) and name this new project PanCodeApp. This creates a single view for the user interface.

2. Click the Main.storyboard file in the Navigator pane. Xcode displays the single view.

3. Click the Library icon to open the Object Library window and drag and drop an image view in the center of the user interface.

4. Click the Align icon in the bottom of the middle Xcode pane. A window appears.

5. Select the Horizontally in Container and Vertically in Container check boxes and then click the Add 2 Constraints button (see Figure 11-10). The image view needs to be in the center to make it easy to mimic pinching gestures in the Simulator.

6. Choose Editor ➤ Resolve Auto Layout Issues ➤ Add Missing Constraints in the top half of the submenu. Xcode adds additional constraints to the image view.

7. Choose View ➤ Assistant Editor ➤ Show Assistant Editor, or click the Assistant Editor icon. Xcode displays the Main.storyboard and ViewController.swift file side by side.

8. Move the mouse pointer over the image view, hold down the Control key, and Ctrl-drag from the image view to the ViewController.swift file underneath the "class ViewController" line.

9. Release the Control key and the left mouse button. A popup window appears.

10. Click in the Name text field, type **topImageView**, and click the Connect button. Xcode creates an IBOutlet variable as follows:

    ```
    @IBOutlet var topImageView: UIImageView!
    ```

11. Choose View ➤ Standard Editor ➤ Show Standard Editor, or click the Standard Editor icon in the upper right corner of the Xcode window.

12. Click the ViewController.swift file in the Navigator pane.

13. Add the following lines underneath the IBOutlet:

    ```
    var panMe: UIPanGestureRecognizer?
    var xOrigin:CGFloat = 0
    var yOrigin:CGFloat = 0
    ```

    This defines a global variable that represents the rotation gesture along with defining two CGFloat variables.

14. Edit the viewDidLoad method as follows:

    ```
    override func viewDidLoad() {
        super.viewDidLoad()

        xOrigin = topImageView.center.x
        yOrigin = topImageView.center.y
    ```

```
topImageView.isUserInteractionEnabled = true
topImageView.backgroundColor = UIColor.green
let panGesture = UIPanGestureRecognizer(target: self,
action: #selector(handlePan))
topImageView.addGestureRecognizer(panGesture)
panMe = panGesture
// Do any additional setup after loading the view,
typically from a nib.
}
```

This code stores the image view's center points in the xOrigin and yOrigin variables. Then it turns on the User Interaction Enabled setting for the image view and defines its background color as green to make it visible. Next, it defines a pan gesture recognizer (instead of dragging and dropping a Pan Gesture Recognizer from the Object Library window), defines a function called handlePan to respond to the pan gesture, and links the pan gesture to the image view so pans only affect the image view. Finally, it assigns the pan gesture recognizer to the panMe variable.

15. Add the following function underneath the viewDidLoad method:

```
@objc func handleRotation() {
    topImageView.transform = CGAffineTransform(rotationAngle:
    rotateMe!.rotation)
}
```

The entire ViewController.swift file should look like this:

```
import UIKit

class ViewController: UIViewController {

    @IBOutlet var topImageView: UIImageView!
    var rotateMe: UIRotationGestureRecognizer?

    override func viewDidLoad() {
        super.viewDidLoad()
        topImageView.isUserInteractionEnabled = true
```

```
        topImageView.backgroundColor = UIColor.green
        let rotationGesture = UIRotationGestureRecognizer(target:
        self, action: #selector(handleRotation))
        topImageView.addGestureRecognizer(rotationGesture)
        rotateMe = rotationGesture
        // Do any additional setup after loading the view,
        typically from a nib.
    }

    @objc func handleRotation() {
        topImageView.transform = CGAffineTransform(rotationAngle:
        rotateMe!.rotation)
    }
}
```

16. Click the Run button or choose Product ➤ Run. The Simulator
     window appears.

17. Hold down the left mouse button and drag the mouse to simulate
     a pan gesture. Notice that as the pan gesture moves, the image
     view also moves.

18. Choose Simulator ➤ Quit Simulator to return to Xcode.

Detecting Screen Edge Pan Gestures

One unique gesture that an app can detect is called a screen edge pan. This occurs
when the user slides a fingertip from the top, bottom, left, or right edge of the screen. By
default, iOS uses top edge pans to display notifications and bottom edge pans to display
the Control Center. You'll need to override these default iOS edge pans if you want your
own app to detect top or bottom edge pans.

When creating a screen edge pan gesture, you'll also need to create a separate
screen edge pan gesture recognizer for each edge you want to detect. So if you want your
app to detect a bottom and a left edge pan, you'll need to create two separate gesture
recognizers, one to detect bottom edge pans and a second to detect left edge pans.

To see how to use a screen edge pan gestures, follow these steps:

1. Create a new iOS project using the Single View App template (see Chapter 1) and name this new project EdgePanApp. This creates a single view for the user interface.

2. Click the Main.storyboard file in the Navigator pane. Xcode displays the single view.

3. Click the Library icon to open the Object Library window and look for the Screen Edge Pan Gesture Recognizer as shown in Figure 11-14.

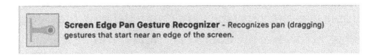

Figure 11-14. *The Screen Edge Pan Gesture Recognizer in the Object Library window*

4. Drag and drop the Screen Edge Pan Gesture Recognizer onto the view. Xcode displays the Screen Edge Pan Gesture Recognizer in the Document Outline and above the View Controller.

5. Choose View ➤ Inspectors ➤ Show Attributes Inspector, or click the Attributes Inspector icon in the upper right corner of the Xcode window. The Attributes Inspector pane appears as shown in Figure 11-15.

Figure 11-15. *The Attributes Inspector pane for the Screen Edge Pan Gesture Recognizer*

6. Select the Bottom check box to recognize bottom screen edge pan
    gestures.

Note   You can only choose one check box to define a screen edge even though it
appears you can select two or more check boxes.

---

7. Choose View ➤ Assistant Editor ➤ Show Assistant Editor, or click
    the Assistant Editor icon. Xcode displays the Main.storyboard and
    ViewController.swift file side by side.

8. Move the mouse pointer over the Screen Edge Pan Gesture
    Recognizer at the top of the View Controller or in the Document
    Outline, hold down the Control key, and Ctrl-drag above the last
    curly bracket at the bottom of the ViewController.swift file.

9. Release the Control key and the left mouse button. A popup
    window appears.

10. Click in the Name text field and type **bottomEdgeDetected**,
    click in the Type popup menu and choose
    UIScreenEdgePanGestureRecognizer, then click the Connect
    button.

11. Edit this bottomEdgeDetected IBAction method as follows:

    ```
    @IBAction func bottomEdgeDetected(_ sender:
    UIScreenEdgePanGestureRecognizer) {
        print ("Bottom edge pan gesture")
    }
    ```

12. Click the Screen Edge Pan Gesture Recognizer in the Document
    Outline and press ENTER. Xcode highlights the entire name.

13. Type **Bottom Edge Gesture** and press ENTER to rename your
    gesture recognizer.

14. Add the following method underneath the viewDidLoad method:

```
override var preferredScreenEdgesDeferringSystemGestures:
UIRectEdge {
    return UIRectEdge.bottom
}
```

This method overrides the default behavior of iOS to display the Control Center when the user pans up from the bottom edge of the screen. If you only want to detect left or right pan edge gestures, you do not need the preceding code.

15. Click the Main.storyboard in the Navigator pane.

16. Click the Library icon to open the Object Library window.

17. Drag and drop another Screen Edge Pan Gesture Recognizer onto the view. Xcode displays the second Screen Edge Pan Gesture Recognizer in the Document Outline and above the View Controller.

18. Click the Screen Edge Pan Gesture Recognizer in the Document Outline and press ENTER to highlight the entire name. Then type **Left Edge Gesture** and press ENTER.

19. Click this Left Edge Gesture in the Document Outline and choose View ➤ Inspectors ➤ Show Attributes Inspector, or click the Attributes Inspector icon in the upper right corner of the Xcode window.

20. Select the Left check box to define it to detect left screen edge pan gestures.

21. Move the mouse pointer over the Left Edge Gesture in the Document Outline, hold down the Control key, and Ctrl-drag above the last curly bracket at the bottom of the ViewController. swift file.

22. Release the Control key and the left mouse button. A popup window appears.

23. Click in the Name text field, type **leftEdgeDetected**, click in the Type popup menu and choose UIScreenEdgePanGestureRecognizer, then click the Connect button.

24. Edit this leftEdgeDetected IBAction method as follows:

```
@IBAction func leftEdgeDetected(_ sender:
UIScreenEdgePanGestureRecognizer) {
    print ("Left edge pan gesture")
}
```

25. Click the Run button or choose Product ➤ Run. The Simulator window appears.

26. Move the mouse pointer just underneath the bottom of the view, hold down the left mouse button, and drag the mouse up. Notice that the Debug Area in the Xcode window displays multiple "Bottom edge pan gesture" lines, indicating that the app recognized the bottom screen edge pan gesture.

27. Move the mouse pointer just left of the view, hold down the left mouse button, and drag the mouse to the right. Notice that the Debug Area in the Xcode window displays multiple "Left edge pan gesture" lines, indicating that the app recognized the left screen edge pan gesture.

28. Choose Simulator ➤ Quit Simulator to return to Xcode.

This example defined the screen edge pan gesture visually by dragging the Screen Edge Pan Gesture Recognizer from the Object Library. Now let's see how to duplicate this process through Swift code alone.

1. Create a new iOS project using the Single View App template (see Chapter 1) and name this new project EdgePanCodeApp. This creates a single view for the user interface.

2. Click the Main.storyboard file in the Navigator pane.

3. Choose View ➤ Assistant Editor ➤ Show Assistant Editor, or click the Assistant Editor icon. Xcode displays the Main.storyboard and ViewController.swift file side by side.

4. Move the mouse pointer over the view (the entire screen of the simulated iOS device), hold down the Control key, and Ctrl-drag underneath the "class ViewController" line in the ViewController. swift file.

5. Release the Control key and the left mouse button. A popup window appears.

6. Click in the Name text field and type **myView**, then click the Connect button. Xcode creates an IBOutlet as follows:

    @IBOutlet var myView: UIView!

7. Choose View ➤ Standard Editor ➤ Show Standard Editor, or click the Standard Editor icon.

8. Click the ViewController.swift file in the Navigator pane.

9. Modify the viewDidLoad method as follows:

```swift
override func viewDidLoad() {
    super.viewDidLoad()
    let bottomEdgeGesture = UIScreenEdgePanGestureRecognizer
    (target: self, action: #selector(handleBottomEdge))
    myView.addGestureRecognizer(bottomEdgeGesture)
    bottomEdgeGesture.edges = .bottom

    let leftEdgeGesture = UIScreenEdgePanGestureRecognizer
    (target: self, action: #selector(handleLeftEdge))
    myView.addGestureRecognizer(leftEdgeGesture)
    leftEdgeGesture.edges = .left
    // Do any additional setup after loading the view,
    typically from a nib.
}
```

This code creates two screen edge pan gesture recognizers named bottomEdgeGesture and leftEdgeGesture. Then it links both gestures to the view (myView) and defines the bottomEdgeGesture to recognize bottom screen edge pans and the leftEdgeGesture to recognize left screen edge pans.

Finally, it calls on two functions called handleBottomEdge and handleLeftEdge to respond to each screen edge pan gesture.

10. Add the following code underneath the viewDidLoad method:

```
override var preferredScreenEdgesDeferringSystemGestures:
UIRectEdge {
    return UIRectEdge.bottom
}

@objc func handleBottomEdge() {
    print ("Bottom edge pan gesture")
}

@objc func handleLeftEdge() {
    print ("Left edge pan gesture")
}
```

11. Click the Run button or choose Product ➤ Run. The Simulator window appears.

12. Move the mouse pointer just underneath the bottom of the view, hold down the left mouse button, and drag the mouse up. Notice that the Debug Area in the Xcode window displays multiple "Bottom edge pan gesture" lines, indicating that the app recognized the bottom screen edge pan gesture.

13. Move the mouse pointer just left of the view, hold down the left mouse button, and drag the mouse to the right. Notice that the Debug Area in the Xcode window displays multiple "Left edge pan gesture" lines, indicating that the app recognized the left screen edge pan gesture.

14. Choose Simulator ➤ Quit Simulator to return to Xcode.

Detecting Swipe Gestures

Swipe gestures occur when the user swipes across the screen in one of the four directions: up, down, left, or right. You can define how many fingertips are needed for a swipe and also the direction you want the gesture recognizer to detect.

Each swipe gesture recognizer can only detect swipes in a single direction. That means if you want to detect an up and down swipe, you'll need to define two separate swipe gesture recognizers where one recognizes only up swipes and the second only recognizes down swipes.

To see how to use a swipe gesture, follow these steps:

1. Create a new iOS project using the Single View App template (see Chapter 1) and name this new project SwipeApp. This creates a single view for the user interface.

2. Click the Main.storyboard file in the Navigator pane. Xcode displays the single view.

3. Click the Library icon to open the Object Library window and look for the Pan Gesture Recognizer as shown in Figure 11-16.

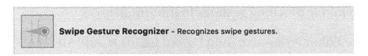

Figure 11-16. *The Swipe Gesture Recognizer in the Object Library window*

4. Drag and drop the Swipe Gesture Recognizer onto the view. Xcode displays the Swipe Gesture Recognizer in the Document Outline and above the View Controller.

5. Click the Swipe Gesture Recognizer in the Document Outline and press ENTER. Then type **Right Swipe Gesture** and press ENTER.

6. Drag and drop a second Swipe Gesture Recognizer onto the view. Xcode displays the Swipe Gesture Recognizer in the Document Outline and above the View Controller.

7. Click the Swipe Gesture Recognizer in the Document Outline and press ENTER. Then type **Up Swipe Gesture** and press ENTER.

8. Click the Library icon to open the Object Library window and drag and drop an image view in the center of the user interface.

9. Choose View ➤ Inspectors ➤ Show Attributes Inspector or click the Attributes Inspector icon in the upper right corner of the Xcode window.

10. Click in the Background popup menu and choose a color such as green or blue. This will make the image view easy to find when you run the app in the Simulator. Without a background color, the default white background of the image view will blend in with the white background of the view.

11. Select the User Interaction Enabled check box. This allows the image view to respond to the user.

12. Click the Align icon in the bottom of the middle Xcode pane. A window appears.

13. Select the Horizontally in Container and Vertically in Container check boxes and then click the Add 2 Constraints button (see Figure 11-10). The image view needs to be in the center to make it easy to mimic pinching gestures in the Simulator.

14. Choose Editor ➤ Resolve Auto Layout Issues ➤ Add Missing Constraints in the top half of the submenu. Xcode adds additional constraints to the image view.

15. Move the mouse pointer over the image view, hold down the Control key, and Ctrl-drag from the image view to the Right Swipe Gesture icon in the Document Outline or at the top of the View Controller.

16. Release the Control key and the left mouse button. A window appears.

17. Choose gestureRecognizers. This link lets the image view detect right swipe gestures.

18. Move the mouse pointer over the image view, hold down the Control key, and Ctrl-drag from the image view to the Up Swipe Gesture icon in the Document Outline or at the top of the View Controller.

19. Release the Control key and the left mouse button. A window appears.

20. Choose gestureRecognizers. This link lets the image view detect up swipe gestures.

21. Click Up Swipe Gesture in the Document Outline and choose View ➤ Inspectors ➤ Show Attributes Inspector, or click the Attributes Inspector icon in the upper right corner of the Xcode window.

22. Click in the Swipe popup menu and choose Up as shown in Figure 11-17. (By default, every swipe gesture recognizer only recognizes right swipes unless you define it otherwise.)

Figure 11-17. *Choosing a swipe direction to recognize for a swipe gesture recognizer*

23. Choose View ➤ Assistant Editor ➤ Show Assistant Editor, or click the Assistant Editor icon. Xcode displays the Main.storyboard and ViewController.swift file side by side.

24. Move the mouse pointer over the image view, hold down the Control key, and Ctrl-drag from the image view to the ViewController.swift file underneath the "class ViewController" line.

25. Release the Control key and the left mouse button. A popup window appears.

26. Click in the Name text field, type **topImageView**, and click the Connect button. Xcode creates an IBOutlet variable as follows:

```
@IBOutlet var topImageView: UIImageView!
```

27. Move the mouse pointer over the Right Swipe Gesture icon in the Document Outline or at the top of the View Controller, hold down the Control key, and Ctrl-drag from the Right Swipe Gesture to above the last curly bracket in the ViewController.swift file.

28. Release the Control key and the left mouse button. A popup window appears.

29. Click in the Name text field, type **rightSwipeDetected**, click in the Type popup menu and choose UISwipeGestureRecognizer, and click the Connect button. Xcode creates an IBAction method.

30. Edit the rightSwipeDetected IBAction method as follows:

```
@IBAction func rightSwipeDetected(_ sender:
UISwipeGestureRecognizer) {
    topImageView.center = CGPoint(x: topImageView.center.x +
    topImageView.frame.width, y: topImageView.center.y)
}
```

31. Move the mouse pointer over the Up Swipe Gesture icon in the Document Outline or at the top of the View Controller, hold down the Control key, and Ctrl-drag from the Right Swipe Gesture to above the last curly bracket in the ViewController.swift file.

32. Release the Control key and the left mouse button. A popup window appears.

33. Click in the Name text field, type **upSwipeDetected**, click in the Type popup menu and choose UISwipeGestureRecognizer, and click the Connect button. Xcode creates an IBAction method.

34. Edit the upSwipeDetected IBAction method as follows:

```
@IBAction func upSwipeDetected(_ sender:
UISwipeGestureRecognizer) {
    topImageView.center = CGPoint(x: topImageView.center.x, y:
    topImageView.center.y - topImageView.frame.height)
}
```

Note   Notice that this code subtracts from the image view center because, for the y-axis, positive numbers increase downward and decrease upward since the origin appears in the upper left corner of the view.

The entire ViewController.swift file should look like this:

```swift
import UIKit

class ViewController: UIViewController {

    @IBOutlet var topImageView: UIImageView!

    override func viewDidLoad() {
        super.viewDidLoad()
        // Do any additional setup after loading the view,
        typically from a nib.
    }

    @IBAction func rightSwipeDetected(_ sender:
    UISwipeGestureRecognizer) {
        topImageView.center = CGPoint(x: topImageView.center.x +
        topImageView.frame.width, y: topImageView.center.y)
    }

    @IBAction func upSwipeDetected(_ sender:
    UISwipeGestureRecognizer) {
        topImageView.center = CGPoint(x: topImageView.center.x, y:
        topImageView.center.y - topImageView.frame.height)
    }
}
```

35. Click the Run button or choose Product ➤ Run. The Simulator window appears.

36. Move the mouse pointer over the image view, hold down the left mouse button, move the mouse to the right, and let go of the left mouse button to simulate a right swipe gesture. Notice that the image view moves to the right.

37. Move the mouse pointer over the image view, hold down the left mouse button, move the mouse up, and let go of the left mouse button to simulate an up swipe gesture. Notice that the image view moves upward.

38. Repeat steps 36 and 37 until the image view disappears out of sight.

39. Choose Simulator ➤ Quit Simulator to return to Xcode.

This example defined the swipe gesture visually by dragging the Swipe Gesture Recognizer from the Object Library. Now let's see how to duplicate this process through Swift code alone.

1. Create a new iOS project using the Single View App template (see Chapter 1) and name this new project SwipeCodeApp. This creates a single view for the user interface.

2. Click the Main.storyboard file in the Navigator pane. Xcode displays the single view.

3. Click the Library icon to open the Object Library window and drag and drop an image view in the center of the user interface.

4. Click the Align icon in the bottom of the middle Xcode pane. A window appears.

5. Select the Horizontally in Container and Vertically in Container check boxes and then click the Add 2 Constraints button (see Figure 11-10). The image view needs to be in the center to make it easy to mimic pinching gestures in the Simulator.

6. Choose Editor ➤ Resolve Auto Layout Issues ➤ Add Missing Constraints in the top half of the submenu. Xcode adds additional constraints to the image view.

7. Choose View ➤ Assistant Editor ➤ Show Assistant Editor, or click the Assistant Editor icon. Xcode displays the Main.storyboard and ViewController.swift file side by side.

8. Move the mouse pointer over the image view, hold down
    the Control key, and Ctrl-drag from the image view to the
    ViewController.swift file underneath the "class ViewController" line.

9. Release the Control key and the left mouse button. A popup
    window appears.

10. Click in the Name text field, type **topImageView**, and click the
    Connect button. Xcode creates an IBOutlet variable as follows:

    ```
    @IBOutlet var topImageView: UIImageView!
    ```

11. Choose View ➤ Standard Editor ➤ Show Standard Editor, or click
    the Standard Editor icon in the upper right corner of the Xcode
    window.

12. Click the ViewController.swift file in the Navigator pane.

13. Edit the viewDidLoad method as follows:

    ```
    override func viewDidLoad() {
        super.viewDidLoad()

        topImageView.isUserInteractionEnabled = true
        topImageView.backgroundColor = UIColor.green

        let downSwipeGesture = UISwipeGestureRecognizer(target:
        self, action: #selector(handleDownSwipe))
        topImageView.addGestureRecognizer(downSwipeGesture)
        downSwipeGesture.direction = .down

        let leftSwipeGesture = UISwipeGestureRecognizer(target:
        self, action: #selector(handleLeftSwipe))
        topImageView.addGestureRecognizer(leftSwipeGesture)
        leftSwipeGesture.direction = .left
        // Do any additional setup after loading the view,
        typically from a nib.
    }
    ```

This code turns on the User Interaction Enabled setting for the image view and defines its background color as green to make it visible. Next, it defines two swipe gesture recognizers (instead of dragging and dropping a Swipe Gesture Recognizer from the Object Library window), defines a function called handleDownSwipe and handleLeftSwipe to respond to the two swipe gestures, and links the swipe gestures to the image view. In addition, it also defines the direction each swipe gesture can recognize such as down and left.

14. Add the following functions underneath the viewDidLoad method:

```
@objc func handleDownSwipe() {
    topImageView.center = CGPoint(x: topImageView.center.x, y:
    topImageView.center.y + topImageView.frame.height)
}

@objc func handleLeftSwipe() {
    topImageView.center = CGPoint(x: topImageView.center.x -
    topImageView.frame.width, y: topImageView.center.y)
}
```

The entire ViewController.swift file should look like this:

```
import UIKit

class ViewController: UIViewController {

    @IBOutlet var topImageView: UIImageView!

    override func viewDidLoad() {
        super.viewDidLoad()

        topImageView.isUserInteractionEnabled = true
        topImageView.backgroundColor = UIColor.green

        let downSwipeGesture = UISwipeGestureRecognizer(target:
        self, action: #selector(handleDownSwipe))
        topImageView.addGestureRecognizer(downSwipeGesture)
        downSwipeGesture.direction = .down
```

```
    let leftSwipeGesture = UISwipeGestureRecognizer(target:
    self, action: #selector(handleLeftSwipe))
    topImageView.addGestureRecognizer(leftSwipeGesture)
    leftSwipeGesture.direction = .left
    // Do any additional setup after loading the view,
    typically from a nib.
}

@objc func handleDownSwipe() {
    topImageView.center = CGPoint(x: topImageView.center.x, y:
    topImageView.center.y + topImageView.frame.height)
}

@objc func handleLeftSwipe() {
    topImageView.center = CGPoint(x: topImageView.center.x -
    topImageView.frame.width, y: topImageView.center.y)
}

}
```

15.   Click the Run button or choose Product ➤ Run. The Simulator
      window appears.

16.   Move the mouse pointer over the image view, hold down the left
      mouse button, move the mouse to the left, and let go of the left
      mouse button to simulate a left swipe gesture. Notice that the
      image view moves to the left.

17.   Move the mouse pointer over the image view, hold down the left
      mouse button, move the mouse down, and let go of the left mouse
      button to simulate a down swipe gesture. Notice that the image
      view moves down.

18.   Repeat steps 16 and 17 until the image view disappears out of
      sight.

19.   Choose Simulator ➤ Quit Simulator to return to Xcode.

Detecting Long Press Gestures

A long press gesture occurs when the user presses one or more fingertips on the screen for a fixed amount of time where the fingertips don't move very far. To define a long press, you can modify the following properties:

- .minimumPressDuration – Defines how long one or more fingertips must press down on the screen until the long press is recognized

- .numberOfTouchesRequired – Defines how many fingertips must press on the screen until the longer press gesture is recognized

- .allowableMovement – Defines how far fingertips can move before the long press gesture fails

To see how to use a long press gesture, follow these steps:

1. Create a new iOS project using the Single View App template (see Chapter 1) and name this new project LongPressApp. This creates a single view for the user interface.

2. Click the Main.storyboard file in the Navigator pane. Xcode displays the single view.

3. Click the Library icon to open the Object Library window and look for the Long Press Gesture Recognizer as shown in Figure 11-18.

Figure 11-18. *The Long Press Gesture Recognizer in the Object Library window*

4. Drag and drop the Long Press Gesture Recognizer onto the view. Xcode displays the Long Press Gesture Recognizer in the Document Outline and above the View Controller.

5. Click the Library icon to open the Object Library window and drag and drop an image view on the user interface.

6. Choose View ➤ Inspectors ➤ Show Attributes Inspector or click the Attributes Inspector icon in the upper right corner of the Xcode window.

7. Click in the Background popup menu and choose a color such as green or blue. This will make the image view easy to find when you run the app in the Simulator. Without a background color, the default white background of the image view will blend in with the white background of the view.

8. Select the User Interaction Enabled check box. This allows the image view to respond to the user.

9. Click the Align icon in the bottom of the middle Xcode pane. A window appears.

10. Select the Horizontally in Container and Vertically in Container check boxes and then click the Add 2 Constraints button (see Figure 11-10). The image view needs to be in the center to make it easy to mimic pinching gestures in the Simulator.

11. Choose Editor ➤ Resolve Auto Layout Issues ➤ Add Missing Constraints in the top half of the submenu. Xcode adds additional constraints to the image view.

12. Move the mouse pointer over the image view, hold down the Control key, and Ctrl-drag from the image view to the Long Press Gesture Recognizer icon in the Document Outline or at the top of the View Controller.

13. Release the Control key and the left mouse button. A window appears.

14. Choose gestureRecognizers. This link lets the image view detect long press gestures.

15. Choose View ➤ Assistant Editor ➤ Show Assistant Editor, or click the Assistant Editor icon. Xcode displays the Main.storyboard and ViewController.swift file side by side.

16. Move the mouse pointer over the image view, hold down the Control key, and Ctrl-drag from the image view to the ViewController.swift file underneath the "class ViewController" line.

17. Release the Control key and the left mouse button. A popup window appears.

18. Click in the Name text field, type **topImageView**, and click the Connect button. Xcode creates an IBOutlet variable as follows:

```
@IBOutlet var topImageView: UIImageView!
```

19. Move the mouse pointer over the Long Press Gesture Recognizer icon in the Document Outline or at the top of the View Controller, hold down the Control key, and Ctrl-drag from the Long Press Gesture Recognizer above the last curly bracket in the ViewController.swift file.

20. Release the Control key and the left mouse button. A popup window appears.

21. Click in the Name text field, type **longPressDetected**, click in the Type popup menu and choose UILongPressGestureRecognizer, and click the Connect button. Xcode creates an IBAction method.

22. Edit the longPressDetected IBAction method as follows:

```
@IBAction func longPressDetected(_ sender:
UILongPressGestureRecognizer) {
    topImageView.backgroundColor = UIColor.red
}
```

The longPressDetected IBAction method changes the background color of the image view to red when it recognizes the long press gesture. The entire ViewController.swift file should look like this:

```
import UIKit

class ViewController: UIViewController {

    @IBOutlet var topImageView: UIImageView!

    override func viewDidLoad() {
        super.viewDidLoad()
        // Do any additional setup after loading the view,
        typically from a nib.
    }
```

```
@IBAction func longPressDetected(_ sender:
UILongPressGestureRecognizer) {
    topImageView.backgroundColor = UIColor.red
}
}
```

23. Click the Run button or choose Product ➤ Run. The Simulator window appears.

24. Move the mouse pointer over the image view, then hold down the left mouse button. When the image view detects the long press gesture, it turns the image view background color to red.

25. Choose Simulator ➤ Quit Simulator to return to Xcode.

This example defined the long press gesture visually by dragging the Long Press Gesture Recognizer from the Object Library. Now let's see how to duplicate this process through Swift code alone.

1. Create a new iOS project using the Single View App template (see Chapter 1) and name this new project LongPressCodeApp. This creates a single view for the user interface.

2. Click the Main.storyboard file in the Navigator pane. Xcode displays the single view.

3. Click the Library icon to open the Object Library window and drag and drop an image view in the center of the user interface.

4. Click the Align icon in the bottom of the middle Xcode pane. A window appears.

5. Select the Horizontally in Container and Vertically in Container check boxes and then click the Add 2 Constraints button (see Figure 11-10). The image view needs to be in the center to make it easy to mimic pinching gestures in the Simulator.

6. Choose Editor ➤ Resolve Auto Layout Issues ➤ Add Missing Constraints in the top half of the submenu. Xcode adds additional constraints to the image view.

7. Choose View ➤ Assistant Editor ➤ Show Assistant Editor, or click the Assistant Editor icon. Xcode displays the Main.storyboard and ViewController.swift file side by side.

8. Move the mouse pointer over the image view, hold down the Control key, and Ctrl-drag from the image view to the ViewController.swift file underneath the "class ViewController" line.

9. Release the Control key and the left mouse button. A popup window appears.

10. Click in the Name text field, type **topImageView**, and click the Connect button. Xcode creates an IBOutlet variable as follows:

    ```
    @IBOutlet var topImageView: UIImageView!
    ```

11. Choose View ➤ Standard Editor ➤ Show Standard Editor, or click the Standard Editor icon in the upper right corner of the Xcode window.

12. Click the ViewController.swift file in the Navigator pane.

13. Edit the viewDidLoad method as follows:

    ```
    override func viewDidLoad() {
        super.viewDidLoad()

        topImageView.isUserInteractionEnabled = true
        topImageView.backgroundColor = UIColor.green

        let longPressGesture = UILongPressGestureRecognizer(target:
        self, action: #selector(handleLongPress))
        topImageView.addGestureRecognizer(longPressGesture)
        // Do any additional setup after loading the view,
        typically from a nib.
    }
    ```

This code turns on the User Interaction Enabled setting for the image view and defines its background color as green to make it visible. Next, it defines a long press gesture recognizer (instead of dragging and dropping a Long Press Gesture Recognizer from the Object Library window), defines a function called handleLongPress to respond to the long press gesture, and links the long press gesture to the image view.

14. Add the following function underneath the viewDidLoad method:

```
@objc func handleLongPress() {
    topImageView.backgroundColor = UIColor.red
}
```

The entire ViewController.swift file should look like this:

```
import UIKit

class ViewController: UIViewController {

    @IBOutlet var topImageView: UIImageView!

    override func viewDidLoad() {
        super.viewDidLoad()

        topImageView.isUserInteractionEnabled = true
        topImageView.backgroundColor = UIColor.green

        let longPressGesture = UILongPressGestureRecognizer
        (target: self, action: #selector(handleLongPress))
        topImageView.addGestureRecognizer(longPressGesture)
        // Do any additional setup after loading the view,
        typically from a nib.
    }

    @objc func handleLongPress() {
        topImageView.backgroundColor = UIColor.red
    }

}
```

15. Click the Run button or choose Product ➤ Run. The Simulator window appears.

16. Move the mouse pointer over the image view, then hold down the left mouse button to mimic a long press. Notice that the image view changes color from green to red.

17. Choose Simulator ➤ Quit Simulator to return to Xcode.

Summary

Touch gestures give commands to an app without placing an object on the user interface such as a button. Gestures can often work with one or more fingertips that you can define using either the Attributes Inspector pane or through Swift code.

There are two ways to add gesture recognizers to an app. First, you can add a gesture recognizer to a storyboard through the Object Library. Once you add a gesture recognizer to a project, you'll need to Ctrl-drag from an object to the gesture recognizer to make that object recognize that particular gesture. Next you'll need to create an IBAction method to respond when the gesture is recognized.

A second method involves writing Swift code to create a gesture recognizer, adding a gesture recognizer to an IBOutlet object, and then writing a function to handle the gesture when it's recognized. Both methods work identically so it's a matter of choosing the method you prefer.

Adding gestures to an app can make the user interface less cluttered and more intuitive by letting users directly manipulate objects on the screen.

CHAPTER 12

Using Alerts and Pickers

Almost every app needs to display and accept data from the user. The simplest way to display data is through a label, but sometimes you need to display data and give the user a way to respond. In that case, you need to use an alert controller.

An alert controller can display a sheet that pops up on the screen, giving the user a chance to respond. Alert controllers appear over the user interface to force the user to respond by tapping a button to make a choice or dismiss the alert controller as shown in Figure 12-1.

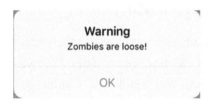

Figure 12-1. *An alert controller typically displays a message and one or more buttons*

Besides displaying data, user interfaces also need to let people input data. If that data is text, then you can use a text field to let the user type anything in that text field such as a name or telephone number. A text field is perfect for accepting any type of data, but when you need to offer the user a list of valid choices, you'll want to use a picker instead.

Xcode offers two different types of pickers:

- Date Picker – Displays dates and times as shown in Figure 12-2
- Picker View – Displays a spinning wheel of different options

© Wallace Wang 2019
W. Wang, *Beginning iPhone Development with Swift 5*, https://doi.org/10.1007/978-1-4842-4865-2_12

Sat Jan 19	6	27	
Sun Jan 20	7	28	
Mon Jan 21	8	29	AM
Today	**9**	**30**	**PM**
Wed Jan 23	10	31	
Thu Jan 24	11	32	
Fri Jan 25	12	33	

Figure 12-2. *A Date Picker makes it easy for users to choose dates and times*

A picker contains a limited number of options on one or more wheels that the user can spin around to select a particular option. The available number of options can be as small as two (such as the AM and PM option for choosing a time), but typically the available options are greater than two. Pickers insure that the user can never choose a non-valid option such as typing a number for a name or typing a city incorrectly.

Using an Alert Controller

Every user interface needs to display data back to the user. In some cases, this data can be displayed just in a label, but sometimes you need to make sure the user sees certain information. In those situations, you should use an alert controller.

An alert controller appears over an app's user interface and can be customized by changing the following properties:

- Title – Text that appears at the top of the alert controller, often in bold and a large font size

- Message – Text that appears underneath the title in a smaller font size

- Preferred style – Defines the appearance of the alert controller as an action sheet (as shown in Figure 12-3) that appear at the bottom of the screen or as an alert (see Figure 12-1) that appear in the middle of the screen

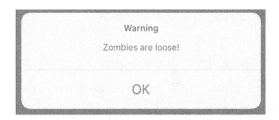

Figure 12-3. *An action sheet appears at the bottom of the screen*

A title typically consists of a single word or short phrase that explains the purpose of the alert controller such as displaying "Warning" or "Log In".

To dismiss an alert controller, an alert controller always needs at least one button. However, an alert controller can display two or more buttons to give user a choice. Besides displaying buttons, alert controllers can also text fields to allow users to enter data as well.

You can create an alert controller solely by writing Swift code. First, you must create the alert controller that defines a title, message, and style. Second, you must define an alert action for each button or text field you want to display on the alert controller. Third, you must actually present that alert controller on the user interface.

To see how to create a simple alert controller that does nothing but display a title, a message, and a button to dismiss it, follow these steps:

1.   Create a new iOS project using the Single View App template (see Chapter 1) and name this new project AlertControllerApp. This creates a single view for the user interface.

2.   Click the Main.storyboard file in the Navigator pane. Xcode displays the single view.

3.   Click the Library icon to open the Object Library window.

4.   Drag and drop a button anywhere on the view.

5.   Choose Editor ➤ Resolve Auto Layout Issues ➤ Reset to Suggested Constraints. Xcode adds constraints to the button.

6.   Choose View ➤ Assistant Editor ➤ Show Assistant Editor. Xcode displays the Main.storyboard and ViewController.swift file side by side.

7.   Move the mouse pointer over the button, hold down the Control key, and Ctrl-drag from the image view to the ViewController.swift file above the last curly bracket at the bottom of the file.

8. Release the Control key and the left mouse button. A popup
    window appears.

9. Click in the Name text field, type **buttonTapped**, click the Type
    popup menu and choose UIButton, and click the Connect button.
    Xcode creates an IBAction method.

10. Edit this buttonTapped IBAction method as follows:

```
@IBAction func buttonTapped(_ sender: UIButton) {
    let alert = UIAlertController(title: "Warning", message:
    "Zombies are loose!", preferredStyle: .alert)

    let okAction = UIAlertAction(title: "OK", style: .default,
    handler: { action -> Void in
        //Just dismiss the action sheet
    })
    alert.addAction(okAction)

    self.present(alert, animated: true, completion: nil)
}
```

11. Click the Run button or choose Product ➤ Run. The Simulator
    screen appears.

12. Click the button. Notice that the alert controller appears in the
    middle of the screen because the preferredStyle were .alert. (If
    the preferredStyle property were .actionSheet, then the alert
    controller would appear at the bottom of the screen.)

13. Tap the OK button on the alert controller to make it go away.

14. Choose Simulator ➤ Quit Simulator to return to Xcode.

Change the title and message properties to display different text and run the app
again to see how it changes the appearance of the alert controller. Also change the
preferredStyle property from .alert to .actionSheet to see how it affects the appearance of
the alert controller as well.

Displaying and Responding to Multiple Buttons

The simplest alert controller displays a single button that allows the user to dismiss it. However, you may want to give the user more than one option to choose and then respond differently depending on which button the user taps.

For each button you want to display on an alert controller, you need to add a UIAlertAction. When the user taps a button on an alert controller, the alert controller goes away. If you want the button to do more, then you need to call a separate function that does some action.

To see how to create an alert controller that displays two buttons and responds differently to each button, follow these steps:

1. Create a new iOS project using the Single View App template (see Chapter 1) and name this new project AlertControllerButtonsApp. This creates a single view for the user interface.

2. Click the Main.storyboard file in the Navigator pane. Xcode displays the single view.

3. Click the Library icon to open the Object Library window.

4. Drag and drop a button and a label anywhere on the view.

5. Choose Editor ➤ Resolve Auto Layout Issues ➤ Reset to Suggested Constraints on the bottom half of the submenu. Xcode adds constraints to the button and label.

6. Choose View ➤ Assistant Editor ➤ Show Assistant Editor. Xcode displays the Main.storyboard and ViewController.swift file side by side.

7. Move the mouse pointer over the label, hold down the Control key, and Ctrl-drag from the image view to the ViewController.swift file under the "class ViewController" line.

8. Release the Control key and the left mouse button. A popup window appears.

9. Click in the Name text field, type **labelResult,** and click the Connect button. Xcode creates an IBOutlet variable as follows:

    ```
    @IBOutlet var labelResult: UILabel!
    ```

10. Move the mouse pointer over the button, hold down the Control key, and Ctrl-drag from the image view to the ViewController.swift file above the last curly bracket at the bottom of the file.

11. Release the Control key and the left mouse button. A popup window appears.

12. Click in the Name text field, type **buttonTapped**, click in the Type popup menu and choose UIButton, and click the Connect button. Xcode creates an IBAction method.

13. Choose View ➤ Standard Editor ➤ Show Standard Editor, or click the Standard Editor icon in the upper right corner of the Xcode window.

14. Click the ViewController.swift file in the Navigator pane.

15. Modify the viewDidLoad method as follows:

```
override func viewDidLoad() {
    super.viewDidLoad()
    labelResult.numberOfLines = 0
    // Do any additional setup after loading the view,
    typically from a nib.
}
```

Setting the numberOfLines property of the label to 0 allows it to expand in width no matter the size of text stored in it. If this numberOfLines property is left at its default value of 1, then the label will not resize automatically and risks cutting text off if the text is longer than the width of the label.

16. Edit this buttonTapped IBAction method as follows:

```
@IBAction func buttonTapped(_ sender: UIButton) {
    let alert = UIAlertController(title: "Warning", message:
    "Zombies are loose!", preferredStyle: .alert)

    let okAction = UIAlertAction(title: "OK", style: .default,
    handler: { action -> Void in
```

```
        self.labelResult.text = "OK"
    })
    let cancelAction = UIAlertAction(title: "Cancel", style:
    .cancel, handler: { action -> Void in
        self.labelResult.text = "Cancel"
    })
    let destroyAction = UIAlertAction(title: "Destroy", style:
    .destructive, handler: { action -> Void in
        self.labelResult.text = "Destroy"
    })
    alert.addAction(okAction)
    alert.addAction(cancelAction)
    alert.addAction(destroyAction)

    self.present(alert, animated: true, completion: nil)
}
```

The code to define each UIAlertAction simply changes the text
displayed in the label. If you need each button to perform more
complicated tasks, you can put the name of one or more functions
in the handler. Then you'll need to create those functions such as:

```
    let destroyAction = UIAlertAction(title: "Destroy", style:
    .destructive, handler: { action -> Void in
        self.labelResult.text = "Destroy"
        self.callFunctionOne()
        self.callFunctionTwo()
    })

func callFunctionOne(){
    // Code here
}

func callFunctionTwo(){
    // Code here
}
```

The entire ViewController.swift file should look like this:

```swift
import UIKit

class ViewController: UIViewController {

    @IBOutlet var labelResult: UILabel!

    override func viewDidLoad() {
        super.viewDidLoad()
        labelResult.numberOfLines = 0
        // Do any additional setup after loading the view,
        // typically from a nib.
    }

    @IBAction func buttonTapped(_ sender: UIButton) {
        let alert = UIAlertController(title: "Warning", message:
        "Zombies are loose!", preferredStyle: .alert)

        let okAction = UIAlertAction(title: "OK", style: .default,
        handler: { action -> Void in
            self.labelResult.text = "OK"
        })
        let cancelAction = UIAlertAction(title: "Cancel", style:
        .cancel, handler: { action -> Void in
            self.labelResult.text = "Cancel"
        })
        let destroyAction = UIAlertAction(title: "Destroy", style:
        .destructive, handler: { action -> Void in
            self.labelResult.text = "Destroy"
        })
        alert.addAction(okAction)
        alert.addAction(cancelAction)
        alert.addAction(destroyAction)

        self.present(alert, animated: true, completion: nil)
    }

}
```

17. Click the Run button or choose Product ➤ Run. The Simulator screen appears.

18. Click the button. The alert controller appears as shown in Figure 12-4.

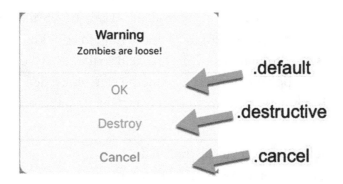

Figure 12-4. *The alert controller displaying three types of buttons, .default, .destructive, and .cancel*

19. Click the OK button, which appears using the .default style. Notice that the label now displays "OK" and dismisses the alert controller.

20. Click the Destroy button, which appears using the .destructive style. Notice that the label now displays "Destroy" and dismisses the alert controller.

21. Click the Cancel button, which appears using the .cancel style. Notice that the label now displays "Cancel" and dismisses the alert controller.

22. Choose Simulator ➤ Quit Simulator to return to Xcode.

Displaying a Text Field on an Alert Controller

Buttons let an alert controller accept choices from the user. Based on those choices, your code can then respond. However, sometimes you might want to display a text field on an alert controller to allow the user to type in data. Then you'll need to store this data.

Note   You can only add text fields on an alert controller that appears in the .alert preferredStyle. You cannot display text fields on an alert controller that appears as the .actionSheet preferredStyle.

When you add a text field to an alert controller, you can modify that text field like any text field such as defining a background color or font. In addition, you must also create a constant to store the contents of that text field so the rest of your app can access whatever data the user typed into the text field on the alert controller.

To see how to display a text field on an alert controller and access its contents, follow these steps:

1. Create a new iOS project using the Single View App template (see Chapter 1) and name this new project AlertControllerTextFieldApp. This creates a single view for the user interface.

2. Click the Main.storyboard file in the Navigator pane. Xcode displays the single view.

3. Click the Library icon to open the Object Library window.

4. Drag and drop a button and a label anywhere on the view.

5. Choose Editor ➤ Resolve Auto Layout Issues ➤ Reset to Suggested Constraints on the bottom half of the submenu. Xcode adds constraints to the button and label.

6. Choose View ➤ Assistant Editor ➤ Show Assistant Editor. Xcode displays the Main.storyboard and ViewController.swift file side by side.

7. Move the mouse pointer over the label, hold down the Control key, and Ctrl-drag from the image view to the ViewController.swift file under the "class ViewController" line.

8. Release the Control key and the left mouse button. A popup window appears.

9. Click in the Name text field, type **labelResult**, and click the Connect button. Xcode creates an IBOutlet variable as follows:

    @IBOutlet var labelResult: UILabel!

10. Move the mouse pointer over the button, hold down the Control key, and Ctrl-drag from the image view to the ViewController.swift file above the last curly bracket at the bottom of the file.

11. Release the Control key and the left mouse button. A popup window appears.

12. Click in the Name text field, type **buttonTapped**, click in the Type popup menu and choose UIButton, and click the Connect button. Xcode creates an IBAction method.

13. Choose View ➤ Standard Editor ➤ Show Standard Editor, or click the Standard Editor icon in the upper right corner of the Xcode window.

14. Click the ViewController.swift file in the Navigator pane.

15. Modify the viewDidLoad method as follows:

    ```
    override func viewDidLoad() {
        super.viewDidLoad()
        labelResult.numberOfLines = 0
        // Do any additional setup after loading the view,
        typically from a nib.
    }
    ```

Setting the numberOfLines property of the label to 0 allows it to expand in width no matter the size of text stored in it. If this numberOfLines property is left at its default value of 1, then the label will not resize automatically and risks cutting text off if the text is longer than the width of the label.

16.   Add the following to the buttonTapped IBAction method as
follows:

```
let alert = UIAlertController(title: "Log In", message:
"Enter Password", preferredStyle: .alert)

alert.addTextField(configurationHandler: {(textField) in
    textField.placeholder = "Password here"
    textField.isSecureTextEntry = true
})
```

The first line creates an alert controller that displays the title
"Log In" and underneath the message "Enter Password". Because
we want to display a text field on the alert controller, the alert
controller's preferredStyle must be .alert.

The second line adds a text field to the alert controller and
configures the text field to display "Password here" as placeholder
text and also sets its isSecureTextEntry property to true which
hides the characters as the user types them in the text field. Any
code listed here simply customized the text field.

17.   Add the following to the buttonTapped IBAction method as
follows:

```
let okAction = UIAlertAction(title: "OK", style: .default,
handler: { action -> Void in
    let savedText = alert.textFields![0] as UITextField
    self.labelResult.text = savedText.text
})

alert.addAction(okAction)
self.present(alert, animated: true, completion: nil)
```

The first line defines a button with the title "OK" and a .default
style. Inside the handler section of the code, this line defines a
constant called savedText, which represents the first text field (note
the index value of 0) on the alert controller. If you add more than
one text field to an alert controller, you'll need to define additional
constants to represent those other text fields. Finally, this line

stores the text from the text field (savedText) and displays it in the labelResult IBOutlet that's linked to the label on the user interface.

The second line adds the button to the alert controller and the third line presents or displays the alert controller.

The entire ViewController.swift file should look like this:

```swift
import UIKit

class ViewController: UIViewController {

    @IBOutlet var labelResult: UILabel!

    override func viewDidLoad() {
        super.viewDidLoad()
        labelResult.numberOfLines = 0
        // Do any additional setup after loading the view,
        typically from a nib.
    }

    @IBAction func buttonTapped(_ sender: UIButton) {
        let alert = UIAlertController(title: "Log In", message:
        "Enter Password", preferredStyle: .alert)

        alert.addTextField(configurationHandler: {(textField) in
            textField.placeholder = "Password here"
            textField.isSecureTextEntry = true
        })

        let okAction = UIAlertAction(title: "OK", style: .default,
        handler: { action -> Void in
            let savedText = alert.textFields![0] as UITextField
            self.labelResult.text = savedText.text
        })

        alert.addAction(okAction)

        self.present(alert, animated: true, completion: nil)
    }
}
```

18. Click the Run button or choose Product ➤ Run. The Simulator screen appears.

19. Click the button. The alert controller appears as shown in Figure 12-5.

Figure 12-5. *An alert controller displaying a text field and a button*

20. Type some text in the text field on the alert controller. Notice that as you type, the text field masks the characters because its isSecureTextEntry property is set to true.

21. Click the OK button. Notice that whatever text you typed into the text field now appears in the label.

22. Choose Simulator ➤ Quit Simulator to return to Xcode.

Using a Date Picker

When an app needs the user to input a date and/or a time, it's best to use the Date Picker to provide a list of valid options. By spinning different wheels on a Date Picker, users can pick days, dates, and times without typing a thing.

After dragging and dropping a Date Picker from the Object Library window to a view, you can customize a Date Picker by modifying the following options in the Attributes Inspector as shown in Figure 12-6:

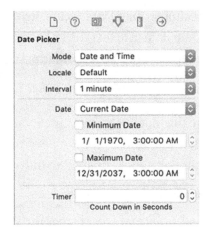

Figure 12-6. *The Attributes Inspector pane lets you customize a Date Picker*

- Mode – Defines the Date Picker to display Time, Date, Time and Date, or Count Down Timer as shown in Figure 12-7

- Locale – Overrides the system default locale property that defines the local language such as American English or Australian English

- Interval – Defines the time interval in minutes from 1 minute up to 30 minutes

- Date – Defines the date to display initially

- Minimum Date – Defines the minimum date allowed

- Maximum Date – Defines the maximum date allowed

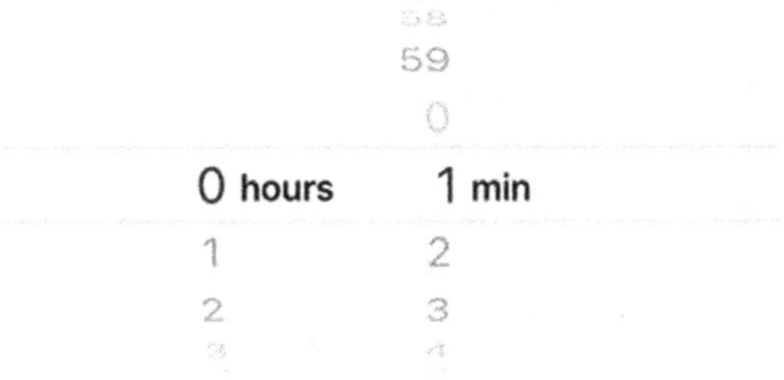

58
59
0

0 hours   1 min

1   2

2   3

Figure 12-7. *Changing the Mode of a Date Picker to a Count Down Timer*

No matter what mode you choose for a Date Picker, its value is stored as an NSDate data type. To convert this NSDate data into text, you need a two-step process. First, you need to create a constant that represents a DateFormatter such as

```
let dateFormatter: DateFormatter = DateFormatter()
```

Second, you have to define the .dateStyle and .timeStyle properties to display the date and time. To define the date and time style, you need to set the .dateStyle and .timeStyle properties of the DateFormatter constant to one of the following options:

- .none – Does not display the date or time

- .short – Displays dates in this format "11/23/19" and times in this format "3:48 PM"

- .medium – Displays dates in this format "Nov 23, 2019" and times in this format "3:48:21 PM"

- .long – Displays dates in this format "November 23, 2019" and times in this format "3:48:21 PM EST"

- .full – Displays dates in this format "Saturday, November 23, 2019 AD" and times in this format "3:48 PM Eastern Standard Time"

```
dateFormatter.dateStyle = .short
dateFormatter.timeStyle = .short
```

Finally, you have to retrieve the date/time currently displayed in the Date Picker. Since the date/time value stored in the Date Picker is in the NSDate data type, you have to convert its .date property to a string by using code such as this:

```
let selectedDate: String = dateFormatter.string(from: myDatePicker.date)
```

In the following example, we'll see how to retrieve the value displayed in a Date Picker in two different ways. First, we'll retrieve the Date Picker value any time the user changes the Date Picker. Second, we'll retrieve the Date Picker value and display it on an alert controller.

To see how to define the title on a button, follow these steps:

1. Create a new iOS project using the Single View App template (see Chapter 1) and name this new project DatePickerApp. This creates a single view for the user interface.

2. Click the Main.storyboard file in the Navigator pane. Xcode displays the single view.

3. Click the Library icon to open the Object Library window.

4. Drag and drop a button and a Date Picker anywhere on the view as shown in Figure 12-8.

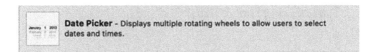

Figure 12-8. *The Date Picker in the Object Library window*

5. Choose Editor ➤ Resolve Auto Layout Issues ➤ Set to Suggested Constraints. Xcode adds constraints to your button and Date Picker.

6. Choose View ➤ Assistant Editor ➤ Show Assistant Editor. Xcode displays the Main.storyboard and ViewController.swift file side by side.

7. Move the mouse pointer over the Date Picker, hold down the Control key, and Ctrl-drag from the Date Picker to the ViewController.swift file underneath the "class ViewController" line.

8. Release the Control key and the left mouse button. A popup window appears.

9. Click in the Name text field, type **myDatePicker**, and click the Connect button. Xcode creates an IBOutlet variable as follows:

```
@IBOutlet var myDatePicker: UIDatePicker!
```

10. Underneath the IBOutlet add the following line to define a date formatter:

```
let dateFormatter: DateFormatter = DateFormatter()
```

11.   Edit the viewDidLoad method as follows:

```
override func viewDidLoad() {
    super.viewDidLoad()
    dateFormatter.dateStyle = .short
    dateFormatter.timeStyle = .short
    // Do any additional setup after loading the view,
    typically from a nib.
}
```

These lines of code define the .dateStyle and .timeStyle properties to .short. You can experiment by changing these values to .medium, .long, and .full to see how it defines the date and time differently.

12.   Underneath the viewDidLoad method, add the following function which will accept a string and display it in an alert controller:

```
func ShowAlert(dateTime : String) {
    let alert = UIAlertController(title: "Selected Date and
    Time", message: "\(dateTime)", preferredStyle: .alert)

    let okAction = UIAlertAction(title: "OK", style: .default,
    handler: { action -> Void in
        //Just dismiss the action sheet
    })
    alert.addAction(okAction)

    self.present(alert, animated: true, completion: nil)
}
```

13.   Move the mouse pointer over the button, hold down the Control key, and Ctrl-drag from the button to the ViewController.swift file above the last curly bracket at the bottom of the file.

14.   Release the Control key and the left mouse button. A popup window appears.

15.   Click in the Name text field, type **getCurrentDateTime**, click
      in the Type popup menu and choose UIButton, and click the
      Connect button. Xcode creates an IBAction method.

16.   Edit this getCurrentDateTime IBAction method as follows:

```
@IBAction func getCurrentDateTime(_ sender: UIButton) {
    let selectedDate: String = dateFormatter.string(from:
    myDatePicker.date)
    ShowAlert(dateTime: selectedDate)
}
```

      This IBAction method retrieves the value of the myDatePicker
      IBOutlet (that represents the Date Picker) and converts this
      date and time into a string that gets stored in the selectedDate
      constant. Then it passes this selectedDate constant to the Show
      Alert function to display it on the alert controller.

17.   Move the mouse pointer over the Date Picker, hold down
      the Control key, and Ctrl-drag from the Date Picker to the
      ViewController.swift file above the last curly bracket at the bottom
      of the file.

18.   Release the Control key and the left mouse button. A popup
      window appears.

19.   Click in the Name text field, type **dateChanged**, click in the Type
      popup menu and choose UIDatePicker, and click the Connect
      button. Xcode creates an IBAction method.

20.   Edit this dateChanged IBAction method as follows:

```
@IBAction func dateChanged(_ sender: UIDatePicker) {
    let selectedDate: String = dateFormatter.string(from:
    sender.date)
    ShowAlert(dateTime: selectedDate)
}
```

      This dateChanged IBAction method runs every time the user
      changes the date or time in the Date Picker. It retrieves the
      .date property from the Date Picker and converts it into a string,

which it stores in the selectedDate constant. Then it passes this selectedDate constant into the Show Alert function that displays it on an alert controller.

The entire ViewController.swift file should look like this:

```swift
import UIKit

class ViewController: UIViewController {

    @IBOutlet var myDatePicker: UIDatePicker!
    let dateFormatter: DateFormatter = DateFormatter()

    override func viewDidLoad() {
        super.viewDidLoad()
        dateFormatter.dateStyle = .short
        dateFormatter.timeStyle = .short
        // Do any additional setup after loading the view,
        // typically from a nib.
    }

    func ShowAlert(dateTime : String) {
        let alert = UIAlertController(title: "Selected Date and
        Time", message: "\(dateTime)", preferredStyle: .alert)

        let okAction = UIAlertAction(title: "OK", style: .default,
        handler: { action -> Void in
            //Just dismiss the action sheet
        })
        alert.addAction(okAction)

        self.present(alert, animated: true, completion: nil)
    }

    @IBAction func dateChanged(_ sender: UIDatePicker) {
        let selectedDate: String = dateFormatter.string(from:
        sender.date)
        ShowAlert(dateTime: selectedDate)
    }
```

```
@IBAction func getCurrentDateTime(_ sender: UIButton) {
    let selectedDate: String = dateFormatter.string(from:
    myDatePicker.date)
    ShowAlert(dateTime: selectedDate)
}
}
```

21. Click the Run button or choose Product ➤ Run. The Simulator screen appears.

22. Click the button. An alert controller appears, displaying the current date and time displayed in the Date Picker.

23. Click the button to dismiss the alert controller.

24. Change the date or time in the Date Picker. Notice another alert controller appears, displaying the modified date/time displayed in the Date Picker.

25. Click the button to dismiss the alert controller.

26. Choose Simulator ➤ Quit Simulator to return to Xcode.

Go back to step 11 and change the .dateStyle and .timeStyle properties from .short to .medium, .long, or .full and see how this affects the way dates and times appear. If you change the .dateStyle or .timeStyle to .none, then the date or time displayed in the Date Picker will be ignored.

Creating a Custom Picker

The Date Picker is fine for letting the user choose dates and times, but many times you want to offer users a limited range of options that are not dates or times. In these situations, you need to use the standard picker object and also create the data to display in the picker.

To use a picker, you must define a delegate and data source. The delegate defines the file that contains functions that define how many columns of data to display (such as a day and month), the total number of options to display in the picker, and which data the user chose in the picker.

The data source defines the file that contains the data to display in the picker. This data can be an array or a database.

To see how to use a Picker View, follow these steps:

1. Create a new iOS project using the Single View App template (see Chapter 1) and name this new project PickerApp. This creates a single view for the user interface.

2. Click the Main.storyboard file in the Navigator pane. Xcode displays the single view.

3. Click the Library icon to open the Object Library window.

4. Drag and drop a button and a Picker View anywhere on the view as shown in Figure 12-9.

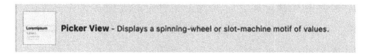

Figure 12-9. *The Picker View in the Object Library window*

5. Choose Editor ➤ Resolve Auto Layout Issues ➤ Set to Suggested Constraints in the bottom half of the submenu. Xcode adds constraints to your button and Picker View.

6. Choose View ➤ Assistant Editor ➤ Show Assistant Editor. Xcode displays the Main.storyboard and ViewController.swift file side by side.

7. Edit the class ViewController line as follows:

```
class ViewController: UIViewController, UIPickerViewDataSource,
UIPickerViewDelegate {
```

This makes the ViewController.swift file the Picker View's data source and delegate.

8. Move the mouse pointer over the Picker View, hold down the Control key, and Ctrl-drag from the Picker View to the ViewController.swift file underneath the "class ViewController" line.

9.   Release the Control key and the left mouse button. A popup
     window appears.

10. Click in the Name text field, type **myPicker**, and click the Connect
     button. Xcode creates an IBOutlet variable as follows:

```
@IBOutlet var myPicker: UIDatePicker!
```

11. Underneath the IBOutlet add the following line to define a
     variable to hold an array of strings:

```
var pickerData: [String] = [String]()
```

12. Edit the viewDidLoad method as follows:

```
override func viewDidLoad() {
    super.viewDidLoad()
    myPicker.delegate = self
    myPicker.dataSource = self
    pickerData = ["cat", "dog", "hamster", "lizard", "parrot",
    "goldfish"]
    // Do any additional setup after loading the view,
    typically from a nib.
}
```

These lines of code declare the ViewController.swift file to be both
the delegate and data source for the Picker View. Then it defines
an array of strings to store in the pickerData variable.

13. Underneath the viewDidLoad method, add the following function
     to define how many components will appear in the Picker View.
     Since we're only displaying a single wheel of options, the number
     of components is just one:

```
func numberOfComponents(in pickerView: UIPickerView) -> Int {
    return 1
}
```

14. Add another function underneath to define how many items will appear in the Picker View. This number can be found by using the .count method on the pickerData array:

```
func pickerView(_ pickerView: UIPickerView,
numberOfRowsInComponent component: Int) -> Int {
    return pickerData.count
}
```

15. Add a third function underneath to display data in the Picker View:

```
func pickerView(_ pickerView: UIPickerView, titleForRow row:
Int, forComponent component:
        Int) -> String? {
        return pickerData[row]
}
```

16. Move the mouse pointer over the button, hold down the Control key, and Ctrl-drag from the button to the ViewController.swift file above the last curly bracket at the bottom of the file.

17. Release the Control key and the left mouse button. A popup window appears.

18. Click in the Name text field, type **buttonTapped**, click in the Type popup menu and choose UIButton, and click the Connect button. Xcode creates an IBAction method.

19. Edit this buttonTapped IBAction method as follows:

```
@IBAction func buttonTapped(_ sender: UIButton) {
    let pickerIndex = myPicker.selectedRow(inComponent: 0)
    let alert = UIAlertController(title: "Your Choice",
    message: "\(pickerData[pickerIndex])", preferredStyle:
    .alert)

    let okAction = UIAlertAction(title: "OK", style: .default,
    handler: { action -> Void in
        //Just dismiss the action sheet
```

```
    })
    alert.addAction(okAction)

    self.present(alert, animated: true, completion: nil)
}
```

The first line in the buttonTapped IBAction method retrieves the index number of the choice currently displayed in the Picker View where the first item has an index of 0, the second item has an index of 1, and so on. Then it uses this index value to determine which item in the pickerData array to display in an alert controller.

The entire ViewController.swift file should look like this:

```
import UIKit

class ViewController: UIViewController, UIPickerViewDataSource,
UIPickerViewDelegate {

    @IBOutlet var myPicker: UIPickerView!
    var pickerData: [String] = [String]()

    override func viewDidLoad() {
        super.viewDidLoad()
        myPicker.delegate = self
        myPicker.dataSource = self
        pickerData = ["cat", "dog", "hamster", "lizard", "parrot",
        "goldfish"]
        // Do any additional setup after loading the view,
        typically from a nib.
    }

    func numberOfComponents(in pickerView: UIPickerView) -> Int {
        return 1
    }

    func pickerView(_ pickerView: UIPickerView,
    numberOfRowsInComponent component: Int) -> Int {
        return pickerData.count
    }
```

```swift
    func pickerView(_ pickerView: UIPickerView, titleForRow row:
    Int, forComponent component:
        Int) -> String? {
        return pickerData[row]
    }

    @IBAction func buttonTapped(_ sender: UIButton) {
        let pickerIndex = myPicker.selectedRow(inComponent: 0)
        let alert = UIAlertController(title: "Your Choice", message:
        "\(pickerData[pickerIndex])", preferredStyle: .alert)

        let okAction = UIAlertAction(title: "OK", style: .default,
        handler: { action -> Void in
            //Just dismiss the action sheet
        })
        alert.addAction(okAction)

        self.present(alert, animated: true, completion: nil)
    }
}
```

20. Click the Run button or choose Product ➤ Run. The Simulator
     screen appears as shown in Figure 12-10.

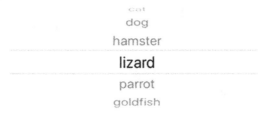

Figure 12-10. *The Picker View on the app*

21. Spin the Picker View and choose an option.

22. Click the button. An alert controller appears, displaying the option
     you chose in the Picker View.

23. Click the button to dismiss the alert controller.

24. Repeat steps 20–22 and choose a different option in the Picker View.

25. Choose Simulator ➤ Quit Simulator to return to Xcode.

Displaying a Multiple-Component Picker View

If you look at the Date Picker, it displays separate wheels or components for the day, hour, minute, and whether it's AM or PM. The simple Picker View we created in the previous example just displayed a single wheel or component listing different types of pets.

For each component you want to display in a Picker View, you need to define a separate data source. Then you need to define how many total components you want the Picker View to display (such as two or three) along with displaying all components and storing the data in each component.

To see how to create a Picker View that consists of three components, follow these steps:

1. Create a new iOS project using the Single View App template (see Chapter 1) and name this new project ThreePickerApp. This creates a single view for the user interface.

2. Click the Main.storyboard file in the Navigator pane. Xcode displays the single view.

3. Click the Library icon to open the Object Library window.

4. Drag and drop a button and a Picker View anywhere on the view (see Figure 12-9).

5. Choose Editor ➤ Resolve Auto Layout Issues ➤ Set to Suggested Constraints in the bottom half of the submenu. Xcode adds constraints to your button and Picker View.

6. Edit the class ViewController line as follows:

    class ViewController: UIViewController, UIPickerViewDataSource, UIPickerViewDelegate {

    This makes the ViewController.swift file the Picker View's data source and delegate.

7. Choose View ➤ Assistant Editor ➤ Show Assistant Editor. Xcode displays the Main.storyboard and ViewController.swift file side by side.

8. Move the mouse pointer over the Picker View, hold down
    the Control key, and Ctrl-drag from the Picker View to the
    ViewController.swift file underneath the "class ViewController" line.

9. Release the Control key and the left mouse button. A popup
    window appears.

10. Click in the Name text field, type **myPicker**, and click the Connect
    button. Xcode creates an IBOutlet variable as follows:

```
@IBOutlet var myPicker: UIDatePicker!
```

11. Underneath the IBOutlet add the following three lines to define
    three variables to hold an array of strings:

```
var componentOne: [String] = [String]()
var componentTwo: [String] = [String]()
var componentThree: [String] = [String]()
```

12. Edit the viewDidLoad method as follows:

```
override func viewDidLoad() {
    super.viewDidLoad()
    myPicker.delegate = self
    myPicker.dataSource = self
    componentOne = ["cat", "dog", "hamster", "lizard",
    "parrot", "goldfish"]
    componentTwo = ["house", "apartment", "condo", "RV"]
    componentThree = ["indoor", "outdoor"]
    // Do any additional setup after loading the view,
    typically from a nib.
}
```

These lines of code declare the ViewController.swift file to be both
the delegate and data source for the Picker View. Then it defines
three arrays of strings that will appear in each component of the
Picker View.

13. Underneath the viewDidLoad method, add the following function
    to define how many components will appear in the Picker View.
    Since we're only displaying a single wheel of options, the number
    of components is just one:

```
func numberOfComponents(in pickerView: UIPickerView) -> Int {
    return 3
}
```

14. Add another function underneath to define how many items will
    appear in the Picker View. This number can be found by using
    the .count method on the three different arrays, so we need a
    switch statement to define how many elements appear in each
    component. The first component will display different pets
    ("hamster"), the second component will display different homes
    ("apartment"), and the third component will display different
    locations ("indoor"):

```
func pickerView(_ pickerView: UIPickerView,
numberOfRowsInComponent component: Int) -> Int {
    switch component {
        case 0: return componentOne.count
        case 1: return componentTwo.count
    default: return componentThree.count
    }
}
```

15. Add a third function underneath to display data in the Picker
    View where the first component (0) displays pets, the second
    component (1) displays homes, and the third component (2)
    displays locations:

```
func pickerView(_ pickerView: UIPickerView, titleForRow row:
Int, forComponent component:
    Int) -> String? {
    switch component {
        case 0: return componentOne[row]
        case 1: return componentTwo[row]
```

```
        default: return componentThree[row]
        }
    }
```

16. Move the mouse pointer over the button, hold down the Control key, and Ctrl-drag from the button to the ViewController.swift file above the last curly bracket at the bottom of the file.

17. Release the Control key and the left mouse button. A popup window appears.

18. Click in the Name text field, type **buttonTapped**, click in the Type popup menu and choose UIButton, and click the Connect button. Xcode creates an IBAction method.

19. Edit this buttonTapped IBAction method as follows:

```
@IBAction func buttonTapped(_ sender: UIButton) {
    let petIndex = myPicker.selectedRow(inComponent: 0)
    let homeIndex = myPicker.selectedRow(inComponent: 1)
    let placeIndex = myPicker.selectedRow(inComponent: 2)

    let alert = UIAlertController(title: "Your
    Choice", message: "\(componentOne[petIndex]) \
    (componentTwo[homeIndex]) \(componentThree[placeIndex])",
    preferredStyle: .alert)

    let okAction = UIAlertAction(title: "OK", style: .default,
    handler: { action -> Void in
        //Just dismiss the action sheet
    })
    alert.addAction(okAction)

    self.present(alert, animated: true, completion: nil)
}
```

The three lines in the buttonTapped IBAction method retrieves the index number of the choice currently displayed in the Picker View where the first item has an index of 0, the second item has an index of 1, and so on. Then it uses this index value to determine which item in the three different arrays to display in an alert controller.

The entire ViewController.swift file should look like this:

```swift
import UIKit

class ViewController: UIViewController, UIPickerViewDataSource,
UIPickerViewDelegate {

    @IBOutlet var myPicker: UIPickerView!
    var componentOne: [String] = [String]()
    var componentTwo: [String] = [String]()
    var componentThree: [String] = [String]()

    override func viewDidLoad() {
        super.viewDidLoad()
        myPicker.delegate = self
        myPicker.dataSource = self
        componentOne = ["cat", "dog", "hamster", "lizard",
        "parrot", "goldfish"]
        componentTwo = ["house", "apartment", "condo", "RV"]
        componentThree = ["indoor", "outdoor"]
        // Do any additional setup after loading the view,
        // typically from a nib.
    }

    func numberOfComponents(in pickerView: UIPickerView) -> Int {
        return 3
    }

    func pickerView(_ pickerView: UIPickerView,
    numberOfRowsInComponent component: Int) -> Int {
        switch component {
            case 0: return componentOne.count
            case 1: return componentTwo.count
        default: return componentThree.count
        }
    }
```

```
func pickerView(_ pickerView: UIPickerView, titleForRow row:
Int, forComponent component:
    Int) -> String? {
    switch component {
        case 0: return componentOne[row]
        case 1: return componentTwo[row]
    default: return componentThree[row]
    }
}

@IBAction func buttonTapped(_ sender: UIButton) {
    let petIndex = myPicker.selectedRow(inComponent: 0)
    let homeIndex = myPicker.selectedRow(inComponent: 1)
    let placeIndex = myPicker.selectedRow(inComponent: 2)

    let alert = UIAlertController(title: "Your
    Choice", message: "\(componentOne[petIndex]) \
    (componentTwo[homeIndex]) \(componentThree[placeIndex])",
    preferredStyle: .alert)

    let okAction = UIAlertAction(title: "OK", style: .default,
    handler: { action -> Void in
        //Just dismiss the action sheet
    })
    alert.addAction(okAction)

    self.present(alert, animated: true, completion: nil)
    }

}
```

20. Click the Run button or choose Product ➤ Run. The Simulator
    screen appears as shown in Figure 12-11.

cat

dog   house   indoor

hamster   apartment   outdoor

lizard   condo

parrot   RV

goldfish

Figure 12-11. *A Picker View with three components*

21. Spin the Picker View and choose an option from each wheel or
     component such as hamster, apartment, outdoor.

22. Click the button. An alert controller appears, displaying all the
     options you chose in the Picker View.

23. Click the button to dismiss the alert controller.

24. Repeat steps 20–22 and choose different options in the Picker View

25. Choose Simulator ➤ Quit Simulator to return to Xcode.

Summary

Alerts display information either in the middle of the screen (.alert) or at the bottom of
the screen (.actionSheet). An alert can display a title and a message in a smaller font
underneath, along with at least one button to dismiss the alert. However, an alert can
display multiple buttons and even a text field as well.

Depending on which button a user taps, the app can respond differently. If an alert
displays a text field, you can customize the text field's appearance and behavior and
store the contents of the text field to use or manipulate later. Alerts interrupt the user by
displaying important information that the user needs to know right away.

When your app needs to give users a limited range of options, you can use a Date
Picker or a Picker View. A Date Picker lets the user choose different dates and times.
You can define the format of the date and time retrieved to be short or long, depending
on how you want this information displayed. A Picker View lets you define the type
of choices to appear and display multiple components or wheels so users can select
multiple options.

Use alerts when you need to display information to the user and get immediate
feedback. Use a Date Picker or a Picker View when you need to restrict a user's choices to
a limited range of valid options.

CHAPTER 13

Constraints and Stack Views

Since the iPhone and iPad come in different screen sizes, every iOS app needs to adapt to these different screen sizes depending on the type of iOS device it's running on. To define the position and spacing of different user interface objects, you can use constraints.

Constraints can define the following:

- Position (such as the center of the screen)

- Size (such as the width or height of an object)

- Distance (such as the space between two objects)

Without constraints, objects on the user interface might look good on one size iOS screen but look completely skewered on another one. That's why you need constraints on all objects placed on the user interface.

The simplest way to add constraints is to let Xcode do it for you. However, you may need to modify constraints since Xcode may not always add constraints accurately. You can add, delete, and modify constraints until your user interface looks perfectly on all different size iOS screens.

If you have multiple objects on a user interface, adding multiple constraints can be clumsy, especially if you need to rearrange objects. To simplify putting constraints on individual objects, you can organize objects into stacks. This lets you move groups of objects around and place constraints on that group rather than on all individual objects in that group.

Both constraints and stack views make it easy to create and organize objects on the user interface so they appear correctly no matter what iOS screen size the app runs on.

341

© Wallace Wang 2019
W. Wang, *Beginning iPhone Development with Swift 5*, https://doi.org/10.1007/978-1-4842-4865-2_13

Understanding Constraints

Constraints define a position, size, or distance using three criteria:

- Constant – Defines the numeric value of the constraint

- Priority – Defines which constraints are more important than others ranging from a required (1000) to high (750) to low (250)

- Multiplier – Multiplies the constant to define the total value of the constraint

The three choices for a constant are a numeric value such as 37, a Standard Value, or a Canvas Value as shown in Figure 13-1.

Figure 13-1. *The three options for defining a constant value in a constraint*

A numeric value defines a specific value such as 12 or 84. When you create constraints, Xcode uses numeric values.

A Standard Value uses Xcode's recommended value. Because your app may run on different size iOS screens, Standard Values are generally the safest option to choose.

A Canvas Value is similar to a specific numeric value except it's tied to the current iOS screen size of your storyboard. That means if your app runs on a different screen size, the constraint may not keep objects the proper distance or position.

Note   As a general rule in programming, it's usually a good idea to avoid relying on specific values known as "magic numbers". A "magic number" appears as an abstract numeric value that does not explain what it means or how the programmer arrived at that value. In most cases, use Standard Values for constraints.

When defining values for a constraint, there are three choices:

- Equal (=) – The constraint must exactly equal a specific value.

- Less than or equal (≤) – The constraint can be less than or equal to a specific value.

- Greater than or equal (≥) – The constraint can be greater than or equal to a specific value.

By defining a constraint to be less than or equal or greater than or equal to a value, you allow more flexibility for the constraint to still work even if screen sizes or orientation changes.

The priority defines the importance of a constraint. By default, every constraint is assigned the required (1000) priority. However when you add multiple constraints, two or more constraints might conflict. For example, one constraint can define that a button appears 97 points from the left edge and a second constraint might define the button to appear 232 points from the right edge.

This may work just fine when an iPhone appears in portrait mode, but when tilted on its side in landscape mode, maintaining a distance of 97 points from the left and 232 points from the right means the button must stretch in width to satisfy both constraints. If the button's width is also constrained to a certain size such as 46 points, then it will be impossible for all three constraints to work as shown in Figure 13-2.

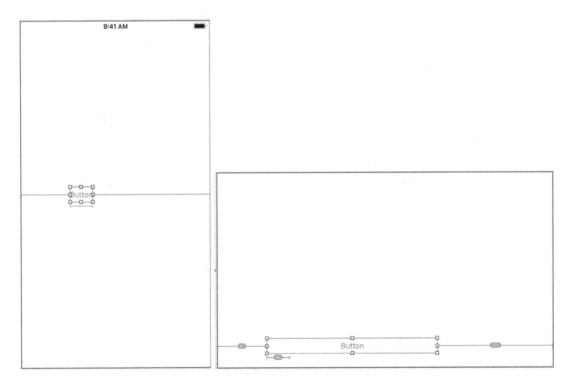

Figure 13-2. *Constraints can conflict with each other in different orientations or screen sizes*

To avoid multiple constraints conflicting, you can assign different priority values to each constraint. The most important constraints get a higher value (such as 1000), while other less important constraints get lower values (such as 750 or 250). Now Xcode first follows the highest priority constraints before trying to follow lower priority constraints. If the lower priority constraints cannot be satisfied, then the higher priority constraints take precedence and the lower priority constraint gets ignored.

The multiplier can define a percentage relationship between two objects. The default multiplier value is 1, but you can change this to make the multiplier value less than or greater than 1 such as 0.5 or 1.5.

Objects typically need two or more constraints to accurately define their size and position on a user interface. When you add constraints to an object, Xcode uses colors to let you know how effective your constraints are. The meanings of these different colors are

- Blue – The object has all the necessary constraints to accurately define its size and position on the user interface.

- Orange – The object does not have enough constraints to define its size and position on the user interface.

- Red – The object has conflicting constraints that either need to be modified or deleted.

When you add constraints, Xcode also displays a frame around your selected object. That frame normally appears around the border of an object, but if you apply constraints and then move the object, you'll see the frame as a dotted-line rectangle. The frame shows where an object will appear even if the object appears somewhere else on the user interface as shown in Figure 13-3.

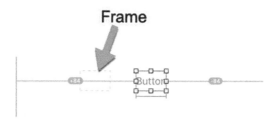

Figure 13-3. *Frames show where an object will appear because of its constraints*

To create a constraint on an object, select the object and then choose one of the following methods:

- Choose Editor ➤ Resolve Auto Layout Issues and choose an option to let Xcode define constraints automatically.

- Click the Align or Add new constraints icon at the bottom of the Xcode window.

- Ctrl-drag from an object to another object.

The Resolve Auto Layout Issues submenu displays identical commands in a top and bottom half as shown Figure 13-4. The top submenu affects only the selected object, while the bottom submenu affects all objects in the currently displayed view.

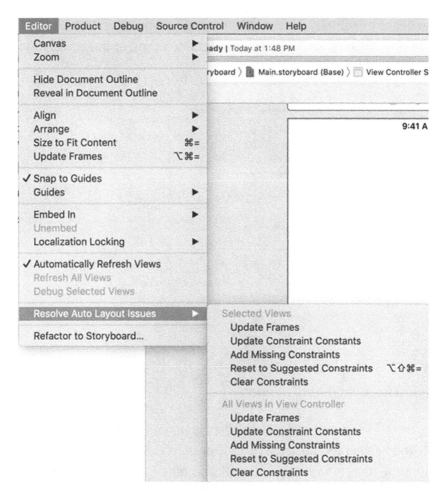

Figure 13-4. *The Resolve Auto Layout submenu*

The available options on the Resolve Auto Layout Issues submenu include

- Update Frames – Used to move an object to the location of its frame

- Update Constraint Constants – Used to move the frame and all constraints to the current position of the object

- Add Missing Constraints – Adds new constraints to any existing constraints on an object

- Reset to Suggested Constraints – Deletes any existing constraints and adds new constraints that Xcode thinks the object needs

- Clear Constraints – Deletes all constraints on the object

Clicking the Align icon displays a popup window that lets you define the position of an object such as horizontally or vertically in a view. If you select two or more objects, you can align one object to another object by its sides, tops, or bottoms as shown in Figure 13-5.

Figure 13-5. *The Align popup window*

Clicking the Add new constraints icon displays a popup window that lets you define sizes (width and height) and distances to nearby objects as shown in Figure 13-6. If you select two or more objects, you can define all selected objects to have the same width or height as well.

Add New Constraints
icon

Figure 13-6. *The Add new constraints popup window*

A third way to add constraints to an object is to Ctrl-drag from an object to a screen edge or onto another object. When you Ctrl-drag and release the Control key and the left mouse button, a popup window appears letting you choose different constraints as shown in Figure 13-7. The available constraints that appear in this popup menu differ depending on where you Ctrl-drag.

Figure 13-7. *A popup menu appears when you Ctrl-drag to create a constraint*

To see how to create, edit, and delete a constraint and use frames, follow these steps:

1. Create a new iOS project using the Single View App template (see Chapter 1) and name this new project ConstraintApp. This creates a single view for the user interface.

2. Click the Main.storyboard file in the Navigator pane. Xcode displays the single view.

3. Click the Library icon to open the Object Library window.

4. Drag and drop a button and a label anywhere on the view. Make sure the button appears lower than the label.

5. Move the mouse pointer over the button, hold down the Control key, and Ctrl-drag the mouse until the mouse pointer appears over the label.

6. Release the Control key and the left mouse button. A popup window appears (see Figure 13-7).

7. Choose Vertical Spacing. Xcode displays this constraint in red to let you know there aren't enough constraints to properly define the button's position on the user interface.

8. Click the button to select it.

9. Click the Add new constraints icon at the bottom of the Xcode window. A popup window appears.

10. Click the two dotted lines that represent a constraint to the right and bottom of the screen as shown in Figure 13-8.

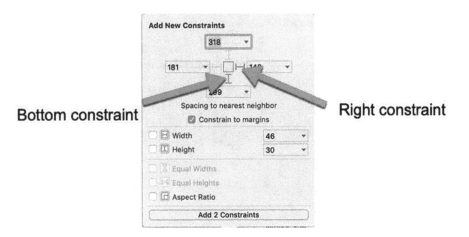

Figure 13-8. *Defining constraints to the right and bottom of the screen*

11. Click the Add 2 Constraints button. Xcode adds two more constraints. Notice that all constraints now appear in blue, which means you have enough constraints on the button to properly place it no matter what iOS device the app runs on.

12. Move the mouse pointer over the button and drag the button to a new position on the user interface. Notice that Xcode now displays a dotted rectangle to define the frame. The frame shows where the button will appear when the app runs, even though the button appears somewhere else as shown in Figure 13-9.

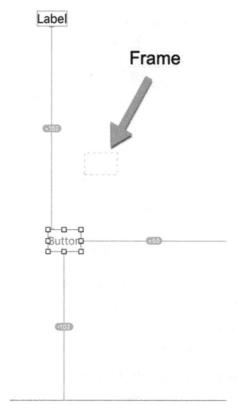

Figure 13-9. *Frames show where an object will appear based on its constraints*

13. Choose Editor ➤ Resolve Auto Layout Issues ➤ Update Frames. Xcode moves the button to the frame's position.

14. Choose Edit ➤ Undo or press Command + Z. Xcode moves the button back to its previous position, displaying the frame again.

15. Choose Editor ➤ Resolve Auto Layout Issues ➤ Update Constraint Constants. Xcode keeps the button in its current position and changes its constraints to display the button at its current location.

Note   The Update Frames command moves an object back to its frame, while the Update Constraint Constants command moves the frame and all constraints to the object's current position.

---

16. Hold down the SHIFT key and click the button and label to select both of them.

17. Click the Align icon at the bottom of the Xcode window. A popup window appears.

18. Select the Leading Edges check box (leading edges define the left side of an object while trailing edges define the right side of an object) as shown in Figure 13-10.

19. Click the Add 1 Constraint button. Notice that Xcode aligns the label and button by their leading (left) edges.

Figure 13-10. *Aligning two objects by leading edges*

20. Click the button to select it and choose View ➤ Inspectors ➤ Show Size Inspector, or click the Size Inspector icon in the upper right corner of the Xcode window. A list of constraints appears in the Constraints category as shown in Figure 13-11.

Figure 13-11. *Constraints appear in the Size Inspector pane*

21. Click the Edit button that appears on the right side of every constraint. A popup window appears, listing the constant, priority, and multiplier values for the constraint as shown in Figure 13-12.

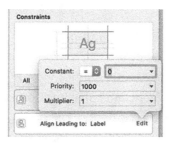

Figure 13-12. *Editing a constraint*

22. Click in the Constant popup menu and you can define an =, ≤, or ≥.

23. Click in the downward-pointing arrow that appears to the right of the text field displaying a value. A popup menu appears, letting you choose a Standard Value or a Canvas Value.

24. Click in the downward-pointing arrow that appears to the right of the Priority text field displaying a value. A popup menu appears, letting you choose different priorities. (You can always type a value in this text field.)

25. Click the button to display all constraints.

26. Click a constraint to select it, then press BACKSPACE or DELETE to delete that constraint. This lets you delete individual constraints.

27. Choose Editor ➤ Resolve Auto Layout Issues ➤ Clear Constraints at the bottom of the submenu. This deletes constraints for all objects on the view.

In this exercise, you learned how to add constraints, edit them, and delete them. Every user interface you design must have constraints defined to make sure objects appear correctly on the user interface no matter what size screen the app runs on.

Using Stack Views

When you have multiple objects on a user interface, it can be troublesome defining constraints for all of them. Even worse, once you define constraints for multiple objects, you might later want to move one or more objects to a different location. That means redefining constraints all over again.

To use a stack view, just drag and drop a stack view from the Object Library window onto a view. Then drag and drop other objects into the stack view. The stack view insures that objects align vertically or horizontally, so you just need to add constraints to the stack view itself. This eliminates the need to add constraints to the objects inside the stack view.

Some of the properties you can modify in a stack view include

- Axis – Displays objects vertically or horizontally

- Alignment – Defines how objects appear inside a stack view with the following options: Fill, Top, Center, Bottom, First Baseline, and Last Baseline

- Distribution – Defines how objects appear inside a stack view with the following options: Fill, Fill Equally, Fill Proportionally, Equal Spacing, and Equal Centering

- Spacing – Defines the distance between objects inside the stack view

Changing the axis lets you define how objects appear inside a stack view. Horizontally displays objects in a row. Vertically displays objects in a column as shown in Figure 13-13. Although the Object Library window offers Horizontal and Vertical Stack Views, you can simply modify the Axis property to change either stack view to act differently.

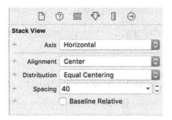

Figure 13-13. *The Attributes Inspector pane for a stack view*

The Alignment property defines how objects appear arranged in a stack view:

- Fill – Expands the height (horizontal stack) or width (vertical stack) of all objects to match the tallest or widest object

- Center – Centers all objects horizontally or vertically

- Leading (vertical stacks only) – Aligns all objects to the left side of the stack view

- Trailing (vertical stacks only) – Aligns all objects to the right side of the stack view

- Top (horizontal stacks only) – Aligns all objects to the top of the stack view

- Bottom (horizontal stacks only) – Aligns all objects to the bottom of the stack view

- First Baseline (horizontal stacks only) – Aligns all objects by the bottom of the first line of text (First Baseline) as shown in Figure 13-14

- Last Baseline (horizontal stacks only) – Aligns all objects by the bottom of the last line of text (First Baseline) as shown in Figure 13-15

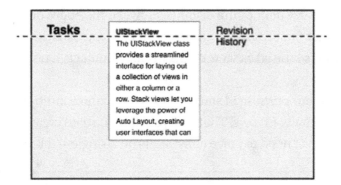

Figure 13-14. *The First Baseline is the bottom of the first line of text*

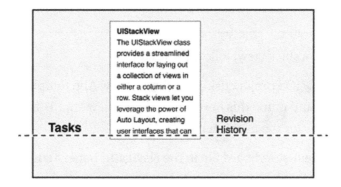

Figure 13-15. *The Last Baseline is the bottom of the last line of text*

The Distribution property defines how objects resize themselves within a stack view:

- Fill – The stack view expands or shrinks to make sure all objects are visible.

- Fill Equally – Resizes all objects so they are the same width (horizontal stack) or height (vertical stack) based on the widest or tallest object.

- Fill Proportionally – Resizes the stack view to expand or shrink so all objects inside remain their original size.

- Equal Spacing – Adds an equal amount of space between all objects in the stack view.

- Equal Centering – Maintains equal spacing between the centers of neighboring objects in addition to maintaining the value defined by the spacing property to define distances between neighboring objects.

The Spacing property defines the distance between the edges of neighboring objects in a stack view. Rather than resize a stack view directly, you can resize it by modifying its various properties so the stack view conforms to the objects it holds with no wasted space at the ends.

Ultimately, the main purpose of stack views is to organize multiple objects vertically in columns or horizontally in rows. That way you don't have to create constraints on multiple objects but just need to place constraints on a single stack view.

Note   Unlike other objects that let you define the height and width, stack views automatically adjust their height and width based on the objects stored inside that stack view.

To see how to use a stack view, follow these steps:

1. Create a new iOS project using the Single View App template (see Chapter 1) and name this new project StackViewApp. This creates a single view for the user interface.

2. Click the Main.storyboard file in the Navigator pane. Xcode displays the single view.

3. Click the Library icon to open the Object Library window.

4. Drag and drop a horizontal or a vertical stack view on the view as shown in Figure 13-16. Although a stack view appears as a large rectangle, its size will adjust based on the number and types of objects you put inside that stack view.

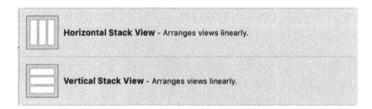

Figure 13-16.   *The Horizontal and Vertical Stack Views in the Object Library window*

5. Click the Library icon to open the Object Library window, and drag and drop the following items into the stack view:

- Label

- Button

- Text field

Because the stack view automatically adjusts its size when you add any object to it, you can easily drag and drop one object directly onto the stack view displayed on the user interface. Afterward, you'll need to add any additional objects onto the stack view by dragging and dropping them underneath the stack view in the Document Outline as shown in Figure 13-17.

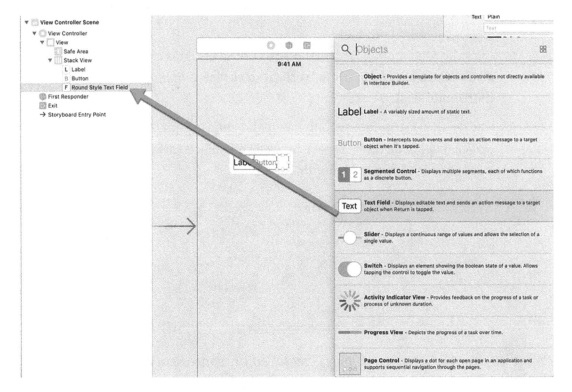

Figure 13-17. *Dragging and dropping objects into the Document Outline*

6. Click the stack view in the Document Outline to select it.

7. Move the mouse pointer over the stack view until the mouse pointer turns into a hand icon. Then drag the mouse to move the stack view. Notice that moving the stack view also moves all objects together in a group.

8. Choose View ➤ Inspectors ➤ Show Attributes Inspector, or click the Attributes Inspector icon in the upper right corner of the Xcode window. The Attributes Inspector pane for the stack view appears (see Figure 13-13).

9. Click in the Axis popup menu and switch back and forth between horizontal and vertical. Whether you start with a horizontal or vertical stack view, you can always modify its orientation later just by changing its Axis property.

10. Make sure the Axis property is vertical. Then click in the Spacing text field and type 40.

11. Click the Alignment popup menu and choose Fill. This causes all objects to expand in width (vertical stack views) or height (horizontal stack views).

12. Click in the Distribution popup menu and choose Equal Spacing. Notice that Xcode creates space between all objects inside the stack view as shown in Figure 13-18.

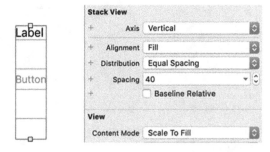

Figure 13-18. *The Spacing property creates empty space between objects in a stack view*

13. Click the Alignment popup menu and choose Center. Notice that the stack view now defines its width based on the largest object as shown in Figure 13-19.

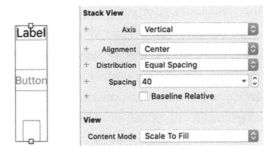

Figure 13-19. *Center alignment defines the stack width based on the widest object*

14. Click the Alignment popup menu and choose Leading. Notice that the stack view aligns all objects on the left side.

15. Click the Alignment popup menu and choose Trailing. Notice that the stack view aligns all objects on the right side.

16. Click in the Axis popup menu and choose Horizontal.

17. Click in the Alignment popup menu and choose Top. Notice that the stack view aligns all objects by their tops.

18. Click in the Alignment popup menu and choose Bottom. Notice that the stack view aligns all objects by their bottoms.

19. Click in the Distribution popup menu and choose Fill Equally. Notice that all objects inside the stack view now appear with the same width. Experiment with different options to see how they affect the appearance of objects inside the stack view.

Once you have defined the appearance of objects inside a stack view, then you can apply constraints on the stack view. Stack views let you organize objects in rows or columns without applying constraints on each object individually.

Summary

Designing a user interface involves placing objects on a view. However, the exact position of these objects can change depending on the screen size that the app runs on. If you design a user interface for a larger screen, then it might look too cramped when viewed on a smaller screen. If you design a user interface for a small screen, it might look empty and out of balance on a larger screen.

To make sure a user interface looks good on all size screens, you need to add constraints. Constraints can define an object's size (width and height), position, or distance to nearby objects. You can define specific values and relationships such as equal, less than or equal to, or greater than or equal to. When adding constraints, Xcode uses colors to let you know if you have enough constraints (blue), do not have enough constraints (orange), or have conflicting constraints (red).

At any time, you can add, delete, or modify a constraint. Since applying constraints to multiple objects can be troublesome, you can group objects into vertical columns or horizontal rows by storing them inside stack views. Then you can apply constraints to the stack view.

Constraints and stack views provide two ways to design your user interface and insure that they look good no matter what screen size your app runs on.

CHAPTER 14

Using Table Views

Table views are one of the most common user interface objects for displaying large amounts of information in a list of rows. The Mail and Photos apps use table views to let users scroll through information. Table views appear to create an endless list because the moment the user scrolls up or down, new data constantly appears to take its place. Table views consist of cells that contain one or more objects such as labels or image views as shown in Figure 14-1.

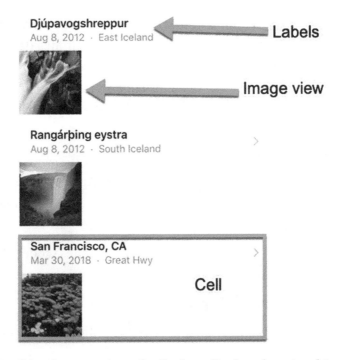

Figure 14-1. *A table view consists of cells that display data in objects such as labels and image view*

To create a table view, you can drag a table view from the Object Library window and drop it on a view. Another alternative is to drag and drop a Table View Controller from

361

© Wallace Wang 2019
W. Wang, *Beginning iPhone Development with Swift 5*, https://doi.org/10.1007/978-1-4842-4865-2_14

the Object Library window and place it as part of the storyboard. A Table View Controller is nothing more than a View Controller with a table view on it.

To use a table view, you need to do the following:

- Define a cell that contains the information you want the table view to display.

- Define a data source that will put information into each cell of a table view.

- Define a delegate .swift file that contains methods to define the number of sections and rows in addition to defining the cell that will make up the table view.

Creating a Simple Table View

If you have an existing view, you can drag and drop a Table View onto that view. Once you have a table view, you must fill the table view with data (from a data source) and define how many sections and rows the table will hold. Data can come from anywhere but should consist of the same number of items. For example, if you want a table view to display names and pictures, then each chunk of data should contain text (for a name) and an image (for a picture).

To see how to create and fill a table view, follow these steps:

1. Create a new iOS project using the Single View App template (see Chapter 1) and name this new project TableViewApp. This creates a single view for the user interface.

2. Click the Main.storyboard file in the Navigator pane. Xcode displays the single view.

3. Click the Library icon to open the Object Library window.

4. Drag and drop a table view, as shown in Figure 14-2, anywhere on the view.

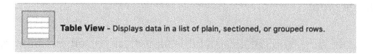

Figure 14-2. *A table view in the Object Library window*

5. Resize the table view so it fills the entire screen.

6. Choose Editor ➤ Resolve Auto Layout Issues ➤ Reset to Suggested
    Constraints. Xcode adds constraints to the table view as shown in
    Figure 14-3.

Figure 14-3. *The table view with constraints*

7. Choose View ➤ Assistant Editor ➤ Show Assistant Editor,
    or click the Assistant Editor icon in the upper right corner of
    the Xcode window.

8. Move the mouse pointer over the table view, hold down the
    Control key, and Ctrl-drag under the "class ViewController" line in
    the ViewController.swift file.

9. Release the Control key and the left mouse button. A popup
    window appears.

10. Click in the Name text field, type **petTable**, and click the Connect button. Xcode creates an IBOutlet as follows:

```
@IBOutlet var petTable: UITableView!
```

11. Choose View ➤ Standard Editor ➤ Show Standard Editor, or click the Standard Editor icon in the upper right corner of the Xcode window.

12. Click the ViewController.swift file in the Navigator pane.

13. Modify the class ViewController line by adding UITableViewDelegate, UITableViewDataSource as follows:

```
class ViewController: UIViewController, UITableViewDelegate,
UITableViewDataSource {
```

The purpose of this code is to identify the ViewController.swift file as both the delegate and data source for the table view.

14. Underneath the class ViewController line, add the following array:

```
let petArray = ["cat", "dog", "parakeet", "parrot", "canary",
"finch", "tropical fish", "goldfish", "sea horses", "hamster",
"gerbil", "rabbit", "turtle", "snake", "lizard", "hermit crab"]
```

15. Underneath this array, add the following line:

```
let cellID = "cellID"
```

The purpose of this code is to create an arbitrary constant name for a cell. A table view consists of rows of cells, so we need to identify the cells for storing data in later.

16. Modify the viewDidLoad method as follows:

```
override func viewDidLoad() {
    super.viewDidLoad()
    petTable.dataSource = self
    petTable.delegate = self
    // Do any additional setup after loading the view,
    typically from a nib.
}
```

The purpose of this code is to define that the table (IBOutlet petTable) gets its data from the ViewController.swift file that it's stored in (self). In addition, the delegate is defined as the ViewController.swift file (self). This means the ViewController.swift file needs to contain functions that define how many rows the table needs and where to find its data, which is the petArray.

17. Add the following function underneath the viewDidLoad method:

```
func tableView(_ tableView: UITableView, numberOfRowsInSection
section: Int) -> Int {
    return petArray.count
}
```

This code defines how many rows are needed in the table. The number of rows is defined by the total number of items stored in the petArray.

18. Add the following function underneath the viewDidLoad method:

```
func tableView(_ tableView: UITableView, cellForRowAt
indexPath: IndexPath) -> UITableViewCell {
    var cell = tableView.dequeueReusableCell(withIdentifier:
    cellID)
    if (cell == nil) {
        cell = UITableViewCell(
            style: UITableViewCell.CellStyle.default,
            reuseIdentifier: cellID)
    }
    cell?.textLabel?.text = petArray[indexPath.row]
    return cell!
}
```

This function runs whenever the table view needs to put data in its rows. This can occur the first time the table view appears as well as when the user scrolls up or down to display data previously hidden because there weren't enough rows to display all of the data at once. Since each row in the table view is defined by a cell, it needs to create a cell with a name:

```
var cell = tableView.dequeueReusableCell(withIdentifier: cellID)
```

If a cell is empty, then the if statement defines the cell's style and gives it the arbitrary cellID name to identify it:

```
if (cell == nil) {
    cell = UITableViewCell(
        style: UITableViewCell.CellStyle.default,
        reuseIdentifier: cellID)
}
```

Next, it takes data from the petArray, and based on the cell's position in the table view (its row number), it stores that data in the text property of the cell's textLabel. Then it returns the cell so it appears in the table view:

```
cell?.textLabel?.text = petArray[indexPath.row]
return cell!
```

The complete ViewController.swift file should look like this:

```
import UIKit

class ViewController: UIViewController, UITableViewDelegate,
UITableViewDataSource {

    @IBOutlet var petTable: UITableView!

    let petArray = ["cat", "dog", "parakeet", "parrot", "canary",
    "finch", "tropical fish", "goldfish", "sea horses", "hamster",
    "gerbil", "rabbit", "turtle", "snake", "lizard", "hermit crab"]
```

```
let cellID = "cellID"

override func viewDidLoad() {
    super.viewDidLoad()
    petTable.dataSource = self
    petTable.delegate = self
    // Do any additional setup after loading the view,
    typically from a nib.
}

func tableView(_ tableView: UITableView, numberOfRowsInSection
section: Int) -> Int {
    return petArray.count
}


func tableView(_ tableView: UITableView, cellForRowAt
indexPath: IndexPath) -> UITableViewCell {
    var cell = tableView.dequeueReusableCell(withIdentifier:
    cellID)
    if (cell == nil) {
        cell = UITableViewCell(
            style: UITableViewCell.CellStyle.default,
            reuseIdentifier: cellID)
    }
    cell?.textLabel?.text = petArray[indexPath.row]
    return cell!
}

}
```

19. Click the Run button or choose Product ➤ Run. The Simulator window appears, displaying the data in your table view as shown in Figure 14-4.

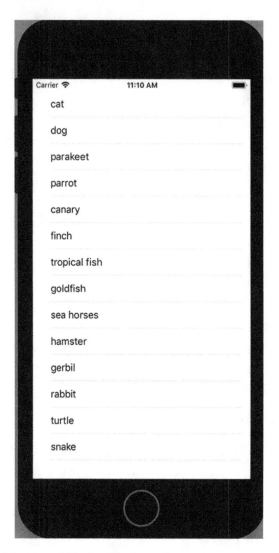

Figure 14-4. *The table view filled with data from the array*

20. Scroll up and down the table view to see how data scrolls off the
     top and bottom of the screen.

21. Choose Simulator ➤ Quit Simulator to return to Xcode.

The basic steps to creating a table view are

- Drag and drop a table view from the Object Library window onto a view.

- Define a .swift file to be the delegate and data source for the table view.

- Create or retrieve data to store in the table view.

- Write a function that defines how many rows the table view needs to display.

- Write a function that stores data in different rows in the table view.

In the previous example, we created and filled a table view by writing code in the ViewController.swift file. Since Xcode gives you multiple ways to accomplish the same task through code or visually, let's see how to duplicate the exact same table view project except with less code.

We'll do this in two ways. First, we'll define the delegate and data source visually and eliminate these three lines of code:

```
@IBOutlet var petTable: UITableView!
      petTable.dataSource = self
      petTable.delegate = self
```

Next, we'll drag and drop a cell from the Object Library window onto the table view so we can eliminate this code:

```
let cellID = "cellID"
   if (cell == nil) {
       cell = UITableViewCell(
           style: UITableViewCell.CellStyle.default,
           reuseIdentifier: "cellID")
   }
```

Reducing the amount of code used to create an app allows you to focus on code that makes your app unique. The drawback of eliminating code though is that you must realize that the code has been replaced in other ways that aren't always obvious at first glance.

To see how to create a table view visually, follow these steps:

1. Create a new iOS project using the Single View App template (see Chapter 1) and name this new project TableViewVisualApp. This creates a single view for the user interface.

2. Click the Main.storyboard file in the Navigator pane. Xcode displays the single view.

3. Click the Library icon to open the Object Library window.

4. Drag and drop a table view (see Figure 14-2) anywhere on the view.

5. Resize the table view so it fills the entire screen.

6. Choose Editor ➤ Resolve Auto Layout Issues ➤ Reset to Suggested Constraints. Xcode adds constraints to the table view (see Figure 14-3).

7. Click the Library icon to open the Object Library window. Then drag and drop a Table View Cell onto the top as shown in Figure 14-5.

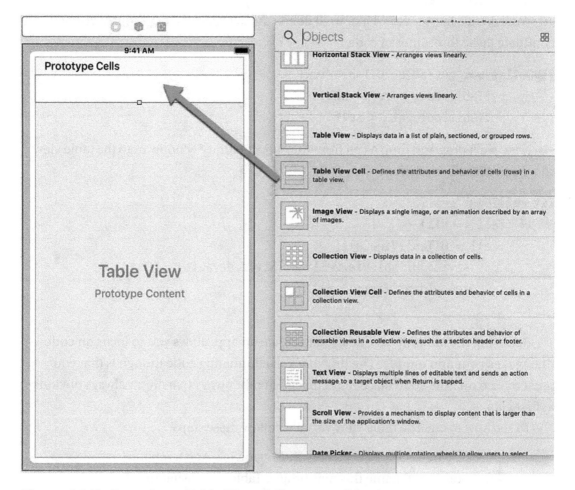

Figure 14-5. *Dragging a Table View Cell onto a table view*

8. Choose View ➤ Inspectors ➤ Show Attributes Inspector, or click the Attributes Inspector icon in the upper right corner of the Xcode window.

9.   Click in the Identifier text field as shown in Figure 14-6, type
     cellID (which can be an arbitrary name you wish to give it), and
     press ENTER.

Figure 14-6.   *The Identifier text field in the Attributes Inspector*

10.   Click the table view to select it and choose View ➤ Inspectors ➤
      Show Connections Inspector, or click the Connections Inspector
      icon in the upper right corner of the Xcode window.

11.   Click in the circle that appears to the right of dataSource and drag
      the mouse over the ViewController icon at the top of the View
      Controller or in the Document Outline as shown in Figure 14-7.

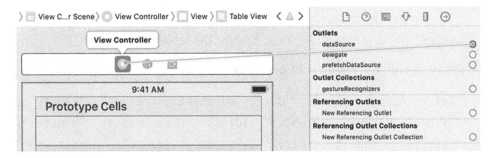

Figure 14-7.   *The Connections Inspector pane lets you connect the dataSource and*
delegate to the View Controller

12.   Release the left mouse button.

13.   Click in the circle that appears to the right of delegate and drag
      the mouse over the ViewController icon at the top of the View
      Controller or in the Document Outline.

14. Release the left mouse button. The Connections Inspector pane should show that the ViewController file is now the dataSource and delegate as shown in Figure 14-8.

Figure 14-8. *Connecting the delegate and dataSource to the ViewController. swift file*

15. Click the ViewController.swift file in the Navigator pane.

16. Modify the class ViewController line by adding UITableViewDelegate, UITableViewDataSource as follows:

```
class ViewController: UIViewController, UITableViewDelegate,
UITableViewDataSource {
```

The purpose of this code is to identify the ViewController.swift file as both the delegate and data source for the table view.

17. Underneath the class ViewController line, add the following array:

```
let petArray = ["cat", "dog", "parakeet", "parrot", "canary",
"finch", "tropical fish", "goldfish", "sea horses", "hamster",
"gerbil", "rabbit", "turtle", "snake", "lizard", "hermit crab"]
```

18. Underneath the viewDidLoad method, add the following function to define the total number of rows needed:

```
func tableView(_ tableView: UITableView, numberOfRowsInSection
section: Int) -> Int {
    return petArray.count
}
```

19. Underneath the viewDidLoad method, add the following function to load data into the table:

```swift
func tableView(_ tableView: UITableView, cellForRowAt
indexPath: IndexPath) -> UITableViewCell {
    let cell = tableView.dequeueReusableCell(withIdentifier:
    "cellID")
    cell?.textLabel?.text = petArray[indexPath.row]
    return cell!
}
```

This code references the cell that has the "cellID" Identifier, which is what we defined the Table View Cell in step 9. The entire ViewController.swift file should look like this:

```swift
import UIKit

class ViewController: UIViewController, UITableViewDelegate,
UITableViewDataSource {

    let petArray = ["cat", "dog", "parakeet", "parrot", "canary",
    "finch", "tropical fish", "goldfish", "sea horses", "hamster",
    "gerbil", "rabbit", "turtle", "snake", "lizard", "hermit crab"]

    override func viewDidLoad() {
        super.viewDidLoad()
        // Do any additional setup after loading the view,
        typically from a nib.
    }

    func tableView(_ tableView: UITableView, numberOfRowsInSection
    section: Int) -> Int {
        return petArray.count
    }
```

```
func tableView(_ tableView: UITableView, cellForRowAt
indexPath: IndexPath) -> UITableViewCell {
    let cell = tableView.dequeueReusableCell(withIdentifier:
    "cellID")
    cell?.textLabel?.text = petArray[indexPath.row]
    return cell!
}

}
```

20. Click the Run button or choose Product ➤ Run. The Simulator window appears, displaying the data in your table view (see Figure 14-4).

21. Scroll up and down the table view to see how data scrolls off the top and bottom of the screen.

22. Choose Simulator ➤ Quit Simulator to return to Xcode.

Selecting an Item in a Table View

A table view displays rows of data for the user to select. To detect which row the user tapped to select, we need another function called didSelectRowAt, which can identify the row selected and retrieve the data from that row. To see how to select an item in a table view, follow these steps:

1. Make sure the TableViewApp project is loaded in Xcode.

2. Click the ViewController.swift file in the Navigator pane. Xcode displays the single view.

3. Add the following function underneath the viewDidLoad method:

```
func tableView(_ tableView: UITableView, didSelectRowAt
indexPath: IndexPath) {
    let selectedItem = petArray[indexPath.row]
    let alert = UIAlertController(title: "Your Choice",
    message: "\(selectedItem)", preferredStyle: .alert)
```

```swift
    let okAction = UIAlertAction(title: "OK", style: .default,
    handler: { action -> Void in
        //Just dismiss the action sheet
    })
    alert.addAction(okAction)

    self.present(alert, animated: true, completion: nil)
}
```

This function returns the indexPath, which can be used to identify the row the user tapped. Based on this index, we can retrieve the proper item from the petArray that filled the table view with data. Then it displays an alert controller to identify what item the user tapped on. The entire ViewController.swift file should look like this:

```swift
import UIKit

class ViewController: UIViewController, UITableViewDelegate,
UITableViewDataSource {

    let petArray = ["cat", "dog", "parakeet", "parrot", "canary",
    "finch", "tropical fish", "goldfish", "sea horses", "hamster",
    "gerbil", "rabbit", "turtle", "snake", "lizard", "hermit crab"]

    override func viewDidLoad() {
        super.viewDidLoad()
        // Do any additional setup after loading the view,
        typically from a nib.
    }

    func tableView(_ tableView: UITableView, numberOfRowsInSection
    section: Int) -> Int {
        return petArray.count
    }
```

```
func tableView(_ tableView: UITableView, cellForRowAt
indexPath: IndexPath) -> UITableViewCell {
    let cell = tableView.dequeueReusableCell(withIdentifier:
    "cellID")
    cell?.textLabel?.text = petArray[indexPath.row]
    return cell!
}

func tableView(_ tableView: UITableView, didSelectRowAt
indexPath: IndexPath) {
    let selectedItem = petArray[indexPath.row]
    let alert = UIAlertController(title: "Your Choice",
    message: "\(selectedItem)", preferredStyle: .alert)

    let okAction = UIAlertAction(title: "OK", style: .default,
    handler: { action -> Void in
        //Just dismiss the action sheet
    })
    alert.addAction(okAction)

    self.present(alert, animated: true, completion: nil)
}

}
```

4. Click the Run button or choose Product ➤ Run. The Simulator window appears, displaying the data in your table view (see Figure 14-4).

5. Click an item in the table view. An alert controller appears to identify your choice as shown in Figure 14-9.

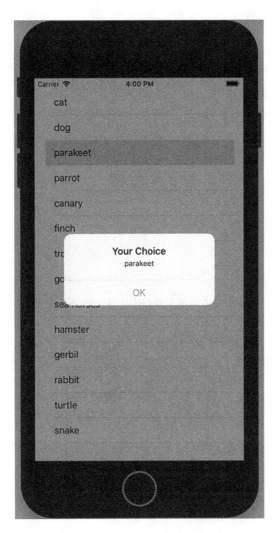

Figure 14-9. *An alert appears to identify the selected choice*

6.   Click OK to dismiss the alert controller.

7.   Choose Simulator ➤ Quit Simulator to return to Xcode.

Creating Grouped Tables

Our current examples of a table simply list data in endless rows, which is known as
a plain table style. To help organize data displayed in a table view, you can create a
grouped table style that divides data into sections where each section has a header title
as shown in Figure 14-10.

377

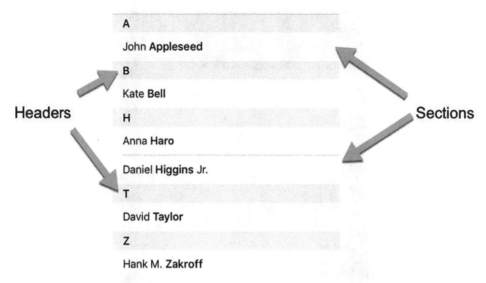

Figure 14-10. *Grouped tables divide data into sections with headers*

Creating a grouped table involves several additional steps:

- Define the table view as a grouped style.

- Write a numberOfSections function that defines how many sections the table view contains.

- Write a numberOfRowsInSection function that defines how many rows appear in each section.

- Write a titleForHeaderInSection function that defines the header that appears for each section.

To define sections, data must be arranged differently. In the previous example, we simply had an array of strings. However to display data in sections, we need an array of arrays. Each array of strings represents a different section such as:

```
let petArray = [["Mammal", "cat", "dog", "hamster", "gerbil", "rabbit"],
["Bird", "parakeet", "parrot", "canary", "finch"], ["Fish", "tropical
fish", "goldfish", "sea horses"], ["Reptile", "turtle", "snake", "lizard"]]
```

The preceding array contains four arrays of strings where the first item in each array defines a header for that section. So the first array's header is "Mammal", the second array's header is "Bird", the third array's header is "Fish", and the fourth array's header is "Reptile".

When determining the number of rows in each section, we need to subtract 1 because the section header appears at the beginning of each array. So the numberOfRowsInSection function subtracts 1 to accurately count the rows in each section like this:

```
func tableView(_ tableView: UITableView, numberOfRowsInSection section:
Int) -> Int {
    return petArray[section].count - 1
}
```

Displaying data in a table view involves identifying the section and then the row. However, since the first element of each array contains a section header, we need to skip over this header by adding 1 to the array index like this line, which appears inside the cellForRowAt function:

```
cell?.textLabel?.text = petArray[indexPath.section][indexPath.row + 1]
```

In addition, we need to identify the item the user tapped on with this code in the didSelectRowAt function:

```
let selectedItem = petArray[indexPath.section][indexPath.row + 1]
```

Identifying the number of sections is simply a matter of counting all the elements (arrays) in the petArray like this:

```
func numberOfSections(in tableView: UITableView) -> Int {
    return petArray.count
}
```

To display the header, we need to retrieve the first element from each section like this:

```
func tableView(_ tableView: UITableView, titleForHeaderInSection
section: Int) -> String? {
    return petArray[section][0]
}
```

To see how to create a grouped table, follow these steps:

1. Create a new iOS project using the Single View App template (see Chapter 1) and name this new project GroupTableViewApp. This creates a single view for the user interface.

2. Click the Main.storyboard file in the Navigator pane. Xcode displays the single view.

3. Click the Library icon to open the Object Library window.

4. Drag and drop a table view (see Figure 14-2) anywhere on the view.

5. Resize the table view so it fills the entire screen.

6. Choose Editor ➤ Resolve Auto Layout Issues ➤ Reset to Suggested Constraints. Xcode adds constraints to the table view (see Figure 14-3).

7. Choose View ➤ Inspectors ➤ Show Attributes Inspector, or click the Attributes Inspector icon in the upper right corner of the Xcode window.

8. Click the Style popup menu and choose Grouped as shown in Figure 14-11.

Figure 14-11. *Defining a table view as a grouped table*

9. Choose View ➤ Assistant Editor ➤ Show Assistant Editor, or click the Assistant Editor icon in the upper right corner of the Xcode window.

10. Move the mouse pointer over the table view, hold down the Control key, and Ctrl-drag under the "class ViewController" line in the ViewController.swift file.

11. Release the Control key and the left mouse button. A popup window appears.

12. Click in the Name text field, type **petTable**, and click the Connect button. Xcode creates an IBOutlet as follows:

```
@IBOutlet var petTable: UITableView!
```

13. Choose View ➤ Standard Editor ➤ Show Standard Editor, or click the Standard Editor icon in the upper right corner of the Xcode window.

14. Click the ViewController.swift file in the Navigator pane.

15. Modify the class ViewController line by adding UITableViewDelegate, UITableViewDataSource as follows:

```
class ViewController: UIViewController, UITableViewDelegate,
UITableViewDataSource {
```

The purpose of this code is to identify the ViewController.swift file as both the delegate and data source for the table view.

16. Underneath the class ViewController line, add the following array:

```
let petArray = [["Mammal", "cat", "dog", "hamster", "gerbil",
"rabbit"], ["Bird", "parakeet", "parrot", "canary", "finch"],
["Fish", "tropical fish", "goldfish", "sea horses"], ["Reptile",
"turtle", "snake", "lizard"]]
```

17. Underneath this array, add the following line:

```
let cellID = "cellID"
```

The purpose of this code is to create an arbitrary constant name for a cell. A table view consists of rows of cells, so we need to identify the cells for storing data in later.

18. Modify the viewDidLoad method as follows:

```
override func viewDidLoad() {
    super.viewDidLoad()
    petTable.dataSource = self
    petTable.delegate = self
    // Do any additional setup after loading the view,
    typically from a nib.
}
```

The purpose of this code is to define that the table (IBOutlet petTable) gets its data from the ViewController.swift file that it's stored in (self). In addition, the delegate is defined as the

ViewController.swift file (self). This means the ViewController.
swift file needs to contain functions that define how many rows
the table needs and where to find its data, which is the petArray.

19. Underneath the viewDidLoad method, add the following function
to count the number of rows in each section:

```swift
func tableView(_ tableView: UITableView, numberOfRowsInSection
section: Int) -> Int {
    return petArray[section].count - 1
}
```

20. Underneath the previous function, add the following function to
fill the table view with data:

```swift
func tableView(_ tableView: UITableView, cellForRowAt
indexPath: IndexPath) -> UITableViewCell {
    var cell = tableView.dequeueReusableCell(withIdentifier:
    cellID)
    if (cell == nil) {
        cell = UITableViewCell(
            style: UITableViewCell.CellStyle.default,
            reuseIdentifier: cellID)
    }
    cell?.textLabel?.text = petArray[indexPath.section]
    [indexPath.row + 1]
    return cell!
}
```

21. Underneath the previous function, add the following function to
identify which item the user selected:

```swift
func tableView(_ tableView: UITableView, didSelectRowAt
indexPath: IndexPath) {
    let selectedItem = petArray[indexPath.section][indexPath.
    row + 1]
    let alert = UIAlertController(title: "Your Choice",
    message: "\(selectedItem)", preferredStyle: .alert)
```

```
    let okAction = UIAlertAction(title: "OK", style: .default,
    handler: { action -> Void in
        //Just dismiss the action sheet
    })
    alert.addAction(okAction)

    self.present(alert, animated: true, completion: nil)
}
```

22. Underneath the previous function, add the following function to count the number of sections to display in the table view:

```
func numberOfSections(in tableView: UITableView) -> Int {
    return petArray.count
}
```

23. Underneath the previous function, add the following function to display the first item in each array as the header for that group:

```
func tableView(_ tableView: UITableView,
titleForHeaderInSection section: Int) -> String? {
    return petArray[section][0]
}
}
```

The entire ViewController.swift file should look like this:

```
import UIKit

class ViewController: UIViewController, UITableViewDelegate,
UITableViewDataSource {

    @IBOutlet var petTable: UITableView!

    let petArray = [["Mammal", "cat", "dog", "hamster", "gerbil",
    "rabbit"], ["Bird", "parakeet", "parrot", "canary", "finch"],
    ["Fish", "tropical fish", "goldfish", "sea horses"],
    ["Reptile", "turtle", "snake", "lizard"]]
```

```swift
let cellID = "cellID"

override func viewDidLoad() {
    super.viewDidLoad()
    petTable.dataSource = self
    petTable.delegate = self
    // Do any additional setup after loading the view,
    typically from a nib.
}

func tableView(_ tableView: UITableView, numberOfRowsInSection
section: Int) -> Int {
    return petArray[section].count - 1
}

func tableView(_ tableView: UITableView, cellForRowAt
indexPath: IndexPath) -> UITableViewCell {
    var cell = tableView.dequeueReusableCell(withIdentifier:
    cellID)
    if (cell == nil) {
        cell = UITableViewCell(
            style: UITableViewCell.CellStyle.default,
            reuseIdentifier: cellID)
    }
    cell?.textLabel?.text = petArray[indexPath.section]
    [indexPath.row + 1]
    return cell!
}

func tableView(_ tableView: UITableView, didSelectRowAt
indexPath: IndexPath) {
    let selectedItem = petArray[indexPath.section][indexPath.
    row + 1]
    let alert = UIAlertController(title: "Your Choice",
    message: "\(selectedItem)", preferredStyle: .alert)
```

```
    let okAction = UIAlertAction(title: "OK", style: .default,
    handler: { action -> Void in
        //Just dismiss the action sheet
    })
    alert.addAction(okAction)

    self.present(alert, animated: true, completion: nil)
}

// Code for creating a grouped table
// First, change the Style property of the table view to
Grouped in the Attributes Inspector pane
func numberOfSections(in tableView: UITableView) -> Int {
    return petArray.count
}

func tableView(_ tableView: UITableView,
titleForHeaderInSection section: Int) -> String? {
    return petArray[section][0]
}

}
```

24. Click the Run button or choose Product ➤ Run. The Simulator
    window appears, displaying the grouped data in the table view as
    shown in Figure 14-12.

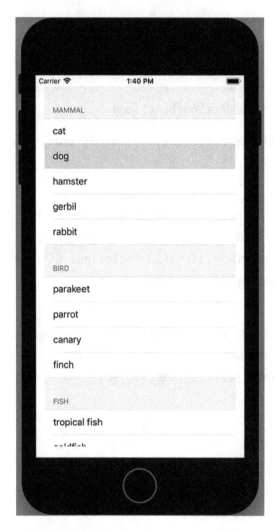

Figure 14-12. *A grouped table view*

25. Click an item in the table view. An alert controller appears to identify your choice.

26. Click OK to dismiss the alert controller.

27. Choose Simulator ➤ Quit Simulator to return to Xcode.

Displaying Indexes

When a table view displays large amounts of data, it can be cumbersome for users to scroll from one end of the table view list to the other. To solve this problem, table views can display an index, which appears on the far right of the screen. Now users can tap an item in the index to jump to a specific section right away.

Note   Table views can only display an index if the table view style is plain, not grouped.

An index typically consists of letters from A to Z but can represent any characters, including emoji. The position of each index item corresponds to each section. So the first item displayed in the index takes users to the first section, the second item displayed in the index takes users to the second section, and so on.

To see how to create an index, follow these steps:

1. Create a new iOS project using the Single View App template (see Chapter 1) and name this new project TableViewIndexApp. This creates a single view for the user interface.

2. Click the Main.storyboard file in the Navigator pane. Xcode displays the single view.

3. Click the Library icon to open the Object Library window.

4. Drag and drop a table view (see Figure 14-2) anywhere on the view.

5. Resize the table view so it fills the entire screen.

6. Choose Editor ➤ Resolve Auto Layout Issues ➤ Reset to Suggested Constraints. Xcode adds constraints to the table view (see Figure 14-3).

7. Choose View ➤ Inspectors ➤ Show Attributes Inspector, or click the Attributes Inspector icon in the upper right corner of the Xcode window.

8. Choose View ➤ Assistant Editor ➤ Show Assistant Editor, or click the Assistant Editor icon in the upper right corner of the Xcode window.

9. Move the mouse pointer over the table view, hold down the Control key, and Ctrl-drag under the "class ViewController" line in the ViewController.swift file.

10. Release the Control key and the left mouse button. A popup window appears.

11. Click in the Name text field, type **petTable**, and click the Connect button. Xcode creates an IBOutlet as follows:

```
@IBOutlet var petTable: UITableView!
```

12. Choose View ➤ Standard Editor ➤ Show Standard Editor, or click the Standard Editor icon in the upper right corner of the Xcode window.

13. Click the ViewController.swift file in the Navigator pane.

14. Modify the class ViewController line by adding UITableViewDelegate, UITableViewDataSource as follows:

```
class ViewController: UIViewController, UITableViewDelegate,
UITableViewDataSource {
```

The purpose of this code is to identify the ViewController.swift file as both the delegate and data source for the table view.

15. Underneath the class ViewController line, add the following array:

```
let petArray = [["Bird", "parakeet", "parrot", "canary", "finch",
"cockatiel"], ["Fish", "tropical fish", "goldfish", "sea horses",
"eel"], ["Mammal", "cat", "dog", "hamster", "gerbil", "rabbit",
"mouse"], ["Reptile", "turtle", "snake", "lizard"]]
```

This petArray contains multiple string arrays where each string array represents a different section. The first item in each string array represents the section header.

16. Underneath the petArray, add this second array:

```
let indexArray = ["🐦B", "🐠F", "🐭M", "🦎R"]
```

Each item in this indexArray represents each section. Since petArray contains four sections, indexArray contains four items. While you could use ordinary letters, you can also add emoji. To insert emoji into your code, choose Edit ➤ Emoji & Symbols to open the Character View.

Then click Emoji ➤ Animals & Nature as shown in Figure 14-13. Now move the cursor where you want to insert an emoji and double-click the emoji to place it in your code. Click a bird, fish, mammal, and reptile emoji.

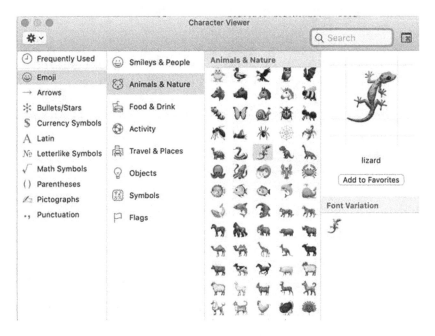

Figure 14-13. *The Character View window for inserting emoji into code*

17. Add the following line underneath the indexArray:

```
let cellID = "cellID"
```

18. Modify the viewDidLoad method as follows:

```
override func viewDidLoad() {
    super.viewDidLoad()
    petTable.dataSource = self
    petTable.delegate = self
    petTable.sectionIndexColor = UIColor.white
    petTable.sectionIndexBackgroundColor = UIColor.black
    petTable.sectionIndexTrackingBackgroundColor = UIColor.
    darkGray
```

```
// Do any additional setup after loading the view,
typically from a nib.
}
```

The sectionIndexColor, sectionIndexBackgroundColor, and
sectionIndexTrackingBackgroundColor make the index easier to
see by displaying white text against a black background.

19. Underneath the viewDidLoad method, add the following function
to define how many rows appear in each section, subtracting one
to account for the header at the beginning of each section:

```
func tableView(_ tableView: UITableView, numberOfRowsInSection
section: Int) -> Int {
    return petArray[section].count - 1
}
```

20. Underneath the previous function, add the following function to
fill the table view with data from the petArray:

```
func tableView(_ tableView: UITableView, cellForRowAt
indexPath: IndexPath) -> UITableViewCell {
    var cell = tableView.dequeueReusableCell(withIdentifier:
    cellID)
    if (cell == nil) {
        cell = UITableViewCell(
            style: UITableViewCell.CellStyle.default,
            reuseIdentifier: cellID)
    }
    cell?.textLabel?.text = petArray[indexPath.section]
    [indexPath.row + 1]
    return cell!
}
```

21. Underneath the previous function, add the following function to
display the item the user selected from the table view:

```
func tableView(_ tableView: UITableView, didSelectRowAt
indexPath: IndexPath) {
```

```
let selectedItem = petArray[indexPath.section][indexPath.
row + 1]
let alert = UIAlertController(title: "Your Choice",
message: "\(selectedItem)", preferredStyle: .alert)

let okAction = UIAlertAction(title: "OK", style: .default,
handler: { action -> Void in
    //Just dismiss the action sheet
})
alert.addAction(okAction)

self.present(alert, animated: true, completion: nil)
}
```

22. Underneath the previous function, add the following function to define the number of sections in the table view:

```
func numberOfSections(in tableView: UITableView) -> Int {
    return petArray.count
}
```

23. Underneath the previous function, add the following function to define the header for each section, which is the first item in each string array:

```
func tableView(_ tableView: UITableView,
titleForHeaderInSection section: Int) -> String? {
    return petArray[section][0]
}
```

24. Underneath the previous function, add the following function to define the index that appears on the right side of the table view:

```
func sectionIndexTitles(for tableView: UITableView) ->
[String]? {
    return indexArray
}
```

The entire ViewController.swift file should look like this:

```swift
import UIKit

class ViewController: UIViewController, UITableViewDelegate,
UITableViewDataSource {

    @IBOutlet var petTable: UITableView!

    let petArray = [["Bird", "parakeet", "parrot", "canary",
    "finch", "cockatiel"], ["Fish", "tropical fish", "goldfish",
    "sea horses", "eel"], ["Mammal", "cat", "dog", "hamster",
    "gerbil", "rabbit", "mouse"], ["Reptile", "turtle", "snake",
    "lizard"]]

    let indexArray = ["🐤B", "🐟F", "🐒M", "🦎R"]

    let cellID = "cellID"

    override func viewDidLoad() {
        super.viewDidLoad()
        petTable.dataSource = self
        petTable.delegate = self
        petTable.sectionIndexColor = UIColor.white
        petTable.sectionIndexBackgroundColor = UIColor.black
        petTable.sectionIndexTrackingBackgroundColor = UIColor.
        darkGray
        // Do any additional setup after loading the view,
        typically from a nib.
    }

    func tableView(_ tableView: UITableView, numberOfRowsInSection
    section: Int) -> Int {
        return petArray[section].count - 1
    }
```

```swift
func tableView(_ tableView: UITableView, cellForRowAt
indexPath: IndexPath) -> UITableViewCell {
    var cell = tableView.dequeueReusableCell(withIdentifier:
    cellID)
    if (cell == nil) {
        cell = UITableViewCell(
            style: UITableViewCell.CellStyle.default,
            reuseIdentifier: cellID)
    }
    cell?.textLabel?.text = petArray[indexPath.section]
    [indexPath.row + 1]
    return cell!
}

func tableView(_ tableView: UITableView, didSelectRowAt
indexPath: IndexPath) {
    let selectedItem = petArray[indexPath.section][indexPath.
    row + 1]
    let alert = UIAlertController(title: "Your Choice",
    message: "\(selectedItem)", preferredStyle: .alert)

    let okAction = UIAlertAction(title: "OK", style: .default,
    handler: { action -> Void in
        //Just dismiss the action sheet
    })
    alert.addAction(okAction)

    self.present(alert, animated: true, completion: nil)
}

func numberOfSections(in tableView: UITableView) -> Int {
    return petArray.count
}

func tableView(_ tableView: UITableView,
titleForHeaderInSection section: Int) -> String? {
    return petArray[section][0]
}
```

```
func sectionIndexTitles(for tableView: UITableView) ->
[String]? {
    return indexArray
}

}
```

25.   Click the Run button or choose Product ➤ Run. The Simulator
window appears, displaying the grouped data in the table view as
shown in Figure 14-14.

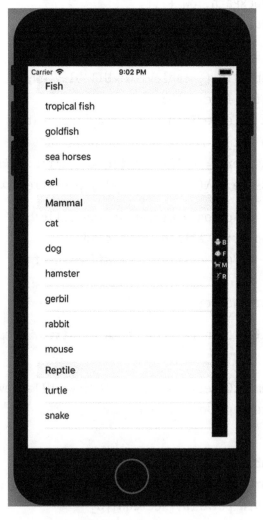

Figure 14-14. *An index appears on the far right of the table view*

26. Click the R index listing. Notice that the table view jumps to the fourth section because the letter "R" is the fourth item in the index.

27. Click the B index listing. Notice that the table view jumps to the first section because the letter "B" is the first item in the index.

28. Click the other two index entries ("F" and "M") to see how the table view jumps to each section.

29. Choose Simulator ➤ Quit Simulator to return to Xcode.

Using a Table View Controller

Through this chapter, we've created a Single View App project and added a table view from the Object Library window. A second way to create a table view is to add a Table View Controller to a storyboard. The main difference between a table view and a Table View Controller is that the Table View Controller consists of the following:

- A View Controller

- A table view on that View Controller

- A Table View Cell on the table view

To see how to use a Table View Controller, follow these steps:

1. Create a new iOS project using the Single View App template (see Chapter 1) and name this new project TableViewControllerApp. This creates a single view for the user interface.

2. Click the Main.storyboard file in the Navigator pane. Xcode displays the single view that automatically appears with every Single View App project.

3. Click View Controller Scene in the Document Outline as shown in Figure 14-15.

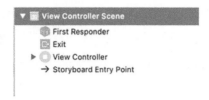

Figure 14-15. *Selecting a View Controller*

4. Press the BACKSPACE or DELETE key to delete the View
    Controller from the storyboard. Xcode removes the selected View
    Controller from the storyboard.

5. Click the ViewController.swift file in the Navigator pane. This .swift
    file was connected to the View Controller we just deleted so we
    don't need it anymore.

6. Press the BACKSPACE or DELETE key to delete the
    ViewController.swift file. A dialog appears, asking if you want to
    remove the file's reference or move it to the trash as shown in
    Figure 14-16.

Figure 14-16. *Deleting a .swift file gives you options*

7. Click Move to Trash. Xcode deletes the ViewController.swift file.

8. Click the Library icon to open the Object Library window and look
    for the yellow Table View Controller icon as shown in Figure 14-17.

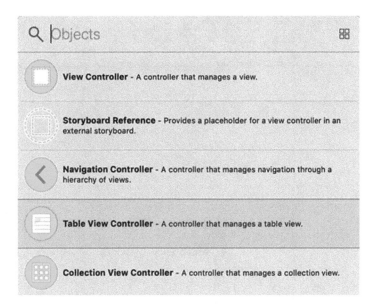

Figure 14-17. *The Table View Controller in the Object Library window*

9. Drag and drop the Table View Controller from the Object Library
    window to the empty storyboard. Xcode displays the Table View
    Controller as shown in Figure 14-18.

Figure 14-18. *The Table View Controller in the storyboard*

10.   Choose View ➤ Inspectors ➤ Show Attributes Inspector, or click
      the Attributes Inspector icon in the upper right corner of the
      Xcode window.

11.   Select the Is Initial View Controller check box as shown in
      Figure 14-19. Notice that when you select this check box, an arrow
      appears pointing to the left side of the Table View Controller.

Note   Only one View Controller can be designated as the initial View Controller.
The initial View Controller defines the first View Controller that appears when the
app runs.

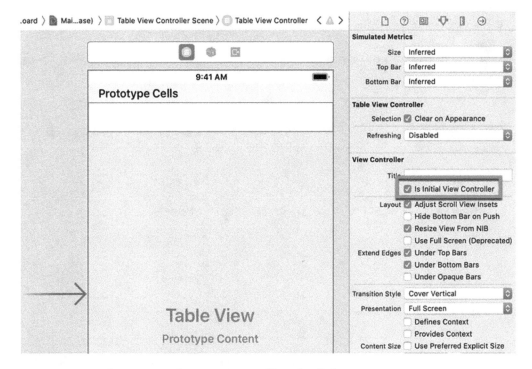

Figure 14-19. *The Is Initial View Controller check box*

Now that we have a Table View Controller in the storyboard, we need to connect it to a .swift file. That involves a two-step process of first creating a .swift file and then connecting it to the Table View Controller.

12. Choose File ➤ New ➤ File. A template dialog appears as shown in Figure 14-20.

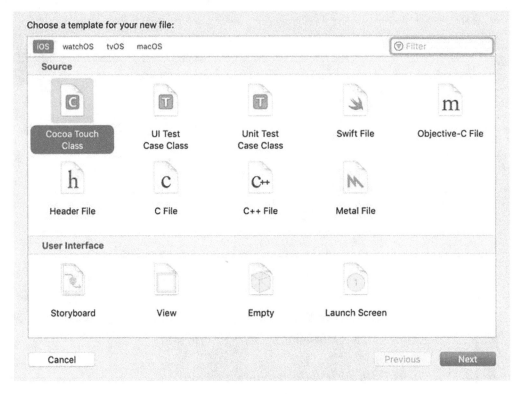

Figure 14-20. *The file template dialog*

13.   Click Cocoa Touch Class and click the **Next** button. Another dialog appears.

14.   Click in the Class text field, delete the existing text, and type **TableViewController**. (This class name can be any arbitrary name you wish.)

15.   Click in the Subclass of text field and choose UITableViewController as shown in Figure 14-21. Then click the **Next** button.

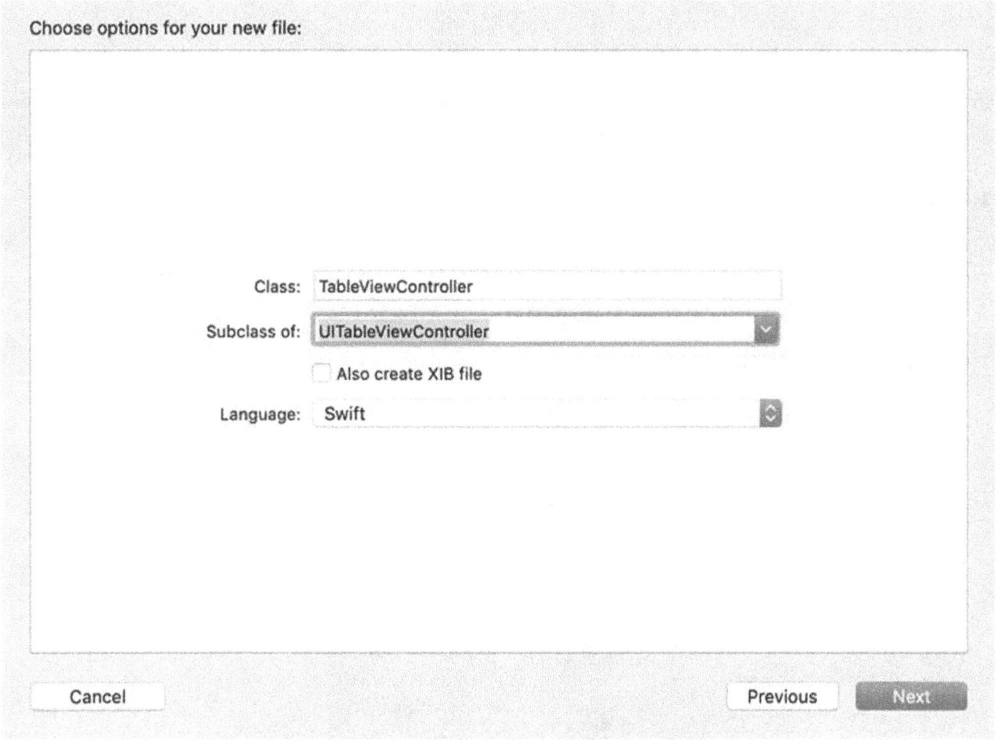

Choose options for your new file:

Class: TableViewController

Subclass of: UITableViewController

Also create XIB file

Language: Swift

Cancel   Previous   Next

Figure 14-21. *Naming the .swift file and defining its subclass*

16. Another dialog appears to ask you where to store this .swift file. Click the **Create** button. Xcode creates the TableViewController.swift file. Now the next step is to connect this .swift file to the Table View Controller.

17. Click the Main.storyboard file in the Navigator pane.

18. Click the Table View Controller Scene in the Document Outline or the Table View Controller icon above the Table View Controller in the storyboard.

19. Choose View ➤ Inspectors ➤ Show Identity Inspector, or click the Identity Inspector icon in the upper right corner of the Xcode window.

20. Click the Class popup menu and choose TableViewController (or whatever name you gave your .swift file in step 14) as shown in Figure 14-22. Connecting a .swift file to a View Controller now lets you create IBOutlets, IBAction methods, and Swift code to work with the Table View Controller.

Figure 14-22. *Connecting a .swift file to the Table View Controller*

21. Click Table View Cell in the Document Outline. (You may need to click the gray disclosure triangle to find the Table View Cell.)

22. Choose View ➤ Inspectors ➤ Show Attributes Inspector, or click the Attributes Inspector icon in the upper right corner of the Xcode window.

23. Click in the Identifier text field and type **cellID** as shown in Figure 14-23. (This can be any arbitrary name.) Then press ENTER.

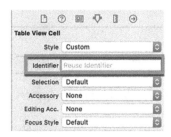

Figure 14-23. *Defining an Identifier for the Table View Cell*

24. Click the TableViewController.swift file in the Navigator pane.

25. Add the following code underneath the class TableViewController line as follows:

```
let petArray = ["cat", "dog", "parakeet", "parrot", "canary",
"finch", "tropical fish", "goldfish", "sea horses", "hamster",
"gerbil", "rabbit", "turtle", "snake", "lizard", "hermit crab"]
```

26. Edit the numberOfSections function as follows:

```
override func numberOfSections(in tableView: UITableView) -> Int {
    return 1
}
```

27. Edit the numberOfRowsInSection function as follows:

```
override func tableView(_ tableView: UITableView,
numberOfRowsInSection section: Int) -> Int {
    return petArray.count
}
```

28. Add the following cellForRowAt function to store data in the Table
View Cell:

```
override func tableView(_ tableView: UITableView, cellForRowAt
indexPath: IndexPath) -> UITableViewCell {
    let cell = tableView.dequeueReusableCell(withIdentifier:
    "cellID")
    cell?.textLabel?.text = petArray[indexPath.row]
    return cell!
}
```

29. Add the following didSelectRowAt function to identify which item
the user selected:

```
override func tableView(_ tableView: UITableView, didSelectRowAt
indexPath: IndexPath) {
        let selectedItem = petArray[indexPath.row]
        let alert = UIAlertController(title: "Your Choice",
        message: "\(selectedItem)", preferredStyle: .alert)

        let okAction = UIAlertAction(title: "OK", style: .default,
        handler: { action -> Void in
            //Just dismiss the action sheet
        })
        alert.addAction(okAction)

        self.present(alert, animated: true, completion: nil)
}
```

30. Click the Main.storyboard file in the Navigator pane.

31. Click the Run button or choose Product ➤ Run. The Simulator window appears, displaying the data in your table view (see Figure 14-4).

32. Click an item in the table view. An alert controller appears to identify your choice (see Figure 14-9).

33. Click OK to dismiss the alert controller.

34. Choose Simulator ➤ Quit Simulator to return to Xcode.

Summary

Table views display rows of data that users can select. A table view requires a data source and functions to define how many rows to display. A simple table view displays one section, but a table view can display multiple sections where each section contains different numbers of rows.

Each row in a table view is defined by a cell. You can define a cell using Swift code or visually by dragging and dropping a Table View Cell onto a table view. You must give this cell an identifying name so your swift code can reference this cell to store data in it.

When using a Table View Controller, you need to connect it to its own .swift file that you can define to make it represent a UITableViewController. This eliminates the need to declare the .swift file as the table view's delegate and data source.

The main difference between a table view and a Table View Controller is that a table view appears on an existing view while a Table View Controller appears in the storyboard.

CHAPTER 15

Customizing Table View Cells

Chapter 14 explained how to create different types of table views including plain and grouped tables along with section indexes. So far, we've only used a simple cell that displays a single line of text. In this chapter you'll learn how to customize a cell to display additional text and images. In addition, you'll also learn how to modify the appearance of cells.

Cells in a table view can display the following as shown in Figure 15-1:

- textLabel – Defines the main text displayed in a cell

- detailTextLabel – Defines the secondary text that appears in a smaller font size than the textLabel text

- imageView – Defines an image that appears in a cell

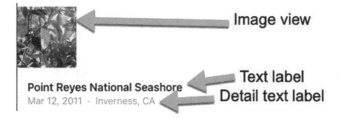

Figure 15-1. *The parts of a Table View Cell*

© Wallace Wang 2019
W. Wang, *Beginning iPhone Development with Swift 5*, https://doi.org/10.1007/978-1-4842-4865-2_15

Customizing a Table View Cell in Swift

Table View Cells can appear in different styles, which define how text, detail text, and images appear. The four different types of cell styles are shown in Figure 15-2:

- .default – Displays a text label, but no detail text label. An image view can appear on the left.

- .value1 – Displays a text label on the left and a detail text label on the right. An image view can appear on the left.

- .value2 – Displays a text label in blue indented from the left and a detail text label indented from the right. Does not display an image view.

- .subtitle – Displays a text label on the left and a detail text label underneath in a smaller font size. An image view can appear on the left.

Text label		.default
Text label	Detail text label	.value1
Text label Detail text label		.value2
Text label Detail text label		.subtitle

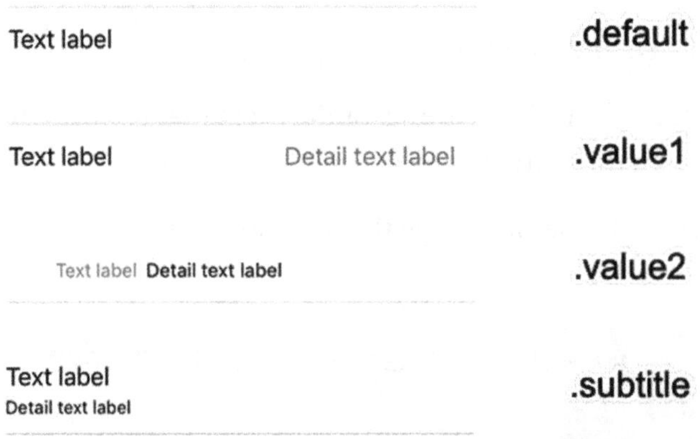

Figure 15-2. *The four different styles for a cell*

Note   The .default cell style is the only one that does not allow a detail text label to appear. The .value2 cell style is the only one that does not allow an image view to appear.

Before creating a table view that can display images, we'll need some images. Some sources of free, public domain images include

- icons8.com

- iconarchive.com

- aiconica.net

For this example, we'll need four different images, preferably of the same size and file format such as .png or .jpg. The exact name of each image doesn't matter but we'll need to be able to identify each image.

In this example, we'll display four items in the table view. To simplify matters, we'll use three different arrays containing four items, one for the text label, one for the detail text label, and one for the image view. In a real app, you'll likely want to use a single data structure such as a dictionary to keep related data together.

Displaying text in a Table View Cell involves assigning the Table View Cell's textLabel. text and detailTextLabel.text properties to a string such as:

```
cell?.textLabel?.text = "String or string variable"
cell?.detailTextLabel?.text = "String or string variable"
```

Displaying an image in a Table View Cell involves assigning the image file name to the image view's Image property such as:

```
cell?.imageView?.image = UIImage(named: "Image file name")
```

To see how to create and fill a table view with text, detail text, and an image, follow these steps:

1. Create a new iOS project using the Single View App template (see Chapter 1) and name this new project TableCellApp. This creates a single view for the user interface.

2. Click the Main.storyboard file in the Navigator pane. Xcode displays the single view.

3. Click the Library icon to open the Object Library window.

4. Drag and drop a table view on the view.

5. Resize the table view so it fills the entire screen.

6. Choose Editor ➤ Resolve Auto Layout Issues ➤ Reset to Suggested
    Constraints. Xcode adds constraints to the table view.

7. Choose View ➤ Assistant Editor ➤ Show Assistant Editor, or click
    the Assistant Editor icon in the upper right corner of the Xcode
    window.

8. Move the mouse pointer over the table view, hold down the
    Control key, and Ctrl-drag under the "class ViewController" line in
    the ViewController.swift file.

9. Release the Control key and the left mouse button. A popup
    window appears.

10. Click in the Name text field, type **tableData**, and click the Connect
    button. Xcode creates an IBOutlet as follows:

    ```
    @IBOutlet var tableData: UITableView!
    ```

11. Choose View ➤ Standard Editor ➤ Show Standard Editor, or click
    the Standard Editor icon in the upper right corner of the Xcode
    window.

12. Click the ViewController.swift file in the Navigator pane.

13. Modify the class ViewController line by adding
    UITableViewDelegate, UITableViewDataSource as follows:

    ```
    class ViewController: UIViewController, UITableViewDelegate,
    UITableViewDataSource {
    ```

    The purpose of this code is to identify the ViewController.swift file
    as both the delegate and data source for the table view.

14. Drag and drop four images into the Navigator pane as shown in
    Figure 15-3. A dialog appears, asking how to add the files to your
    project.

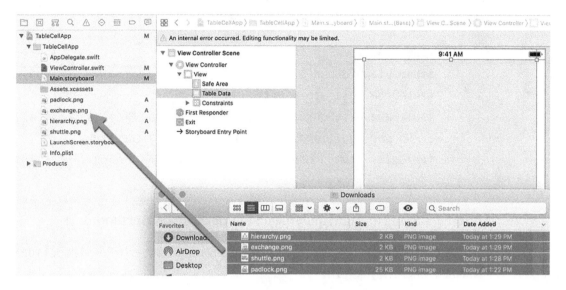

Figure 15-3. *Dragging and dropping image files into the Navigator pane*

15. Click the Finish button. Note the exact names of all the image files.

16. Underneath the class ViewController line, add the following three arrays to fill the table view with four rows of data:

```
let mainArray = ["Shuttle bus", "Hierarchy", "Exchange",
"Padlock"]
let detailArray = ["6am - 10pm", "Acme corporation", "Ideas
worth sharing", "Access denied"]
let imageArray = ["shuttle.png", "hierarchy.png", "exchange.
png", "padlock.png"]
```

For the imageArray, replace these file names with the names of the image files you dragged and dropped into the Navigator pane in step 14.

17. Underneath this array, add the following line:

```
let cellID = "cellID"
```

The purpose of this code is to create an arbitrary constant name for a cell. A table view consists of rows of cells, so we need to identify the cells for storing data in later.

18.   Modify the viewDidLoad method as follows:

```swift
override func viewDidLoad() {
    super.viewDidLoad()
    tableData.delegate = self
    tableData.dataSource = self
    // Do any additional setup after loading the view,
    typically from a nib.
}
```

19.   Add the following function underneath the viewDidLoad method:

```swift
func tableView(_ tableView: UITableView, numberOfRowsInSection
section: Int) -> Int {
    return mainArray.count
}
```

20.   Add the following function underneath the viewDidLoad method:

```swift
func tableView(_ tableView: UITableView, cellForRowAt
indexPath: IndexPath) -> UITableViewCell {
    var cell = tableView.dequeueReusableCell(withIdentifier:
    cellID)
    if (cell == nil) {
        cell = UITableViewCell(
            style: UITableViewCell.CellStyle.subtitle,
            reuseIdentifier: cellID)
    }
    cell?.textLabel?.text = mainArray[indexPath.row]
    cell?.detailTextLabel?.text = detailArray[indexPath.row]
    cell?.imageView?.image = UIImage(named: imageArray
    [indexPath.row])
    return cell!
}
```

This function stores the data from the array into the table view. Since each row in the table view is defined by a cell, it needs to create a cell with a name:

```
var cell = tableView.dequeueReusableCell(withIdentifier: cellID)
```

If a cell is empty, then the if statement defines the cell's style and gives it the arbitrary cellID name to identify it and defines the cell style as .subtitle (feel free to change this to .default or .value1):

```
if (cell == nil) {
    cell = UITableViewCell(
        style: UITableViewCell.CellStyle.subtitle,
        reuseIdentifier: cellID)
}
```

Next it takes data from the mainArray to store in the text label, takes data from detailArray to store in the detail text label, and takes data from the imageArray to identify which image to put in the image view:

```
cell?.textLabel?.text = mainArray[indexPath.row]
cell?.detailTextLabel?.text = detailArray[indexPath.row]
cell?.imageView?.image = UIImage(named:
imageArray[indexPath.row])
```

21. Add the following function underneath the viewDidLoad method to detect which item the user selected:

```
func tableView(_ tableView: UITableView, didSelectRowAt
indexPath: IndexPath) {
    let selectedItem = mainArray[indexPath.row]
    let alert = UIAlertController(title: "Your Choice",
    message: "\(selectedItem)", preferredStyle: .alert)

    let okAction = UIAlertAction(title: "OK", style: .default,
    handler: { action -> Void in
        //Just dismiss the action sheet
    })
```

```
    alert.addAction(okAction)

    self.present(alert, animated: true, completion: nil)
}
```

The complete ViewController.swift file should look like this:

```swift
import UIKit

class ViewController: UIViewController, UITableViewDelegate,
UITableViewDataSource {

    @IBOutlet var tableData: UITableView!

    let mainArray = ["Shuttle bus", "Hierarchy", "Exchange",
    "Padlock"]
    let detailArray = ["6am - 10pm", "Acme corporation", "Ideas
    worth sharing", "Access denied"]
    let imageArray = ["shuttle.png", "hierarchy.png", "exchange.
    png", "padlock.png"]

    let cellID = "cellID"

    override func viewDidLoad() {
        super.viewDidLoad()
        tableData.delegate = self
        tableData.dataSource = self
        // Do any additional setup after loading the view,
        typically from a nib.
    }

    func tableView(_ tableView: UITableView, numberOfRowsInSection
    section: Int) -> Int {
        return mainArray.count
    }

    func tableView(_ tableView: UITableView, cellForRowAt
    indexPath: IndexPath) -> UITableViewCell {
        var cell = tableView.dequeueReusableCell(withIdentifier:
        cellID)
```

```swift
    if (cell == nil) {
        cell = UITableViewCell(
            style: UITableViewCell.CellStyle.subtitle,
            reuseIdentifier: cellID)
    }
    cell?.textLabel?.text = mainArray[indexPath.row]
    cell?.detailTextLabel?.text = detailArray[indexPath.row]
    cell?.imageView?.image = UIImage(named:
    imageArray[indexPath.row])
    return cell!
    }

    func tableView(_ tableView: UITableView, didSelectRowAt
    indexPath: IndexPath) {
        let selectedItem = mainArray[indexPath.row]
        let alert = UIAlertController(title: "Your Choice",
        message: "\(selectedItem)", preferredStyle: .alert)

        let okAction = UIAlertAction(title: "OK", style: .default,
        handler: { action -> Void in
            //Just dismiss the action sheet
        })
        alert.addAction(okAction)

        self.present(alert, animated: true, completion: nil)
    }
}
```

22. Click the Run button or choose Product ➤ Run. The Simulator
    window appears, displaying the data in your table view as shown
    in Figure 15-4.

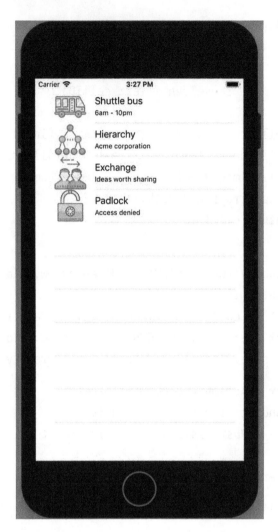

Figure 15-4. *The table view displaying a text label, detail text label, and image view*

23. Click an item to see an alert controller display the item you chose. Then click OK to dismiss the alert controller.

24. Choose Simulator ➤ Quit Simulator to return to Xcode.

Experiment with different cell styles such as .default, .value1, .value2, and .subtitle to see how it changes the appearance of the table view. Notice that if you change the cell style to .value2, the image view does not appear.

Designing a Custom Table View Cell

By changing the Table View Cell style, we can change the way each row in a table view displays text, detail text, and an image. For more flexibility, we can also design a custom Table View Cell by dragging and dropping objects from the Object Library window onto the Table View Cell.

Not only can you define the position of labels in a custom cell but you can also customize the font and font size of the text that appears in the label. To see how to create a custom Table View Cell, follow these steps:

1. Create a new iOS project using the Single View App template (see Chapter 1) and name this new project TableViewCellVisualApp. This creates a single view for the user interface.

2. Click the Main.storyboard file in the Navigator pane. Xcode displays the single view.

3. Click the Library icon to open the Object Library window.

4. Drag and drop a table view anywhere on the view.

5. Resize the table view so it fills the entire screen.

6. Choose Editor ➤ Resolve Auto Layout Issues ➤ Reset to Suggested Constraints. Xcode adds constraints to the table view.

7. Click the Library icon to open the Object Library window.

8. Drag and drop a Table View Cell, as shown in Figure 15-5, on the table view.

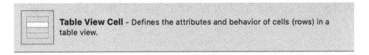

Figure 15-5. *The Table View Cell in the Object Library window*

9. Click the Library icon to open the Object Library window and drag and drop an image view to the far left of the Table View Cell.

10. Click the Library icon to open the Object Library window and drag and drop two labels onto the Table View Cell.

11. Move one label to the top right of the image view.

12. Move the second label underneath the first label and indented to the right.

13. Click this second label and choose View ➤ Inspectors ➤ Attributes Inspector, or click the Attributes Inspector icon in the upper right corner of the Xcode window.

14. Click the T inside a square icon in the Font text field to display a popup window.

15. Click the Family popup menu and choose Courier New.

16. Click in the Size text field and type 12 as shown in Figure 15-6. The entire Table View Cell should look similar to Figure 15-7.

Figure 15-6. *Customizing the text in a label for a Table View Cell*

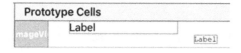

Figure 15-7. *The design of two labels and an image view on the Table View Cell*

17. Click the Table View Cell in the Document Outline and choose
     View ➤ Inspectors ➤ Show Attributes Inspector, or click the
     Attributes Inspector icon in the upper right corner of the Xcode
     window.

18. Click in the Identifier text field, type **customCell**, and press
     ENTER as shown in Figure 15-8.

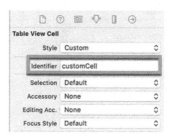

Figure 15-8. *Changing the Identifier of the Table View Cell*

19. Choose File ➤ New ➤ File. A template window appears.

20. Choose Cocoa Touch Class and click the **Next** button. Another
     dialog appears asking for a name and subclass for your file.

21. Click in the Class text field and type **TableViewCell**.

22. Click in the Subclass of popup menu and choose UITableViewCell
     as shown in Figure 15-9.

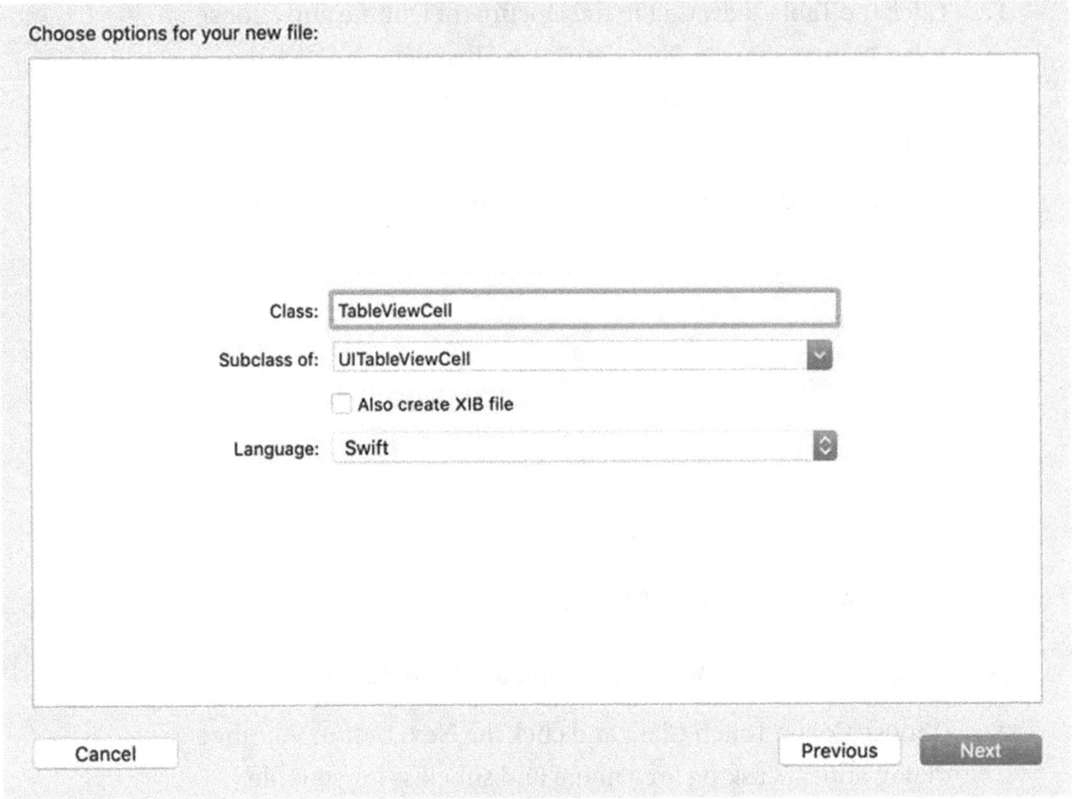

Choose options for your new file:

Class:	TableViewCell
Subclass of:	UITableViewCell
	☐ Also create XIB file
Language:	Swift

Cancel   Previous   Next

Figure 15-9. *Defining a class name and subclass type of a new Cocoa Touch Class file*

23. Click the **Next** button. Xcode asks for a location to store your file. Click the **Create** button. Xcode displays the TableViewCell.swift file in the Navigator pane.

24. Click the Main.storyboard file in the Navigator pane.

25. Click customCell in the Document Outline and then choose View ➤ Inspectors ➤ Show Identity Inspector, or click the Identity Inspector icon in the upper right corner of the Xcode window.

26. Click in the Class popup menu and choose TableViewCell, which is the .swift file you just created as shown in Figure 15-10.

Custom Class
Class TableViewCell
Module TableViewCellVisualApp
Inherit Module From Target

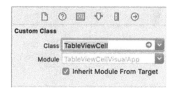

Figure 15-10. *Connecting the Table View Cell to the TableViewCellswift file*

27. Choose View ➤ Assistant Editor ➤ Show Assistant Editor, or click the Assistant Editor icon in the upper right corner of the Xcode window. This displays the Main.storyboard file on the left and a .swift file on the right.

28. Click the icon that looks like two circles intertwined at the top of the Assistant Editor as shown in Figure 15-11. A popup menu appears.

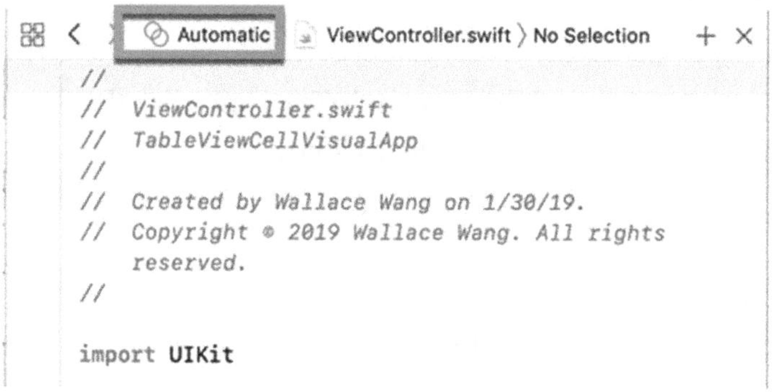

Automatic
ViewController.swift 〉 No Selection
//
// ViewController.swift
// TableViewCellVisualApp
//
// Created by Wallace Wang on 1/30/19.
// Copyright © 2019 Wallace Wang. All rights reserved.
//
import UIKit

Figure 15-11. *The icon of two intertwined circles*

29. Choose Manual ➤ TableViewCellVisualApp ➤ TableViewCellVisualApp ➤ TableViewCell.swift as shown in Figure 15-12. Xcode now displays the TableViewCell.swift file to the right of the Main.storyboard file.

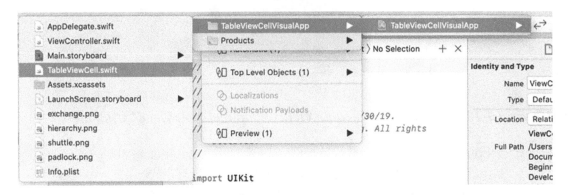

Figure 15-12. *Navigating to the TableViewCell.swift file*

30. Move the mouse pointer over the top label, hold down the Control key, and Ctrl-drag under the "class TableViewCell" line in the TableViewCell.swift file.

31. Release the Control key and the left mouse button. A popup window appears.

32. Click in the Name text field, type **mainText**, and click the Connect button. Xcode creates an IBOutlet as follows:

@IBOutlet var mainText: UILabel!

33. Move the mouse pointer over the bottom label, hold down the Control key, and Ctrl-drag under the IBOutlet line.

34. Release the Control key and the left mouse button. A popup window appears.

35. Click in the Name text field, type **detailText**, and click the Connect button. Xcode creates an IBOutlet as follows:

@IBOutlet var detailText: UILabel!

36. Move the mouse pointer over the image view, hold down the Control key, and Ctrl-drag under the IBOutlet line.

37. Release the Control key and the left mouse button. A popup window appears.

38. Click in the Name text field, type **cellImage**, and click the Connect button. Xcode creates an IBOutlet as follows:

```
@IBOutlet var cellImage: UIImageView!
```

The entire TableViewCell.swift file should look like this:

```
import UIKit

class TableViewCell: UITableViewCell {

    @IBOutlet var mainText: UILabel!
    @IBOutlet var detailText: UILabel!
    @IBOutlet var cellImage: UIImageView!

    override func awakeFromNib() {
        super.awakeFromNib()
        // Initialization code
    }

    override func setSelected(_ selected: Bool, animated: Bool) {
        super.setSelected(selected, animated: animated)

        // Configure the view for the selected state
    }

}
```

39. Choose View ➤ Standard Editor ➤ Show Standard Editor, or click the Standard Editor icon in the upper right corner of the Xcode window.

40. Click the ViewController.swift file in the Navigator pane.

41. Modify the class ViewController line as follows:

```
class ViewController: UIViewController, UITableViewDelegate,
UITableViewDataSource {
```

42. Drag and drop four images into the Navigator pane (see Figure 15-3). A dialog appears, asking how to add the files to your project.

43. Click the Finish button. Note the exact names of all the image files.

44. Underneath the class ViewController line, add the following three
     arrays:

```
let mainArray = ["Shuttle bus", "Hierarchy", "Exchange",
"Padlock"]
let detailArray = ["6am - 10pm", "Acme corporation", "Ideas
worth sharing", "Access denied"]
let imageArray = ["shuttle.png", "hierarchy.png", "exchange.
png", "padlock.png"]
```

     For the imageArray, make sure you change the file names to
     match the actual image files you dragged and dropped in the
     Navigator pane in step 42. In a real app, you would likely use a
     data structure that would keep all related data together rather
     than stored in three separate arrays.

45. Underneath the viewDidLoad method, add the following function
     to count the number of rows in each section:

```
func tableView(_ tableView: UITableView, numberOfRowsInSection
section: Int) -> Int {
    return mainArray.count
}
```

46. Underneath the previous function, add the following function to
     fill the table view with data:

```
func tableView(_ tableView: UITableView, cellForRowAt
indexPath: IndexPath) -> UITableViewCell {
    let cell: TableViewCell = tableView.dequeueReusableCell
    (withIdentifier: "customCell") as! TableViewCell

    cell.mainText?.text = self.mainArray[indexPath.row]
    cell.detailText?.text = self.detailArray[indexPath.row]
    cell.imageView?.image = UIImage(named: self.
    imageArray[indexPath.row])
    return cell
}
```

The first line defines a cell based on the TableViewCell.swift file. Then it stores the mainArray strings in the mainText IBOutlet, the detailArray strings in the detailText IBOutlet, and the imageArray files in the image view IBOutlet of the TableViewCell.swift file.

47. Underneath the previous function, add the following function to identify which item the user selected:

```swift
func tableView(_ tableView: UITableView, didSelectRowAt
indexPath: IndexPath) {
    let selectedItem = mainArray[indexPath.row]
    let alert = UIAlertController(title: "Your Choice",
    message: "\(selectedItem)", preferredStyle: .alert)

    let okAction = UIAlertAction(title: "OK", style: .default,
    handler: { action -> Void in
        //Just dismiss the action sheet
    })
    alert.addAction(okAction)

    self.present(alert, animated: true, completion: nil)
}
```

The entire ViewController.swift file should look like this:

```swift
import UIKit

class ViewController: UIViewController, UITableViewDelegate,
UITableViewDataSource {

    let mainArray = ["Shuttle bus", "Hierarchy", "Exchange",
    "Padlock"]
    let detailArray = ["6am - 10pm", "Acme corporation", "Ideas
    worth sharing", "Access denied"]
    let imageArray = ["shuttle.png", "hierarchy.png", "exchange.
    png", "padlock.png"]

    func tableView(_ tableView: UITableView, numberOfRowsInSection
    section: Int) -> Int {
        return mainArray.count
    }
```

```swift
func tableView(_ tableView: UITableView, cellForRowAt
indexPath: IndexPath) -> UITableViewCell {
    let cell: TableViewCell = tableView.dequeueReusableCell
    (withIdentifier: "customCell") as! TableViewCell

    cell.mainText?.text = self.mainArray[indexPath.row]
    cell.detailText?.text = self.detailArray[indexPath.row]
    cell.imageView?.image = UIImage(named: self.
    imageArray[indexPath.row])
    return cell
}

override func viewDidLoad() {
    super.viewDidLoad()
    // Do any additional setup after loading the view,
    typically from a nib.
}

func tableView(_ tableView: UITableView, didSelectRowAt
indexPath: IndexPath) {
    let selectedItem = mainArray[indexPath.row]
    let alert = UIAlertController(title: "Your Choice",
    message: "\(selectedItem)", preferredStyle: .alert)

    let okAction = UIAlertAction(title: "OK", style: .default,
    handler: { action -> Void in
        //Just dismiss the action sheet
    })
    alert.addAction(okAction)

    self.present(alert, animated: true, completion: nil)
}
}
```

48. Click the Run button or choose Product ➤ Run. The Simulator
     window appears, displaying the image and text in the two labels
     as shown in Figure 15-13. Notice that the bottom label appears
     indented from the left and appears in a different font and size,
     which we had customized earlier.

Figure 15-13. *The table view displaying the custom Table View Cell*

49. Click an item in the table view. An alert controller appears to identify your choice.

50. Click OK to dismiss the alert controller.

51. Choose Simulator ➤ Quit Simulator to return to Xcode.

Swipe to Add and Delete a Row

Table views can display large amounts of data in multiple rows. However, besides viewing data, you might also want to be able to add or delete data to a table view. One way to modify a table view to add or delete items is to use a left swiping gesture. When the user swipes left on a table view row, one or more buttons can appear, letting the user choose an option such as adding a new item or deleting the existing item.

To allow a left swiping gesture on a table view, row, we need an editActionsForRowAt function such as:

```
func tableView(_ tableView: UITableView, editActionsForRowAt indexPath:
IndexPath) -> [UITableViewRowAction]? {

}
```

Inside this function, we can define one or more buttons such as:

```
        let addAction = UITableViewRowAction(style:
        UITableViewRowAction.Style.normal, title: "Add", handler:
        {(action: UITableViewRowAction, indexPath: IndexPath) in

    })

    let deleteAction = UITableViewRowAction(style: UITableViewRowAction.
    Style.destructive, title: "Delete", handler: {(action:
    UITableViewRowAction, indexPath: IndexPath) in

    })

    return [deleteAction, addAction]
```

The preceding code defines two buttons labeled "Add" and "Delete". The "Add" button appears with the .normal style, which makes it appear light gray. The "Delete" button appears with the .destructive style so it appears as bright red. The last line returns the two UITableViewRowAction constants that represent the "Add" and "Delete" buttons.

To see how to add and delete items in a table view using a swiping gesture, follow these steps:

1. Create a new iOS project using the Single View App template (see Chapter 1) and name this new project EditRowApp. This creates a single view for the user interface.

2. Click the Main.storyboard file in the Navigator pane. Xcode displays the single view.

3. Click the Library icon to open the Object Library window.

4. Drag and drop a table view anywhere on the view.

5. Resize the table view so it fills the entire screen.

6. Choose Editor ➤ Resolve Auto Layout Issues ➤ Reset to Suggested Constraints. Xcode adds constraints to the table view.

7. Choose View ➤ Inspectors ➤ Show Attributes Inspector, or click the Attributes Inspector icon in the upper right corner of the Xcode window.

8. Choose View ➤ Assistant Editor ➤ Show Assistant Editor, or click the Assistant Editor icon in the upper right corner of the Xcode window.

9. Move the mouse pointer over the table view, hold down the Control key, and Ctrl-drag under the "class ViewController" line in the ViewController.swift file.

10. Release the Control key and the left mouse button. A popup window appears.

11. Click in the Name text field, type **tableView**, and click the Connect button. Xcode creates an IBOutlet as follows:

```
@IBOutlet var tableView: UITableView!
```

12. Choose View ➤ Standard Editor ➤ Show Standard Editor, or click the Standard Editor icon in the upper right corner of the Xcode window.

13. Click the ViewController.swift file in the Navigator pane.

14. Modify the class ViewController line by adding UITableViewDelegate, UITableViewDataSource as follows:

```
class ViewController: UIViewController, UITableViewDelegate,
UITableViewDataSource {
```

The purpose of this code is to identify the ViewController.swift file as both the delegate and data source for the table view.

15. Underneath the class ViewController line, add the following array:

```
var petArray = ["cat", "dog", "parakeet", "parrot", "canary",
"finch", "tropical fish", "goldfish", "sea horses", "hamster",
"gerbil", "rabbit", "turtle", "snake", "lizard", "hermit crab"]
```

Notice that this petArray is declared as "var", which means we'll be able to modify it by adding or deleting items to this array. If we declared this petArray with "let", then we wouldn't be able to add or delete items from the array.

16. Add the following line underneath the petArray:

```
let cellID = "cellID"
```

17. Modify the viewDidLoad method as follows:

```
        override func viewDidLoad() {
           super.viewDidLoad()
           tableView.dataSource = self
           tableView.delegate = self
           // Do any additional setup after loading the view,
           typically from a nib.
        }
```

18. Underneath the viewDidLoad method, add the following function
to define how many rows appear in the table view, which consists
of only one section:

```
func tableView(_ tableView: UITableView, numberOfRowsInSection
section: Int) -> Int {
    return petArray.count
}
```

19. Underneath the previous function, add the following function to
fill the table view with data from the petArray:

```
func tableView(_ tableView: UITableView, cellForRowAt
indexPath: IndexPath) -> UITableViewCell {
    var cell = tableView.dequeueReusableCell(withIdentifier:
    cellID)
    if (cell == nil) {
        cell = UITableViewCell(
            style: UITableViewCell.CellStyle.default,
            reuseIdentifier: cellID)
    }
    cell?.textLabel?.text = petArray[indexPath.row]
    return cell!
}
```

20. Underneath the previous function, add the following function to
display the item the user selected from the table view:

```
func tableView(_ tableView: UITableView, didSelectRowAt
indexPath: IndexPath) {
    let selectedItem = petArray[indexPath.row]
    let alert = UIAlertController(title: "Your Choice",
    message: "\(selectedItem)", preferredStyle: .alert)

    let okAction = UIAlertAction(title: "OK", style: .default,
    handler: { action -> Void in
        //Just dismiss the action sheet
    })
```

```
        alert.addAction(okAction)

        self.present(alert, animated: true, completion: nil)
    }
```

21. Underneath the previous function, add the following function to
     display an alert controller with a text field, letting the user type in
     data to add a new row to the table view:

```
func displayAlert(location: Int) {
    let alert = UIAlertController(title: "Add", message: "New
    Pet", preferredStyle: .alert)

    alert.addTextField(configurationHandler: {(textField) in
        textField.placeholder = "Pet type here"
    })

    let okAction = UIAlertAction(title: "OK", style: .default,
    handler: { action -> Void in
        let savedText = alert.textFields![0] as UITextField
        self.petArray.insert(savedText.text ?? "default", at:
        location)
        self.tableView.reloadData()
    })

    let cancelAction = UIAlertAction(title: "Cancel", style:
    .default, handler: { action -> Void in
        // Do nothing
    })

    alert.addAction(okAction)
    alert.addAction(cancelAction)
    self.present(alert, animated: true, completion: nil)
}
```

This displayAlert function accepts an integer that represents an
index location value that identifies the current item selected in the
petArray. Then it displays an alert controller that shows a text field
and two buttons labeled "OK" and "Cancel".

If the user taps the "Cancel" button, nothing happens and the alert controller goes away. If the user taps the "OK" button, then the alert controller takes the contents in the text field and inserts it into the petArray. Then it reloads the entire table view to display the modified array contents.

22. Underneath the previous function, add the following function to display two buttons when the user swipes on the table view row:

```
func tableView(_ tableView: UITableView, editActionsForRowAt
indexPath: IndexPath) -> [UITableViewRowAction]? {
    let addAction = UITableViewRowAction(style:
    UITableViewRowAction.Style.normal, title: "Add", handler:
    {(action: UITableViewRowAction, indexPath: IndexPath) in
        self.displayAlert(location: indexPath.row)
    })

    let deleteAction = UITableViewRowAction(style:
    UITableViewRowAction.Style.destructive, title: "Delete",
    handler: {(action: UITableViewRowAction, indexPath:
    IndexPath) in
        self.petArray.remove(at: indexPath.row)
        tableView.deleteRows(at: [indexPath], with:
        UITableView.RowAnimation.fade)
    })

    return [deleteAction, addAction]
}
```

The addAction line defines an "Add" button using the .normal style that displays the button in gray. Tapping the "Add" button runs the displayAlert function, passing the current index value of the item selected in the table view.

The deleteAction line defines a "Delete" button that removes the selected item from both the petArray and the table view.

The entire ViewController.swift file should look like this:

```swift
import UIKit

class ViewController: UIViewController, UITableViewDelegate,
UITableViewDataSource {

    @IBOutlet var tableView: UITableView!

    var petArray = ["cat", "dog", "parakeet", "parrot", "canary",
    "finch", "tropical fish", "goldfish", "sea horses", "hamster",
    "gerbil", "rabbit", "turtle", "snake", "lizard", "hermit crab"]

    let cellID = "cellID"

    override func viewDidLoad() {
        super.viewDidLoad()
        tableView.dataSource = self
        tableView.delegate = self
        // Do any additional setup after loading the view,
        typically from a nib.
    }

    func tableView(_ tableView: UITableView, numberOfRowsInSection
    section: Int) -> Int {
        return petArray.count
    }

    func tableView(_ tableView: UITableView, cellForRowAt
    indexPath: IndexPath) -> UITableViewCell {
        var cell = tableView.dequeueReusableCell(withIdentifier:
        cellID)
        if (cell == nil) {
            cell = UITableViewCell(
                style: UITableViewCell.CellStyle.default,
                reuseIdentifier: cellID)
        }
        cell?.textLabel?.text = petArray[indexPath.row]
        return cell!
    }
```

```swift
func tableView(_ tableView: UITableView, didSelectRowAt
indexPath: IndexPath) {
    let selectedItem = petArray[indexPath.row]
    let alert = UIAlertController(title: "Your Choice",
    message: "\(selectedItem)", preferredStyle: .alert)

    let okAction = UIAlertAction(title: "OK", style: .default,
    handler: { action -> Void in
        //Just dismiss the action sheet
    })
    alert.addAction(okAction)

    self.present(alert, animated: true, completion: nil)
}

func displayAlert(location: Int) {
    let alert = UIAlertController(title: "Add", message: "New
    Pet", preferredStyle: .alert)

    alert.addTextField(configurationHandler: {(textField) in
        textField.placeholder = "Pet type here"
    })

    let okAction = UIAlertAction(title: "OK", style: .default,
    handler: { action -> Void in
        let savedText = alert.textFields![0] as UITextField
        self.petArray.insert(savedText.text ?? "default", at:
        location)
        self.tableView.reloadData()
    })

    let cancelAction = UIAlertAction(title: "Cancel", style:
    .default, handler: { action -> Void in
        // Do nothing
    })

    alert.addAction(okAction)
    alert.addAction(cancelAction)
    self.present(alert, animated: true, completion: nil)
}
```

```swift
func tableView(_ tableView: UITableView, editActionsForRowAt
indexPath: IndexPath) -> [UITableViewRowAction]? {
    let addAction = UITableViewRowAction(style:
    UITableViewRowAction.Style.normal, title: "Add", handler:
    {(action: UITableViewRowAction, indexPath: IndexPath) in
        self.displayAlert(location: indexPath.row)
    })

    let deleteAction = UITableViewRowAction(style:
    UITableViewRowAction.Style.destructive, title: "Delete",
    handler: {(action: UITableViewRowAction, indexPath:
    IndexPath) in
        self.petArray.remove(at: indexPath.row)
        tableView.deleteRows(at: [indexPath], with:
        UITableView.RowAnimation.fade)
    })

    return [deleteAction, addAction]
}

}
```

23. Click the Run button or choose Product ➤ Run. The Simulator window appears, displaying the table view.

24. Move the mouse pointer over "tropical fish", hold down the left mouse button, and drag to the left. The Add and Delete buttons appear as shown in Figure 15-14.

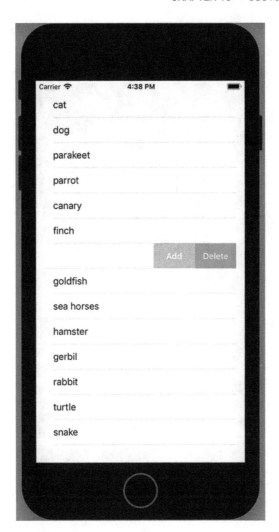

Figure 15-14. *Swiping to the left reveals an Add and a Delete button*

25.   Click the Add button. An alert controller appears displaying a text field as shown in Figure 15-15.

Figure 15-15.   *The alert controller lets the user type in new text*

26.   Click in the text field (that displays "Pet type here" as placeholder text), type **tarantula**, and click the OK button. Notice that the table view now displays "tarantula".

27.   Move the mouse pointer over "rabbit", hold down the left mouse button, and drag to the left. The Add and Delete buttons appear (see Figure 15-14).

28.   Click the Delete button. Notice the row containing "rabbit" disappears.

29.   Choose Simulator ➤ Quit Simulator to return to Xcode.

Summary

By defining different Table View Cell styles, you can display main text, detail text that often appears in a smaller font size, and an image. Images and detail text can make data displayed in a table view more visually interesting and descriptive.

As an alternative to choosing different cell styles, you can also design a custom Table View Cell by dragging and dropping a Table View Cell from the Object Library window onto a table view. Once you've created a custom Table View Cell, you can drag and drop other objects onto this cell such as multiple labels and image views where you can customize each label or image view to create a unique visual effect.

While table views can be handy for displaying data, they can also be useful to allow editing such as adding or deleting rows in a table view. To do this, you can include a left swipe gesture that lets a row display buttons. By clicking a button, users can add a new item to a table view or delete an existing row.

By customizing Table View Cells and implementing left swipe gestures to add or delete rows in a table view, you can define table views unique to your app.

CHAPTER 16

Using Collection Views

Table views are great for displaying large amounts of data in rows that the user can scroll through. While table views are perfect for the smaller, narrower screen of the iPhone, they are limited to scrolling rows of data up and down. If you want to scroll data horizontally or display multiple columns of data, you can use a Collection View instead.

Like table views, Collection Views need a data source and a delegate that implements methods that define how much data will appear in the Collection View. Think of Collection Views as more versatile table views.

Creating a Collection View

Collection Views display data in cells that make up a grid that can scroll vertically or horizontally. To see how to create a simple Collection View, follow these steps:

1. Create a new iOS project using the Single View App template (see Chapter 1) and name this new project SimpleCollectionViewApp. This creates a single view for the user interface.

2. Click the Main.storyboard file in the Navigator pane. Xcode displays the single view.

3. Click the Library icon to open the Object Library window.

4. Drag and drop a Collection View, as shown in Figure 16-1, on the view.

Collection View - Displays data in a collection of cells.

Figure 16-1. *A Collection View in the Object Library window*

© Wallace Wang 2019
W. Wang, *Beginning iPhone Development with Swift 5*, https://doi.org/10.1007/978-1-4842-4865-2_16

5. Resize the Collection View so it fills the entire screen.

6. Choose Editor ➤ Resolve Auto Layout Issues ➤ Reset to Suggested Constraints. Xcode adds constraints to the Collection View.

7. Click Collection View Cell in the Document Outline.

8. Choose View ➤ Inspectors ➤ Show Attributes Inspector, or click the Attributes Inspector icon in the upper right corner of the Xcode window.

9. Click in the Identifier text field, type **customCell**, and press ENTER as shown in Figure 16-2.

Figure 16-2. *The Identifier text field appears in the Collection View Cell's Attributes Inspector pane*

10. Choose View ➤ Assistant Editor ➤ Show Assistant Editor, or click the Assistant Editor icon in the upper right corner of the Xcode window.

11. Move the mouse pointer over the Collection View, hold down the Control key, and Ctrl-drag under the "class ViewController" line in the ViewController.swift file.

12. Release the Control key and the left mouse button. A popup window appears.

13. Click in the Name text field, type **collectionView**, and click the Connect button. Xcode creates an IBOutlet as follows:

```
@IBOutlet var collectionView: UICollectionView!
```

14. Choose View ➤ Standard Editor ➤ Show Standard Editor, or click the Standard Editor icon in the upper right corner of the Xcode window.

15. Click the ViewController.swift file in the Navigator pane.

16. Modify the class ViewController line by adding
     UITableViewDelegate, UITableViewDataSource as follows:

```
class ViewController: UIViewController, UICollectionViewDataSource,
UICollectionViewDelegate {
```

The purpose of this code is to identify the ViewController.swift file
as both the delegate and data source for the Collection View.

17. Underneath the class ViewController line, add the following:

```
var cellColor = true
```

18. Modify the viewDidLoad method as follows:

```
override func viewDidLoad() {
    super.viewDidLoad()
    collectionView.dataSource = self
    collectionView.delegate = self
    // Do any additional setup after loading the view.
}
```

19. Add the following function underneath the viewDidLoad method
     to define how many items appear in the Collection View section.
     By default, a Collection View has one section:

```
func collectionView(_ collectionView: UICollectionView,
numberOfItemsInSection section: Int) -> Int {
    return 100
}
```

20. Add the following function underneath the viewDidLoad method
     to fill the Collection View Cells with data:

```
func collectionView(_ collectionView: UICollectionView,
cellForItemAt indexPath: IndexPath) -> UICollectionViewCell {
    let cell = collectionView.dequeueReusableCell(withReuseIde
    ntifier: "customCell", for: indexPath)
    // Alternate colors in the Collection View cells
```

```
        if cellColor {
            cell.backgroundColor = UIColor.yellow
        } else {
            cell.backgroundColor = UIColor.green
        }

        cellColor = !cellColor

        return cell
    }
```

This function defines the Collection View Cell by its identifier "customCell":

```
let cell = collectionView.dequeueReusableCell(withReuseIdentifier:
"customCell", for: indexPath)
```

Next, if the value of cellColor is true, then it fills the Collection View Cell with the color yellow. Otherwise if the value of cellColor is false, then it fills the Collection View Cell with the color green.

```
        if cellColor {
            cell.backgroundColor = UIColor.yellow
        } else {
            cell.backgroundColor = UIColor.green
        }
```

Finally it changes the value of cellColor from true to false (or false to true) and returns the cell.

The complete ViewController.swift file should look like this:

```
import UIKit
```

```
class ViewController: UIViewController, UICollectionViewDataSource,
UICollectionViewDelegate {

    @IBOutlet var collectionView: UICollectionView!

    var cellColor = true

    override func viewDidLoad() {
```

```
    super.viewDidLoad()
    collectionView.dataSource = self
    collectionView.delegate = self
    // Do any additional setup after loading the view.
}

func collectionView(_ collectionView: UICollectionView,
numberOfItemsInSection section: Int) -> Int {
    return 100
}

func collectionView(_ collectionView: UICollectionView,
cellForItemAt indexPath: IndexPath) -> UICollectionViewCell {
    let cell = collectionView.dequeueReusableCell(withReuseIde
    ntifier: "customCell", for: indexPath)
    // Alternate colors in the Collection View cells
    if cellColor {
        cell.backgroundColor = UIColor.yellow
    } else {
        cell.backgroundColor = UIColor.green
    }

    cellColor = !cellColor

    return cell
}

}
```

21. Click the Run button or choose Product ➤ Run. The Simulator
     window appears, displaying the Collection View showing
     alternating green and yellow cells as shown in Figure 16-3.

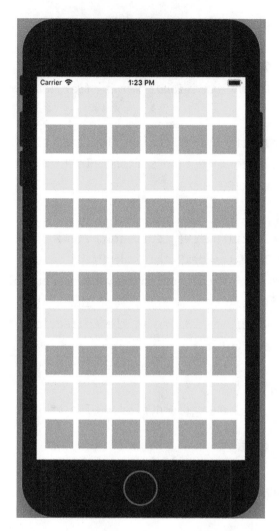

Figure 16-3. *The Collection View displaying alternating cell colors*

22. Scroll up and down.

23. Choose Simulator ➤ Quit Simulator to return to Xcode.

24. Click the Main.storyboard file and click Collection View in the Document Outline.

25. Choose View ➤ Inspectors ➤ Show Attributes Inspector, or click the Attributes Inspector icon in the upper right corner of the Xcode window.

26. Click the Scroll Direction popup menu and choose Horizontal as shown in Figure 16-4.

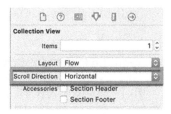

Figure 16-4. *The Scroll Direction popup menu lets you choose between Vertical or Horizontal scrolling*

27.   Click the Run button or choose Product ➤ Run. The Simulator window appears, displaying the Collection View showing alternating green and yellow cells (see Figure 16-3).

28.   Notice that you can now scroll left and right but not up or down.

29.   Choose Simulator ➤ Quit Simulator to return to Xcode.

Displaying Data in a Collection View

The main purpose of a Collection View is to display information in cells. To display information in a cell takes several steps:

- Drag and drop objects onto the Collection View Cell.

- Create a new .swift class file to represent the Collection View Cell.

- Connect this new .swift class file to the Collection View Cell in the Identity Inspector pane.

- Ctrl-drag from the objects on the Collection View Cell to the .swift class file to create IBOutlet variables to represent each object.

- Write code in the cellForItemAt function to store data in each Collection View Cell.

When designing a Collection View Cell, you can resize its height and width. In addition, you can also define the spacing between cells along with how much space cells appear away from the top, left, bottom, or right edges of the screen.

To see how to display text in a Collection View Cell, follow these steps:

1.   Create a new iOS project using the Single View App template (see Chapter 1) and name this new project CollectionViewDataApp. This creates a single view for the user interface.

2. Click the Main.storyboard file in the Navigator pane. Xcode displays the single view.

3. Click the Library icon to open the Object Library window.

4. Drag and drop a Collection View anywhere on the view.

5. Resize the Collection View so it fills the entire screen.

6. Choose Editor ➤ Resolve Auto Layout Issues ➤ Reset to Suggested Constraints. Xcode adds constraints to the Collection View.

7. Choose File ➤ New ➤ File. Xcode displays a list of templates.

8. Choose Cocoa Touch Class under the iOS category and click the **Next** button. Another dialog appears, asking for a class name and subclass.

9. Click in the Class text field and type **itemCell**.

10. Click in the Subclass of popup menu and choose UICollectionViewCell as shown in Figure 16-5.

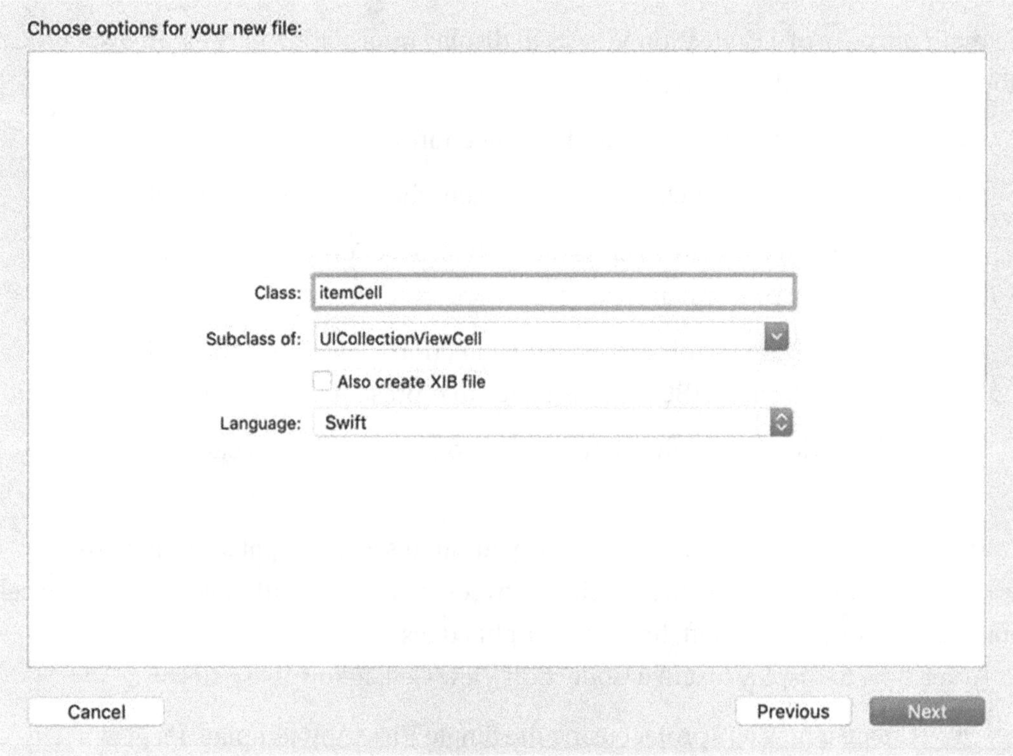

Choose options for your new file:

Class: itemCell

Subclass of: UICollectionViewCell

☐ Also create XIB file

Language: Swift

Cancel   Previous   Next

Figure 16-5. *Creating a new .swift class file for the Collection View Cell*

11.   Click the **Next** button. Xcode asks where to store the file.

12.   Click the **Create** button. Xcode displays the itemCell.swift file in the Navigator pane.

13.   Click the Main.storyboard in the Navigator pane, click the Collection View Cell in the Document Outline and choose View ➤ Inspectors ➤ Show Attributes Inspector, or click the Attributes Inspector icon in the upper right corner of the Xcode window.

14.   Click in the identifier text field, type **customCell**, and press ENTER as shown in Figure 16-6.

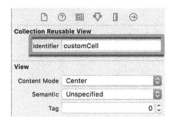

Figure 16-6. *Defining the Collection View Cell's identifier the Attributes Inspector pane.*

15.   Click in the Background color popup menu and choose a color such as yellow. Xcode highlights the Collection View Cell.

16.   Choose View ➤ Inspectors ➤ Show Identity Inspector, or click the Identity Inspector icon in the upper right corner of the Xcode window.

17.   Click in the Class popup menu and choose itemCell as shown in Figure 16-7.

Figure 16-7. *Connecting the Collection View Cell to the itemCell.swift file*

18. Click the Library icon to open the Object Library window and drag and drop a label in the center of the Collection View Cell.

19. Click the Align icon at the bottom of the Xcode window and select the Horizontally in Container and Vertically in Container check boxes. Then click the Add 2 Constraints button. Xcode adds constraints to make sure the label is centered inside the Collection View Cell as shown in Figure 16-8.

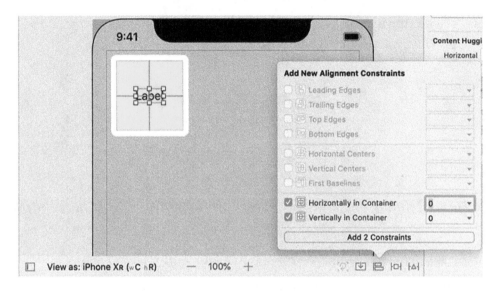

Figure 16-8. *Centering a label inside a Collection View label*

20. Click Collection View in the Document Outline and then choose View ➤ Inspectors ➤ Show Size Inspector, or click the Size Inspector icon in the upper right corner of the Xcode window.

21. Click in the Cell Size Width text fields, type 100, and press ENTER.

22. Click in the Cell Size Height text fields, type 100, and press ENTER.

23. Click in the Min Spacing For Cells text field, type 20, and press ENTER.

24. Click in the Section Insets Top text field, type 15, and press ENTER. Xcode moves the Collection View Cell down from the top.

25. Click in the Section Insets Left text field, type 15, and press ENTER. Xcode moves the Collection View Cell away from the left edge as shown in Figure 16-9.

Figure 16-9. *Modifying the cell size and spacing in a Collection View*

26. Choose View ➤ Assistant Editor ➤ Show Assistant Editor, or click the Assistant Editor icon in the upper right corner of the Xcode window. This displays the Main.storyboard file on the left and the ViewController.swift file on the right.

27. Move the mouse pointer over the Collection View in the Document Outline, hold down the Control key, and Ctrl-drag from the Collection View to the ViewController.swift file underneath the "class ViewController" line.

28. Release the Control key and the left mouse button. A popup window appears.

29. Click in the Name text field and type **collectionView**. Then click the Connect button. Xcode creates an IBOutlet as follows:

    @IBOutlet var collectionView: UICollectionView!

30. Move the mouse pointer over Label under customCell in the Document Outline. If Xcode does not display the itemCell.swift file in the Assistant Editor, click the two intertwined circles icon at the top of the Assistant Editor to display a menu.

31. Choose Automatic ➤ itemCell.swift as shown in Figure 16-10.

Figure 16-10. *Choosing the itemCell.swift file to appear in the Assistant Editor*

32. Move the mouse pointer over the Label, hold down the Control key, and Ctrl-drag from the Label under the "class TableViewCell" line in the itemCell.swift file.

33. Release the Control key and the left mouse button. A popup window appears.

34. Click in the Name text field, type **itemLabel**, and click the Connect button. Xcode creates an IBOutlet as follows:

```
@IBOutlet var itemLabel: UILabel!
```

The entire itemCell.swift file should look like this:

```
import UIKit

class itemCell: UICollectionViewCell {

    @IBOutlet var itemLabel: UILabel!

}
```

35. Choose View ➤ Standard Editor ➤ Show Standard Editor, or click the Standard Editor icon in the upper right corner of the Xcode window.

36. Click the ViewController.swift file in the Navigator pane.

37. Edit the class ViewController line as follows:

```
class ViewController: UIViewController, UICollectionViewDataSource,
UICollectionViewDelegate {
```

38. Type the following underneath the IBOutlet:

```
let petArray = ["cat", "dog", "parakeet", "parrot", "canary",
"finch", "tropical fish", "goldfish", "sea horses", "hamster",
"gerbil", "rabbit", "turtle", "snake", "lizard", "hermit crab"]
```

39. Edit the viewDidLoad method as follows:

```
override func viewDidLoad() {
    super.viewDidLoad()
    collectionView.dataSource = self
    collectionView.delegate = self
    // Do any additional setup after loading the view.
}
```

40. Add the following function under the viewDidLoad method:

```
func collectionView(_ collectionView: UICollectionView,
numberOfItemsInSection section: Int) -> Int {
    return petArray.count
}
```

41. Add the following function under the previous function:

```
func collectionView(_ collectionView: UICollectionView,
cellForItemAt indexPath: IndexPath) -> UICollectionViewCell {
    let cell = collectionView.dequeueReusableCell(withReuseIde
    ntifier: "customCell", for: indexPath) as! itemCell
    cell.itemLabel.text = petArray[indexPath.row]
    return cell
}
```

42. Add the following function under the previous function:

```
func collectionView(_ collectionView: UICollectionView,
didSelectItemAt indexPath: IndexPath) {
    let alert = UIAlertController(title: "Your Choice", message:
    "\(petArray[indexPath.row])", preferredStyle: .alert)
    let action = UIAlertAction(title: "OK", style: .default,
    handler: nil)
    alert.addAction(action)
```

```
    self.present(alert, animated: true, completion: nil)
}
```

The entire ViewController.swift file should look like this:

```
import UIKit

class ViewController: UIViewController, UICollectionViewDataSource,
UICollectionViewDelegate {

    @IBOutlet var collectionView: UICollectionView!

    let petArray = ["cat", "dog", "parakeet", "parrot", "canary",
    "finch", "tropical fish", "goldfish", "sea horses", "hamster",
    "gerbil", "rabbit", "turtle", "snake", "lizard", "hermit crab"]

    override func viewDidLoad() {
        super.viewDidLoad()
        collectionView.dataSource = self
        collectionView.delegate = self
        // Do any additional setup after loading the view.
    }

    func collectionView(_ collectionView: UICollectionView,
    numberOfItemsInSection section: Int) -> Int {
        return petArray.count
    }

    func collectionView(_ collectionView: UICollectionView,
    cellForItemAt indexPath: IndexPath) -> UICollectionViewCell {
        let cell = collectionView.dequeueReusableCell(withReuseIde
        ntifier: "customCell", for: indexPath) as! itemCell
        cell.itemLabel.text = petArray[indexPath.row]
        return cell
    }

    func collectionView(_ collectionView: UICollectionView,
    didSelectItemAt indexPath: IndexPath) {
        let alert = UIAlertController(title: "Your Choice", message:
        "\(petArray[indexPath.row])", preferredStyle: .alert)
```

```
let action = UIAlertAction(title: "OK", style: .default,
handler: nil)
alert.addAction(action)
self.present(alert, animated: true, completion: nil)
}

}
```

43. Click the Run button or choose Product ➤ Run. The Simulator
window appears, displaying text inside the Collection View labels
as shown in Figure 16-11.

Figure 16-11. *Displaying text from an array in multiple Collection View Cells*

44. Click a cell. An alert appears, listing the item you selected.

45. Click OK to dismiss the alert controller.

46. Choose Simulator ➤ Quit Simulator to return to Xcode.

Making any data appear in a Collection View Cell involves dragging and dropping objects inside that Collection View Cell. This example used a label but you can also add image views to display pictures inside each Collection View Cell as well.

Displaying Section Headers in a Collection View

The simplest Collection View consists of one section, which displays a grid of items on the screen. However, it's more likely that data can be divided into two or more groups or sections. When this occurs, a Collection View can display section headers to divide items on the screen.

Creating a section header involves several steps:

- Enable a section header in the Attributes Inspector pane of the Collection View.

- Define an arbitrary identifier name for the header.

- Drag and drop one or more objects into the section header such as a label.

- Connect the section header objects to IBOutlets in a .swift file.

- Implement the viewForSupplementaryElementOfKind method to define what appears in the header.

To see how to create and display section headers in a Collection View, follow these steps:

1. Create a new iOS project using the Single View App template (see Chapter 1) and name this new project CollectionViewSectionApp. This creates a single view for the user interface.

2. Click the Main.storyboard file in the Navigator pane. Xcode displays the single view.

3. Click the Library icon to open the Object Library window.

4. Drag and drop a Collection View anywhere on the view.

5. Resize the Collection View so it fills the entire screen.

6. Choose Editor ➤ Resolve Auto Layout Issues ➤ Reset to Suggested Constraints. Xcode adds constraints to the Collection View.

7. Choose View ➤ Inspectors ➤ Show Size Inspector, or click the Size Inspector icon in the upper right corner of the Xcode window.

8. Click in the Cell Size Width text field, type 100, and press ENTER.

9. Click in the Cell Size Height text field, type 100, and press ENTER.

10. Choose View ➤ Inspectors ➤ Show Attributes Inspector, or click the Attributes Inspector icon in the upper right corner of the Xcode window.

11. Select the Section Header check box as shown in Figure 16-12. Xcode creates a Collection Reusable View (section header) in the Document Outline and on the view as shown in Figure 16-13.

Figure 16-12. *Selecting the Section Header check box in the Attributes Inspector*

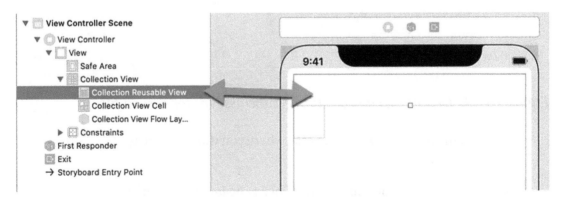

Figure 16-13. *The Collection Reusable View (section header)*

12. Click in the Background popup menu and choose a color to make the section header easy to see.

13. Choose File ➤ New ➤ File. A template dialog appears.

14. Click Cocoa Touch Class under the iOS category and click the **Next** button. Another dialog appears.

15. Click in the Class text field, type **itemCell**, and press ENTER.

16. Click in the Subclass of popup menu and choose UICollectionViewCell as shown in Figure 16-14.

Figure 16-14. *Defining a class name and subclass type for a .swift file*

17. Click the **Next** button. Xcode asks where you want to store the itemCell.swift file.

18. Click the **Create** button. Xcode displays the itemCell.swift file in the Navigator pane.

19. Click Collection Reusable View in the Document Outline and choose View ➤ Inspectors ➤ Show Attributes Inspector, or click the Attributes Inspector icon in the upper right corner of the Xcode window.

20. Click in the Identifier text field, type **headerView**, and press ENTER as shown in Figure 16-15.

Figure 16-15. *Defining an identifier for the section header*

21. Choose View ➤ Inspectors ➤ Show Identity Inspector, or click the Identity Inspector icon in the upper right corner of the Xcode window.

22. Click in the Class popup menu and choose itemCell as shown in Figure 16-16.

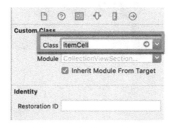

Figure 16-16. *Connecting the itemCell.swift file to the Collection Reusable View*

23. Click the Collection View Cell in the Document Outline.

24. Choose View ➤ Inspectors ➤ Show Identity Inspector, or click the Identity Inspector icon in the upper right corner of the Xcode window.

25. Click in the Class popup menu and choose itemCell (see Figure 16-16).

26. Choose View ➤ Inspectors ➤ Show Attributes Inspector, or click the Attributes Inspector icon in the upper right corner of the Xcode window.

27. Click in the Identifier text field, type **customCell**, and press ENTER.

28. Click in the Background popup menu and choose a color to make the Collection View Cell easy to see.

29. Click the Library icon to display the Object Library window.

30. Drag and drop a label in the center of the cell.

31. Click the Align icon at the bottom of the Xcode window, select the Horizontally in Container and Vertically in Container check boxes, then click the Add 2 Constraints button.

32. Click the Library icon to display the Object Library window.

33. Drag and drop a label in the center of the section header.

34. Click the Align icon at the bottom of the Xcode window, select the Horizontally in Container and Vertically in Container check boxes, then click the Add 2 Constraints button. The user interface should look like Figure 16-17.

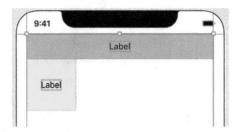

Figure 16-17. *A label in the center of the cell and section header*

35. Choose View ➤ Assistant Editor ➤ Show Assistant Editor, or click the Assistant Editor icon in the upper right corner of the Xcode window. The Main.storyboard appears in the left side.

36. Click the two entwined circles at the top of the Assistant Editor on the right side and choose Manual. Then navigate through the folders to select itemCell.swift.

37. Move the mouse pointer over the label in the section header, hold down the Control key, and Ctrl-drag under the "class ViewController" line in the itemCell.swift file.

38. Release the Control key and the left mouse button. A popup window appears.

39. Click in the Name text field, type **headerLabel**, and click the Connect button. Xcode creates an IBOutlet as follows:

    @IBOutlet var headerLabel: UILabel!

40. Move the mouse pointer over the label in the Collection View Cell, hold down the Control key, and Ctrl-drag under the "class ViewController" line in the itemCell.swift file.

41. Release the Control key and the left mouse button. A popup window appears.

42. Click in the Name text field, type **itemLabel**, and click the Connect button. Xcode creates an IBOutlet as follows:

    @IBOutlet var itemLabel: UILabel!

The entire itemCell.swift file should look like this:

import UIKit

class itemCell: UICollectionViewCell {

    @IBOutlet var headerLabel: UILabel!
    @IBOutlet var itemLabel: UILabel!
}

43. Choose View ➤ Standard Editor ➤ Show Standard Editor, or click the Standard Editor icon in the upper right corner of the Xcode window.

44. Click the ViewController.swift file in the Navigator pane.

45. Modify the class ViewController line by adding UICollectionViewDelegate, UICollectionViewDataSource as follows:

```
class ViewController: UIViewController, UICollectionViewDataSource,
UICollectionViewDelegate {
```

The purpose of this code is to identify the ViewController.swift file as both the delegate and data source for the Collection View.

46. Underneath the class ViewController line, add the following array:

```
let petArray = [["Mammal", "cat", "dog", "hamster", "gerbil",
"rabbit"], ["Bird", "parakeet", "parrot", "canary", "finch"],
["Fish", "tropical fish", "goldfish", "sea horses"], ["Reptile",
"turtle", "snake", "lizard"]]
```

This petArray consists of four string arrays where the first item in each array defines the section header such as "Mammal" or "Bird".

47. Click the Main.storyboard file in the Navigator pane.

48. Choose View ➤ Assistant Editor ➤ Show Assistant Editor, or click the Assistant Editor icon in the upper right corner of the Xcode window. The Main.storyboard appears on the left side and the ViewController.swift file should appear on the right side.

49. Move the mouse pointer over Collection View in the Document Outline, hold down the Control key, and Ctrl-drag under the "class ViewController" line in the itemCell.swift file.

50. Release the Control key and the left mouse button. A popup window appears.

51. Click in the Name text field, type **collectionView**, and click the Connect button. Xcode creates an IBOutlet as follows:

```
@IBOutlet var collectionView: UICollectionView!
```

52. Choose View ➤ Standard Editor ➤ Show Standard Editor, or click the Standard Editor icon in the upper right corner of the Xcode window.

53. Click the ViewController.swift file in the Navigator pane.

54. Modify the viewDidLoad method as follows:

```
override func viewDidLoad() {
    super.viewDidLoad()
    collectionView.delegate = self
    collectionView.dataSource = self
    // Do any additional setup after loading the view.
}
```

55. Underneath the viewDidLoad method, add the following function to define how many sections appear in the Collection View:

```
func numberOfSections(in collectionView: UICollectionView) ->
Int {
    return petArray.count
}
```

56. Underneath the previous function, add the following function to identify the number of items in each section:

```
func collectionView(_ collectionView: UICollectionView,
numberOfItemsInSection section: Int) -> Int {
    return petArray[section].count - 1
}
```

This function returns a value counting all items in each string array except one because one item in each string array is the section header name such as "Mammal".

57. Underneath the previous function, add the following function to fill the Collection View with data from the petArray:

```
func collectionView(_ collectionView: UICollectionView,
cellForItemAt indexPath: IndexPath) -> UICollectionViewCell {
```

```
let cell = collectionView.dequeueReusableCell(withReuseIde
ntifier: "customCell", for: indexPath) as! itemCell
cell.itemLabel.text = petArray[indexPath.section]
[indexPath.row + 1]
return cell
}
```

58. Underneath the previous function, add the following function to display the item the user selected from the Collection View:

```
func collectionView(_ collectionView: UICollectionView,
didSelectItemAt indexPath: IndexPath) {
    let alert = UIAlertController(title: "Your Choice", message:
    "\(petArray[indexPath.section][indexPath.row + 1])",
    preferredStyle: .alert)
    let action = UIAlertAction(title: "OK", style: .default,
    handler: nil)
    alert.addAction(action)
    self.present(alert, animated: true, completion: nil)
}
```

59. Underneath the previous function, add the following function to fill the section headers with the first item in each string array:

```
func collectionView(_ collectionView: UICollectionView,
viewForSupplementaryElementOfKind kind: String, at indexPath:
IndexPath) -> UICollectionReusableView {
    let headerView = collectionView.dequeueReusableSupplement
    aryView(ofKind: kind, withReuseIdentifier: "headerView",
    for: indexPath) as! itemCell
    headerView.headerLabel.text = petArray[indexPath.section][0]
    return headerView
}
```

The entire ViewController.swift file should look like this:

```swift
import UIKit

class ViewController: UIViewController, UICollectionViewDataSource,
UICollectionViewDelegate {

    @IBOutlet var collectionView: UICollectionView!

    let petArray = [["Mammal", "cat", "dog", "hamster", "gerbil",
    "rabbit"], ["Bird", "parakeet", "parrot", "canary", "finch"],
    ["Fish", "tropical fish", "goldfish", "sea horses"],
    ["Reptile", "turtle", "snake", "lizard"]]

    override func viewDidLoad() {
        super.viewDidLoad()
        collectionView.delegate = self
        collectionView.dataSource = self
        // Do any additional setup after loading the view.
    }

    func numberOfSections(in collectionView: UICollectionView) ->
    Int {
        return petArray.count
    }

    func collectionView(_ collectionView: UICollectionView,
    numberOfItemsInSection section: Int) -> Int {
        return petArray[section].count - 1
    }

    func collectionView(_ collectionView: UICollectionView,
    cellForItemAt indexPath: IndexPath) -> UICollectionViewCell {
        let cell = collectionView.dequeueReusableCell(withReuseIde
        ntifier: "customCell", for: indexPath) as! itemCell
        cell.itemLabel.text = petArray[indexPath.section]
        [indexPath.row + 1]
        return cell
    }
```

```
func collectionView(_ collectionView: UICollectionView,
didSelectItemAt indexPath: IndexPath) {
    let alert = UIAlertController(title: "Your Choice", message:
    "\(petArray[indexPath.section][indexPath.row + 1])",
    preferredStyle: .alert)
    let action = UIAlertAction(title: "OK", style: .default,
    handler: nil)
    alert.addAction(action)
    self.present(alert, animated: true, completion: nil)
}

func collectionView(_ collectionView: UICollectionView,
viewForSupplementaryElementOfKind kind: String, at indexPath:
IndexPath) -> UICollectionReusableView {
    let headerView = collectionView.dequeueReusableSupplement
    aryView(ofKind: kind, withReuseIdentifier: "headerView",
    for: indexPath) as! itemCell
    headerView.headerLabel.text = petArray[indexPath.section][0]
    return headerView
}

}
```

60. Click the Run button or choose Product ➤ Run. The Simulator
     window appears, displaying the Collection View divided into
     sections as shown in Figure 16-18.

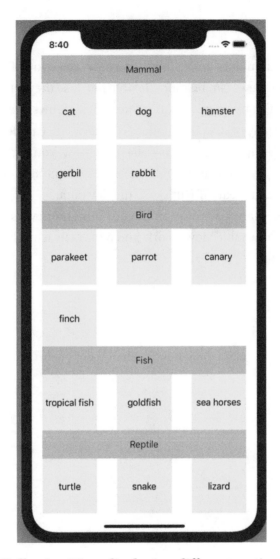

Figure 16-18. *The Collection View displaying different sections*

61. Click any item. An alert controller appears, displaying the item you chose.

62. Click OK to dismiss the alert controller.

63. Choose Simulator ➤ Quit Simulator to return to Xcode.

Summary

Collection Views work similar to table views where you need to define a delegate and a data source. Collection Views can be more flexible because they let you scroll horizontally or vertically and display items in grids rather than stacked rows like a table view.

To organize the display of data in a Collection View, you can define section headers. To further customize the appearance of a Collection View, you can drag and drop objects onto a Collection View Cell such as a label and create a separate .swift class file to link to this cell. That way you can create IBOutlets to display data.

Think of Collection Views as more complicated and more versatile table views. Once you understand how table views work, you can easily learn how to create and use Collection Views in your future apps.

CHAPTER 17

Using the Navigation Controller

Only the simplest apps consist of a single view such as the Calculator app. Most apps usually need two or more views to display information. While you could create buttons and link them to different views, this can be a clumsy solution. A far better solution is to organize related views together.

Xcode offers two ways to group related views together. One option is to use a Navigation Controller. This allows the user to browse through a list of views in sequential order where each view can open the next view and a special back button returns to the previous view as shown in Figure 17-1.

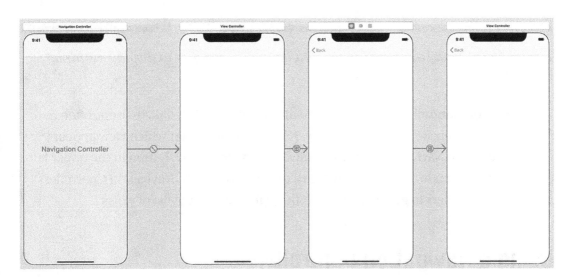

Figure 17-1. *A Navigation Controller can display multiple views in sequential order*

© Wallace Wang 2019

W. Wang, *Beginning iPhone Development with Swift 5*, https://doi.org/10.1007/978-1-4842-4865-2_17

Many of the apps that come with iOS rely on the Navigation Controller such as Mail, Photos, and the Settings app. Typically an app will display a list of options as rows in a table view. Selecting an option then displays another list of options until you finally reach the last screen that displays information as shown in Figure 17-2.

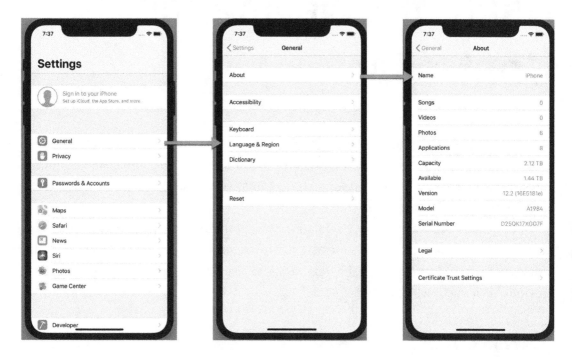

Figure 17-2. *Many apps rely on the Navigation Controller to display multiple options*

Navigation Controllers are designed to display hierarchical data to users, often in rows of information stored in a table view. Notice that no matter which view appears on the screen, the Navigation Controller always provides a Back button in the upper left corner of the screen to allow users to return to a previous view. Navigation Controllers make it easy for users to go back and forth through a sequential list of views.

Using a Navigation Controller

A Navigation Controller acts as a frame around a root view. The root view displays data while the Navigation Controller provides a navigation bar at the top of every view that can show a title and buttons as shown in Figure 17-3.

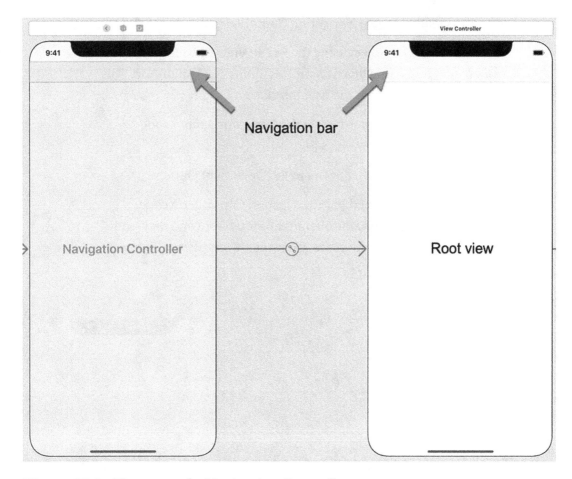

Figure 17-3. *The parts of a Navigation Controller*

Every Navigation Controller needs exactly one root view. By itself, a Navigation Controller and its root view does nothing more than display data. What makes the Navigation Controller useful is when the root view connects to another view through a link called a segue.

A segue consists of an identifying name and a visual link from one view to another. The first view needs a button or some other item for the user to trigger the segue and make it display the second view. Then the Navigation Controller automatically displays a Back button on the navigation bar of the second view, which allows the user to return to the first view. The only code needed to display another view is this:

```
performSegue(withIdentifier: "segueIdentifier", sender: self)
```

To see how to create a simple Navigation Controller, follow these steps:

1. Create a new iOS project using the Single View App template (see Chapter 1) and name this new project SimpleNavigationApp. This creates a single view for the user interface.

2. Click the Main.storyboard file in the Navigator pane. Xcode displays the single view.

3. Click the View Controller Scene in the Document Outline.

4. Choose Editor ➤ Embed In ➤ Navigation Controller. Xcode displays a Navigation Controller in the storyboard and makes the single view the root view of the Navigation Controller as shown in Figure 17-4.

Figure 17-4. *Embedding a view inside a Navigation Controller*

5. Click the Library icon to open the Object Library window.

6. Drag and drop a View Controller from the Object Library window
    to the storyboard as shown in Figure 17-5.

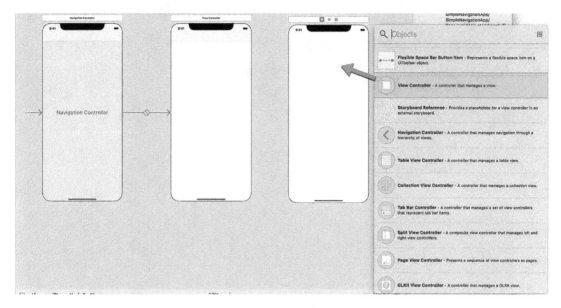

Figure 17-5. *Dragging and dropping a View Controller onto the storyboard*

7. Click View in the Document Outline under the View Controller
    that you just added to the storyboard. Xcode highlights the view.
    This view appears on the View Controller that is not connected to
    the Navigation Controller as shown in Figure 17-6.

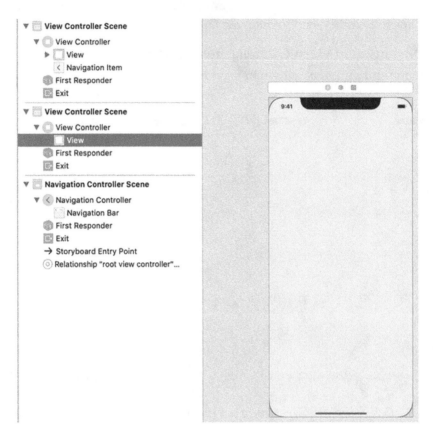

Figure 17-6. *Selecting the view of the newly added View Controller*

8. Choose View ➤ Inspectors ➤ Show Attributes Inspector, or click the Attributes Inspector icon in the upper right corner of the Xcode window.

9. Click Background popup menu and choose a color. Xcode fills the view of this newly added View Controller with a color. This color will make it easy to verify when this View Controller appears.

10. Click the View Controller icon of the root controller, hold down the Control key, and Ctrl-drag the mouse to point inside the newly added View Controller as shown in Figure 17-7.

Figure 17-7. *Creating a segue between the root controller and a separate View Controller*

11.   Release the Control key and the left mouse button. A popup menu appears as shown in Figure 17-8.

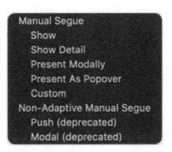

Figure 17-8. *A popup menu lets you define the segue*

12.   Choose Show. Xcode draws an arrow (segue) linking the root view to the newly added View Controller as shown in Figure 17-9.

Figure 17-9. *A segue links two views within a Navigation Controller*

13.   Click Show segue to "View Controller" in the Document Outline. Xcode highlights the segue between the two views as shown in Figure 17-10.

Figure 17-10. *Selecting the segue between two views*

14. Choose View ➤ Inspectors ➤ Show Attributes Inspector, or click the Attributes Inspector icon in the upper right corner of the Xcode window.

15. Click in the Identifier text field, type **firstLink**, and press ENTER as shown in Figure 17-11.

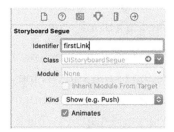

Figure 17-11. *Defining an identifier name for a segue*

16.   Click the ViewController.swift file in the Navigator pane.

17.   Add the following function:

```
override func touchesBegan(_ touches: Set<UITouch>, with
event: UIEvent?) {
    performSegue(withIdentifier: "firstLink", sender: self)
}
```

The purpose of this code is to identify the segue named "firstLink" and follow that segue to open another view, which is the view with a different background color.

The complete ViewController.swift file should look like this:

```
import UIKit

class ViewController: UIViewController {

    override func viewDidLoad() {
        super.viewDidLoad()
        // Do any additional setup after loading the view.
    }

    override func touchesBegan(_ touches: Set<UITouch>, with event:
    UIEvent?) {
        performSegue(withIdentifier: "firstLink", sender: self)
    }
}
```

18.   Click the Run button or choose Product ➤ Run. The Simulator window appears, displaying a blank screen.

19.   Click anywhere inside the Simulator window. This causes the touchesBegan function to run and call the performSegue command. Notice that the second view, with the colored background, now appears and displays a Back button in the upper left corner that was created automatically by the Navigation Controller.

20.   Choose Simulator ➤ Quit Simulator to return to Xcode.

Passing Data to Other Views

When an app displays multiple views in a Navigation Controller, data selected or entered in one view may need to be used in another view. Since the whole purpose of object-oriented programming is to isolate data, the solution is to pass data from one view to the other.

To receive data, a view needs the following:

- A .swift Cocoa Touch Class file connected to its View Controller.

- Properties defined with the "var" keyword in this .swift file. Any data stored in a property can then be copied into any objects on the user interface connected by an IBOutlet variable.

To send data, a view needs the following in its own .swift Cocoa Touch Class file:

- A prepare for segue function that defines a constant that represents the segue destination

- Data assigned to properties defined by the receiving view's .swift file

To see how to pass data from one view to another in a Navigation Controller, follow these steps:

1. Make sure the CollectionViewDataApp is loaded in Xcode.

2. Click the Main.storyboard file in the Navigator pane. Xcode displays storyboard.

3. Click the Library icon to open the Object Library window.

4. Drag and drop a label anywhere on the second (colored) view.

5. Resize the label's width so it can display more than a single word of text.

6. Choose Editor ➤ Resolve Auto Layout Issues ➤ Reset to Suggested Constraints. Xcode adds constraints to the label.

7. Choose File ➤ New ➤ File. Xcode displays a list of templates.

8. Choose Cocoa Touch Class under the iOS category and click the **Next** button. Another dialog appears, asking for a class name and subclass.

9.   Click in the Class text field and type **SecondViewController**.

10.   Click in the Subclass of popup menu and choose UIViewController.

11.   Click the **Next** button. Xcode asks where to store the file.

12.   Click the **Create** button. Xcode displays the SecondViewController.swift file in the Navigator pane.

13.   Click the Main.storyboard in the Navigator pane.

14.   Click the View Controller icon above the second view to select it.

15.   Choose View ➤ Inspectors ➤ Show Identity Inspector, or click the Identity Inspector icon in the upper right corner of the Xcode window.

16.   Click in the Class popup menu and choose SecondViewController as shown in Figure 17-12. This connects the SecondViewController.swift file to the second View Controller with the colored background.

Figure 17-12. *Connecting the SecondViewControllerswift file to the second View Controller*

17.   Choose View ➤ Assistant Editor ➤ Show Assistant Editor, or click the Assistant Editor icon in the upper right corner of the Xcode window. This displays the Main.storyboard file on the left and the SecondViewController.swift file on the right.

18. Move the mouse pointer over the label on the second view, hold down the Control key, and Ctrl-drag from the label to the SecondViewController.swift file underneath the "class SecondViewController" line.

19. Release the Control key and the left mouse button. A popup window appears.

20. Click in the Name text field and type **labelDisplay**. Then click the Connect button. Xcode creates an IBOutlet as follows:

```
@IBOutlet var labelDisplay: UILabel!
```

21. Add the following underneath this IBOutlet:

```
var receivedString = ""
```

22. Edit the viewDidLoad method as follows:

```
        override func viewDidLoad() {
            super.viewDidLoad()
            labelDisplay.text = receivedString
            // Do any additional setup after loading the view.
        }
```

This viewDidLoad method takes whatever data is stored in the receivedString property and stores it in the labelDisplay.text property so the text can appear on the label on the user interface.

The entire SecondViewController.swift file should look like this:

```
import UIKit

class SecondViewController: UIViewController {

    @IBOutlet var labelDisplay: UILabel!

    var receivedString = ""
```

```
override func viewDidLoad() {
    super.viewDidLoad()
    labelDisplay.text = receivedString
    // Do any additional setup after loading the view.
}
```

}

23. Choose View ➤ Standard Editor ➤ Show Standard Editor, or click
    the Standard Editor icon in the upper right corner of the Xcode
    window.

24. Click the ViewController.swift file in the Navigator pane.

25. Add the following function in the ViewController.swift file:

```
override func prepare(for segue: UIStoryboardSegue, sender:
Any?) {
    let nextVC = segue.destination as! SecondViewController
    nextVC.navigationItem.title = "Second View Title"
    nextVC.receivedString = "Passed text"
}
```

The entire ViewController.swift file should look like this:

```
import UIKit

class ViewController: UIViewController {

    override func viewDidLoad() {
        super.viewDidLoad()
        // Do any additional setup after loading the view.
    }

    override func touchesBegan(_ touches: Set<UITouch>, with event:
    UIEvent?) {
        performSegue(withIdentifier: "firstLink", sender: self)
    }
```

```
override func prepare(for segue: UIStoryboardSegue, sender: Any?) {
    let nextVC = segue.destination as! SecondViewController
    nextVC.navigationItem.title = "Second View Title"
    nextVC.receivedString = "Passed text"
  }
}
```

This first line declares a constant named nextVC (which can be any arbitrary name), which represents the segue.destination as the SecondViewController, which is the name of the .swift file connected to the destination of the segue (the second View Controller).

The Navigation Controller displays a navigation bar at the top of every view. Accessing this navigation bar involves using navigationItem and accessing the Title property to store the "Second View Title" text.

We can then access the receivedString property, defined in the SecondViewController.swift file, and store the "Passed text" string.

26. Click the Run button or choose Product ➤ Run. The Simulator window appears, displaying a blank screen.

27. Click the screen. The second (colored) view appears, displaying "Second View Title" at the top and "Passed text" in the label as shown in Figure 17-13.

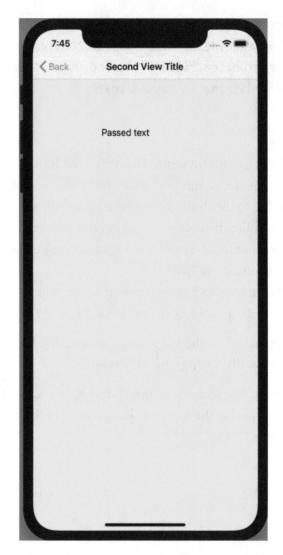

Figure 17-13. *The passed text appears in the title and the label*

28.   Click the Back button to return to the first (white) view.

29.   Choose Simulator ➤ Quit Simulator to return to Xcode.

Displaying Multiple Views in a Navigation Controller

Every Navigation Controller needs a root view. However to be useful, a Navigation Controller also needs at least one other view. That way users can move from the root view to the second view and back to the root view again. Of course, a Navigation Controller can display more than a single view to work with the root view. By storing multiple views in a sequential list, a Navigation Controller can display more information.

Each time you add a new View Controller to a storyboard, you need to do the following:

- Create a new .swift Cocoa Touch Class file and connect it to the View Controller.

- Create a segue link from the last View Controller in the Navigation Controller to the newly added view.

- Define an identifying name for this new segue link.

- Write Swift code in the last view's .swift file to open the next display when triggered by user interaction such as tapping a button or the screen.

To see how to add more views to a Navigation Controller, follow these steps:

1. Create a new iOS project using the Single View App template (see Chapter 1) and name this new project MultipleNavigationApp. This creates a single view for the user interface.

2. Click the Main.storyboard file in the Navigator pane. Xcode displays the single view.

3. Click the View Controller Scene in the Document Outline.

4. Choose Editor ➤ Embed In ➤ Navigation Controller. Xcode displays a Navigation Controller in the storyboard and makes the single view the root view of the Navigation Controller (see Figure 17-4).

5. Click the Library icon to open the Object Library window.

6. Drag and drop two View Controllers to the right of the root view. There should be a Navigation Controller and three View Controllers as shown in Figure 17-14. At this point, the ViewController.swift file is connected to the root view of the Navigation Controller (the one connected to the Navigation Controller by an arrow). We'll need to create separate .swift Cocoa Touch Class files for each of the other two View Controllers and connect them.

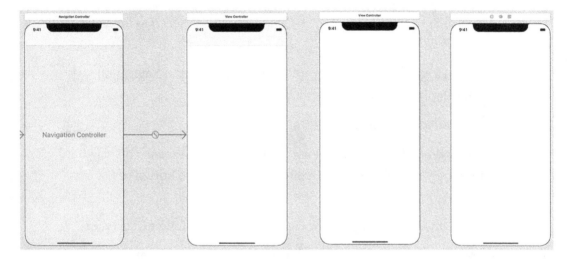

Figure 17-14. *Two View Controllers separate from a Navigation Controller and its root view*

7. Choose File ➤ New ➤ File. Xcode displays a list of templates.

8. Choose Cocoa Touch Class under the iOS category and click the **Next** button. Another dialog appears, asking for a class name and subclass.

9. Click in the Class text field and type **SecondViewController**.

10. Click in the Subclass of popup menu and choose UIViewController.

11. Click the **Next** button. Xcode asks where to store the file.

12. Click the **Create** button. Xcode displays the SecondViewController.swift file in the Navigator pane.

13.   Choose File ➤ New ➤ File. Xcode displays a list of templates.

14.   Choose Cocoa Touch Class under the iOS category and click the
       Next button. Another dialog appears, asking for a class name and
       subclass.

15.   Click in the Class text field and type **ThirdViewController**.

16.   Click in the Subclass of popup menu and choose
       UIViewController.

17.   Click the **Next** button. Xcode asks where to store the file.

18.   Click the **Create** button. Xcode displays the ThirdViewController.
       swift file in the Navigator pane.

19.   Click the Main.storyboard in the Navigator pane.

20.   Click the View Controller icon above the View Controller that
       appears to the right of the Navigation Controller root view as
       shown in Figure 17-15.

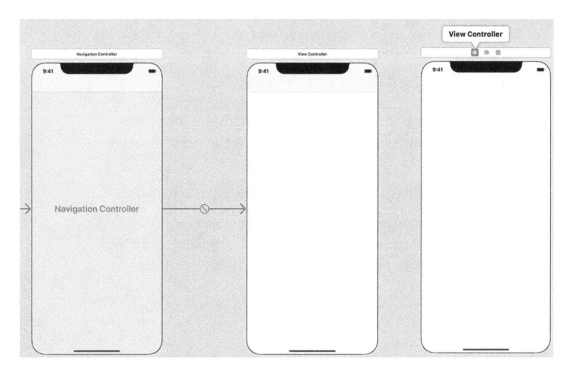

Figure 17-15. *Selecting the second View Controller*

21. Choose View ➤ Inspectors ➤ Show Identity Inspector, or click
     the Identity Inspector icon in the upper right corner of the Xcode
     window.

22. Click in the Class popup menu and choose SecondViewController.

23. Click the View Controller icon above the View Controller that
     appears on the far right as shown in Figure 17-16.

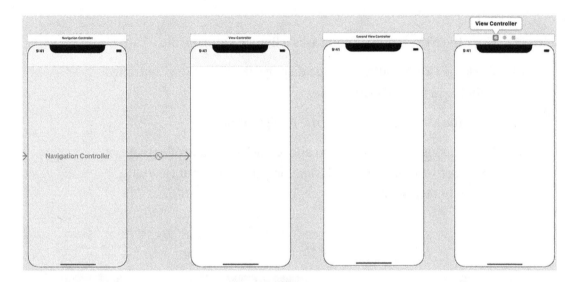

Figure 17-16. *Selecting the third View Controller*

24. Choose View ➤ Inspectors ➤ Show Identity Inspector, or click
     the Identity Inspector icon in the upper right corner of the Xcode
     window.

25. Click in the Class popup menu and choose ThirdViewController.

26. Move the mouse pointer over the View Controller icon above the
     root view, hold down the Control key, and Ctrl-drag over the View
     Controller to the right as shown in Figure 17-17.

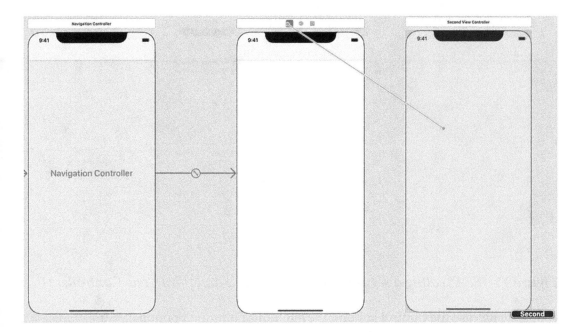

Figure 17-17. *Creating a segue between the root view and the next View Controller*

27. Release the Control key and the left mouse button. A popup menu appears (see Figure 17-8).

28. Choose Show. Xcode creates a segue between the root view and the second View Controller.

29. Click this segue and choose View ➤ Inspectors ➤ Show Attributes Inspector, or click the Attributes Inspector icon in the upper right corner of the Xcode window.

30. Click in the Identifier text field, type **firstLink**, and press ENTER.

31. Move the mouse pointer over the View Controller icon above the second View Controller, hold down the Control key, and Ctrl-drag over the third View Controller as shown in Figure 17-18.

Figure 17-18. *Creating a segue between the second and third View Controllers*

32. Release the Control key and the left mouse button. A popup menu appears (see Figure 17-8).

33. Choose Show. Xcode creates a segue between the second View Controller and the third View Controller.

34. Click this segue and choose View ➤ Inspectors ➤ Show Attributes Inspector, or click the Attributes Inspector icon in the upper right corner of the Xcode window.

35. Click in the Identifier text field, type **secondLink**, and press ENTER.

36. Click in the ViewController.swift file in the Navigator pane and add the following two functions:

```
override func touchesBegan(_ touches: Set<UITouch>, with
event: UIEvent?) {
    performSegue(withIdentifier: "firstLink", sender: self)
}

override func prepare(for segue: UIStoryboardSegue, sender:
Any?) {
    let nextVC = segue.destination as! SecondViewController
    nextVC.navigationItem.title = "Second View Controller"
}
```

The entire ViewController.swift file should look like this:

```swift
import UIKit

class ViewController: UIViewController {

    override func viewDidLoad() {
        super.viewDidLoad()
        // Do any additional setup after loading the view.
    }

    override func touchesBegan(_ touches: Set<UITouch>, with event:
    UIEvent?) {
        performSegue(withIdentifier: "firstLink", sender: self)
    }

    override func prepare(for segue: UIStoryboardSegue, sender: Any?) {
        let nextVC = segue.destination as! SecondViewController
        nextVC.navigationItem.title = "Second View Controller"
    }
}
```

37. Click in the SecondViewController.swift file in the Navigator pane
    and add the following two functions:

```swift
        override func touchesBegan(_ touches: Set<UITouch>, with
        event: UIEvent?) {
            performSegue(withIdentifier: "secondLink", sender: self)
        }

        override func prepare(for segue: UIStoryboardSegue, sender:
        Any?) {
            let nextVC = segue.destination as! ThirdViewController
            nextVC.navigationItem.title = "Third View Controller"
        }
```

The entire SecondViewController.swift file should look like this:

```swift
import UIKit

class SecondViewController: UIViewController {

    override func viewDidLoad() {
        super.viewDidLoad()
        // Do any additional setup after loading the view.
    }

    override func touchesBegan(_ touches: Set<UITouch>, with event:
    UIEvent?) {
        performSegue(withIdentifier: "secondLink", sender: self)
    }

    override func prepare(for segue: UIStoryboardSegue, sender: Any?) {
        let nextVC = segue.destination as! ThirdViewController
        nextVC.navigationItem.title = "Third View Controller"
    }

}
```

38. Click the Run button or choose Product ➤ Run. The Simulator
     window appears, displaying the blank root view screen.

39. Click the screen. The second view appears, displaying the title
     "Second View Controller" along with a Back button in the upper
     left corner as shown in Figure 17-19.

Figure 17-19. *Displaying the second View Controller*

40. Click the view. The third View Controller appears, displaying the title "Third View Controller".

41. Click the Back button and click the views to move back and forth between all three View Controllers.

42. Choose Simulator ➤ Quit Simulator to return to Xcode.

Customizing the Navigation Bar

The Navigation Controller automatically displays a navigation bar at the top of every view. At the very least, this navigation bar displays a Back button in the upper left corner so that way users can always return to a previous view.

By default, this Back button always displays "Back", but you can customize this text to represent the title of the previous view. You can also add your own buttons on the navigation bar to display additional options. Customizing the navigation bar can create a more distinct visual experience for your app's users as shown in Figure 17-20.

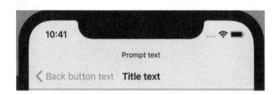

Figure 17-20. *Displaying custom text for a prompt, title, and back button*

Some different ways to customize the navigation bar include

- Prompt – Displays a single line of additional text at the top of the navigation bar

- Title – Defines the text that appears in the middle of the navigation bar

- Back button – Changes the back button's default text of "Back" to something more descriptive

- Color – Defines the color of the navigation bar

Modifying the Prompt and Title Text

By default, the navigation bar doesn't show a prompt or title text. A title text typically displays the name or category of the information displayed on the screen such as the title text identifying different categories of data in the Settings app as shown in Figure 17-21.

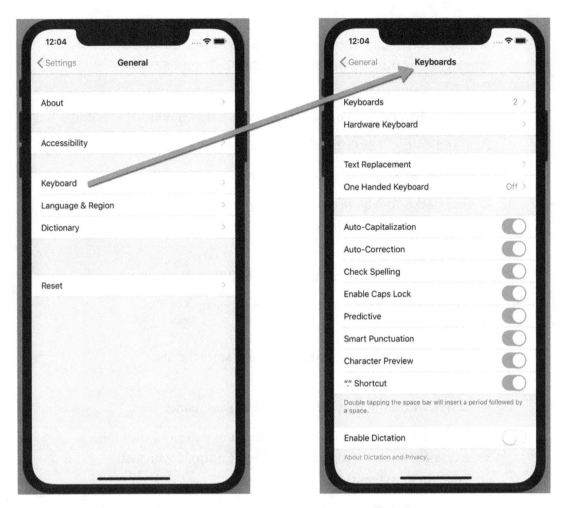

Figure 17-21. *Titles typically display the option chosen from the previous view*

Prompt text is used less often but can display helpful information to the user. To see how to modify the prompt and title text of a navigation bar, follow these steps:

1. Create a new iOS project using the Single View App template (see Chapter 1) and name this new project NavigationTextApp. This creates a single view for the user interface.

2. Click the Main.storyboard file in the Navigator pane. Xcode displays the single view.

3. Click the View Controller Scene in the Document Outline.

4. Choose Editor ➤ Embed In ➤ Navigation Controller. Xcode displays a Navigation Controller in the storyboard and makes the single view the root view of the Navigation Controller (see Figure 17-4).

5. Click the Library icon to open the Object Library window.

6. Drag and drop a View Controller to the right of the root view.

7. Choose File ➤ New ➤ File. Xcode displays a list of templates.

8. Choose Cocoa Touch Class under the iOS category and click the **Next** button. Another dialog appears, asking for a class name and subclass.

9. Click in the Class text field and type **SecondViewController**.

10. Click in the Subclass of popup menu and choose UIViewController.

11. Click the **Next** button. Xcode asks where to store the file.

12. Click the **Create** button. Xcode displays the SecondViewController.swift file in the Navigator pane.

13. Click the Main.storyboard file in the Navigator pane and click the View Controller icon at the top of the View Controller you just added to the storyboard.

14. Choose View ➤ Inspectors ➤ Show Identity Inspector, or click the Identity Inspector icon in the upper right corner of the Xcode window.

15. Click in the Class popup menu and choose SecondViewController.

16. Move the mouse pointer over the View Controller icon of the root view, hold down the Control key, and Ctrl-drag over the second View Controller you just added as shown in Figure 17-22.

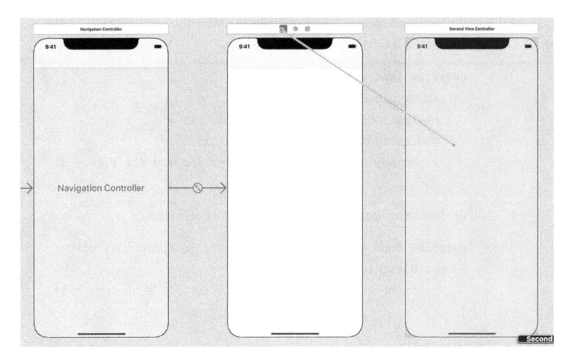

Figure 17-22. *Connecting the root view to the newly added View Controller*

17. Release the Control key and the left mouse button. A popup menu appears (see Figure 17-8).

18. Choose Show. Xcode draws an arrow (segue) linking the root view to the newly added View Controller (see Figure 17-9).

19. Click Show segue to "Second View Controller" in the Document Outline. Xcode highlights the segue between the two views.

20. Choose View ➤ Inspectors ➤ Show Attributes Inspector, or click the Attributes Inspector icon in the upper right corner of the Xcode window.

21. Click in the Identifier text field, type **firstLink**, and press ENTER.

22. Click the ViewController.swift file in the Navigator pane.

23.   Edit the viewDidLoad method as follows to define the prompt and title text for the root view:

```
override func viewDidLoad() {
    super.viewDidLoad()
    navigationItem.prompt = "Prompt text"
    navigationItem.title = "Title text"
    // Do any additional setup after loading the view.
}
```

24.   Add the following function under the viewDidLoad method:

```
override func touchesBegan(_ touches: Set<UITouch>, with
event: UIEvent?) {
    performSegue(withIdentifier: "firstLink", sender: self)
}
```

25.   Add the following function underneath the previous function:

```
override func prepare(for segue: UIStoryboardSegue, sender:
Any?) {
    let nextVC = segue.destination as! SecondViewController
    nextVC.navigationItem.prompt = "New prompt here"
    nextVC.navigationItem.title = "New title here"
}
```

This function defines new prompt and title text for the second View Controller.

26.   Click the Run button or choose Product ➤ Run. The Simulator window appears, displaying the root view screen with "Prompt text" at the top and "Title text" underneath as shown in Figure 17-23.

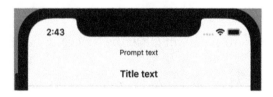

Figure 17-23. *Displaying prompt and title text on the root view*

27.   Click the screen to display the second View Controller. Notice that the prompt now displays "New prompt here" and the title displays "New title here". Also notice that the Back button displays the title of the previous view as shown in Figure 17-24. (If the previous view does not have a title, then the Back button would simply display the default text of "Back".)

Figure 17-24. *Different prompt and title text on the second View Controller*

28.   Choose Simulator ➤ Quit Simulator to return to Xcode.

Modifying the Back Button

The Navigation Controller always displays a Back button in the upper left corner of a view so users can return to a previous view. You can modify both the color and text that appears on the Back button. The three ways to modify the text on the Back button are as follows:

- If the previous view does not have a title, then the Back button defaults to displaying "Back".

- If the previous view has a title, then the Back button displays that title.

- If you customize the backBarButtonItem property, you can define new Back button text.

The default text color for the Back button text is light blue, but you can define a different color by modifying the navigation bar's tintColor property. To see how to change the Back button text and color, follow these steps:

1.   Make sure the NavigationTextApp project is loaded into Xcode.

2.   Click the ViewController.swift file in the Navigator pane.

3. Modify the prepare for segue function as follows:

```
override func prepare(for segue: UIStoryboardSegue, sender:
Any?) {
    let nextVC = segue.destination as! SecondViewController
    nextVC.navigationItem.prompt = "New prompt here"
    nextVC.navigationItem.title = "New title here"

    let customButton = UIBarButtonItem()
    customButton.title = "New back text"
    navigationItem.backBarButtonItem = customButton
}
```

These last three lines create a new UIBarButtonItem, define a new title, and then store this new bar button in the backBarButtonItem property to define new text to appear in the Back button.

4. Modify the viewDidLoad method as follows:

```
override func viewDidLoad() {
    super.viewDidLoad()
    navigationItem.prompt = "Prompt text"
    navigationItem.title = "Title text"

    navigationController?.navigationBar.tintColor = UIColor.red
    // Do any additional setup after loading the view.
}
```

The tintColor property on the navigation bar (which is defined by the Navigation Controller) defines the color of the Back button text. The preceding code changes the Back button text to red, but you can choose any color such as yellow or green.

The entire ViewController.swift file should look like this:

```
import UIKit

class ViewController: UIViewController {
```

```swift
override func viewDidLoad() {
    super.viewDidLoad()
    navigationItem.prompt = "Prompt text"
    navigationItem.title = "Title text"

    navigationController?.navigationBar.tintColor = UIColor.red
    // Do any additional setup after loading the view.
}

override func touchesBegan(_ touches: Set<UITouch>, with event:
UIEvent?) {
    performSegue(withIdentifier: "firstLink", sender: self)
}

override func prepare(for segue: UIStoryboardSegue, sender: Any?) {
    let nextVC = segue.destination as! SecondViewController
    nextVC.navigationItem.prompt = "New prompt here"
    nextVC.navigationItem.title = "New title here"

    let customButton = UIBarButtonItem()
    customButton.title = "New back text"
    navigationItem.backBarButtonItem = customButton
}

}
```

5. Click the Run button or choose Product ➤ Run. The Simulator window appears, displaying the root view screen with "Prompt text" at the top and "Title text" underneath (see Figure 17-23).

6. Click the screen. The next view appears. Notice that this second view displays the Back button text as "New back text" and it appears in red.

7. Choose Simulator ➤ Quit Simulator to return to Xcode.

Modifying the Color of the Navigation Bar

The barTintColor property defines the color of the navigation bar. Keep in mind that whatever color you choose for the navigation bar should contrast with any colors defined for the Back button to make it easy to see.

To see how to change the color of the navigation bar, follow these steps:

1. Make sure the NavigationTextApp project is loaded into Xcode.

2. Click the ViewController.swift file in the Navigator pane.

3. Modify the viewDidLoad method as follows:

```swift
override func viewDidLoad() {
    super.viewDidLoad()
    navigationItem.prompt = "Prompt text"
    navigationItem.title = "Title text"

    navigationController?.navigationBar.tintColor = UIColor.red

    navigationController?.navigationBar.barTintColor =
    UIColor.green
    // Do any additional setup after loading the view.
}
```

Notice that the tintColor property of the navigation bar defines the Back button text, while the barTintColor property defines the color of the navigation bar.

4. Click the Run button or choose Product ➤ Run. The Simulator window appears. Notice that the navigation bar now appears in green.

5. Click the screen. The next view appears.

6. Choose Simulator ➤ Quit Simulator to return to Xcode.

Adding Buttons to a Navigation Bar

The navigation bar always displays a Back button on all but the root view. However, you can always add more buttons on the right side of the navigation bar. Then you can connect these buttons to IBAction methods to make them actually do something.

Besides customizing your own button titles, Xcode also includes several common types of button types that you can choose such as Save, Done, Reply, Camera, Play, Search, or Undo as shown in Figure 17-25.

Figure 17-25. *Common types of buttons to place on a navigation bar*

To see how to add and customize a button on the navigation bar, follow these steps:

1. Create a new iOS project using the Single View App template (see Chapter 1) and name this new project NavigationButtonApp. This creates a single view for the user interface.

2. Click the Main.storyboard file in the Navigator pane. Xcode displays the single view.

3. Click the View Controller Scene in the Document Outline.

4. Choose Editor ➤ Embed In ➤ Navigation Controller. Xcode displays a Navigation Controller in the storyboard and makes the single view the root view of the Navigation Controller (see Figure 17-4).

5. Click the Library icon to open the Object Library window.

6. Drag and drop a View Controller to the right of the root view.

7. Choose File ➤ New ➤ File. Xcode displays a list of templates.

8. Choose Cocoa Touch Class under the iOS category and click the **Next** button. Another dialog appears, asking for a class name and subclass.

9. Click in the Class text field and type **SecondViewController**.

10. Click in the Subclass of popup menu and choose UIViewController.

11. Click the **Next** button. Xcode asks where to store the file.

12. Click the **Create** button. Xcode displays the SecondViewController.swift file in the Navigator pane.

13. Click the Main.storyboard file in the Navigator pane and click the View Controller icon at the top of the View Controller you just added to the storyboard.

14. Choose View ➤ Inspectors ➤ Show Identity Inspector, or click the Identity Inspector icon in the upper right corner of the Xcode window.

15. Click in the Class popup menu and choose SecondViewController.

16. Move the mouse pointer over the View Controller icon of the root view, hold down the Control key, and Ctrl-drag over the second View Controller you just added (see Figure 17-22).

17. Release the Control key and the left mouse button. A popup menu appears (see Figure 17-8).

18. Choose Show. Xcode draws an arrow (segue) linking the root view to the newly added View Controller (see Figure 17-9).

19. Click Show segue to "Second View Controller" in the Document Outline. Xcode highlights the segue between the two views.

20. Choose View ➤ Inspectors ➤ Show Attributes Inspector, or click the Attributes Inspector icon in the upper right corner of the Xcode window.

21. Click in the Identifier text field, type **firstLink**, and press ENTER.

22. Click the ViewController.swift file in the Navigator pane.

23. Add the following function underneath the viewDidLoad method:

```
override func touchesBegan(_ touches: Set<UITouch>, with
event: UIEvent?) {
    performSegue(withIdentifier: "firstLink", sender: self)
}
```

24. Click the Main.storyboard file in the Navigator pane.

25. Click the Library icon to open the Object Library window.

26. Drag and drop a Bar Button Item to the far right of the navigation bar on the root view as shown in Figure 17-26.

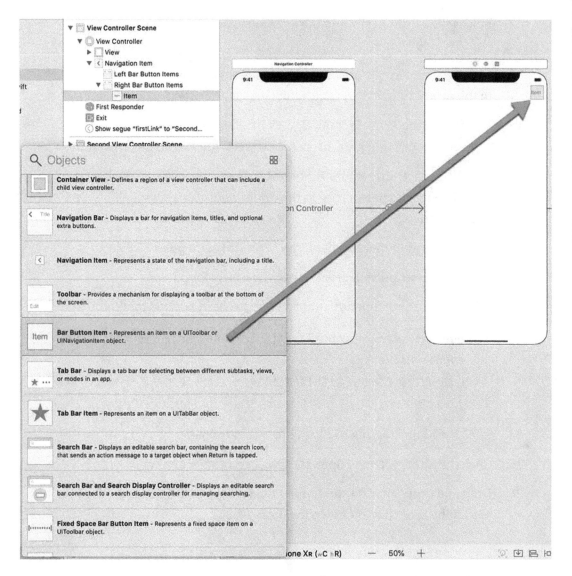

Figure 17-26. *Dragging a Bar Button Item to the navigation bar on the root view*

27. Choose View ➤ Inspectors ➤ Show Attributes Inspector, or click the Attributes Inspector icon in the upper right corner of the Xcode window.

28. Click in the System Item popup menu and choose Action. Notice that Xcode displays an icon on the bar button as shown in Figure 17-27.

Figure 17-27. *Choosing Action from the System Item popup menu*

29. Choose View ➤ Assistant Editor ➤ Show Assistant Editor. Xcode displays the Main.storyboard and ViewController.swift file side by side.

30. Move the mouse pointer over the bar button that displays the Action icon, hold down the Control key, and Ctrl-drag from the bar button to the space above the last curly bracket in the bottom of the ViewController.swift file.

31. Release the Control key and the left mouse button. A popup window appears.

32. Click in the Name text field and type **buttonTapped**.

33. Click in the Type popup menu, choose UIBarButtonItem, and then click the Connect button. Xcode creates an IBAction method.

34. Edit the buttonTapped IBAction method as follows:

```
@IBAction func buttonTapped(_ sender: UIBarButtonItem) {
    let alert = UIAlertController(title: "Message", message:
    "Bar button tapped", preferredStyle: .alert)

    let okAction = UIAlertAction(title: "OK", style: .default,
    handler: { action -> Void in
        //Just dismiss the action sheet
    })
```

```
            alert.addAction(okAction)

            self.present(alert, animated: true, completion: nil)

    }
```

If you run the app at this point, a view will appear with a button in the upper right corner. Clicking this button will display an alert controller. Clicking the view will display the second view with a Back button in the upper left corner.

If you want navigational bar buttons to appear on this second view, you must first add a navigation item (navigation bar) on this second View Controller. Then you can add a bar button onto the navigation item.

35. Choose View ➤ Standard Editor ➤ Show Standard Editor. Xcode displays the Main.storyboard and ViewController.swift file side by side.

36. Click the Main.storyboard file in the Navigator pane.

37. Click the Second View Controller icon that appears at the top of the second View Controller.

38. Choose Editor ➤ Embed In ➤ Navigation Controller. Xcode embeds the second View Controller inside a Navigation Controller as shown in Figure 17-28.

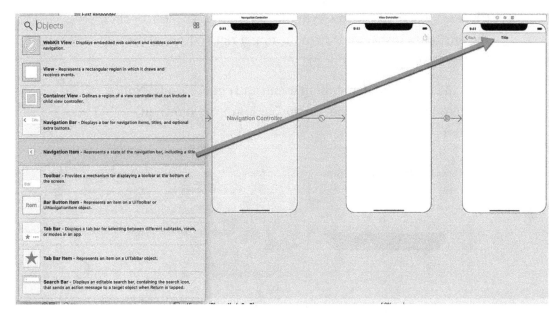

Figure 17-28. *Adding a navigation item to the second View Controller*

39.   Click the Library icon to open the Object Library window.

40.   Drag and drop a Bar Button Item to the far right of the navigation bar
      on the second View Controller's root view as shown in Figure 17-29.

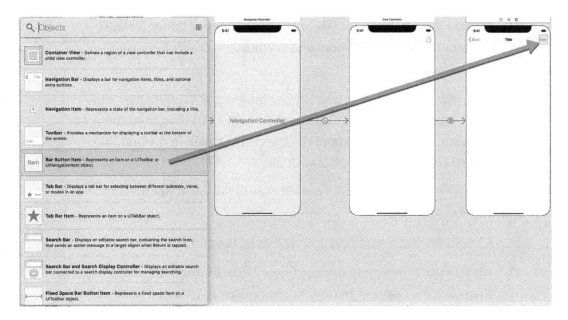

Figure 17-29. *Dragging and dropping a Bar Button Item to the second View
Controller's navigation bar*

41.   Choose View ➤ Inspectors ➤ Show Attributes Inspector, or click the Attributes Inspector icon in the upper right corner of the Xcode window.

42.   Click in the System Item popup menu and choose Done. Notice that Xcode displays "Done" on the bar button as shown in Figure 17-30.

Figure 17-30. *Choosing Done from the System Item popup menu*

43.   Choose View ➤ Assistant Editor ➤ Show Assistant Editor. Xcode displays the Main.storyboard and SecondViewController.swift file side by side.

44.   Move the mouse pointer over the bar button that displays the Done button, hold down the Control key, and Ctrl-drag from the bar button to the space above the last curly bracket in the bottom of the SecondViewController.swift file.

45.   Release the Control key and the left mouse button. A popup window appears.

46.   Click in the Name text field and type **doneTapped**.

47.   Click in the Type popup menu, choose UIBarButtonItem, and then click the Connect button. Xcode creates an IBAction method.

48. Edit the doneTapped IBAction method as follows:

```
@IBAction func doneTapped(_ sender: UIBarButtonItem) {
    let alert = UIAlertController(title: "Message", message:
    "Done button tapped", preferredStyle: .alert)

    let okAction = UIAlertAction(title: "OK", style: .default,
    handler: { action -> Void in
        //Just dismiss the action sheet
    })
    alert.addAction(okAction)

    self.present(alert, animated: true, completion: nil)
}
```

49. Click the Run button or choose Product ➤ Run. The Simulator window appears, displaying the root view screen with the Action icon in the upper right corner.

50. Click the screen. The next view appears. Notice that this second view displays the Back button.

51. Click the Done button in the upper right corner. An alert controller appears.

52. Click OK to dismiss the alert controller.

53. Choose Simulator ➤ Quit Simulator to return to Xcode.

Before you can add Bar Button Items to a navigation bar on anything other than the root view, you need to first add a navigation item. Then you can add a bar button onto this navigation item.

Summary

A Navigation Controller always needs exactly one root view. To link to other views, you need to create segues. When you create a segue, you must also give that segue an identifier name. Then to display the next View Controller connected to a segue, you use this line of code where you replace "Link Identifier" with the identifier name you give to your segue:

```
performSegue(withIdentifier: "Link Identifier", sender: self)
```

The Navigation Controller takes care of automatically displaying a navigation bar on any View Controller that it displays. This navigation bar displays a Back button in the upper left corner. By default, this Back button displays "Back", but if the previous View Controller has a title, this Back button will display that title. You can also define Back button text if you wish.

Since a Navigation Controller can display multiple View Controllers, you can pass data from one View Controller to another. That way information retrieved from one view can be used and displayed in another view.

To make a Navigation Controller look more appealing, you can change the color of the navigation bar or add Bar Button Items. You can link these bar buttons to IBAction methods and display any text on them that you wish. As a shortcut, Xcode can also display icons and common button titles (such as Done or Cancel) on bar buttons.

A Navigation Controller can display a list of View Controllers sequentially. Whenever you need to group related View Controllers together and display them one after another, use a Navigation Controller.

CHAPTER 18

Using Tab Bars and Tool Bars

Like a Navigation Controller, a Tab Bar Controller also groups related View Controllers together. The main difference is that a Navigation Controller can only display View Controllers in sequential order. On the other hand, a Tab Bar Controller can jump to another View Controller directly.

While a Navigation Controller always displays a navigation bar and a Back button on every View Controller it opens, a Tab Bar Controller always displays a list of icons at the bottom of the screen where each icon represents a different View Controller. By tapping on an icon, the user can jump to that particular View Controller right away. Then the user can return to the Tab Bar Controller again to see the list of icons representing the other View Controllers as shown in Figure 18-1.

Note   Because a Tab Bar Controller can only display a limited number of icons at the bottom of the screen, this tends to limit the number of View Controllers that the Tab Bar Controller can contain. As a general rule, five icons is usually the maximum number to appear on a Tab bar to look aesthetically pleasing on an iPhone in portrait orientation.

© Wallace Wang 2019
W. Wang, *Beginning iPhone Development with Swift 5*, https://doi.org/10.1007/978-1-4842-4865-2_18

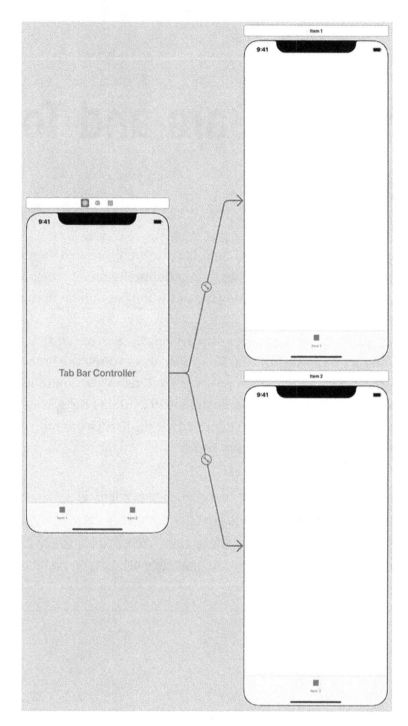

Figure 18-1. *A Tab bar Controller displays icons that represent multiple views*

Similar to a Tab bar is a Toolbar. While a Tab bar is strictly for navigating to different views, a Toolbar displays icons that represent actions that the user may want to perform. Many of the apps that come with iOS display a Toolbar at the bottom of the screen such as Mail and the Photos app, which can delete a selected message or photo as shown in Figure 18-2.

Figure 18-2. *Many apps display a Toolbar at the bottom of the screen*

Both tab and Toolbars are limited by the number of icons that can comfortably appear at any given time. The more icons, the more cluttered the Tab bar appearance and the harder it will be for a user to tap the right icon. As a general rule, don't display too many icons on a Tab bar that will make finding or choosing any particular icon too difficult for the user.

The main differences between a Tab Bar bar and a Tool Bar are

- A Tab Bar displays different View Controllers.

- A Tool Bar runs different commands.

Switching View Controllers in a Tab Bar Controller

Tab Bar Controllers make it easy to switch from one view to another in any order you wish. Each icon on the Tab bar represents a different View Controller. The basic steps to using a Tab Bar Controller to represent different views are to add multiple View Controllers to your storyboard and then Ctrl-drag to connect the Tab Bar Controller to a View Controller.

Then the next step is to create a title and icon to represent that View Controller. You may also want to reorder the icons on the Tab bar or delete a View Controller and its Tab bar icon later.

To see how to create a simple Tab Bar Controller, follow these steps:

1. Create a new iOS project using the Single View App template (see Chapter 1) and name this new project TabBarApp. This creates a single view for the user interface.

2. Click the Main.storyboard file in the Navigator pane. Xcode displays the single view.

3. Click the View Controller Scene at the top of the View Controller.

4. Choose Editor ➤ Embed In ➤ Tab Bar Controller. Xcode displays a Tab Bar Controller in the storyboard connected to the existing View Controller as shown in Figure 18-3.

Figure 18-3. *Embedding a view inside a Tab Bar Controller*

5. Click the Library icon to open the Object Library window.

6. Drag and drop a View Controller from the Object Library window to the storyboard as shown in Figure 18-4.

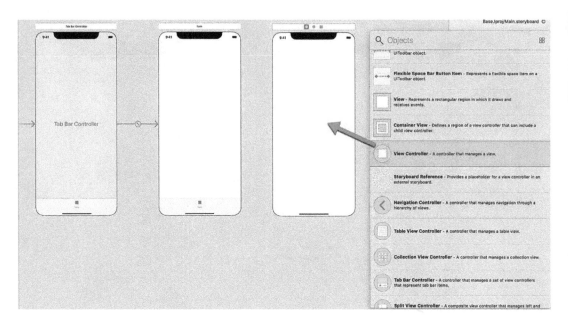

Figure 18-4. *Dragging and dropping a View Controller onto the storyboard*

7.   Move the mouse over the Tab Bar Controller icon at the top of the Tab Bar Controller (or over the Tab Bar Controller in the Document Outline).

8.   Hold down the Control key and Ctrl-drag over the newly added View Controller you just added to the storyboard as shown in Figure 18-5.

Figure 18-5. *Ctrl-dragging from the Tab Bar Controller to the separate View Controller*

9. Release the left mouse button and the Control key. A popup menu appears as shown in Figure 18-6.

Figure 18-6. *A popup menu for connecting a View Controller to a Tab Bar Controller*

10. Choose View Controllers under the Relationship Segue category. Xcode draws an arrow (segue) linking the Tab Bar Controller to the newly added View Controller as shown in Figure 18-7. (You may need to move the View Controller to see that the Tab Bar Controller's segues fork to connect to both View Controllers.)

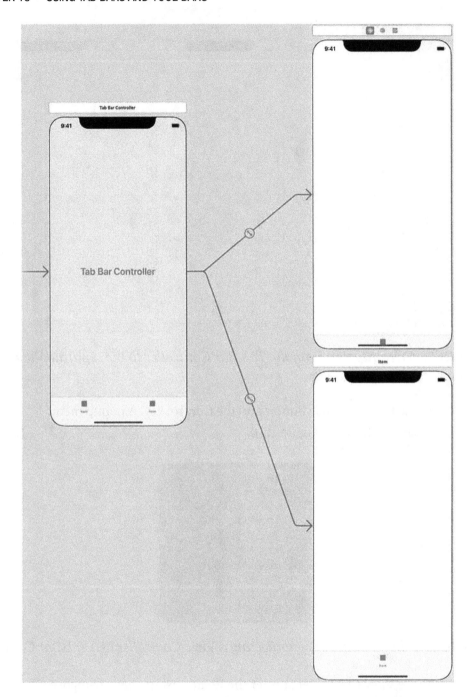

Figure 18-7. *A segue links two views within a Navigation Controller*

11. Click in the middle of the top View Controller (or click view in the Document Outline).

12.   Choose View ➤ Inspectors ➤ Show Attributes Inspector, or click
      the Attributes Inspector icon in the upper right corner of the Xcode
      window.

13.   Click in the Background popup menu and choose a color such as yellow.

14.   Click in the middle of the bottom View Controller (or click view in the
      Document Outline).

15.   Click in the Background popup menu and choose a color such as orange.

16.   Click the Run button or choose Product ➤ Run. The Simulator window
      appears, displaying a colored screen of the first View Controller.

17.   Click the second icon on the Tab bar at the bottom of the screen. The
      second View Controller appears showing a different color.

18.   Choose Simulator ➤ Quit Simulator to return to Xcode.

Customizing Tab Bar Icons

Tab Bar Controllers display icons on a Tab bar at the bottom of the screen. By default,
this icon simply displays a generic label such as "Item", but you can customize this icon
to include more descriptive text and/or an icon. You can create icons using a graphics
editor such as Adobe Illustrator. When creating your own icons, be sure to follow
Apple's guidelines for designing icons (`https://developer.apple.com/design/human-`
`interface-guidelines/ios/icons-and-images/custom-icons/`).

As an alternative to creating your own icons, you can buy or download icons from the
following sites:

- iconbeast.com

- icons8.com

- pixellove.com

To see how to customize Tab bar icons, follow these steps:

1.   Make sure the TabBarApp is loaded in Xcode.

2.   Download two or more free icons from any site that offers free icons.

3.   Click the Assets.xcassets folder.

4.   Click the + icon to display a popup menu as shown in Figure 18-8.

Figure 18-8. *Creating a new image set in the Assets.xcassets folder*

5. Choose New Image Set. Xcode displays an Image item underneath AppIcon.

6. Click this Image item and press ENTER to highlight the text as shown in Figure 18-9.

Figure 18-9. *Editing the Image name*

7. Type **First** and press ENTER.

8. Drag and drop an icon into all the placeholders labeled 1x, 2x, and 3x as shown in Figure 18-10.

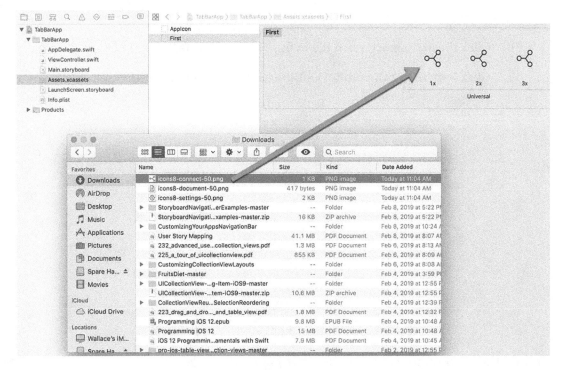

Figure 18-10. *Dragging and dropping icons into the image set*

9. Repeat steps 5–8 but label this image set **Second** and drag and drop a different icon into each 1x, 2x, and 3x placeholder as shown in Figure 18-11.

Figure 18-11. Creating a second image set.

Figure 18-11. *Creating two image sets with icons*

Note   The 1x image appears on older iOS device screens. The 2x image appears on Retina displays. The 3x icon image appears on Retina Display HD displays for the iPhone X and later models.

10.   Click the Main.storyboard file in the Navigator pane.

11.   Click Item in the Document Outline as shown in Figure 18-12.

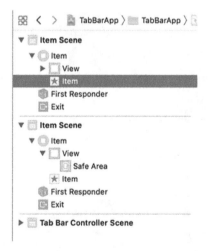

Figure 18-12. *Selecting the Tab bar on a View Controller*

12. Choose View ➤ Inspectors ➤ Show Attributes Inspector, or click the Attributes Inspector icon in the upper right corner of the Xcode window.

13. Click the Image popup menu under the Bar Item category and select First as shown in Figure 18-13.

Figure 18-13. *Choosing an image set for a Tab bar icon*

14. Click in the Title text field, delete the "Item" text, type the color of the View Controller (such as yellow), and press ENTER. Notice that the Tab bar now displays your chosen icon and text.

15. Repeat steps 11–14 for the other Tab bar item except choose Second for its Image and type a different color for its Title.

16. Click the Run button or choose Product ➤ Run. The Simulator window appears showing the two icons on the Tab bar as shown in Figure 18-14.

Figure 18-14. *The Tab bar displaying the custom text and icon*

17. Click the second tab. Notice that the second View Controller appears for that tab.

18. Click the first tab. Notice that the first View Controller appears for that tab.

19. Choose Simulator ➤ Quit Simulator to return to Xcode.

Deleting View Controllers from a Tab Bar Controller

You can connect multiple View Controllers to a Tab Bar Controller. However, if you later want to disconnect a View Controller from a Tab Bar Controller, you have two options:

- Delete the View Controller and its segue from the Tab Bar Controller.

- Delete just the segue from the Tab Bar Controller but keep the View Controller.

Deleting a View Controller will delete both the segue from the Tab Bar Controller and the View Controller, but this also means you'll lose everything stored on that View Controller such as buttons, text fields, and labels. Another option is to delete just the segue and keep the View Controller.

To delete both a View Controller and its segue from a Tab Bar Controller, follow these steps:

1. Click the Main.storyboard in the Navigator pane.

2. Click the Item Scene in the Document Outline that represents the View Controller you want to delete and disconnect from the Tab Bar Controller as shown in Figure 18-15.

Figure 18-15. *Selecting an Item Scene to delete from a Tab Bar Controller*

3. Press BACKSPACE or DELETE. Xcode removes the selected View Controller and the segue connecting it to the Tab Bar Controller.

Note   If you make a mistake deleting a segue and/or its connecting View Controller, choose Edit ➤ Undo or press Command + Z to undo the delete command.

Sometimes you may not want to delete a View Controller. Instead, you just want to disconnect it from a Tab Bar Controller. To disconnect a View Controller's segue to a Tab Bar Controller while keeping the View Controller, follow these steps:

1. Click the Main.storyboard in the Navigator pane.

2. Click a Relationship icon under the Tab Bar Controller Scene in the Document Outline as shown in Figure 18-16.

Figure 18-16. *Selecting a segue in the Document Outline*

3. Press BACKSPACE or DELETE. Xcode removes the segue to the Tab Bar Controller but keeps the View Controller in the storyboard.

Creating a Tool Bar

Similar to Tab Bar Controller is a Tool Bar. While a Tab Bar Controller is designed to display icons at the bottom of the screen that represent different views users can open, a Tool Bar is meant to display icons that represent different commands the user can choose. The two objects to use from the Object Library window are shown in Figure 18-17:

- Tool Bar – Displays a bar at the bottom of the screen

- Bar Button Item – Displays text and/or an icon on a Toolbar

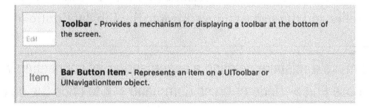

Figure 18-17. *The Toolbar and Bar Button Item on the Object Library window*

To see how to add a Toolbar and icons and connect them to IBAction methods, follow these steps:

1. Create a new iOS project using the Single View App template (see Chapter 1) and name this new project TabBarMethodsApp. This creates a single view for the user interface.

2. Click the Main.storyboard file in the Navigator pane. Xcode displays the single view.

3. Click the Library icon to open the Object Library window.

4. Drag and drop a Tool Bar from the Object Library window to the bottom of the view as shown in Figure 18-18.

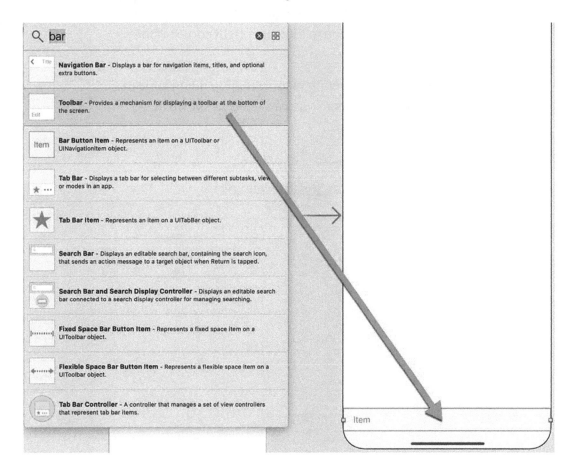

Figure 18-18. *Dragging and dropping a Toolbar onto a view*

5.   Click Item underneath Toolbar in the Document Outline as shown in Figure 18-19. This selects the bar button currently visible on the Toolbar.

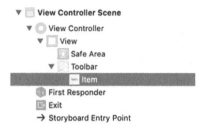

Figure 18-19.   *The Bar Button Item on the Toolbar in the Document Outline*

6.   Choose View ➤ Inspectors ➤ Show Attributes Inspector, or click the Attributes Inspector icon in the upper right corner of the Xcode window.

7.   Click in the System Item popup menu. A popup menu appears, listing common types of icons you can select as shown in Figure 18-20.

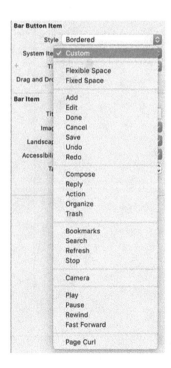

Figure 18-20.   *Clicking the System Item popup menu*

8. Choose Add. Notice that Xcode now displays the bar button as a + icon.

9. Choose View ➤ Assistant Editor ➤ Show Assistant Editor, or click the Assistant Editor icon in the upper right corner of the Xcode window. Xcode displays the Main.storyboard file and the ViewController.swift file side by side.

10. Move the mouse pointer over the Add (+) button on the Toolbar, hold down the Control key, and Ctrl-drag from the Add (+) button just above the last curly bracket at the bottom of the ViewController.swift file.

11. Release the Control key and the left mouse button. A popup window appears.

12. Click in the Name text field and type **addTapped**.

13. Click in the Type popup menu and choose UIBarButtonItem. Then click the Connect button. Xcode creates an addTapped IBAction method.

14. Edit this addTapped IBAction method as follows:

```
@IBAction func addTapped(_ sender: UIBarButtonItem) {
        let alert = UIAlertController(title: "Add", message: "Add
        button tapped", preferredStyle: .alert)

        let okAction = UIAlertAction(title: "OK", style: .default,
        handler: { action -> Void in
            //Just dismiss the action sheet
        })
        alert.addAction(okAction)

        self.present(alert, animated: true, completion: nil)
    }
```

The entire ViewController.swift file should look like this:

```
import UIKit

class ViewController: UIViewController {
```

```
    override func viewDidLoad() {
        super.viewDidLoad()
        // Do any additional setup after loading the view.
    }

    @IBAction func addTapped(_ sender: UIBarButtonItem) {
        let alert = UIAlertController(title: "Add", message: "Add
        button tapped", preferredStyle: .alert)

        let okAction = UIAlertAction(title: "OK", style: .default,
        handler: { action -> Void in
            //Just dismiss the action sheet
        })
        alert.addAction(okAction)

        self.present(alert, animated: true, completion: nil)
    }

}
```

15. Click the Run button or choose Product ➤ Run. The Simulator
     window appears, displaying the Toolbar and the Add (+) button at
     the bottom of the screen.

16. Click the Add (+) button. An alert controller appears.

17. Click OK to dismiss the alert controller.

18. Choose Simulator ➤ Quit Simulator to return to Xcode.

Adding and Deleting Tool Bar Buttons

When you add a Toolbar, it comes with one bar button generically labeled "Item". After
customizing this one bar button, you may want to add more buttons to a Toolbar. If you
add too many bar buttons, you can always delete them. Bar buttons can display icons
and/or text as shown in Figure 18-21.

| Text buttons | Icon buttons |

Figure 18-21. *Bar buttons typically display text or icons*

Note   Although bar buttons can display both text and icons, you can also use one or the other. If you have three or fewer buttons on a Toolbar, text (with no icon) can make each option easier to understand. If you have more than three buttons on a Toolbar, icons (with no text) take up less space but at the sacrifice of the user not understanding what command each icon may represent.

Besides bar buttons, another object you can add to Toolbars is spaces. Xcode offers two different types of spaces as shown in Figure 18-22:

- Fixed space – Defines an exact value for space between two bar buttons

- Flexible space – Acts like a spring that shrinks or expands between two bar buttons when viewed on different size screens such as an iPhone and an iPad

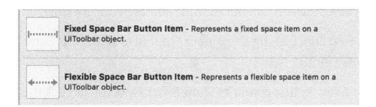

Figure 18-22. *Two types of spaces you can add between bar buttons*

To see how to add, delete, and add spaces on a Toolbar, follow these steps:

1. Create a new iOS project using the Single View App template
    (see Chapter 1) and name this new project ToolBarEditApp. This
    creates a single view for the user interface.

2. Click the Main.storyboard file in the Navigator pane. Xcode
    displays the single view.

3. Click the Library icon to open the Object Library window.

4. Drag and drop a Tool Bar onto the bottom of the view. A generic
    "Item" bar button appears on the Toolbar.

5. Click the Library icon to open the Object Library window and drag
    and drop a Bar Button Item onto the Toolbar. Notice that the two
    bar buttons appear close together as shown in Figure 18-23.

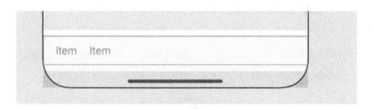

Figure 18-23. *Two bar buttons appear on a Toolbar*

6. Click the Library icon to open the Object Library window and drag
    and drop a Fixed Space Bar Button Item onto the Toolbar in between
    the two existing bar buttons. The Fixed Space Bar Button Item simply
    adds space between two bar buttons and appears invisible.

7. Click Fixed Space in the Document Outline to select the Fixed
    Space Bar Button Item.

8. Choose View ➤ Inspectors ➤ Show Size Inspector, or click the Size
    Inspector icon on the upper right corner of the Xcode window.

9. Click in the Width text field, type **75**, and press ENTER. The Width
    property defines the exact spacing of the Fixed Space Bar Button Item.

10. Click the Run button or choose Product ➤ Run. The Simulator
    window appears, displaying the Toolbar at the bottom of the
    screen with its two bar buttons.

11. Choose Hardware ➤ Rotate Left. Notice that the spacing between the two bar buttons on the Toolbar remains the same as shown in Figure 18-24.

Figure 18-24. *The Fixed Space Bar Button Item maintains an exact distance between two bar buttons*

12. Choose Simulator ➤ Quit Simulator to return to Xcode.

13. Click Fixed Space in the Document Outline and press BACKSPACE or DELETE to remove the Fixed Space Bar Button Item.

14. Click the Library icon to open the Object Library window and drag and drop a Flexible Space Bar Button Item onto the Toolbar in between the two existing bar buttons. Notice that Flexible Space Bar Button pushes the two bar buttons on opposite ends of the Toolbar as shown in Figure 18-25.

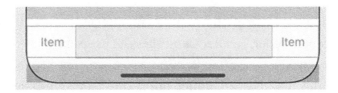

Figure 18-25. *The Flexible Space Bar Button Item acts like a spring between two bar buttons*

15. Click the Run button or choose Product ➤ Run. The Simulator
     window appears, displaying the Toolbar at the bottom of the
     screen with its two bar buttons at opposite ends of the Toolbar.

16. Choose Hardware ➤ Rotate Left. Notice that the spacing between
     the two bar buttons on the Toolbar expands to accommodate the
     wider distance of the iPhone in landscape orientation as shown in
     Figure 18-26.

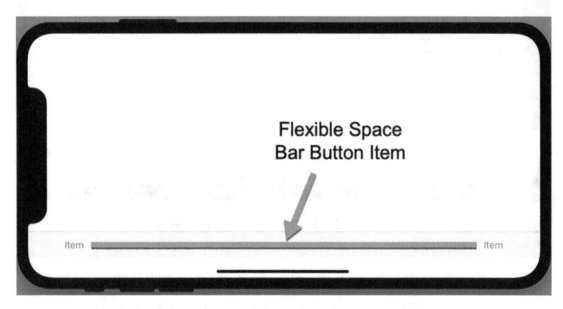

Figure 18-26. *The Flexible Space Bar Button Item pushes two bar buttons regardless of the iOS device orientation*

17. Choose Simulator ➤ Quit Simulator to return to Xcode.

Summary

Tab Bar Controllers display icons at the bottom of the screen that represent different View Controllers. Unlike a Navigation Controller that forces users to display View Controllers in sequential order, Tab Bar Controllers let users navigate to different View Controllers in any order. Because a Tab Bar Controller can only display a limited number of icons, users can only navigate to a limited number of View Controllers.

A Tool Bar also displays icons at the bottom of the screen. While a Tab Bar displays icons that jump to a different View Controller, a Tool Bar displays icons that represent different commands to manipulate data currently displayed on the screen. For example, the Mail app displays icons at the bottom of the screen while showing messages. One icon lets you delete the message, while another lets you forward it. Yet another icon lets you store the message in another folder.

Buttons can display text and an image, although it's more common for buttons to display text or an image, but not necessarily both. Text makes it easy to understand the purpose of each button, but text buttons take up more space. Icons take up far less space but can be harder to understand what they represent.

When placing buttons on a Toolbar, you can also define spacing between buttons using either fixed or flexible spacing. Fixed spacing lets you define a specific value for spacing between two buttons. Flexible spacing lets the spacing between buttons shrink or expand depending on the orientation of the iOS device.

By using Tab Bars to navigate to different View Controllers or Tool Bars to display different types of commands available to manipulating currently displayed data, you can make your app easier to use.

CHAPTER 19

Using the Page View Controller

One unique way to display the contents of two or more View Controllers is through a Page View Controller, which lets users swipe left and right. Each swipe displays a different View Controller like swiping through pages in an e-book.

To use a page controller, you need to add a Page Controller to a storyboard. Then you can customize this Page Controller by defining the following properties in the Attributes Inspector pane as shown in Figure 19-1:

- Navigation – Defines whether the user needs to swipe horizontally or vertically to display the next or previous view

- Transition style – Defines whether views curl like pages in a book (page curl) or whether they simply slide in place (scroll)

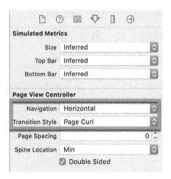

Figure 19-1. *Modifying the behavior of a Page Controller*

© Wallace Wang 2019
W. Wang, *Beginning iPhone Development with Swift 5*, https://doi.org/10.1007/978-1-4842-4865-2_19

After customizing the behavior of the Page Controller, the next step is to create multiple View Controllers that are completely separate from the storyboard (not connected to any existing storyboard scenes through segues). To make these View Controllers appear within a Page Controller, each View Controller needs a unique Storyboard ID that you can define within the Identity Inspector pane.

Finally, you need to create separate .swift files and connect them to each View Controller. In addition, you need to create a separate .swift file and connect it to the Page Controller. Altogether, you need two types of .swift files:

- A single UIPageViewController class file to connect to the Page Controller

- A UIViewController class file to connect to each View Controller you want to appear inside the Page Controller

Once you've added a Page Controller to your storyboard and multiple View Controllers that are not connected to any part of the storyboard through segues, you can then write Swift code to load the multiple View Controllers.

Adding and Customizing a Page Controller

The first step to using a Page Controller is to add one to your storyboard. To see how to place a Page Controller in a storyboard, follow these steps:

1. Create a new iOS project using the Single View App template (see Chapter 1) and name this new project PageControllerApp. This creates a single view for the user interface.

2. Click the Main.storyboard file in the Navigator pane. Xcode displays the single view.

3. Click the Library icon to open the Object Library window.

4. Drag and drop a Page Controller from the Object Library window to the storyboard as shown in Figure 19-2.

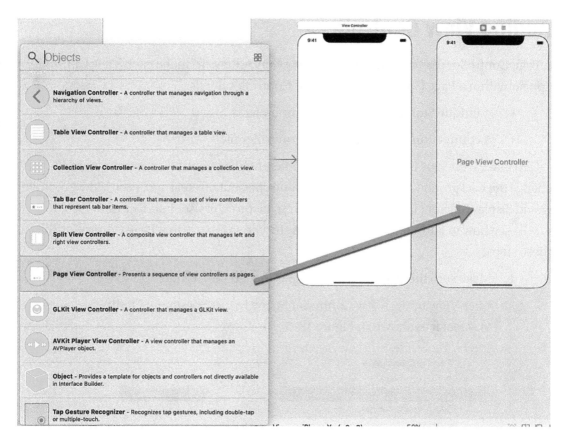

Figure 19-2. *Dragging and dropping a Page Controller onto the storyboard*

5. Click the Page View Controller icon at the top of the Page
    Controller (or on the Page View Controller in the Document
    Outline).

6. Choose View ➤ Inspectors ➤ Show Attributes Inspector, or click
    the Attributes Inspector icon in the upper right corner of the
    Xcode window.

7. Click in the Navigation popup menu and choose Horizontal.

8. Click in the Transition Style popup menu and choose Page Curl.

9. Select the "Is Initial View Controller" check box. Xcode now
    displays an arrow on the left side of the Page Controller in the
    storyboard.

Adding View Controllers

A Page Controller displays one or more View Controllers. To make each View Controller appear within a Page Controller, each View Controller needs

- A unique Storyboard ID (any arbitrary text)
- A connection to a .swift UIViewController file

To make it obvious when we're viewing different View Controllers, we also need to change the background color of each View Controller, but in a real app, each View Controller would display different information such as text, pictures, or user interface designs.

To see how to add View Controllers to a storyboard to use in a Page Controller, follow these steps:

1. Make sure the PageControllerApp is loaded into Xcode.

2. Click View under View Controller Scene in the Document Outline to select it as shown in Figure 19-3.

Figure 19-3. *Selecting the view on the View Controller*

540

3. Choose View ➤ Inspectors ➤ Show Attributes Inspector, or click the Attributes Inspector icon in the upper right corner of the Xcode window.

4. Click the Background popup menu and choose a color such as yellow. We want to display different colors on all View Controllers displayed by the Page Controller so it's obvious we're looking at a different View Controller.

5. Click the View Controller in the Document Outline or click the View Controller icon above the View Controller.

6. Choose View ➤ Inspectors ➤ Show Identity Inspector, or click the Identity Inspector icon in the upper right corner of the Xcode window.

7. Click in the Storyboard ID text field, type **page01**, and press ENTER as shown in Figure 19-4.

Figure 19-4. Each View Controller needs a unique Storyboard ID in the Identity Inspector pane

8. Choose File ➤ New ➤ File. A dialog appears, displaying different templates.

9. Choose Cocoa Touch Class under the iOS category and then click the **Next** button. Another window appears letting you choose a name for your file.

10. Click in the Class text field and type **SecondViewController**. (Make sure the Subclass of popup menu displays UIViewController.)

11. Click the **Next** button and then the **Create** button. Xcode displays the SecondViewController.swift file in the Navigator pane.

12. Repeat steps 8–11 except name this .swift file as **ThirdViewController**. The Navigator pane should now display the ViewController.swift, SecondViewController.swift, and ThirdViewController.swift files as shown in Figure 19-5. (You can rearrange the files in the Navigator pane if you wish.)

Figure 19-5.   *Creating three separate View Controller .swift files*

13. Click the Library icon to open the Object Library window and drag and drop a View Controller from the Object Library window to the storyboard. The storyboard should now contain a Page Controller and two View Controllers.

14. Click the View Controller in the Document Outline or click the View Controller icon above the View Controller.

15. Choose View ➤ Inspectors ➤ Show Identity Inspector, or click the Identity Inspector icon in the upper right corner of the Xcode window.

16. Click in the Class popup menu and choose SecondViewController.

17. Click in the Storyboard ID text field, type **page02**, and press ENTER as shown in Figure 19-6.

Figure 19-6. *Connecting the second View Controller to a .swift class file and giving it a Storyboard ID*

18. Click the View of the second View Controller in the Document Outline, or click in the middle of the second View Controller.

19. Choose View ➤ Inspectors ➤ Show Attributes Inspector, or click the Attributes Inspector icon in the upper right corner of the Xcode window.

20. Click in the Background popup menu and choose a color such as orange.

21. Click the Library icon to open the Object Library window and drag and drop a View Controller from the Object Library window to the storyboard. The storyboard should now contain a Page Controller and three View Controllers.

22. Click the View Controller in the Document Outline or click the View Controller icon above the View Controller.

23. Choose View ➤ Inspectors ➤ Show Identity Inspector, or click the Identity Inspector icon in the upper right corner of the Xcode window.

24. Click in the Class popup menu and choose ThirdViewController.

25. Click in the Storyboard ID text field, type **page03**, and press ENTER.

26. Click the View of the third View Controller in the Document Outline, or click in the middle of the third View Controller.

27. Choose View ➤ Inspectors ➤ Show Attributes Inspector, or click the Attributes Inspector icon in the upper right corner of the Xcode window.

28. Click the Background popup menu and choose a color such as cyan. The storyboard should contain a Page Controller and three View Controllers where each View Controller has a different background color as shown in Figure 19-7.

Figure 19-7. *The storyboard with one Page Controller and three View Controllers*

Making View Controllers Appear in a Page Controller

To make multiple View Controllers appear inside a Page Controller, you must first connect the Page Controller to a .swift UIPageController class file. Then within this UIPageController .swift file, you need to write Swift code to do the following:

- Define an array to hold all the View Controllers to display inside the Page Controller.

- Write a viewControllerBefore method to define which View Controller to display when the user swipes to open the previous view.

- Write a viewControllerAfter method to define which View Controller to display when the user swipes to open the next view.

To see how to write Swift code to make a Page Controller work, follow these steps:

1. Make sure the PageControllerApp is loaded into Xcode.

2. Choose File ➤ New ➤ File. A dialog appears displaying different templates available.

3. Click Cocoa Touch Class under the iOS category and click the **Next** button. Another window appears, asking for a class name and subclass type.

4. Click in the Class text field and type **PageViewController**.

5. Click in the Subclass of popup menu and choose UIPageViewController as shown in Figure 19-8.

Figure 19-8.   *Creating a UIPageViewController .swift class file*

6. Click the **Next** button and then click the **Create** button. Xcode displays the PageViewController.swift file in the Navigator pane.

7. Click the Main.storyboard file in the Navigator pane. Xcode displays the storyboard.

8. Click Page View Controller in the Document Outline, or click the Page View Controller icon at the top of the Page Controller as shown in Figure 19-9.

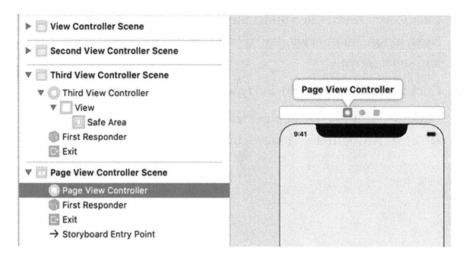

Figure 19-9. *Selecting the Page View Controller*

9. Choose View ➤ Inspectors ➤ Show Identity Inspector, or click the Identity Inspector icon at the top right corner of the Xcode window.

10. Click in the Class popup menu and choose PageViewController as shown in Figure 19-10.

Figure 19-10. *Connecting the Page Controller to the PageViewController.swift file*

11. Click the PageViewController.swift file in the Navigator pane.

12. Edit the class PageViewController line as follows:

```
class PageViewController: UIPageViewController,
UIPageViewControllerDataSource {
```

13. Under the class PageViewController line, add the following line that declares an array of UIViewControllers:

```
var controllerArray: [UIViewController]? = nil
```

14. Modify the viewDidLoad method as follows:

```
override func viewDidLoad() {
    super.viewDidLoad()
    dataSource = self

    let storyBoard = UIStoryboard(name: "Main", bundle: nil)
    let firstVC = storyBoard.instantiateViewController(withIde
    ntifier: "page01")
    let secondVC = storyBoard.instantiateViewController(withId
    entifier: "page02")
    let thirdVC = storyBoard.instantiateViewController(withIde
    ntifier: "page03")

    controllerArray = [firstVC, secondVC, thirdVC]

    self.setViewControllers([controllerArray![0]], direction:
    UIPageViewController.NavigationDirection.forward,
    animated: true, completion: nil)
}
```

The first line defines the PageViewController.swift file as the data source for the Page Controller. The next line creates a storyboard constant named "Main". The next three lines define constants (firstVC, secondVC, and thirdVC) to represent each View Controller to appear inside the Page Controller. Notice that each View Controller uses the Storyboard ID of each View Controller to identify it such as "page01" or "page03".

Next, we store all of these View Controllers into the controllerArray. Finally, we set this array of View Controllers inside the Page Controller.

15. Add the following function to define the View Controller to appear
   when the user displays the previous View Controller:

```
func pageViewController(_ pageViewController:
UIPageViewController, viewControllerBefore viewController:
UIViewController) -> UIViewController? {
    guard let vcIndex = controllerArray!.firstIndex(of:
    viewController) else {
        return nil
    }

    let preIndex = vcIndex - 1

    guard preIndex >= 0 else {
        return controllerArray!.last // loops back to end
    }

    guard controllerArray!.count > preIndex else {
        return nil
    }

    return controllerArray![preIndex]
}
```

The first guard statement checks to make sure that the controller
array contains valid View Controllers. Then it creates a preIndex
constant to represent the previous View Controller. As long as the
value of preIndex is greater than 0, the Page Controller can display
the previous View Controller in the array. The moment the value of
preIndex equals 0 or less, then the next View Controller displayed
is the last one. This creates an infinite loop so the first View
Controller displayed links to the last View Controller in the array.

The last guard statement makes sure that the total number of
View Controllers in the array is greater than the value of preIndex.
Finally this function returns the previous View Controller in the
array.

16. Add the following function to define the View Controller to appear when the user displays the next View Controller:

```swift
func pageViewController(_ pageViewController:
UIPageViewController, viewControllerAfter viewController:
UIViewController) -> UIViewController? {
    guard let vcIndex = controllerArray!.firstIndex(of:
    viewController) else {
        return nil
    }

    let nextIndex = vcIndex + 1

    guard controllerArray!.count != nextIndex else {
        return controllerArray!.first // loops back to beginning
    }

    guard controllerArray!.count > nextIndex else {
        return nil
    }

    return controllerArray![nextIndex]
}
```

The entire PageViewController.swift file should look like this:

```swift
import UIKit

class PageViewController: UIPageViewController,
UIPageViewControllerDataSource {

    var controllerArray: [UIViewController]? = nil

    override func viewDidLoad() {
        super.viewDidLoad()
        dataSource = self

        let storyBoard = UIStoryboard(name: "Main", bundle: nil)
        let firstVC = storyBoard.instantiateViewController
        (withIdentifier: "page01")
```

```swift
    let secondVC = storyBoard.instantiateViewController(withId
    entifier: "page02")
    let thirdVC = storyBoard.instantiateViewController(withIde
    ntifier: "page03")

    controllerArray = [firstVC, secondVC, thirdVC]

    self.setViewControllers([controllerArray![0]], direction:
    UIPageViewController.NavigationDirection.forward,
    animated: true, completion: nil)
    // Do any additional setup after loading the view.
}

func pageViewController(_ pageViewController:
UIPageViewController, viewControllerBefore viewController:
UIViewController) -> UIViewController? {
    guard let vcIndex = controllerArray!.firstIndex(of:
    viewController) else {
        return nil
    }

    let preIndex = vcIndex - 1

    guard preIndex >= 0 else {
        return controllerArray!.last // loops back to end
    }

    guard controllerArray!.count > preIndex else {
        return nil
    }

    return controllerArray![preIndex]
}

func pageViewController(_ pageViewController:
UIPageViewController, viewControllerAfter viewController:
UIViewController) -> UIViewController? {
    guard let vcIndex = controllerArray!.firstIndex(of:
    viewController) else {
```

```swift
        return nil
    }

    let nextIndex = vcIndex + 1

    guard controllerArray!.count != nextIndex else {
        return controllerArray!.first // loops back to beginning
    }

    guard controllerArray!.count > nextIndex else {
        return nil
    }

    return controllerArray![nextIndex]
    }

}
```

17. Click the Run button or choose Product ➤ Run. The Simulator window appears showing the first View Controller.

18. Drag the mouse from the bottom right corner to the left. Notice that the page curl transition makes the View Controller appear like a physical page as shown in Figure 19-11.

Figure 19-11. *The page curl transition style makes the transition between View Controllers look like a physical page turning*

19. Continue swiping left and right. Notice that when you reach the last View Controller, swiping to the left reveals the first View Controller. When you reach the first View Controller, swiping to the left reveals the last View Controller.

20. Choose Simulator ➤ Quit Simulator to return to Xcode.

Summary

The Page Controller offers another way to display multiple View Controllers in sequential order. By using a page curl transition style, swiping can make each View Controller look like a physical page turning at the corner. To use a Page Controller, you must drag and drop a Page Controller from the Object Library window onto your app's storyboard.

After adding a Page Controller to a storyboard, you need to add View Controllers to your storyboard. Each View Controller needs a unique Storyboard ID (any arbitrary text). In addition, each View Controller needs to be connected to a .swift UIViewController class file.

Finally, you need to create a .swift UIPageViewController class file and connect this to the Page Controller. Inside this .swift UIPageViewController, you need to write Swift code to create an array of View Controllers, identifying all View Controllers by their unique Storyboard ID.

Inside the UIPageViewController class file, you need to write two methods to define which view to display before and after the currently displayed View Controller.

By using a Page Controller, you can create interesting visual effects that create the illusion of turning physical pages in a printed book.

CHAPTER 20

Using the Split View Controller

One of the most common user interface objects for displaying lists of information is the table view. When viewed on the narrow screen of an iPhone in portrait orientation, table views look fine. However, when viewed on the much larger iPad screen, especially in landscape orientation, a table view can look unbalanced with text appearing far to one side with empty space filling the majority of the screen as shown in Figure 20-1.

© Wallace Wang 2019
W. Wang, *Beginning iPhone Development with Swift 5*, https://doi.org/10.1007/978-1-4842-4865-2_20

Figure 20-1. *A table view displayed on the larger screen of an iPad*

To avoid this unbalanced, empty look, you can use a Split View Controller for the iPad and for the larger screens on certain iPhone models. Instead of displaying a single table view at a time, a Split View Controller displays two views side by side. The left view (known as the primary or master view) displays additional information in a right view (known as the secondary or detail view) as shown in Figure 20-2.

Master view   Detail view

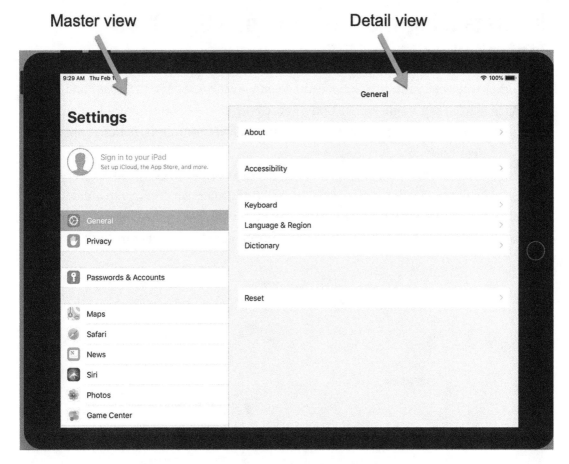

Figure 20-2. *A Split View Controller displays two views side by side to fill a larger screen*

The master view essentially displays the previous table view, while the detail view displays the next table view. By displaying them side by side, you can easily see the relationship between each list such as seeing the About, Accessibility, Keyboard, Language & Region, Dictionary, and Reset options all appear under the General category (see Figure 20-2).

When run on larger iPad and iPhone screens, a Split View Controller divides the screen in two parts to display the master view and the detail view. When run on smaller iPhone screens, a Split View Controller acts like an ordinary table view by displaying a single list of items.

Understanding the Structure of a Split View Controller

While other types of controllers, such as the Page View Controller or a Table View Controller, consist of a single item, a Split View Controller is far more complicated. A Split View Controller must connect to two separate View Controllers, which represent the master-detail side-by-side views.

To define the master view, a Split View Controller must connect to a Navigation Controller. To define the detail view, a Split View Controller can connect to a View Controller. When you drag and drop a Split View Controller from the Object Library, you'll see the basic structure of a Split View Controller as shown in Figure 20-3.

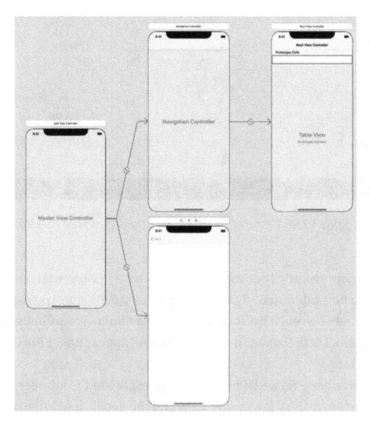

Figure 20-3. *The basic structure of a Split View Controller*

In addition to the Split View Controller relying on at least one Navigation Controller and a View Controller, a Split View Controller also requires Swift code spread across three separate files to work:

- AppDelegate.swift – Controls the two View Controllers that make up the master and detail views

- A .swift file that connects to the master view – Controls the master View Controller

- A .swift file that connects to the detail view – Controls the detail View Controller

To see how a Split View Controller works, follow these steps:

1. Choose File ➤ New ➤ Project. A dialog appears listing different templates.

2. Choose Master-Detail App under the iOS category as shown in Figure 20-4.

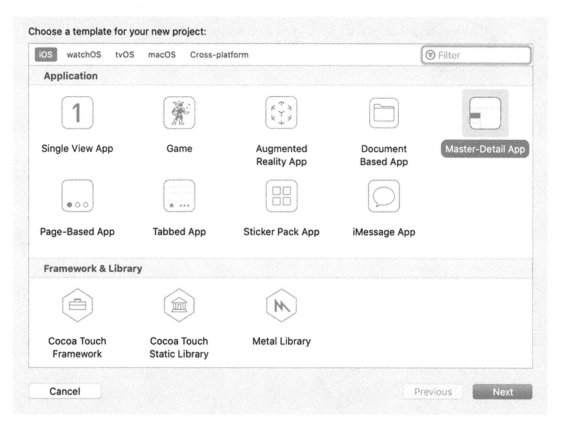

Figure 20-4. *The basic structure of a Split View Controller*

3. Click the **Next** button. Xcode displays another window asking for a Product name.

4. Click in the Product name text field, type **SplitViewApp**, and click the **Next** button. Then click the **Create** button. Xcode displays the Master-Detail App.

5. Click the AppDelegate.swift file in the Navigator pane and notice the Swift code inside.

6. Click the MasterViewController.swift file in the Navigator pane and study the Swift code inside.

7. Click the DetailViewController.swift file in the Navigator pane and study the Swift code inside.

8. Click the Main.storyboard file in the Navigator pane. Notice how the storyboard displays a Split View Controller connected to two Navigation Controllers as shown in Figure 20-5.

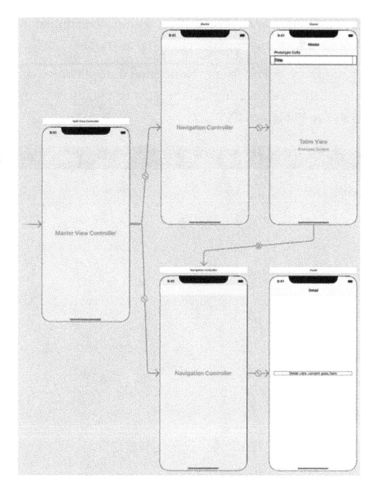

Figure 20-5. *The storyboard of the Master-Detail App*

9. Click the Active Scheme popup menu as shown in Figure 20-6. A popup menu appears.

Figure 20-6. *Clicking the Active Scheme popup menu*

10. Chose an iPad model such as an iPad Air or an iPad Pro.

11.   Click the Run button or choose Product ➤ Run. The Simulator
      window appears, simulating your chosen iPad model.

12.   Choose Hardware ➤ Rotate Left. Notice that the Split View
      Controller displays a table view on the left and a blank view on the
      right as shown in Figure 20-7.

Figure 20-7. *Displaying the Split View Controller*

13.   Click the + icon that appears at the top of the left (master) view.
      Click this + icon multiple times. Each time you click this + icon,
      the time you clicked appears in the left (master) view.

14.   Click any of the times displayed in the left (master) view.
      Notice that the right (detail) view displays that time as shown in
      Figure 20-8.

Figure 20-8. *Selecting an item in the left (master) view displays more information in the right (detail) view*

15. Choose Hardware ➤ Rotate Right. Notice that the Split View Controller now hides the master view and only shows the detail view.

16. Click the < Master button in the upper left corner of the simulated iPad screen. Notice how the master view slides out as shown in Figure 20-9.

Figure 20-9. *The master view slides out from the left*

17. Choose Simulator ➤ Quit Simulator to return to Xcode.

By experimenting with the Split View Controller in the Master-Detail App template, you can see how the Split View Controller changes its appearance based on the simulated iPad's orientation (portrait or landscape).

18. Click the Active Scheme popup menu (see Figure 20-6). A popup menu appears.

19. Choose iPhone XR.

20. Click the Run button or choose Product ➤ Run. The Simulator window appears, simulating an iPhone XR in portrait orientation.

21. Click the + icon in the upper right corner multiple times. Each time you click the + icon, the master view displays the time. Notice that in the smaller screen size of an iPhone in portrait orientation, the Split View Controller looks like a standard table view as shown in Figure 20-10.

Figure 20-10. *The Split View Controller appears as a table view on an iPhone in portrait orientation*

22. Choose Hardware ➤ Rotate Left.

23. Click the < Master button in the upper left corner. Notice that the Split View Controller slides the master view from the left and displays the detail view on the right as shown in Figure 20-11.

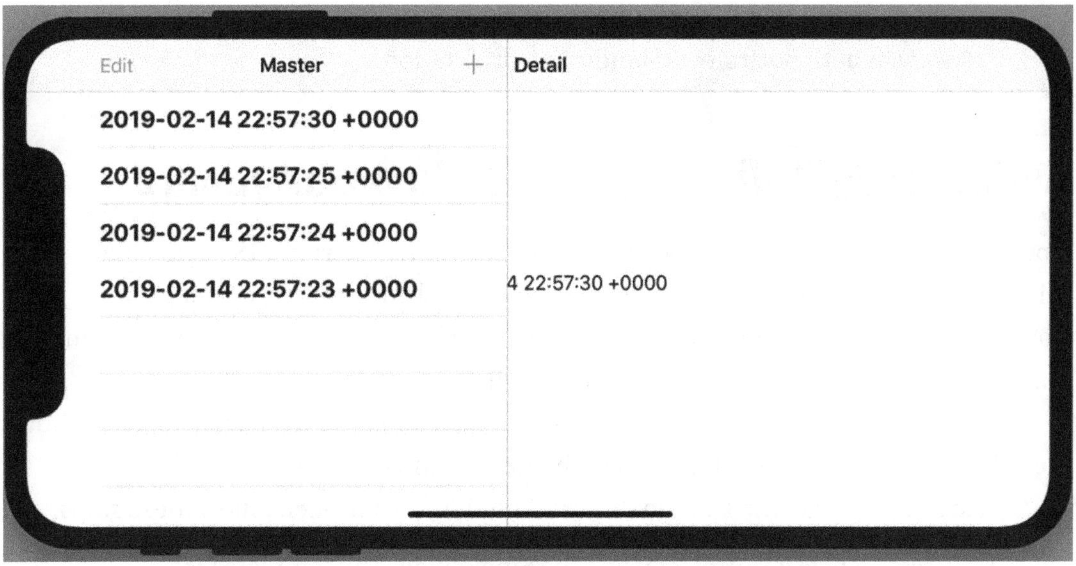

Figure 20-11. *The master view can slide from the left when an iPhone switches to landscape orientation*

24. Choose Hardware ➤ Rotate Right. Notice that the master view disappears again.

25. Choose Simulator ➤ Quit Simulator to return to Xcode.

Try experimenting by running this app in different iOS devices such as a small screen iPhone 5s or a large screen iPad Pro. Then rotate the iOS device left and right. Notice that the Split View Controller behaves differently depending on the iOS device chosen and its orientation:

- On an iPad in portrait orientation, the Split View Controller hides the master view but slides it out when the user requests it.

- On an iPad in landscape orientation, the Split View Controller displays the master view on the left and the detail view on the right.

- On a large screen iPhone in portrait orientation, the Split View Controller displays a table view.

- On a large screen iPhone in landscape orientation, the Split View Controller hides the master view but slides it out when the user requests it.

567

- On a small screen iPhone, the Split View Controller displays a table view in both portrait and landscape orientation.

Adding a Split View Controller to a Storyboard

Once you've seen how a Split View Controller behaves in different iOS devices and orientations, it's time to learn more about creating and customizing a Split View Controller. A Split View Controller typically needs at least one table view to represent the master view and a View Controller to represent the detail view.

That means you need to fill a table view with data and then write code to define how the Split View Controller displays data in the master and detail views.

To see how to create the storyboard for a Split View Controller, follow these steps:

1. Create a new iOS project using the Single View App template (see Chapter 1) and name this new project SplitViewCustomApp. This creates a single view for the user interface.

2. Click the Main.storyboard in the Navigator pane.

3. Click the View Controller Scene in the Document Outline and press BACKSPACE or DELETE to remove the View Controller from the storyboard.

4. Click ViewController.swift in the Navigator pane and choose Edit ➤ Delete. A dialog appears, asking how you want to delete the file.

5. Click the Move to Trash button. The ViewController.swift file disappears from the Navigator pane.

6. Click the Main.storyboard file in the Navigator pane.

7. Click the Library icon to open the Object Library window.

8. Drag and drop a Split View Controller from the Object Library window to the storyboard as shown in Figure 20-12.

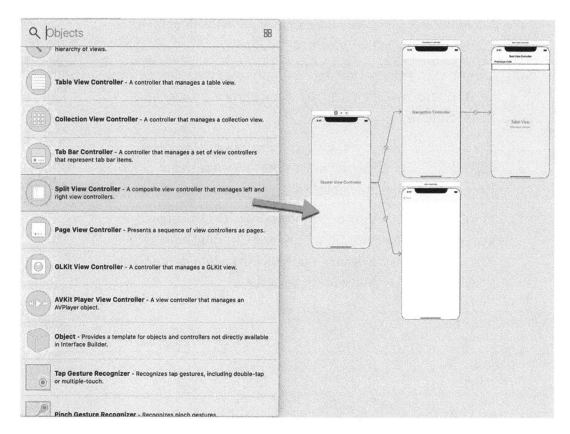

Figure 20-12. *Dragging a Split View Controller onto a storyboard*

9. Click the Split View Controller Scene in the Document Outline.

10. Choose View ➤ Inspectors ➤ Show Attributes Inspector, or click the Attributes Inspector icon in the upper right corner of the Xcode window.

11. Select the "Is Initial View Controller" check box. Xcode displays an arrow pointing to the Split View Controller.

12. Click the View Controller Scene in the Document Outline.

13. Choose Editor ➤ Embed In ➤ Navigation Controller. Xcode embeds the View Controller inside a Navigation Controller. This will allow the View Controller to slide in and out, but we need to create a segue between the table cell and this Navigation Controller, so when the user clicks a table cell, it displays the View Controller inside this Navigation Controller.

14.   Click the Table View Cell under Table View in the Root View
      Controller Scene in the Document Outline.

15.   Choose View ➤ Inspectors ➤ Show Attributes Inspector, or click
      the Attributes Inspector icon in the upper right corner of the
      Xcode window.

16.   Click in the Identifier text field, type **customCell**, and press
      ENTER. Xcode changes the Table View Cell name in the
      Document Outline to customCell.

17.   Move the mouse pointer over customCell in the Document
      Outline, hold down the Control key, and Ctrl-drag from
      customCell to the Navigation Controller that embeds the blank
      View Controller as shown in Figure 20-13.

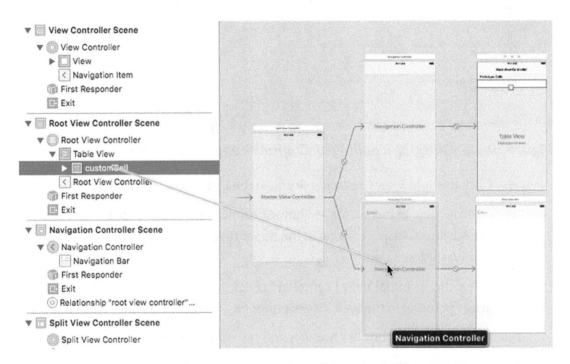

Figure 20-13. *Creating a segue between the Table View Cell and the Navigation*
Controller

18.   Release the Control key and the left mouse button. A popup menu
      appears as shown in Figure 20-14.

Figure 20-14. *A segue popup menu*

19. Choose Show Detail. Xcode create a segue between the Table View Cell (named customCell) and the Navigation Controller that embeds the blank View Controller.

20. Click the Show Detail segue "showDetail" to "Navigation Controller" in the Document Outline. This selects the segue from the Table View Cell (customCell) to the Navigation Controller.

21. Choose View ➤ Inspectors ➤ Show Attributes Inspector, or click the Attributes Inspector icon in the upper right corner of the Xcode window.

22. Click in the Identifier text field, type **showDetail**, and press ENTER as shown in Figure 20-15.

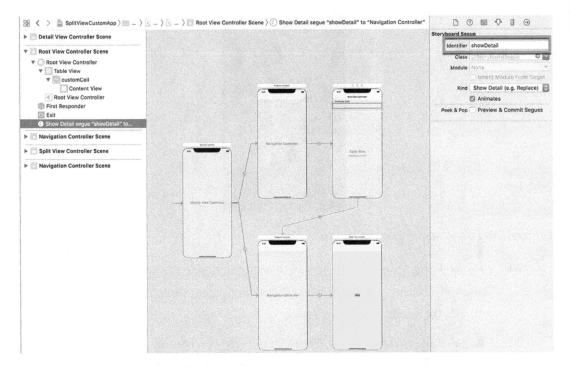

Figure 20-15. *Defining an Identifier name for the segue between the Table View Cell and the Navigation Controller*

23. Click View under View Controller Scene in the Document Outline.

24. Choose View ➤ Inspectors ➤ Show Attributes Inspector, or click the Attributes Inspector icon in the upper right corner of the Xcode window.

25. Click in the Background popup menu and choose a different color such as yellow to make it easy to identify the View Controller when the app runs.

26. Click the Library icon to open the Object Library window.

27. Drag and drop a label in the middle of the view that you just modified to display a background color such as yellow.

28. Click the Align icon at the bottom of the Xcode window to display a popup window.

29. Select the Horizontally in Container and Vertically in Container check boxes. Then click the Add 2 Constraints button.

The storyboard for the Split View Controller is now complete. Now we need to create .swift files for the Split View Controller's master view and detail view.

Creating Class Files

With a Split View Controller, you need two .swift class files, one for the table view (UITableViewController) and one for the View Controller (UIViewController). The UITableViewController .swift file defines the master view that fills the table view rows with data and then detects when the user taps on a particular row. The UIViewController .swift file displays data on the View Controller that represents the detail view.

To create two .swift class files, follow these steps:

1. Make sure the SplitViewCustomApp is loaded into Xcode.

2. Choose File ➤ New ➤ File. A dialog appears displaying different templates available.

3. Click Cocoa Touch Class under the iOS category and click the **Next** button. Another window appears, asking for a class name and subclass type.

4. Click in the Class text field and type **MasterTableViewController**.

5. Click in the Subclass of popup menu and choose UITableViewController.

6. Click the **Next** button and then click the **Create** button. Xcode displays the MasterViewController.swift file in the Navigator pane.

7. Choose File ➤ New ➤ File. A dialog appears displaying different templates available.

8. Click Cocoa Touch Class under the iOS category and click the **Next** button. Another window appears, asking for a class name and subclass type.

9. Click in the Class text field and type **DetailViewController**.

10. Click in the Subclass of popup menu and choose UIViewController.

11. Click the **Next** button and then click the **Create** button. Xcode displays the DetailViewController.swift file in the Navigator pane.

12. Click the Main.storyboard file in the Navigator pane. Xcode displays the storyboard.

13. Click the Root View Controller in the Document Outline.

14. Choose View ➤ Inspectors ➤ Show Identity Inspector, or click the Identity Inspector icon at the top right corner of the Xcode window.

15. Click in the Class popup menu and choose MasterViewController as shown in Figure 20-16.

Figure 20-16. *Connecting the Root View Controller to the MasterViewController. swift file*

16. Click the View Controller Scene in the Document Outline.

17. Choose View ➤ Inspectors ➤ Show Identity Inspector, or click the Identity Inspector icon at the top right corner of the Xcode window.

18. Click the Class popup menu and choose DetailViewController.

Modifying the AppDelegate.swift File

The AppDelegate.swift file typically monitors the app behavior such as loading or terminating. For our example, we need the AppDelegate.swift file to set up the Split View Controller. This means writing Swift code and declaring the AppDelegate.swift file to be the delegate for the Split View Controller.

That means adding these two lines of code to assign the AppDelegate.swift file as the Split View Controller delegate:

```
let splitVC = window!.rootViewController as! UISplitViewController
splitVC.delegate = self
```

The first line declares a splitVC constant that represents the Split View Controller on the storyboard. The second line makes sure that the Split View Controller (the splitVC constant) knows that the AppDelegate.swift file is its delegate, which means that the AppDelegate.swift file will contain Swift code to load the Navigation Controller into the Split View Controller.

The Split View Controller keeps track of all the View Controllers it can display by storing them in an array. Initially, the Split View Controller displays the last item in this array.

```swift
let navigationVC = splitVC.viewControllers.last as? UINavigationController
```

Finally, the Navigation Controller needs a left bar button, which the following code creates:

```swift
navigationVC.topViewController!.navigationItem.leftBarButtonItem = splitVC.displayModeButtonItem
```

To make all these changes, follow these steps:

1. Make sure the SplitViewCustomApp project is loaded in Xcode.

2. Click the AppDelegate.swift file in the Navigator pane.

3. Edit the class AppDelegate line as follows:

   ```swift
   class AppDelegate: UIResponder, UIApplicationDelegate,
   UISplitViewControllerDelegate {
   ```

4. Edit the didFinishLaunchingWithOptions method as follows:

   ```swift
   func application(_ application: UIApplication,
   didFinishLaunchingWithOptions launchOptions: [UIApplication.
   LaunchOptionsKey: Any]?) -> Bool {
       let splitVC = window!.rootViewController as!
       UISplitViewController
       splitVC.delegate = self
       let navigationVC = splitVC.viewControllers.last as?
       UINavigationController
       navigationVC?.topViewController!.navigationItem.
       leftBarButtonItem = splitVC.displayModeButtonItem
       return true
   }
   ```

5. Add the following method at the bottom of the AppDelegate.swift
    file above the last curly bracket:

```swift
func splitViewController(_ splitViewController:
UISplitViewController, collapseSecondary secondaryViewController
:UIViewController, onto primaryViewController:UIViewController)
-> Bool {
    guard let secondaryAsNavController =
    secondaryViewController as? UINavigationController else {
    return false }
    guard let topAsDetailController = secondaryAsNavController.
    topViewController as? DetailViewController else { return
    false }
    if topAsDetailController.detailItem == nil {
        // Return true to indicate that we have handled the
        collapse by doing nothing; the secondary controller
        will be discarded.
        return true
    }
    return false
}
```

This collapseSecondary function takes care of showing or hiding the detail view. The
if statement checks if a detailItem property is nil. This detailItem property holds the data
to appear in the detail view and will be defined in the DetailViewController.swift file so
don't worry if Xcode displays an error message for now.

The entire AppDelegate.swift file should look like this:

```swift
import UIKit

@UIApplicationMain
class AppDelegate: UIResponder, UIApplicationDelegate,
UISplitViewControllerDelegate {

    var window: UIWindow?
```

```
func application(_ application: UIApplication,
didFinishLaunchingWithOptions launchOptions: [UIApplication.
LaunchOptionsKey: Any]?) -> Bool {
    let splitVC = window!.rootViewController as! UISplitViewController
    splitVC.delegate = self
    let navigationVC = splitVC.viewControllers.last as?
    UINavigationController
    navigationVC?.topViewController!.navigationItem.leftBarButtonItem =
    splitVC.displayModeButtonItem
    return true
}

func splitViewController(_ splitViewController: UISplitViewController,
collapseSecondary secondaryViewController:UIViewController, onto primar
yViewController:UIViewController) -> Bool {
    guard let secondaryAsNavController = secondaryViewController as?
    UINavigationController else { return false }
    guard let topAsDetailController = secondaryAsNavController.
    topViewController as? DetailViewController else { return false }
    if topAsDetailController.detailItem == nil {
        // Return true to indicate that we have handled the collapse by
        doing nothing; the secondary controller will be discarded.
        return true
    }
    return false
}
}
```

Modifying the DetailViewController.swift File

The DetailViewController.swift file displays the user's selection. Right now the detail
View Controller displays a label, but this label needs to be connected to an IBOutlet so
Swift code can display data in that label.

In addition, the DetailViewController.swift file also needs to define a detailItem
property. This detailItem property stores data sent from the MasterTableViewController.
swift file, which defines the item in the table view row that the user selected. This data

577

needs to be displayed in the label when the detail View Controller first loads and each time when the user selects a different item in the table view.

To modify the DetailViewController.swift file, follow these steps:

1. Make sure the SplitViewCustomApp project is loaded in Xcode.

2. Click the Main.storyboard file in the Navigator pane.

3. Click the Detail View Controller Scene in the Document Outline.

4. Choose View ➤ Assistant Editor ➤ Show Assistant Editor, or click the Assistant Editor icon in the upper right corner of the Xcode window. This displays the Main.storyboard and DetailViewController.swift file side by side.

5. Move the mouse over the Label under the Detail View Controller Scene in the Document Outline, hold down the Control key, and Ctrl-drag to the "class DetailViewController" line in the DetailViewController.swift file.

6. Release the Control key and the left mouse button. A popup window appears.

7. Click in the Name text field, type **petLabel**, and click the Connect button. Xcode creates an IBOutlet as follows:

@IBOutlet var petLabel: UILabel!

8. Choose View ➤ Standard Editor ➤ Show Standard Editor, or click the Standard Editor icon in the upper right corner of the Xcode window.

9. Click the DetailViewController.swift file in the Navigator pane.

10. Add the following property under the IBOutlet:

```
var detailItem: String? {
    didSet {
        configureView()
    }
}
```

11.   Add the following function under the IBOutlet:

```
func configureView() {
    if let label = petLabel {
        label.text = detailItem
    }
}
```

12.   Modify the viewDidLoad method as follows:

```
override func viewDidLoad() {
    super.viewDidLoad()
    configureView()
}
```

When the view loads for the first time, it calls the configureView function, which stores the detailItem data into the label. Each time the user chooses a different item in the table view displayed on the master view, this chosen item gets stored in the detailItem property.

The complete DetailViewController.swift file should look like this:

```
import UIKit

class DetailViewController: UIViewController {

    @IBOutlet var petLabel: UILabel!

    var detailItem: String? {
        didSet {
            configureView()
        }
    }

    func configureView() {
        if let label = petLabel {
            label.text = detailItem
        }
    }
}
```

```
override func viewDidLoad() {
    super.viewDidLoad()
    configureView()
    // Do any additional setup after loading the view.
}

}
```

Modifying the MasterTableViewController.swift File

The MasterTableViewController.swift file displays a table view for the user to select an item. That means the MasterTableViewController.swift file needs to define how many sections appear in the table view (1) and how many number of rows appear in the table view (the total array count of data) and fill the table view with data from an array. The array simply displays a list of strings where each string appears in a row in the table view.

In addition to filling the table view with data, the MasterTableViewController.swift file also needs to create a variable that represents the detail View Controller and pass that detail View Controller the item selected from the table view by using the segue defined in the storyboard.

To modify the MasterTableViewController.swift file, follow these steps:

1. Make sure the SplitViewCustomApp project is loaded in Xcode.

2. Click the MasterTableViewController.swift file in the Navigator pane.

3. Underneath the "class MasterTableViewController" line, add the following:

   ```
   var detailVC: DetailViewController? = nil
   let petArray = ["cat", "dog", "parakeet", "parrot", "canary",
   "finch", "tropical fish", "goldfish", "sea horses", "hamster",
   "gerbil", "rabbit", "turtle", "snake", "lizard", "hermit crab"]
   ```

4. Modify the viewDidLoad method as follows:

   ```
   override func viewDidLoad() {
       super.viewDidLoad()
   ```

```
    if let split = splitViewController {
        detailVC = (split.viewControllers.last as!
        UINavigationController).topViewController as?
        DetailViewController
    }
}
```

5. Add the following method underneath the viewDidLoad method:

```
override func viewWillAppear(_ animated: Bool) {
    clearsSelectionOnViewWillAppear = splitViewController!.
    isCollapsed
    super.viewWillAppear(animated)
}
```

6. Add the following under the viewWillAppear method to define the
    table view and fill it with data from the array:

```
override func numberOfSections(in tableView: UITableView) -> Int {
    return 1
}

override func tableView(_ tableView: UITableView,
numberOfRowsInSection section: Int) -> Int {
    return petArray.count
}

override func tableView(_ tableView: UITableView, cellForRowAt
indexPath: IndexPath) -> UITableViewCell {
    // Make sure you define the table view's cell Identifier
    in the Attributes Inspector pane
    let cell = tableView.dequeueReusableCell(withIdentifier:
    "customCell", for: indexPath)
    cell.textLabel!.text = petArray[indexPath.row]
    return cell
}
```

7. Add the following prepare for segue function to retrieve data from
    the table view and send it to the DetailViewController.swift file:

```
override func prepare(for segue: UIStoryboardSegue, sender:
Any?) {
    if segue.identifier == "showDetail" {
        if let indexPath = tableView.indexPathForSelectedRow {
            let object = petArray[indexPath.row]
            let controller = (segue.destination as!
            UINavigationController).topViewController as!
            DetailViewController
            controller.detailItem = object
            controller.navigationItem.leftBarButtonItem =
            splitViewController?.displayModeButtonItem
            controller.navigationItem.
            leftItemsSupplementBackButton = true
        }
    }
}
```

8. Click the Run button or choose Product ➤ Run. The Simulator
    window appears, displaying a table view filled with items from the
    petArray.

9. Click any item. Notice that the detail view displays the chosen
    item in its label.

10. Choose Hardware ➤ Rotate Left.

11. Move the mouse to the left of the Simulator and drag to the right
    to pull the master view out as shown in Figure 20-17.

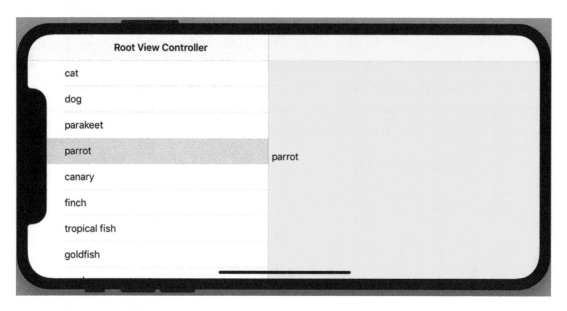

Figure 20-17. *Running the app on a simulated iPhone in landscape orientation*

12. Move the mouse pointer to the right of the master view and drag the mouse to the left to collapse the master view.

13. Choose Hardware ➤ Rotate Right.

14. Choose Simulator ➤ Quit Simulator to return to Xcode.

Summary

A Split View Controller is designed for larger screens such as the iPad or the larger screen models of the iPhone. A Split View Controller can display two views side by side where one side (known as the master view) typically displays a table of items. Selecting an item from this table then transfers this data to the second side (known as the detail view).

When displayed on large screens, Split View Controllers can display both a master view and a detail view side by side. When displayed on smaller screens, Split View Controllers act like ordinary Navigation Controllers in sliding views back and forth.

When using a Split View Controller, make sure you name the segue between the Table View Cell and the Navigation Controller by defining the segue's Identifier property in the Attributes Inspector pane. Also make sure you name the Table View Cell by modifying its Identifier property as well.

The master View Controller and the detail View Controller both need a separate .swift class file to connect to. In addition to writing code in these two .swift files, you'll also need to write code in the AppDelegate.swift file.

Split View Controllers help display data correctly in both large and small screens. Think of a Split View Controller as a fancier version of a Navigation Controller that's especially suited for large screens such as the iPad.

APPENDIX

An Introduction to Swift

While there are numerous programming languages and tools you can use to create iOS apps, the most popular tool is Xcode, which allows you to write iOS apps using two languages: Objective-C and Swift. Originally Objective-C was the only language that Xcode supported, but in 2014, Apple introduced Swift. Two crucial advantages of Swift over Objective-C are that Swift is easier to read and write and is faster than Objective-C. While many older iOS apps are written in Objective-C, Swift is the programming language of the future for not only iOS but also for macOS, tvOS, watchOS, and any future operating systems Apple may develop.

The best way to learn Swift is to use a special feature of Xcode called a playground. A playground lets you write and experiment with Swift code without worrying about a user interface. By doing this, a playground helps you focus solely on learning how to write Swift commands.

To open a playground, follow these steps:

1. Choose File ➤ New ➤ Playground, or click the Get started with a playground on the opening Xcode window as shown in Figure A-1. A window appears displaying different types of playgrounds you can create as shown in Figure A-2.

© Wallace Wang 2019
W. Wang, *Beginning iPhone Development with Swift 5*, https://doi.org/10.1007/978-1-4842-4865-2

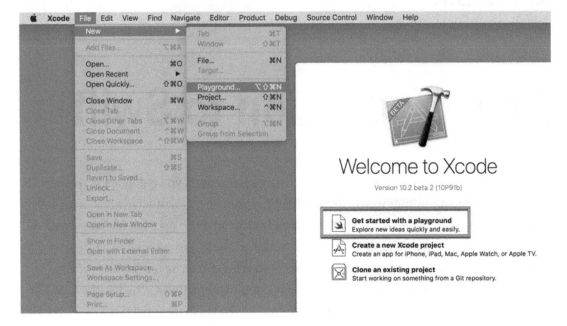

Figure A-1. *Creating a playground in Xcode*

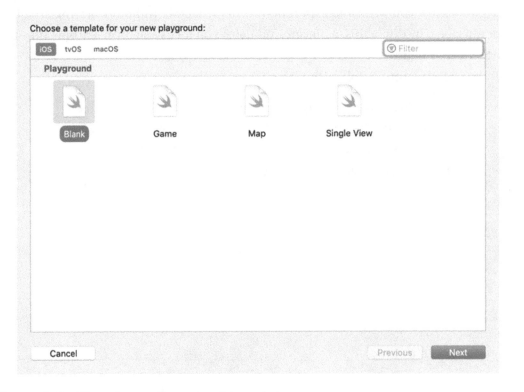

Figure A-2. *Choosing a playground template*

2. Click Blank under the iOS category and click the **Next** button. A dialog appears where you can choose where to save your playground and give it a name beyond the generic MyPlayground name.

3. Choose a folder to store your playground and give it a descriptive name if you wish. Then click the **Create** button. Xcode displays the playground as shown in Figure A-3.

Figure A-3. *An iOS playground*

Notice that in Figure A-3, Xcode colors all Swift code in the following ways:

- Magenta (purple) – Identifies keywords of the Swift language. In Figure A-3, "import" tells the code to access a software framework called UIKit. By replacing UIKit with another name, or adding another import statement, you can access as many software frameworks as you wish. A second keyword is "var" which stands for variable.

- Black – Identifies arbitrarily named text. In Figure A-3, UIKit is a software framework name and "str" is an arbitrarily named variable.

- Red – Identifies a text string bracketed by double quotation marks.

When typing Swift code, use color coding to help identify possible mistakes. For example, if you're typing a string, it should appear in red. If it does not, chances are good you're missing a beginning or ending quotation mark.

You can create as many different playgrounds as you wish to experiment with different features of Swift. Once you get Swift code to work correctly, then you can copy and paste it into an Xcode project.

Note   The first line of every iOS Swift playground begins with the "import UIKit" line, which allows access to Apple's UIKit framework for iOS devices.

Storing Data

Every programming language needs a way to store data. In Swift, you can store data in two ways:

- As a constant

- As a variable

A constant lets you store data in it exactly once. A variable lets you store data multiple times over and over again. Each time you store data in a variable, it deletes any data already stored in that variable.

Every constant or variable needs a name that begins with a letter, although it can use numbers as part of its name such as "Fred2" or "jo903tre". Ideally, the name should be descriptive of the type of data it holds such as "taxReturn" or "Age".

Although not required, Swift programmers typically create names using something known as camel case. That's where a name is made up of two or more words where the first letter is lowercase and the first letter of each additional word is uppercase. Some examples of camel case names are

- nameToDelete

- fly2MoonTomorrow

- sleepLatePlayHard

Apple uses camel case throughout its software frameworks so you should get familiar with camel case and use it for your own code as well.

Each time you create a new Swift playground, it creates a default line that creates or declares a variable called "str" and stores or assigns it a text string "Hello, playground" as shown in Figure A-4.

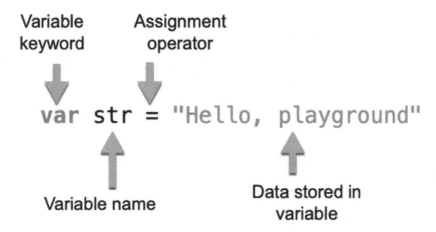

Figure A-4. *The parts of a variable declaration*

Every variable (or constant) declaration begins with the keyword "var" (for variable) or "let" (for a constant). The second part of a variable or constant declaration is the name, which can be any descriptive name you want to use.

Next is the equal sign that assigns data to that name. Finally, the data itself appears on the right side of the equal sign. In this case, the text string "Hello, playground" gets stored in the variable named "str".

To see the difference between constants and variables, follow these steps in the Swift playground:

1. Add the following line in the playground underneath the variable declaration:

    ```
    print (str)
    ```

2. Click the Run button in the left column as shown in Figure A-5.

Figure A-5. *Viewing the output of the print statement*

3. Choose View ➤ Debug Area ➤ Show Debug Area, click the Show/
    Hide Debug Area icon in the lower left corner of the playground
    window, or click the Hide or show Debug Area icon in the upper
    right corner of the playground window. The playground window
    displays the text "Hello, playground" in the right column and the
    Debug Area at the bottom of the window.

The variable declaration simply stores "Hello, playground" into the "str" variable.
Then the print statement prints the contents of that "str" variable, displaying "Hello,
playground" in the right column and in the Debug Area at the bottom of the screen.

Right now, all we've done is store data in a variable once and printed it out. Modify
the code as follows and then click the Run button:

```swift
import UIKit

var str = "Hello, playground"
print (str)
str = "Swift is a great language to learn"
print (str)
```

Notice that the preceding code first stores the string "Hello, playground" into the
"str" variable. Then it prints out the data currently stored in the "str" variable.

Then it stores a new string "Swift is a great language to learn" into the "str" variable
and prints the "str" variable contents out again, which is now "Swift is a great language
to learn".

590

You can store data in a variable as many times as you wish. The only limitation is that

- A variable can only hold one chunk of data at a time

- A variable can only hold one type of data

Storing Different Data Types

We've already seen how the "str" variable can only hold one string at a time. The first time we store data in a variable, we need to define what type of data that variable can hold. By storing a string in that "str" variable, we've told the "str" variable that it can only hold strings but cannot hold any other type of data such as integers or real numbers (decimal numbers such as 3.14 or 49.082).

Modify the code to store a number into the "str" variable a second time as follows and then click the Run button:

```
import UIKit

var str = "Hello, playground"
print (str)
str = 54
print (str)
```

Notice that Xcode flags the line assigning the number 54 to the "str" variable as an error as shown in Figure A-6.

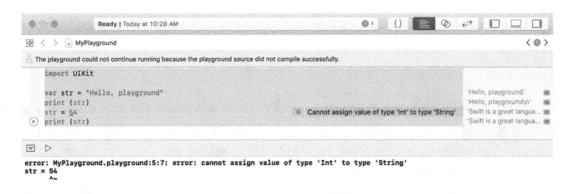

Figure A-6. *An error occurs when you try to store a number into a variable that can only hold string values*

The problem occurs because the first time we store data in the "str" variable, it holds a text string. From now on, that "str" can only hold string data. Let's rewrite the code to make the "str" variable hold an integer. Modify the code as follows and then click the Run button:

```
import UIKit

var str = 7
print (str)
str = 54
print (str)
```

In the preceding code, we first store the number 7 into the "str" variable. From that point on, the "str" variable can only hold numbers, so when we store 54 into the "str" variable a second time, there is no error message.

Note   The first time you store data in a variable, Swift tries to guess the type of data it's storing in a variable, which is called "inference".

In the previous examples, we've created a variable and stored two different strings in it and then two different integers. Let's change the "str" from a variable to a constant by replacing the "var" keyword with "let" as follows:

```
import UIKit

let str = 7
print (str)
str = 54
print (str)
```

Notice that this also creates an error. That's because a constant can only store data exactly once. The first time we stored the number 7 in the "str" constant, which is fine. The problem is that we tried to store 54 into the "str" constant and that's not allowed because "str" is now declared a constant.

If you only need to store data once, use a constant. If you need to store different data over and over again, use a variable.

You might be tempted to simply use a variable all the time, even if you only store data in it once. While this is technically allowed, Xcode will suggest that you use a constant instead. That's because constants use less memory than variables and will make your app run more efficiently.

When creating a variable, you must define the data type you want that variable to hold. The simplest method is to store any data into a variable and let Swift infer the data type. However, inference can sometimes be confusing when it's not clear what type of data is being stored in a variable. Modify the code as follows:

```swift
import UIKit

var str = 7.0
print (str)
str = 54
print (str)
```

When you click the Run button, playground prints the number 7.0 and 54.0, yet we stored the value of 54 in the "str" variable as shown in Figure A-7.

Figure A-7. *Swift infers that all data must be floating-point decimal numbers*

Modify the code to store an integer (7) in the "str" variable first, and then try storing a decimal number (54.0) in the "str" variable later. The first time we store the number 7 in the "str" variable, Swift infers that we'll be storing integer data types from now on. Then when we try storing a decimal number (54.0) in the same "str" variable, Swift raises an error message as shown in Figure A-8.

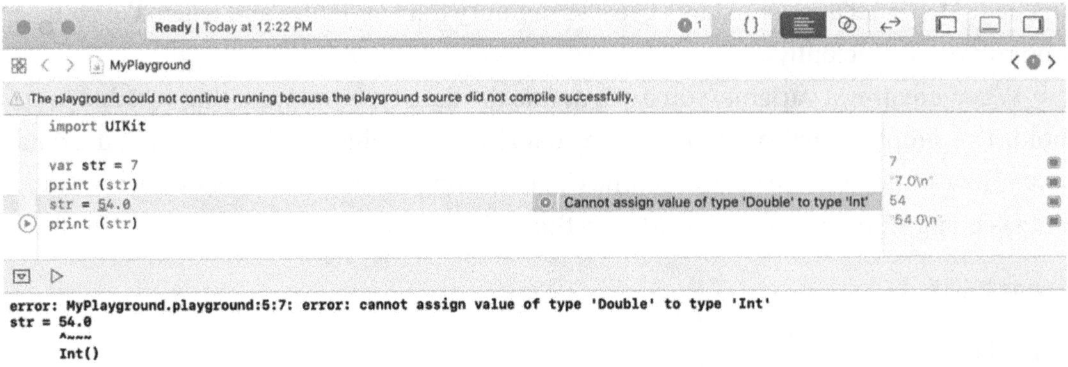

Figure A-8. *Swift raises an error if you try to store different data types in the same variable*

While it's often easier to simply store data in a variable, you might want to make it clear what data type a variable can store. Some common types of data types include:

- Int – Integer or whole numbers such as 8, 92, and 102

- Float – Decimal or floating-point numbers such as 2.13, 98.673, and 0.3784 that stores 32 bits of data

- Double – Decimal or floating-point numbers such as 2.13, 98.673, and 0.3784 except offering greater precision by storing 64 bits of data

- String – Text enclosed by double quotation marks such as "Hello, playground or "78.03"

- Bool – Represents a true or false value

To see how to make the data type of a variable clear, modify the code as follows:

```
import UIKit

var str : Double = 7
print (str)
str = 54.0
print (str)
```

Notice that although the number 7 gets stored in the "str" variable, it's explicitly defined as a Double data type. So rather than storing the number 7 as an integer in the "str" variable, Swift stores the number 7.0 as a Double data type.

Using Optional Data Types

When you explicitly declare a data type for a variable to hold, you can store data in that variable right away like this:

```
var str : Double = 7
```

Another alternative is to define the data type without storing any data in that variable right away like this:

```
var str : Double
```

The preceding line means the "str" variable can only hold Double (decimal) numbers. However, it currently contains nothing. If you create a variable without storing any data in it initially, you cannot use that variable because it contains nothing. Trying to do so will create an error, which you can see by modifying the code as follows:

```
import UIKit

var str : Double
print (str)
str = 54.0
print (str)
```

To avoid this problem, you have two options. One, you can declare a variable and store data in it right away. Two, you can declare an optional variable by adding a question mark at the end of the data type like this:

```
var str : Double?
```

An optional variable initially has a value of nil, so using a variable with a nil value won't cause an error. To see the difference, modify the code as follows and click the Run button:

```
import UIKit

var str : Double?
print (str)
str = 54.0
print (str)
```

Notice that the first print statement prints nil but the second print statement prints Optional(54.0) as shown in Figure A-9.

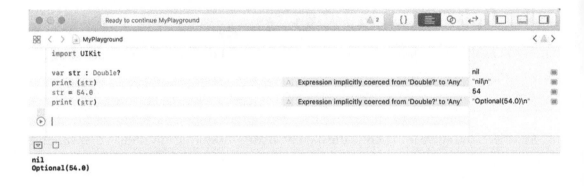

Figure A-9. *Optional variables can be used without data in them*

To access values stored in an optional variable, you can unwrap the data using the exclamation mark symbol (!). To see how to unwrap data, modify the code as follows and click the Run button:

```
import UIKit

var str : Double?
print (str)
str = 54.0
print (str!)
```

Notice that unwrapping optional variables with an exclamation mark retrieves the data as shown in Figure A-10.

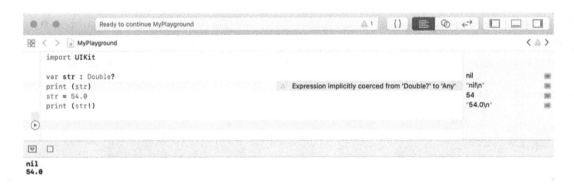

Figure A-10. *Optional variables can be used without data in them*

However, an error will occur if you try unwrapping optional variables that contain a nil value. Modify the code as follows and click the Run button to see the error of trying to unwrap an optional variable that contains a nil value as shown in Figure A-11:

```
import UIKit

var str : Double?
print (str!)
str = 54.0
print (str!)
```

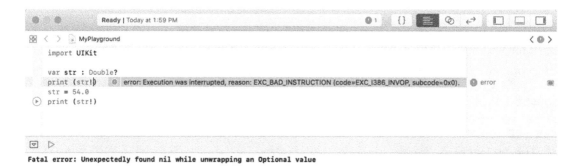

Figure A-11. *You cannot unwrap an optional variable if it contains a nil value*

When using optional variables, you should always check if it contains a nil value first before trying to access its contents. One way to do this is to use an if statement that uses an optional variable only if it does not contain a nil value. To see how this works, modify the code as follows and click the Run button:

```
import UIKit

var str : Double? = 9
if str != nil {
    print (str!)
}
str = 54.0
print (str!)
```

The first print statement never runs because the "str" variable contains a nil value. Change the code as follows and notice that now the first print statement runs:

```
import UIKit

var str : Double?
if str != nil {
    print (str!)
}
str = 54.0
print (str!)
```

Making sure an optional variable does not contain a nil value is one way to safely use optional variables. A second way is to assign a constant to an optional variable, then use that constant. To see how this works, modify the code as follows and click the Run button:

```
import UIKit

var str : Double? = 9
if let myConstant = str {
    print (myConstant)
}
str = 54.0
print (str!)
```

Both methods let you check if an optional variable contains a nil value first before trying to access it. The first method (making sure an optional variable is not equal != to nil) requires you to unwrap the optional variable to use it.

The second method (assigning a constant to an optional value) lets you use the constant without adding exclamation marks to unwrap the data, so this method looks cleaner and is used most often by Swift programmers.

Optional variables are commonly used in Swift so make sure you're familiar with using them. The basics behind optional variables are:

- Optional variables avoid errors when using variables that do not contain any data.

- You must declare an optional variable using a question mark such as

  ```
  var str : Double?
  ```

- You must unwrap an optional variable to access its data.

Using Comments

One crucial feature of every programming language, including Swift, is the ability to add comments to code. Comments are descriptive text meant for humans to read but the computer to ignore. Programmers often add comments to their code for several reasons:

- To identify who wrote the code and when it was last modified

- To define any assumptions in the code

- To explain what the code does

- To temporarily disable code

You can add as many comments as you wish because the computer just ignores them. There are two ways to create comments:

- To comment out a single line of text, type // in front of the text you want to turn into a comment.

- To comment out blocks of text, type /* at the beginning of the text and */ at the end of text:

```
// This is a single line comment

/* This is a multi-line
 comment because the slash
 and asterisk define the
 beginning of a comment
 while the asterisk and
 slash characters define
 the end of a comment
 */
```

To comment out multiple lines of text quickly, you can follow these steps:

1. Select the text you want to turn into a comment.

2. Choose Editor ➤ Structure ➤ Toggle Comments, or press Command+/.

If you repeat the preceding steps, you can previously converted comments back into code again.

As a general rule, use comments generously. Every programmer has their own style, so add comments to your code to make sure someone else can understand what your code means if you aren't around to explain it to someone in person.

Mathematical and String Operators

The whole purpose of any program is to manipulate data and create a useful result. Spreadsheets calculate large amounts of formulas, word processors manipulate text, and even games display animation to challenge the user. The simplest way to manipulate numeric data is to use a mathematical operator. The most common types of mathematical operators are

- + (addition)
- – (subtraction)
- / (division)
- * (multiplication)

When performing mathematical calculations, all data types must be the same. That means you can't add an integer (Int) with a decimal (Double) number.

To convert one numeric data type into another, you just need to define the data type you want followed by the value inside parentheses as shown in Figure A-12.

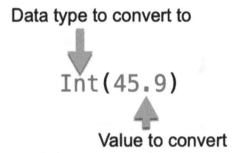

Figure A-12. *Converting numeric data types*

Note   When converting a decimal number to an integer, Swift will drop the decimal value, so the integer value of 45.9 is simply 45.

To see how to use mathematical operators, modify the code as follows and then click the Run button to see the results as shown in Figure A-13:

```swift
import UIKit

var x : Int
var y : Double
var z : Float

x = 90 + Int(45.9)

y = Double(x) - 6.25

z = Float(y) * 4.2

y = Double(z) / 7.3

print (x)
print (y)
print (z)
```

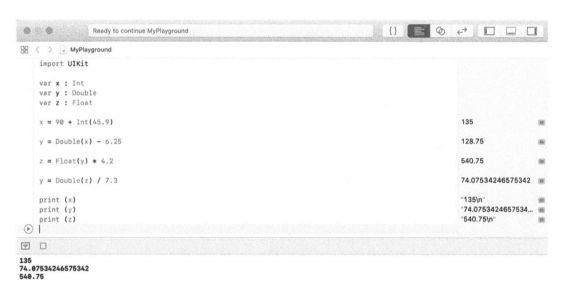

Figure A-13. *Using all four mathematical operators*

Note   When using division, make sure you never divide by zero because this will cause an error.

The addition (+) operator can also be used to concatenate two strings. To see how this works, modify the code as follows and click the Run button:

```
import UIKit

var name = "Swift"
var term : String

term = name + " is a great language"

print (term)
```

The + operator joins two strings together into a single string. Notice that you need to leave a space between two strings when concatenating them or else Swift will jam the two strings together incorrectly like this: "Swiftis a great language" where there should be a space between "Swift" and "is".

If you ever need to add, subtract, multiply, or divide a variable by a fixed value, the straightforward way to do so is like this:

```
x = x + 5 // Add by five
x = x - 3 // Subtract by three
x = x * 2 // Multiply by two
x = x / 6 // Divide by six
```

While this is perfectly fine, you may see shortcuts like this:

```
x += 5 // Add by five
x -= 3 // Subtract by three
x *= 2 // Multiply by two
x /= 6 // Divide by six
```

The first method is longer but easier to understand. The second method is shorter but slightly harder to understand. Experienced programmers often use the shorter method that takes less time to type.

Branching Statements

The simplest program runs through a single list of commands and then stops when it reaches the last command. However, more complicated programs typically offer two or more different sets of commands to follow based on the value of certain data. For example, a program might offer two sets of commands when asking a user to type a password.

One set of commands would run if the user types in a valid password, while a second set of commands would run if the user types an incorrect password. To decide which set of commands to run requires the following:

- A branching statement that offers two or more different sets of commands to run

- A condition to determine which set of commands to run

Using Boolean Values

One data type used in branching statements is the Boolean data type, which can hold one of two values: true or false. At the simplest level, you can simply declare a Boolean variable like this:

```
var flag : Bool = true
```

Of course, declaring a Boolean variable as either true or false can be limiting. A more flexible way to create Boolean value is to use comparison operators that compare two values. Then based on the result of that comparison operator, it returns a value of true or false.

The most common types of comparison operators include

- Equal to (==)
- Not equal to (!=)
- Greater than (>)
- Greater than or equal to (>=)
- Less than (<)
- Less than or equal to (<=)

603

Comparison operators return a true or false Boolean value depending on the comparison. Technically, you could compare two values that will always return a true or false value such as:

```
5 > 98      // Always false
20 == 20    // Always true
```

However, it's far more useful to compare a value to a variable or compare two variables such as:

```
5 > x       // Only true if x is 4 or less
x == y      // Only true if x is exactly equal to y
```

To see how comparison operators evaluate to either true or false, modify the code as follows and click the Run button:

```
import UIKit

var x = 7

print (5 > x)      // Only true if x is 4 or less
print (x <= 6)     // Only true if x is 6

x = 2

print (5 > x)      // Only true if x is 4 or less
print (x <= 6)     // Only true if x is 6
```

The first two print statements evaluate to false and false, but the next two print statements evaluate to true and true as shown in Figure A-14.

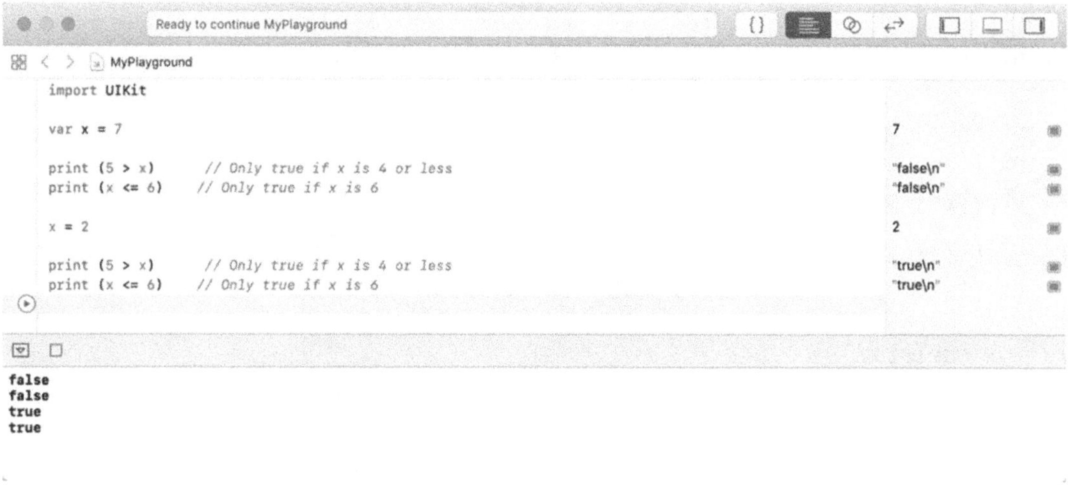

Figure A-14. *Comparison operators evaluate to either true or false*

Using Boolean Operators

Boolean operators let you manipulate Boolean values. The three different types of Boolean operators include

- && – Represents the And operator

- || – Represents the Or operator

- ! – Represents the Not operator

The And operator compares two Boolean values and returns true only if both Boolean values are true. The Or operator compares two Boolean values and returns false only if both Boolean values are false. The Not operator simply changes a true value to false (and vice versa).

To see how these Boolean operators work, modify the following code and click the Run button:

```
import UIKit

var x = 7

// And operator
print ((x > 10) && (x <= 15))   // false && true = false
print ((x > 1) && (x <= 5))     // true && false = false
```

605

```
print ((x > 45) && (x <= 1))    // false && false = false
print ((x > 3) && (x <= 15))    // true && true = true

// Or operator
print ((x > 10) || (x <= 15))    // false || true = true
print ((x > 78) || (x <= 15))    // true || false = true
print ((x > 10) || (x <= 1))     // false || false = false
print ((x > 3) || (x <= 15))     // true || true = true

// Not operator
print (!(x > 6))    // !true = false
print (!(x > 9))    // !false = true
```

Using If Statements

Boolean values and Boolean operators are most often used to determine which set of commands to choose in a branching statement. The most common type of branching statement is an if statement. The basic structure of an if statement checks if a single Boolean value evaluates to true, then it runs one or more commands. If the Boolean value evaluates to false, then it does not run one or more commands.

An if statement looks like this:

```
if (Boolean value) {
    // Run one or more commands
}
```

If the Boolean value is true, then the if statement runs the commands inside its curly brackets. If the Boolean value is false, then the if statement does not run any commands.

A variation of the if statement is called the if-else statement, which creates exactly two mutually exclusive sets of commands to run. If its Boolean value is true, then one set of commands runs, but if its Boolean value is false, then a different set of commands runs. The if-else statement looks like this:

```
if (Boolean value) {
    // Run one or more commands
} else {
    // Run one or more commands
}
```

The if statement either runs a set of commands or does nothing. The if-else statement offers exactly two different sets of commands and always runs one set of commands. If you want to offer more than two different sets of commands, you can use another variation called an if-elseif statement. An if-elseif statement looks like this:

```
if (Boolean value) {
    // Run one or more commands
} else if (Boolean value) {
    // Run one or more commands
} else if (Boolean value) {
    // Run one or more commands
}
```

The if-elseif statement can offer more than two sets of commands and checks a different Boolean value each time. Even with so many sets of commands, it's still possible that an if-elseif statement won't run any commands at all.

The three variations of the if statement are

- The if statement – Only runs one set of commands if a Boolean value is true.

- The if-else statement – Offers exactly two different sets of commands and runs one set of commands if a Boolean value is true and a second set of commands if a Boolean value is false.

- The if-elseif statement – Can offer two or more sets of commands and compares a Boolean value before running any commands. Depending on its different Boolean values, it's possible that an if-elseif statement won't run any commands at all.

To see how different if statements work, modify the following code and click the Run button:

```
import UIKit

var x = 7

if (x > 0) {
    print ("If statement running")
}
```

```
if (x > 10) {
    print ("First half of if-else statement running")
} else {
    print ("Second half of if-else statement running")
}

if (x > 10) {
    print ("First if-elseif commands running")
} else if (x > 5) {
    print ("Second if-elseif commands running")
} else if (x <= 0) {
    print ("Third if-elseif commands running")
}
```

Change the value of x from 7 to 12 and then to 4 to see how the different if statements react when their Boolean values change.

Using Switch Statements

The if-elseif statement offers multiple sets of commands to run depending on different Boolean conditions. However, an if-elseif statement that offers too many different sets of commands can be confusing to read. As an alternative to the if-elseif statement, Swift offers a switch statement.

A switch statement is a cleaner, more organized version of the if-elseif statement. The basic structure of a switch statement looks like this:

```
switch (Variable) {
case (Boolean Value1):
    // Run commands here
case (Boolean Value2):
    // Run commands here
default:
    // Run commands here
}
```

The switch statement makes it easy to provide multiple sets of mutually exclusive commands that run only if a specific Boolean condition becomes true. It's possible that no Boolean conditions in a switch statement will ever be true, so every switch statement ends with a default set of commands.

A switch statement's Boolean values can represent the following types of conditions:

- Equality – A variable is exactly equal to specific value.

- Comparison – A variable is less than, less than or equal to, greater than, or greater than or equal to a specific value.

- Range – A variable falls within a range of two values.

In an if statement, we can test for equality like this:

```
if x == 1 {
    print ("x = 1")
}
```

In a switch statement, we can test for equality like this:

```
switch x {
case 1:
    print ("x = 1")
default:
    print ("x is not equal to 1")
}
```

In an if statement, we can compare a variable to a value using a comparison operator (<, <=, >, or >=). In a switch statement, we must define a new constant and check this constant using a comparison operator such as

```
switch x {
case let y where y < 9:
    print ("x < 9")
default:
    print ("x is not less than 9")
}
```

A switch statement is especially useful to check if a variable falls within a range of two values. If you want to check if a variable is equal or greater than 1, or equal but less than 10, you could do the following:

```
switch x {
case 1...10:
    print ("x is within the range of 1 - 10")
default:
    print ("x is not within the range of 1 - 10")
}
```

Besides checking if a value falls within a range, Swift offers an alternative that checks if a variable is equal to or greater than one value but only less than (not equal) to a second value. This range check looks like this:

```
switch x {
case 1..<10:
    print ("x is within the range of 1 - 10")
default:
    print ("x is not within the range of 1 - 10")
}
```

To see how the switch statement works, modify the code as follows and click the Run button:

```
import UIKit

var x = 1 // Change this to 4, 7, and 10

switch x {
case 1:
    print ("x is 1")
case let y where y < 0:
    print ("x is a negative number")
case 2...5:
    print ("x is a number from 2 - 5")
case 6..<10:
    print ("x is a number from 6 - 9")
```

```
default:
    print ("None of the Boolean values matched")
}
```

Change the value of x from 1 to 4, 7, and 10 and click the Run button each time to see a different result.

Looping Statements

Branching statements like the if or switch statement allows a program to run different sets of commands based on Boolean conditions. Another type of programming statement is called a loop statement. With a loop statement, a program runs a set of commands multiple times until a Boolean value becomes true such as repeating exactly five times or repeating until the user enters a valid password.

Note   Looping statements must always have a way to stop. A loop that fails to stop is called an endless loop, which makes a program stuck running commands but failing to respond to the user. Whenever you use a looping statement, always make sure there's a way to make that loop stop running by changing its Boolean value somehow.

Swift offers the following different looping statements:

- For loops
- While loops
- Repeat-while loops

You can use loop interchangeably but some loops are easier for certain types of tasks. For example, a for loop makes it easy to repeat commands a fixed number of times, but you can duplicate that behavior using any of the other loops instead. By learning what each loop does best, you can write more efficient and understandable code.

Using the For Loop

The for loop is best for running a fixed number of times such as five or sixteen times. This assumes that you know ahead of time exactly how many times you need to repeat a set of commands that will never change. The basic structure of a for loop requires a variable and a range such as:

```swift
for variable in range {
    // Run commands here
}
```

If you want to count from 1 to 10, you could define a range like this:

```swift
for i in 1...10 {
    print (i)
}
```

The preceding code simply prints the numbers 1 through 10 sequentially. If you only wanted to count from 1 to 9, you could define a range up to but not including 10 like this:

```swift
for i in 1..<10 {
    print (i)
}
```

The preceding code prints the numbers 1 through 9 sequentially. Notice that the preceding code defines a variable (i) that counts between a range of numbers. Then a print statement uses this (i) variable. What if you don't need to use this counting variable inside the for loop? Then you can simply use an underscore like this:

```swift
for _ in 1...4 {
    print ("test")
}
```

The preceding code prints "test" four times and then stops. The for loop is best to use whenever you know ahead of time how many times to run a loop.

Normally a for loop counts from a lower value to a higher value such as from 1 to 10. If you want to count backward, you can use the reversed() method like this:

```swift
for i in (1...4).reversed() {
    print (i)
}
```

This code prints the numbers 4, 3, 2, and 1 in that order, reversing the range from 1 to 4 and changing it to 4 to 1.

Besides counting from an arbitrary range of numbers, the for loop can also count the number of items within an array or string. Rather than define a numeric range, you define an item to count such as:

```swift
for i in "Hello" {
    print (i)
}
```

This for loop runs five times and prints each letter from the string "Hello" on a separate line like this:

```
H
e
l
l
o
```

Using the While Loop

The for loop always runs a fixed number of times. However, sometimes you may want a loop that does one or both of the following:

- May not run at all

- May run a different number of times

A while loop checks a Boolean condition first. If this Boolean condition is true, then the loop runs. If this Boolean condition is false, then the while loop won't run at all. The basic structure of a while loop looks like this:

```swift
while Boolean condition {
    // Run commands here
}
```

A while loop needs two commands. One command must appear before the while loop and define the Boolean condition to either true or false. A second command must appear inside the while loop and change that Boolean condition to false eventually.

Note   A while loop absolutely must include a command that can change the Boolean condition to false inside the while loop. Failure to do so can create an endless loop.

Modify the following code as follows and click the Run button to see how both a for loop and a while loop can count and repeat the same number of times:

```
import UIKit

for i in 1...4 {
    print (i)
}

var x = 1

while (x <= 4) {
    print (x)
    x = x + 1
}
```

Notice that although the for loop and while loop perform the exact same task (counting from 1 to 4), the for loop is much simpler and shorter. On the other hand, the while loop requires an additional line to define its Boolean condition and another additional line to eventually change its Boolean condition, which creates a greater chance of mistakes.

Using the Repeat Loop

The while loop checks a Boolean condition before running, which means if that Boolean condition is false, the while loop won't run at all. The repeat loop is like an upside down while loop because it runs at least once and then checks a Boolean condition. If this Boolean condition is false, then it stops running after running at least once. The main features of a repeat loop are

- Always runs at least once

- May run a different number of times

The basic structure of a repeat loop looks like this:

```
repeat {
    // Run commands here
} while (Boolean condition)
```

Like the while loop, the repeat loop also needs two additional commands. One command needs to appear before the repeat loop and help define its Boolean condition. Then a second command needs to appear inside the repeat loop to change the Boolean condition eventually.

To make a repeat loop run four times just like the previous example using the for loop and while loop, modify the code as follows and click the Run button:

```
import UIKit

var x = 1

repeat {
    print (x)
    x = x + 1
} while (x <= 4)
```

The preceding repeat loop simply prints the numbers 1 through 4 sequentially. As a general rule, use for loops to repeat commands a fixed number of times, use while loops in case you may want the loop to run zero or more timers, and use repeat loops to run at least once.

Functions

The more your program needs to do, the longer it will get. While you could write an entire program in one long list of commands, it's far easier to divide a large program into smaller parts called functions. Functions act like building blocks that allow you to create a large, complicated program by solving one task at a time.

Besides breaking a large program into smaller pieces, functions also let you create reusable code that different parts of your program can run. Without functions, you would have to make copies of code. Then if you modified that code, you would have to modify it in every copy.

A far simpler solution is to store your code in a function. Now if you need to modify that code, you just modify it once in a single location. This improves efficiency and reliability.

The simplest function consists of a name followed by a list of commands as follows:

```
func name() {
    // Commands here
}
```

To run or call a function, you simply use the function name as a command like this:

```
name()
```

To see how a simple function can work, modify the code as follows and click the Run button:

```
import UIKit

func greeting() {
    print ("Hello")
}

greeting()
```

This code defines a function called "greeting", which simply prints "Hello". To run or call this function, you simply need the greeting() line, which makes the function actually run.

In case you noticed the empty parentheses after the function name, those empty parentheses define parameters. Parameters let you pass data to a function so the function can use that data somehow. To create parameters to pass, you need to give each parameter a descriptive name and define its data type like this:

```
func name(parameterName: dataType) {
    // Commands here
}
```

To run or call a function with parameters, you must specify the function name along with all parameter names such as:

```
name(parameterName: dataType)
```

To see how a function with parameters can work, modify the code as follows and click the Run button:

```
import UIKit

func greeting(name: String) {
    print ("Hello, " + name)
}

greeting(name: "Fred")
```

The preceding code calls the greeting function and passes it the string "Fred". The greeting function retrieves this passed parameter and uses it in the print statement to print "Hello, Fred".

Functions can have zero or more parameters. Another variation of a function returns a value. A function that returns a value needs to define the data type of the returned value plus define the value to return like this:

```
func name() -> dataType {
    // Commands here
    return value
}
```

To see how to return a value in a function, modify the code as follows and click the Run button:

```
import UIKit

func greeting(name: String) -> String {
    let message = "Hello, " + name
    return message
}

print (greeting(name: "Jack"))
```

This code passes the name "Jack" to the greeting function, which adds the name "Jack" to "Hello, " and returns the entire string back as "Hello, Jack".

Ideally, functions should focus on performing a single task. This keeps the function short, which makes it easy to write and debug. The shorter your code, the easier it will be to debug, which increases the reliability of your overall program.

Data Structures

Earlier you learned about storing data in variables. The problem with using variables to store data is that you need a separate variable for each chunk of data you want to store. Even worse, if you need to store numerous amounts of data, the data gets stored in separate variables, which means there's no connection between related data. To solve this problem, Swift offers different ways to store related data together in what are called data structures. Some common types of data structures include

- Arrays

- Tuples

- Dictionaries

- Structures

Storing Data in Arrays

While variables store data in separate chunks, arrays store data in list as shown in Figure A-15.

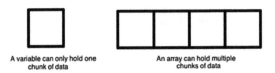

Figure A-15. *Arrays act like a single variable that can hold multiple chunks of data*

The simplest way to declare an array is to store a list of items in square brackets like this:

```
var myArray = [3, 54, 90, 1, 83]
```

This creates an array of integers. If you use an array with a for loop, you can sequentially retrieve each item stored in an array. Modify the code as follows and click the Run button to print each number in the array:

```
import UIKit

var myArray = [3, 54, 90, 1, 83]
```

```
for x in myArray {
    print (x)
}
```

Another way to create an array is to define its data type only like this:

```
var arrayName = [dataType]()
```

So if we wanted to create an array to hold only strings, the declaration would look like this:

```
var arrayName = [String]()
```

Whether you have an array filled with data or just created an empty array, you may want to add new items to that array. To add a new item at the end of an array, you can use the append or insert command.

The append command always adds data to the end of an array. To see how the append command works, modify the code as follows and click the Run button:

```
import UIKit

var myArray = [Int]()

for x in 1...4 {
    myArray.append(x)
    print(myArray)
}
```

The preceding code prints the following:

```
[1]
[1, 2]
[1, 2, 3]
[1, 2, 3, 4]
```

Another way to add items to an array is through the insert command. While the append command always adds a new item to the end of an array, the insert command lets you define where to insert a new item based on an index value.

The index value of an array defines the position of each item where the first item in an array has an index of 0, the second item as an index of 1, and so on. So if you want to always insert new items at index position 0 (the beginning of the array), you could use the insert command. Modify the code as follows and click the Run button:

```
import UIKit

var myArray = [Int]()

for x in 1...4 {
    myArray.insert(x, at: 0)
    print(myArray)
}
```

The preceding code prints the following:

```
[1]
[2, 1]
[3, 2, 1]
[4, 3, 2, 1]
```

To delete an item from an array, you can use the remove command and specify the index position of the item you want to remove. So if you want to remove the third item in an array, you would remove the item at index position 2.

To see how to use the remove command, modify the code as follows and click the Run button:

```
import UIKit

var myArray = [Int]()

for x in 1...4 {
    myArray.insert(x, at: 0)
    print(myArray)
}

myArray.remove(at: 2)
print(myArray)
```

The preceding code prints the following:

```
[1]
[2, 1]
[3, 2, 1]
[4, 3, 2, 1]
[4, 3, 1]
```

One useful command is counting the total number of items in an array using the count command. To see how the count command works, modify the code as follows and click the Run button:

```
import UIKit

var myArray = [Int]()

for x in 1...4 {
    myArray.insert(x, at: 0)
    print(myArray)
}

print(myArray.count)
```

The preceding code prints the following:

```
[1]
[2, 1]
[3, 2, 1]
[4, 3, 2, 1]
4
```

Arrays make it easy to store similar data in one location. Once you create an array, you can add new items to the end (append) or anywhere by specifying an index position (insert). To delete an item from an array, you must specify the index position (remove). Finally, you can use the count command to count the total number of items in an array.

Storing Data in Tuples

If you have two different types of data, such as a name (string) and an age (integer), you would normally need to store them in two separate variables. However it makes more sense to store related data together. To store related data in a single variable, even if they are of different data types, you can use something called a tuple.

To create a tuple, you just need to group all data together and assign it to a variable name such as:

```
var myTuple = ("Joe", 42)
```

You can store two or more chunks of data in a tuple. To retrieve data from a tuple, you need to identify the data position where the first item in a tuple is at position 0, the second item is at position 1, and so on. To see how to create and retrieve data from a tuple, modify the code as follows and click the Run button:

```
import UIKit

var myTuple = ("Joe", 42)

print (myTuple.0)
print (myTuple.1)
```

The first print statement retrieves "Joe" (myTuple.0) and the second print statement retrieves 42 (myTuple.1). Since identifying data in a tuple by its position can be awkward, Swift also allows you to give each position in a tuple a distinct name. That way instead of retrieving data using its position number, you can retrieve data using its name instead.

To see how to use named elements in a tuple, modify the code as follows and click the Run button:

```
import UIKit

var myTuple = (name: "Joe", age: 42)

print (myTuple.name)
print (myTuple.age)
```

The preceding code does the exact same thing as the previous tuple example that references data using its position in the tuple such as myTuple.0 or myTuple.1. Use tuples whenever you need to store related information of different data types in a single variable.

Storing Data in Dictionaries

When you store data in an array, each item gets assigned an index number that represents its position in the array. The first item in the array has an index of 0, the second item has an index of 1, and so on. To retrieve data from an array, you need to know its index number (position) in the array.

So what happens if you want to search for an item but don't know its index number? Then you'll need to exhaustively search the entire array until you find the item you want. For a small array, this won't be a problem, but for a larger array, this can slow down your program.

As an alternative to storing data in an array, Swift gives you the option of storing data in a dictionary. A dictionary acts like an array except that you identify each stored item with an identifying key value. Now to retrieve a value from a dictionary, you just need to know its key. To declare a dictionary, you can use the following:

```swift
var myDictionary: [keyDataType:valueDataType]
```

Both the keyDataType and valueDataType can be any type such as String, Int, or Double. When you store data in a dictionary, you must also assign a unique key value to that data value as well. If you have a list of employees, each employee can be assigned a unique employee ID number such as:

```swift
import UIKit

var myDictionary: [Int: String] = [
    10: "Bob",
    15: "Lucy",
    20: "Kyle",
    25: "Jackie",
    30: "Gile"]

print (myDictionary.count)

for (key, value) in myDictionary {
    print("\(key): \(value)")
}
```

The myDictionary.count command returns the total number of items stored in the dictionary where a single key:value pair is considered one item. Thus myDictionary.count returns a value of 5.

The for-in loop goes through the dictionary and returns each key:value pair stored in the dictionary. Note that the order of data stored in a dictionary doesn't matter. That means the for-in loop does not print 10: Bob first and 15: Lucy second, but may print the data in a wildly different order such as:

25: Jackie
10: Bob
30: Gile
20: Kyle
15: Lucy

To add new data to a dictionary, you need to define a new key and assign it new data like this:

```
myDictionary[35] = "Tom"
```

The preceding code assigns the data "Tom" to a new key 35. If you want to replace data with a key that's already used, you can use the updateValue method to define new data and the existing key for that data such as:

```
myDictionary.updateValue("Howard", forKey: 10)
```

Finally, if you want to remove data from a dictionary, you can use the removeValue method and define the key of the data you want to remove such as:

```
myDictionary.removeValue(forKey: 10)
```

Modify the code as follows and click the Run button:

```
import UIKit

var myDictionary: [Int: String] = [
    10: "Bob",
    15: "Lucy",
    20: "Kyle",
    25: "Jackie",
    30: "Gile"]
```

```
print (myDictionary.count)

for (key, value) in myDictionary {
    print("\(key): \(value)")
}

print ("*****")

myDictionary[35] = "Tom"

print (myDictionary.count)

for (key, value) in myDictionary {
    print("\(key): \(value)")
}

print ("*****")

myDictionary.updateValue("Howard", forKey: 10)

for (key, value) in myDictionary {
    print("\(key): \(value)")
}

print ("*****")

myDictionary.removeValue(forKey: 10)

for (key, value) in myDictionary {
    print("\(key): \(value)")
}
```

This will create output similar to the following (the exact order that the for-in loop prints out data may differ on your computer):

```
5
20: Kyle
25: Jackie
10: Bob
15: Lucy
30: Gile
*****
```

6

35: Tom

20: Kyle

25: Jackie

10: Bob

15: Lucy

30: Gile

*****

35: Tom

20: Kyle

25: Jackie

10: Howard

15: Lucy

30: Gile

*****

35: Tom

20: Kyle

25: Jackie

15: Lucy

30: Gile

Storing Data in Structures

If you need to store someone's name, age, and email address, you could use three separate variables. However, using separate variables won't show you the relationship between all the variables. When you need to group different variables together to show that they're related to each other and should be treated as a single chunk of data, you can use a structure.

A structure lets you group related variables together like this:

```swift
struct myStructure {
    var name: String
    var age: Int
    var email: String
}
```

Every structure needs a distinct name such as myStructure. Then inside the structure you can define as many variables as you want. After defining variables, you need to give each variable an initial value such as:

```swift
struct myStructure {
    var name: String = ""
    var age: Int = 0
    var email: String = ""
}
```

A structure is simply a data type so you don't use a structure directly. Instead, you create a variable and assign the structure to that variable such as:

```swift
var myContacts = myStructure()
```

To store data in a structure, you need to use the variable name (that represents the structure) followed by the structure variable like this:

```swift
import UIKit

struct myStructure {
    var name: String = ""
    var age: Int = 0
    var email: String = ""
}

var myContacts = myStructure()

myContacts.name = "Flora"
myContacts.age = 30
myContacts.email = "flora@yahoo.com"

print (myContacts.name)
print (myContacts.age)
print (myContacts.email)
```

The preceding code simply prints the following:

Flora
30
flora@yahoo.com

Structures are often used with other data structures such as an array that holds a structure rather than a single string or number.

Classes and Object-Oriented Programming

Modern programming languages like Swift support object-oriented programming. Objects are defined by a class file, which determines the following:

- Properties – Variables that allow an object to store data or share it with other objects

- Methods – Functions that perform some action on data

You can treat an object's properties like a variable. To assign a value to an object's property, you just need to specify the object's name and the property you want to access, separated by a period as shown in Figure A-16.

Figure A-16. *Accessing an object's property*

In Figure A-16, we're creating a new object named myButton, based on the UIButton class. Then we can use the backgroundColor property. Object-oriented programming offers three features:

- Encapsulation

- Inheritance

- Polymorphism

Understanding Encapsulation

Encapsulation means that objects can define private and public variables. Private variables can only be accessed and modified by code within that object, which prevents other parts of a program from accidentally modifying a variable used by a different part of a program. Public variables allow an object to share data with other parts of a program.

Note   Encapsulation is meant to eliminate the problem of global variables that allow any part of a program to store and modify data in a variable. If multiple parts of a program can modify the same variable, it can be difficult to identify problems when one part of a program modifies a variable incorrectly.

Public variables are usually called properties and need an initial value. When creating class names, it's customary to start with an uppercase letter such as MyClass instead of myClass. To see how to create a class with properties you can access, modify the code as follows and click the Run button:

```swift
import UIKit

class MyClass {
    var name: String = ""
    var age: Int = 0
}

var person = MyClass()
person.name = "Kate"
person.age = 32

print (person.name)
print (person.age)
```

The preceding code defines a class named MyClass and defines two properties with initial values. Then it creates an object based on that class and stores data in the name and age properties. Finally, it prints out this data ("Kate" and 32).

Besides defining properties, class files typically also define methods, which are functions that manipulate data. Methods typically accept data through parameters. To see how to create and use a method in a class, modify the code as follows and click the Run button:

```
import UIKit

class MyClass {
    var name: String = ""
    var age: Int = 0

    func greeting(human: String) {
        print ("Hello, " + human)
    }
}

var person = MyClass()

person.greeting(human: "Mary")
```

The preceding code calls the greeting method and passes it the string "Mary". The greeting method then prints "Hello, Mary".

Understanding Inheritance

The main idea behind object-oriented programming is to reuse code. Suppose you're making a video game that displays a race car and obstacles such as rocks on the road. A rock needs to store data like a location and size while a car needs to store data like a location, size, speed, and direction.

You could write one chunk of code to define a rock and a second chunk of code to define a car, but this essentially duplicates code. Now if you need to modify the code that defines location or size, you'll have to do it for both the rock and car, which increases the risk of making a mistake or having two different versions of the same code.

Inheritance solves this problem by letting you write code for one object (such as a rock) and inherit that code for a second object (such as a car). Instead of copying code, inheritance points to the code it wants to use. That way there's only one copy of code that can be reused by multiple classes.

Without inheritance, you might define two classes like this:

```swift
class MyPerson {
    var name: String = ""
    var age: Int = 0

    func greeting(human: String) {
        print ("Hello, " + human)
    }
}

class MyDog {
    var name: String = ""
    var age: Int = 0
    var legs: Int = 0

    func greeting(human: String) {
        print ("Hello, " + human)
    }
}
```

Notice the duplication of code in both classes with the properties age and name and the method greeting. By using inheritance, we can eliminate this duplication of code and just focus on adding properties and methods unique to the second class like this:

```swift
class MyPerson {
    var name: String = ""
    var age: Int = 0

    func greeting(human: String) {
        print ("Hello, " + human)
    }
}

class MyDog : MyPerson {
    var rabies: Bool = false
}
```

To inherit code from another class, notice that the MyDog class includes a colon (:) and the MyPerson name. This tells the MyDog class to inherit code from the MyPerson class.

To see how inheritance works, modify the code as follows and click the Run button:

```swift
import UIKit

class MyPerson {
    var name: String = ""
    var age: Int = 0

    func greeting(thing: String) {
        print ("Hello, " + thing)
    }
}

class MyDog : MyPerson {
    var rabies: Bool = false
}

var person = MyPerson()
person.greeting(thing: "Mary")

var pet = MyDog()
pet.name = "Lassie"
pet.age = 3
pet.rabies = true
pet.greeting(thing: pet.name)
```

The preceding code prints "Hello, Mary" and "Hello, Lassie". Even though the MyDog class does not explicitly define a name and age property or a greeting method, it's still possible to use the name and age properties along with the greeting method through inheritance.

Understanding Polymorphism

Even though one class can inherit from another class, there still might be a problem with the names of methods stored in each class. In a video game, there might be a method called move() that defines how different objects move. However, a race car can only move in two dimensions while a bird can move in three dimensions.

Ideally, you'd want to move both a race car and a bird using the same method name move(). However, the code within each move() method needs to be different. A clumsy solution is to create different method names such as move() for a race car and fly() for a bird, but if the bird class inherits from the car class, the bird class will still inherit the move() method anyway.

Polymorphism solves this problem by letting you use the same method name but fill it with different code. When you want to reuse a method name but use different code, you have to use the override command in front of the method name. To see how polymorphism works, modify the code as follows and click the Run button:

```swift
import UIKit

class MyPerson {
    var name: String = ""
    var age: Int = 0

    func greeting(thing: String) {
        print ("Hello, " + thing)
    }
}

class MyDog : MyPerson {
    var rabies: Bool = false
    override func greeting(thing: String) {
        print ("Barking at you, " + thing)
    }
}

var person = MyPerson()
person.greeting(thing: "Mary")

var pet = MyDog()
pet.name = "Lassie"
pet.age = 3
pet.rabies = true
pet.greeting(thing: pet.name)
```

Notice that the MyDog class overrides the greeting method it inherited from the MyPerson class. The MyPerson class greeting method prints "Hello, Mary", while the MyDog greeting method prints "Barking at you, Lassie". So even though the greeting method name remains the same, the result can be different because of polymorphism.

You'll be using object-oriented programming extensively when creating an iOS app. User interface objects are derived from different classes that inherit from each other. If you browse through Apple's documentation for their various software frameworks, you'll see how different classes inherit from others as shown in Figure A-17.

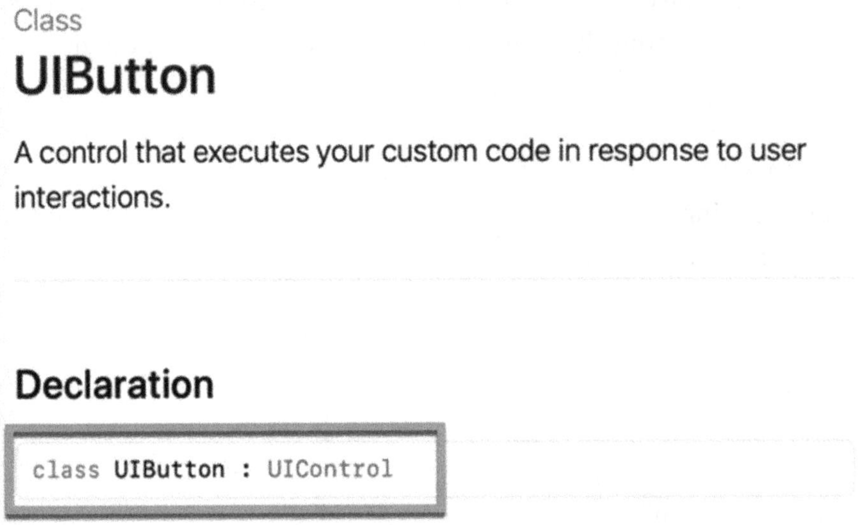

Class
UIButton

A control that executes your custom code in response to user interactions.

Declaration

```
class UIButton : UIControl
```

Figure A-17. *Identifying inheritance in different classes used to design a user interface*

Summary

Since 2014, Swift has been Apple's official programming language. Swift is designed to be simpler, easier to read and write, and faster than Apple's previous programming language, Objective-C. While many older apps are still written in Objective-C, most newer apps are written in Swift. If you're going to learn iOS programming, learn Swift first because that's the future of programming for all of Apple's devices including the Macintosh (macOS), Apple Watch (watchOS), and Apple TV (tvOS).

If you're familiar with other programming languages, you'll find Swift easy to learn. If you've never programmed before, learn Swift by using Xcode's playgrounds. A playground gives you a safe way to experiment with Swift without the additional distraction of designing an iOS user interface.

Besides letting you learn about Swift in a safe environment, playgrounds also give you a way to experiment with different Swift features before using them in an actual project. That way you can make sure your Swift code works before you rely on it.

By learning Swift and iOS programming, you'll be able to program all of Apple's products now and in the future.

Index

© Wallace Wang 2019
W. Wang, *Beginning iPhone Development with Swift 5*, https://doi.org/10.1007/978-1-4842-4865-2

T